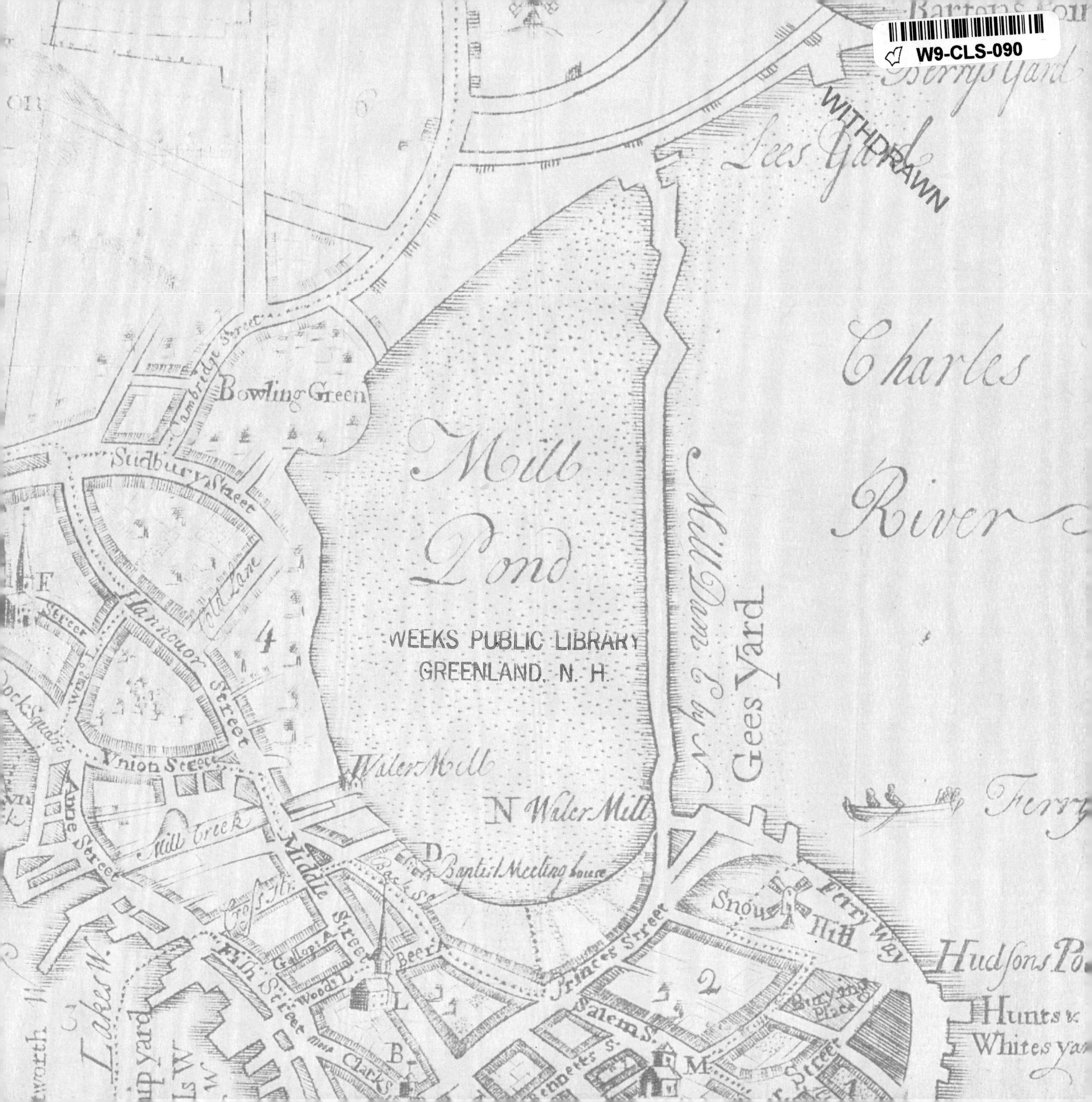

WITHDRAWN

Lees Garden

Charles

River

Bowling Green

Cambridge Street

Sudbury Street

Old Lane

Mill

Pond

Mill Dam ?

Gees Yard

Ferry

Water Mill

N Water Mill

Baptist Meeting house

Back St

Snows Mill

Ferry Way

Hudsons Po

Mill Creek

Middle Street

Princes Street

Hunts v.

Whites yard

Union Street

Anne Street

Hannover Street

Dock Square

Mapping Boston

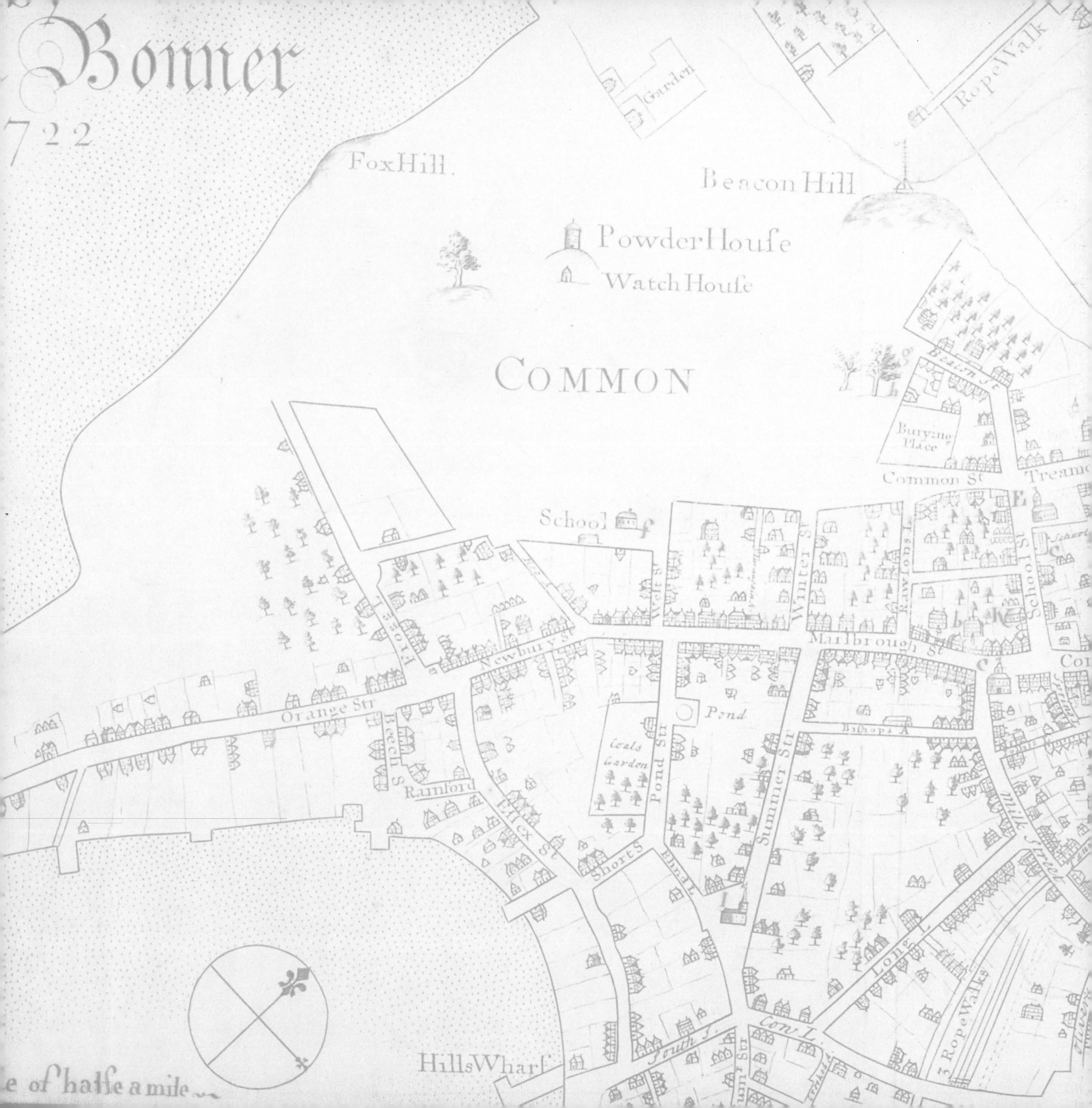

Bonner

1722

Fox Hill.

Beacon Hill

Powder Houfe

Watch Houfe

COMMON

Garden

Rope Walk

Beacon St

Buryine Place

Common St   Treame

School

Winter St

Rawfons

School St

Marlbrough St

Welt St

Newbury St

Pond

North

Orange Str

Beech S

Rainford

Effex St

Coals Garden

Pond Str

Bifhops A

Summer Str

Milk Street

Shores

Broad

Lane

Rope Walks

Con L

South J

Rope Walks

e of halfe a mile

Hills Wharf

Mapping Boston

edited by
Alex Krieger and David Cobb with Amy Turner

contributing essays by
David Bosse
James Carroll
David Cobb
Alex Krieger
Barbara McCorkle
Nancy S. Seasholes
Sam Bass Warner, Jr.

vignettes accompanying the plates
Anne Mackin

map descriptions
Nancy S. Seasholes and David Cobb

This book was set in Garamond 3 and Snell Roundhand by The MIT Press.

Printed and bound in the United States of America.

Library of Congress Cataloging-in-Publication Data

Mapping Boston/edited by Alex Krieger and David Cobb, with Amy Turner;
    contributing essays by David Bosse . . . [et al.]; vignettes accompanying the plates,
    Anne Mackin; map descriptions, David Cobb and Nancy S. Seasholes.
        p.   cm.
    Includes bibliographical references and index.
    ISBN 0-262-11244-2 (hc.:alk. paper)
    1. Cartography—Massachusetts—Boston. 2. Boston (Mass.) Maps.
    I. Krieger, Alex, 1951– . II Cobb, David A., 1945– .
    III. Turner, Amy. IV. Bosse, David C.
    GA430.M36   1999
    912.744'61—dc21   99-20991
                                                        CIP

Illustration credits are found on p. 259.

http://www.mappingboston.com

Contents

Foreword

Norman B. Leventhal

To read a map is to embark on a journey of the imagination. Since I first became fascinated with maps, I have enjoyed many such journeys, but perhaps the most rewarding has been the one that led to this book. It is a pleasure for me to introduce *Mapping Boston,* which so imaginatively weaves together two strong and common passions: maps of the city and the city of Boston itself.

Mapping Boston traces the growth of the city from its earliest European settlement to the present day. It does so by weaving together 50 plates, essays about maps and the city, a variety of short stories about our history, and nearly 300 illustrations. Just as an old map's original purpose was to educate and inform, we now turn to maps, years or centuries later, to learn many varied stories. From a city's beginnings to its changing neighborhoods to its growth, maps capture history as well as geography, political science, economics, ecology, and sociology. With that purpose in mind, here is a book for a wide spectrum of people—from students to scholars and from lifelong residents to casual visitors.

People of all ages seem to be interested in maps and the history associated with them; they are always asking questions and seeking to learn more. Many of the maps printed here have been displayed for a decade now in the public downtown lobbies of the Boston Harbor Hotel (seventeenth- and eighteenth-century maps) and the Hotel Meridien (eighteenth- and nineteenth-century maps). It is heartwarming to see large numbers of people stop to look at the maps and carefully read the accompanying descriptions, especially when they are young people. Four years ago, a fourth grade teacher called me to ask if her students could view some of the maps on display in my office and the adjacent hotel at Rowes Wharf. Sixteen children came and were interested and inquisitive. The teacher reported to me that it was the best field trip the class had ever made. I couldn't have been happier.

People often ask me when, why, or how I began to collect maps. The easiest question to answer is when. I bought my first historic map of Boston while visiting London with my wife, Muriel, more than twenty-five years ago. My curiosity about maps slowly got the better of me and my collection started to grow—or metastasize, in Muriel's opinion.

The question of why I collect maps is more complex. The answer begins with my lifelong relationship with this wonderful city, but I hope that telling my personal story can be seen as the education of a person and not solely the indulgence of a Foreword writer. I was born and raised in Dorchester and was schooled at the city-wide Boston Latin School. After high school, Harvard accepted me, but it was MIT that gave me a scholarship. So, for want of a hundred dollars to pay Harvard's first quarter tuition, I found myself becoming an engineer, a naval architect, a contractor, and then a real estate developer. It is as a developer that I have become interested and involved in the city of Boston, its history, its growth, and its well-being.

My brother, Robert, and I were very close and became business partners in 1946. We started at first on small projects, but by 1962, when Mayor John Collins and Boston Redevelopment Authority director Ed Logue launched their ambitious plans for rebuilding Boston, we, too, were ready for an ambitious project. Between 1962 and 1967 we worked on the 900-foot-long crescent-shaped Center Plaza office building in Government Center, whose footprint and character had been delineated in a master plan by I. M. Pei. Although many developers were reluctant to build office space in Boston at that time, after the city had endured decades of depression, the Logue-Collins plan did, in fact, breathe life back into the downtown, and the offices of Center Plaza filled up.

Over the years, I have observed that each mayor of Boston in my adult life, John Collins, Kevin White, and Raymond Flynn, has had a similar but individual vision of the city that has changed the face of Boston. And now Mayor Thomas Menino remains faithful to this tradition as he continues to shape the urban landscape for the next century—when a new generation will probably view it through the maps made today.

When my brother Robert died in 1972, it was both a personal tragedy and a professional setback. But our company continued to grow as Boston grew. My son-in-law Ed Sidman and my sons Alan and Mark joined us. We purchased the old Federal Reserve Bank on Pearl Street at Post Office Square and renovated it as the Hotel Meridien with an adjacent office tower. These buildings opened in 1981. From Post Office Square we moved to the waterfront to develop Rowes Wharf, and from there to the old South Station. In these projects and many others, including civic projects such as the creation of a new park at Post Office Square, I have tried to understand how a city changes, and I am fascinated by that process.

And that has to do with why I collect maps. There is no better way to study the growth of a city than through maps. All of the maps in this book, some from my own collection and some from other collections, have given me a better understanding of what our city is all about.

And how did I collect these maps? My small but growing collection took me on an interesting voyage—not just into history but into the world of map dealers and New England's cartographic scholars.

Through an ad in the *New York Times* one Sunday morning in 1982, I found my way to E. Forbes Smiley III, a map dealer who, when he came to understand the focus of my interest, became a lookout for historic materials that might suit the collection's needs. His first find was the 1616 map of New England by Captain John Smith. One day, after we had been doing business together for several years, Mr. Smiley showed up at my door and complained that I now owned such a complete collection of the more important seventeenth- and eighteenth-century maps of New England and Boston that he would surely go out of business with me if I would not consider expanding the scope of my map collection. The next time I saw him he had a smile on his face. In his hands, he held a 1507 Ruysch map, one of the first showing the New World. He proposed that my collection should commence with Columbus's arrival in the New World and proceed to the exploration of the New England Coast and then to the settlement of Boston. And so, in fact, it does.

Creating a collection of maps has been a wonderful journey of learning for me, with some major turning points along the way. For example, in 1988, I attended a presentation of the national Boston Visions competition by the Boston Society of Architects. The speaker, Alex Krieger, now chairman of urban design and planning at Harvard's Graduate School of Design, was using slides of old plans and maps to illustrate the visions for Boston held by earlier generations of planners and dreamers. I knew of Alex's reputation as an architect and planner, but his knowledge of maps was new to me. We talked and before long he became an important source for me on matters of urban history and the history of cartography, as well as a treasured friend.

Together, Alex and I visited the map collections at various institutions around New England, where we met some wonderful people. We met with David Cobb at the Harvard Map Collection at Pusey Library; John Lannon at the Boston Atheneum; Laura Monti, then Keeper of Rare Books at the Boston Public Library; Louis Leonard Tucker at the Massachusetts Historical Society; Sam Bass Warner, Jr., Boston's eminent historian; and Peter and John Loring, stewards of Augustus Loring's distinguished collection of the *English Pilot*, now in the Peabody Essex Museum. Following many conversations among all of these knowledgeable devotees of maps, the Boston Map Society came into being, with David Cobb as its enthusiastic president. The society, now with 200 members, has generated considerable interest. We also visited the John Carter Brown Library at Brown University, where we met the librarian Norman Fiering, who has become a mentor and friend. We organized a planning committee for the Early Mapping of New England Project in 1990, attended by an unusual and distinguished group of scholars, map dealers, and collectors including Richard Arkway, Peter Benes, Edward Dahl, Susan Danforth, J. B. Harley, David Jolly, Kevin Kaufman, Alex Krieger, Barbara McCorkle, Russell Morrison, Kenneth Nebenzahl, Harold Osher,

Richard Wilkie, and David Woodward. In his report of this meeting, Norman Fiering wrote: "No such group had ever been brought together before for this purpose, and it is not likely it can easily be assembled again." The meeting of those illustrious and vibrant minds helped to inspire this book. The maps have also traveled. In addition to displays in the public lobbies of the hotels, some of the maps have been exhibited at Boston's Museum of Science, the Boston Athenaeum, Harvard's Gund Gallery, and MIT's Compton Gallery. Each of these exhibits has been, for me, a special occasion of sharing the maps I love with the public of the city I love.

All of these associations and events have led me to a greater understanding and appreciation of maps and the history relating to them. I am delighted that I have been able to provide a number of maps that appear in *Mapping Boston* and to participate in its creation. I hope the readers of *Mapping Boston* will enjoy these maps as much I have enjoyed collecting and studying them, and that they will lead, as they did with me, to an even greater appreciation for the city of Boston.

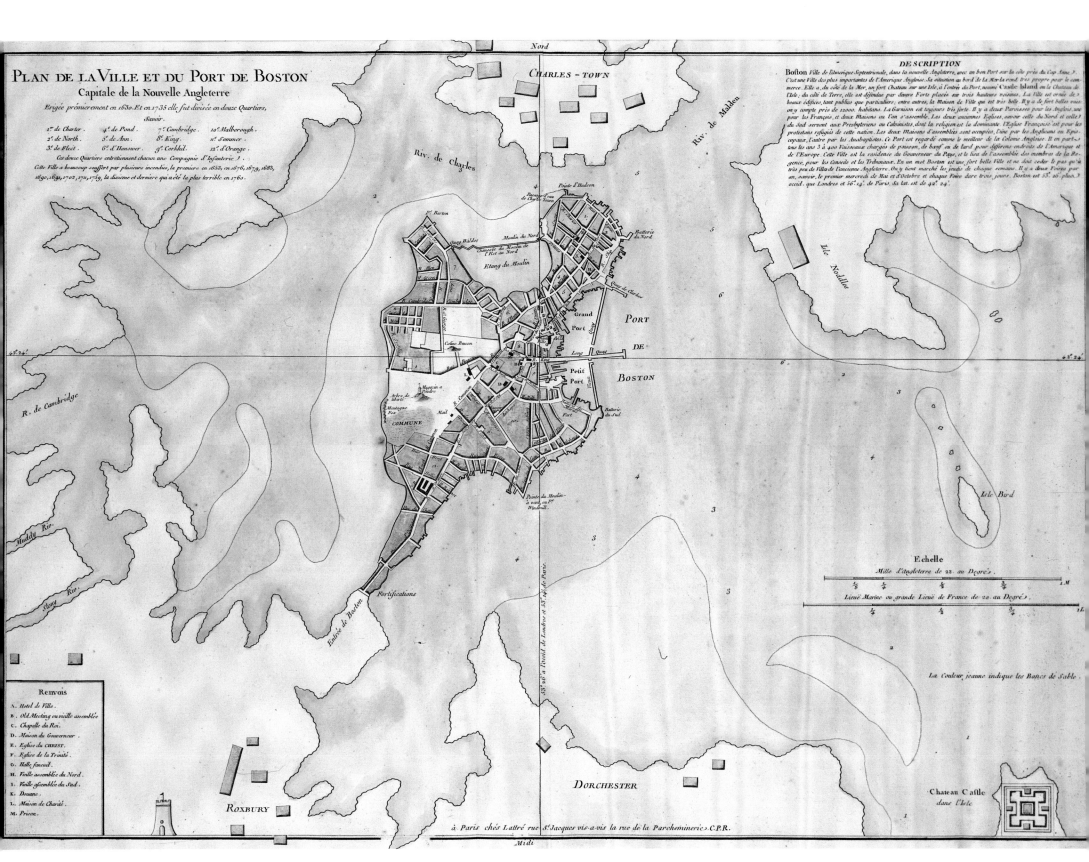

Frontispiece Jacques Nicolas Bellin (1703–1772),
Plan de la Ville et du Port de Boston (Paris, 1764).

Introduction: Revealing a City/Exploring Its Maps

Alex Krieger

It is an extraordinary delight to study, to looke upon a geographical map and to behold, as it were, all the remote Provinces, Towns, Citties of the world . . . what greater pleasure can there be.
—Robert Burton, *The Anatomy of Melancholy,* 1621

It is not down on any map: the true places never are.
—Herman Melville

I can see the whole state just laid out like on a map.
—John H. Glenn, while in orbit around the earth

Immersing oneself in the lines of a map and strolling the streets of a fine old city provide for the explorer/traveler analogous pleasures. *Mapping Boston* sets out to extend such pleasures by presenting the story of a specific city, Boston, through its mapping history. While many books have been written about maps and many more about cities, especially venerable ones such as Boston, relatively few have attempted to cover, concurrently, the story of a place and the landmarks in its mapping. *Mapping Boston* builds connections between specific maps of the city, the places that the maps delineate, and events or people important in the evolution of those places.

Using a map to broaden one's understanding of a place is especially useful for a city like Boston, whose complex social history is matched by its radical geographic transformation over the years, a transformation best recorded in a sequence of maps. Of course, to properly interpret a map requires knowledge of the place it delineates and the milieu out of which the map was created. Thus the dual objective of *Mapping Boston:* to use maps as a vehicle to learn about the city of Boston and to outline Boston's history so that the exploration of its maps is made more meaningful.

For much of human history, maps have served as a primary embodiment of a society's understanding of the physical world. Maps have always been a powerful medium for conveying information and ideas about space, geography, empire, distance, patterns of settlement, and transportation routes. They record historic events and, through the precision of the information collected and the instruments used to record this information, they mark technological advances as well. They are sophisticated means of synthesizing complex fragments of data into, at the least, visual order. Occasionally, maps transcend their primary objective of gathering information about space to become unique works of graphic art.

Modern mapping techniques, enhanced by satellite-borne photography and computer-generated imaging, provide increasingly sophisticated and accurate representations of space. Yet maps yield only partial truths. They are biased by available data, by the tools used to record these data, by prevailing theories about the function of cartography, by what cartographers choose to delineate, by the area of geography that is covered and what is recordable at specific scales, and by the techniques used to project a spherical world onto a flat surface.

Maps are also often prejudiced by the objectives of those who commission or delineate them. As several historians of cartography have pointed out, it is not entirely surprising that the Mercator projection, with its privileging of compass direction, which made it of great utility in sea navigation, tends to exaggerate the size of the countries of Europe, those of the explorers, against that of the places, especially in the southern hemisphere, being explored and colonized. The annals of cartography are full of such exaggerations. Sometimes they are inadvertent, the result of poor information or human error, but across the centuries of mapmaking, ideology, mythology, politics, and even wishful thinking have influenced particular depictions of geography. Like virtually all products of human intellect, maps offer fascinating insights not only about their specified purpose—recording a territory or route—but about the culture that produced them.

Another intriguing aspect of maps is their ability to evoke a sense of adventure or discovery of unfamiliar territory. Precision is relatively unimportant as we attempt to imagine a place sketched out for us on a map. Were the imprecise sixteenth-century maps of a "New World" held in any less awe by contemporaries than we hold computer-enhanced photographs of the surface of Mars? Lacking our multiple technologies for presenting information, the accounts of that earlier age of exploration depended even more on the knowledge (and rush of adrenaline) that a new map of a new territory would bring.

But if there is a future-oriented aspect to newly rendered maps, heightening our desire to explore the places not yet visited or seen, maps delineated long ago draw our minds to the unvisitable past. Every map records a particular moment as well as a particular location, and so a collection of maps of one city across time can serve as a powerful gateway to its history. This returns us to the idea of *Mapping Boston.*

Mapping Boston presents the most extensive graphic presentation of maps of Boston and New England yet assembled under one cover. But the word *mapping* in the title does not only refer to cartography. This chronicle of Boston and Boston-area maps "maps out" several stories about the city and region. Indeed, the ambition was to construct overlapping narratives by which important moments in the cartographic history of Boston could be related to the history of the city's physical development, and both maps and annals of city building could, in turn, be related to—and animated by—knowledge about the region's social and cultural history.

When, for example, on p. 185 Henry Pelham's great 1777 map of Boston is presented along with a brief account of John Singleton Copley (in whose famous painting *Boy with a Squirrel* Copley's half-brother Henry Pelham is portrayed) we learn something about an important American painter, a prominent Boston family, British and American troop placements during a moment of the Revolution (the subject of the map), and

the street layout and topography of the city in 1777. The map, we hope, comes alive in several ways.

Such overlapping narratives are intended to attract at least four kinds of readers: students of New England mapping and cartography; those interested in the topographic, land development, and physical evolution of Boston; people intrigued by the social, cultural, or political history of Boston; and younger readers whose natural wonder about place and geography might be channeled toward a deeper appreciation for the environment in which they live. One goal of *Mapping Boston* is to provide an engaging source of data and insights about their city for young adults being educated in the region's school systems.

Mapping Boston is three books intertwined: a collection of essays, a series of illustrated vignettes written to be accessible to a general audience, and a collection of plates of important maps accompanied by technical descriptions. Each "book" can be read and appreciated independently. Full enjoyment, however, awaits those whose curiosity—like the curiosity aroused by inspecting a map—compels them to read across the narratives.

In the first section of the book, the eminent urban historian Sam Bass Warner, Jr., introduces Boston to those who may not know the city well, while reminding those who are familiar with it about important social, political, and economic milestones. He chronicles the city's evolution from New World outpost, to colonial capital, to fomenter of the Revolution, to port-of-call for successive waves of immigrants, to industrial and mercantile center, to postindustrial metropolis. Warner also takes note of Boston's knack for both cherishing and preserving its history while periodically remaking itself, as is reflected in its post–World War II transformation into a high technology, banking, education, cultural, and tourist center. His essay serves as the social foundation on which the second and third sections of the book are built.

The second section of the book, with essays by Barbara McCorkle, David Bosse, and David Cobb, focuses on the mapping and mapmaking history of New England and Boston from the Age of Discovery to the end of the nineteenth century. Barbara McCorkle reaches for the beginnings of New England cartography by reviewing the landmarks of sixteenth-, seventeenth-, and eighteenth-century New England mapping. The essay, and the sequence of maps she describes, charts the developing European consciousness of the New World, from uncharted oceans to the eventual careful delineation of the New England coastline. The subject matter zooms in from the scale of the continent to the coastline and finally to the city-region itself. Among the revelations is the degree of international interest in the early exploration of New England. McCorkle describes and includes maps produced by Italian, French, Dutch, German, and British interests as each of these empires strove to survey, gain a foothold in, and control portions of the new territories.

While editions of old maps and atlases survive in libraries or private collections, and chronologies of maps published during a particular era are generally researchable, the publishing and selling of maps is less widely understood. David Bosse has produced a unique insight into the map trade of colonial Boston during its period of American dominance in map production and selling. His essay covers the work and influence of the major figures in Boston mapmaking and publishing during the eighteenth century along with their methods of production, financing, and distribution, including Cyprian Southack, John Bonner, William Price, William Burgis, Peter Pelham, Thomas Johnston, James Turner, John and William Norman, Osgood Carleton, and Matthew Clark.

David Cobb introduces modern cartography, focusing on the events of the nineteenth century, the first dominated by American rather than European mapmakers. His essay reviews many of the technical innovations of nineteenth-century mapping and publishing and introduces the familiar names of Colton and Mitchell; the atlas makers of Beers and Bromley; and the beginning of the fire insurance map industry represented by D. A. Sanborn. It also discusses the development of private-enterprise mapping as well as mapping by the federal government, and introduces state-of-the-art electronic maps.

The third section of the book, with essays by Nancy S. Seasholes and Alex Krieger, focuses more explicitly on the physical evolution of Boston, using maps as a primary source of data about the changing city. Nancy S. Seasholes provides a comprehensive overview of the topographic transformations that have enabled Boston to expand its landmass *fourfold.* The story of these topographic changes is both familiar and elusive. No matter how often one goes up to the John Hancock tower observatory to see the Boston 1775 exhibition, no matter how carefully one studies diagrams of the individual land-making initiatives or how frequently one rereads accounts of them in Walter Muir Whitehill's *Boston: A Topographical History*, it remains nearly impossible to appreciate how much of central Boston has been created from the mudflats and marshes that constituted the original shoreline. It is only when one arranges several maps of the city chronologically, like a set of flash cards, that the radical nature and sheer magnitude of the undertakings become evident. While a few of these land-making ventures—like the filling of the Back Bay—are frequently, if incompletely, documented, this essay provides a systematic account of them, in relation to one another and to the civic and entrepreneurial motivations behind each.

Alex Krieger, in "Experiencing Boston: Encounters with the Places on the Maps," relates Seasholes's account of the topographic transformations to the physical environments that residents and visitors experience.

He invites us to experience the urban patterns of Boston; how the city acquired its neighborhoods and special districts, its spatial character and overall sense of place. Boston is often considered the "most European of American cities." This label refers to the city's cultural and social institutions and manners as well as to its physical form, although as in many cities, and certainly the European cities to which it is compared, those institutions are often first encountered, and perhaps best mirrored, in the city's architecture and public places. In highlighting Boston's special domains, Krieger seeks to evoke the aura of the city.

In two sequences of plates, at the end of the second and third sections of essays, fifty Boston and New England maps are featured. The first of these sequences begins with a 1486 Ptolemaic map of the then-known world and ends with an 1898–1900 United States Geological Survey map of Boston Harbor. Across four centuries, first a New World, then the New England coastline, and finally a major urban area and its harbor come into focus. The second sequence, beginning with the 1722 Bonner plan, the first detailed map of any American city, and ending with a contemporary aerial view of Boston, provides a decade-by-decade cartographic description of the growth of the city from colonial times to the present.

Opposite each plate is a "vignette." It is sometimes a story about a map or mapmaking, but more often it introduces a person, event, or place-making venture from the era in which the map was published. Each featured map is, therefore, connected to a specific account of Boston's or the region's history. Conversely, the introduction of a person or event, for example, Mayor Josiah Quincy and the building of the markets that bear his name, is made in relationship to a particular (mapped) depiction of the city. One "sees" the Boston of Mayor Quincy as one reads about one of his major contributions to his city. Anne Mackin is the narrator of these stories, which relate people to events to geography to an epoch and time.

The book concludes with an epilogue by James Carroll, "Map of Good Hope: Boston in the American Imagination," in which Carroll ponders Boston's role within contemporary American culture. Less a description than a discussion of the phenomenon of Boston, the essay examines the prevailing characterizations and myths about the city, how these portrayals mirror the way Bostonians perceive themselves, and the broader lessons about the contemporary nature of civic life that may be drawn from Boston's experience.

It is our hope that this book will inspire further research in several areas. A more comprehensive Boston cartobibliography and historic atlas would surely be welcomed by students of cartography, urban planning, and regional history. The specific relationships between land use planning, real estate development, infrastructure investment, and mapmaking—in short, between the forces of city building and those of recording that process—should be researched with greater thoroughness. Likewise, the research that David Bosse introduces on the mapmaking and publishing industries in Boston might also be extended to other regions. Finally, we hope that other projects follow that use maps and mapmaking as vehicles for educating people about their environment—local, regional, and global.

Mapping Boston has depended on the participation and contributions of many. Norman B. Leventhal must be acknowledged above all others. His love of both maps and of Boston most inspired this effort to relate the two in one manuscript. His energy is felt in every aspect of the book. Second, Amy Turner, whose dedication as the project manager to the enterprise and her command of every detail—and over each of the contributors—enabled the book to get to press. Nancy S. Seasholes's unsurpassed knowledge of the topographical development of Boston, in combination with her willingness to review every facet of the overall manuscript, was also essential and must be noted. A number of people involved in the study of cartography or the collecting of maps were important resources. These include Richard Arkway, Peter Benes, Edward H. Dahl, Susan Danforth, Norman Fiering, J. B. Harley, the late David Jolly, Kevin Kaufman, H. Russell Morrison, Jr., Kenneth Nebenzahl, Harold Osher, Seymour Schwartz, Richard Wilkie, and David Woodward. Librarians and curators of several repositories and research institutions have been most helpful. These include Georgia Barnhill of the American Antiquarian Society, Sally Pierce and Catharina Slautterback of the Boston Athenaeum, Philip Bergen and Doug Southard of the Bostonian Society, Aaron Schmidt of the Boston Public Library Print Department, Eugene Zepp of the Boston Public Library Rare Book Department, Joseph Garver of the Harvard Map Collection, Alix Reiskind of the Frances Loeb Library at Harvard University's Graduate School of Design, Chris Steele of the Massachusetts Historical Society, and Lorna Condon of the Society for the Preservation of New England Antiquities. The original steering committee that formed the Boston Map Society served as early advisors to the project. These include Lois Craig, Alexander von Hoffmann, John Lannon, Peter and John Loring, Laura Monti, George Thrush, and Leonard Tucker. An informal advisory group met regularly to review progress and content. These include Donna Leventhal, Roni Pick, Monique Doyle Spencer, and Hope Sidman. We are grateful to Herb Heidt and Eliza McClennen of MapWorks for their computer wizardry in the production of the outline maps of Boston's growth. Last, Larry Cohen, Michael Sims, and Yasuyo Iguchi of The MIT Press have been impeccable professionals and delightful colleagues in the actual production of this book.

As everyone who has tried understands, getting around Boston requires effort. Instincts alone, even a good sense of direction, are insufficient. Locals blame this on the irregular colonial cowpaths upon which the present streets are believed to have been built, or on some diabolical plot to have all traffic pass through the same half-dozen rotaries. Whether mythic trails or contemporary traffic engineering, or more likely because of the immense changes Bostonians have been making to the region's topography, an accurate mental map of Boston is difficult to construct. Unless one is a native, and even then outside of one's own neighborhood, maps are essential to navigate Boston.

On behalf of all of the authors who have created this book, we dedicate *Mapping Boston* to the many navigators of the city—those who travel through its spaces and those who navigate its history.

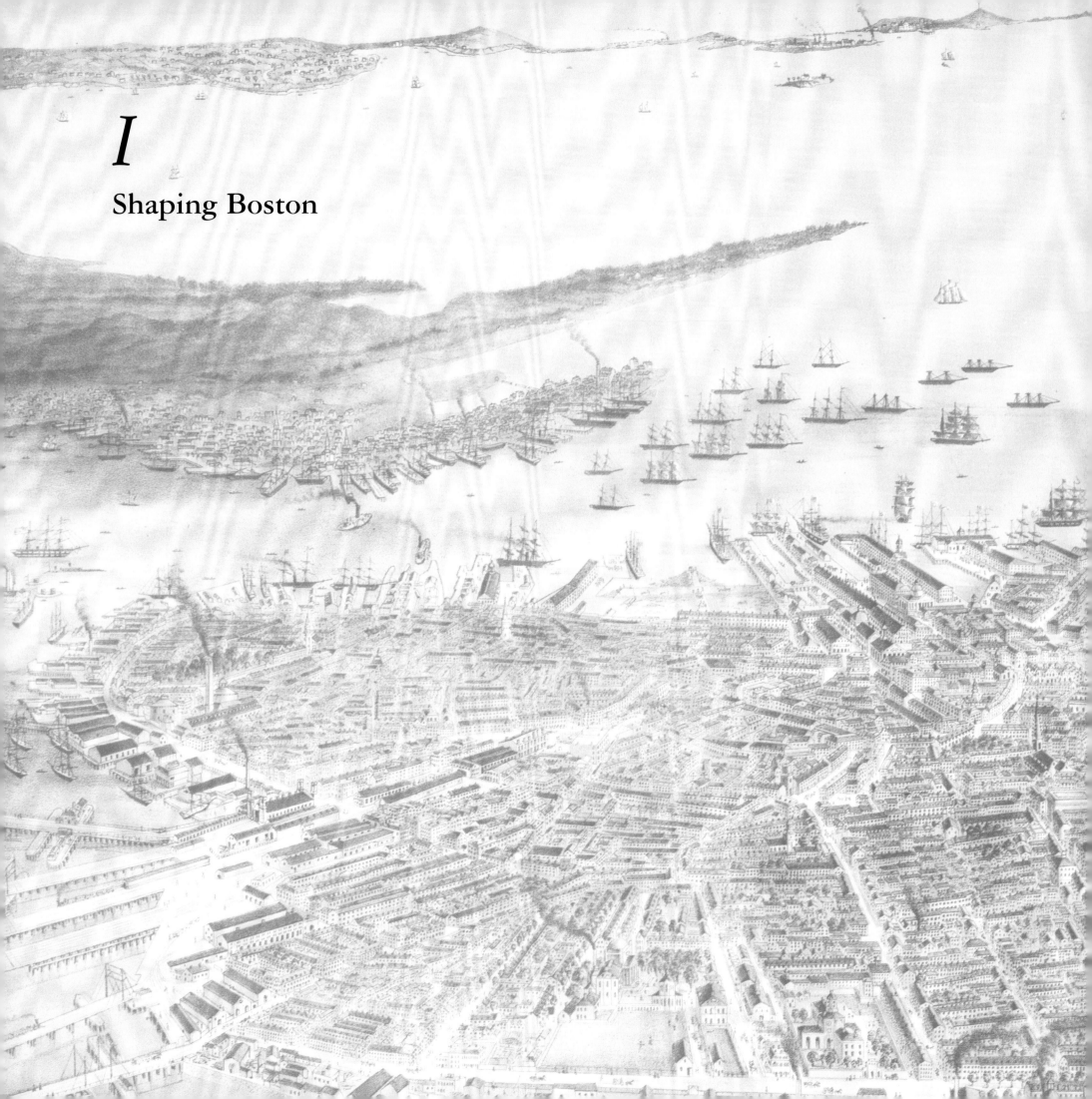

I

Shaping Boston

VIEW OF BOSTON,

July 4ᵗʰ 1870.

Frontispiece F. Fuchs, *View of Boston, July 4th, 1870* (Philadelphia, 1870).

1

A Brief History of Boston

Sam Bass Warner, Jr.

Boston is the largest city in New England, the capital of Massachusetts, and the dominant metropolis of the northeast corner of the United States. An old Atlantic seaport, founded in 1630, it grew up with the country. The metropolitan area's population is 2,870,000, making it the ninth largest in the country. The city of Boston itself, population 574,000, lies at the coastal center of a ring of cities and towns. More than that of most cities in America, its present condition is the result of continuous reworking by successive generations who have drained, filled, leveled, planted, built, and rebuilt the 48.4 square miles that lie within its municipal boundaries.

Boston inherited its beauty and much of its early wealth from the glaciers. The city and its inner suburbs rest within a bowl formed by ancient deposits of volcanic ash, clay, slate, and conglomerate rocks (called Roxbury Pudding Stone here) that have been alternately ground down and piled up by successive waves of glaciers. The deep water port, its many islands, and indeed the peninsula of Boston itself, come from the seas rising around hills left by the glaciers 10,000 years ago.[1]

The land beyond the port and its islands is drained by three rivers, the Mystic, the Charles, and the Neponset, which empty onto tidal marshes and mud flats once rich in fish, scallops, oysters, and clams. Flood plain meadows and rounded hills of gravel and glacial till give the Boston Basin a rolling character of pleasant views. For the Indians, who called the area Shawmut, it was the treasure of the shellfish and the salmon, alewives, and herring that ran up the rivers each spring that drew them to the area. For the Europeans, the flood plain meadows gave grasses for their cattle, the valleys and gentle slopes afforded plow lands, and the gravel hills poured sweet water into their wells. The harbor teemed with fish and gave access to the treasure of the Grand Banks fishing grounds. Today the cod and haddock of the Grand Banks have been fished out, the shellfish beds filled or polluted by the city and its suburbs, and only the sewage-happy lobsters continue as a cash crop in Boston harbor.

PURITAN SETTLEMENT AND ITS LEGACY

In June 1630 eleven ships carried a thousand settlers of the Massachusetts Bay Company from England to Salem, fifteen miles north of Boston. The stony ground there discouraged the party. Their leader, John Winthrop, traveled south to Charlestown, a neck of land between the Charles and Mystic Rivers that had been settled a year before. Winthrop then removed his company to Charlestown, but a sickness broke out that was attributed to bad water from the town's only well.

Fortunately, across the Charles River on the peninsula that is now central Boston, a solitary Reverend William Blaxton had established himself on the western slope of Beacon Hill. He told Winthrop of the fine springs that flowed from the hill, and he welcomed the Charlestown settlers to his peninsula. It was their first patterns of settlement that determined much of the later development of the city, physically and culturally.

The Massachusetts Bay Company group and the many newcomers that soon followed them built their houses around a small inner harbor (East Cove) formed by the slopes of Fort Hill, Beacon and Pemberton Hills, and the back side of Cops Hill in the North End. Reverend Blaxton's farm became the Boston Common (1634), and when the Bostonians piled up the rocks and wooden piles to make their Long Wharf in the middle of this little harbor (1711) the center of the city became fixed in the form that we now know. The Old State House (1713), the town market, stood in a straight street on the high ground above the wharf (figure 1). Later named State Street, it became the business spine of the city. Over the next three hundred years the city spread out from this central axis. The land near the wharf was later filled to allow the building of Faneuil Hall and its market (1742).

The first boatloads of settlers also brought families whose initiative and traditions began enduring cultural streams. John Winthrop's ship, the *Arbella* (1630), also carried on board Sir Richard Saltonstall, the wealthy nephew of the lord mayor of London. He was the progenitor of a later governor of Massachusetts, Leverett Saltonstall (governor 1939–1944). Another passenger was Reverend George Phillips (1593–1644), whose family sired Samuel Phillips (1752–1802), founder of Andover Academy, John Phillips (1719–1795), founder of Exeter Academy, and Wendell Phillips (1811–1884), the abolitionist, and Phillips Brooks (1835–1893), the popular Episcopal bishop. Later, the ship *Griffin* (1633) carried Edmund Quincy, progenitor of three Boston mayors, Josiah Quincy

Figure 1 Revere view of Long Wharf (1770). In 1770, when Paul Revere engraved and published this view, Long Wharf still extended out further than any other wharf on the waterfront. The view shows the arrival in Boston on September 28, 1768, of British troops sent to quell disorders and enforce the Townshend Acts (see plate 27 vignette) and can be compared with a similar view by William Burgis in 1725 (see figure 7 in chapter 4).

(mayor 1823–1828), Josiah P. Quincy (mayor 1845–1849) and Josiah Quincy (mayor 1895–1899).[2]

That the first settlers were English Puritans has also had enduring consequences. Their manner of speech, with the long "a" and the dropped "r," has been passed down from generation to generation to give Boston speech its characteristic sound.[3] The Puritans' respect for a learned clergy and congregation also left an inheritance of a devotion to education that has flowered into a regional specialty. The pioneer institutions were

Harvard College, up the Charles River from Boston (1636) (figure 2); the nation's first public school, Boston Public Latin School, established by a vote of the town meeting and begun two blocks from the Old State House on School Street (1635); and the private Roxbury Latin School, opened in that suburb in 1645. There are now 200,000 college students in the Boston region. The Puritans also believed in government, the public ordering of the common lands, the local economy, and the citizens themselves. This inheritance has continued century after century in the high

Figure 2 Burgis view of Harvard College (1726). This view of Harvard was published in 1726 by William Burgis, who also drew one of the early maps of Boston (see plate 25) and several views of the town (see figure 7 in chapter 4). The view shows what is now Massachusetts Avenue in the foreground and Harvard buildings, of which only Massachusetts Hall, on the right, is still standing.

A Prospect of the Colledges in Cambridge in New England

level of municipal undertakings that the city of Boston attempts. It long has been a city of high taxes and many services.

The unfortunate side of this legacy manifested itself first in intolerance of all others: the execution of Quakers, the warning out of Jews and Baptists. Later the tradition took the form of conflicts over cultural dominance that set Protestant against Catholic, natives against immigrants, and later Catholics against Jews, and whites against African Americans. Today, like all American cities, Boston struggles with its race relations, a troubled ambivalence about new immigrants, a tendency of its religious residents to doubt the morals of those who differ, and the failure of its public schools to educate large numbers of the city's children.

From the vantage point of the present, a good way to comprehend the history of the city is to think in terms of six long waves of alternating growth and depression. The colonial wave of prosperity lasted from 1630 to about 1740. It was followed by half a century of war, revolution, and hard times. A second wave of prosperity opened with the trading opportunities of the English wars against revolutionary and Napoleonic France. This mercantile success continued until after the Civil War.

In the midst of this trading prosperity, waves of new immigrants, first from Ireland and later from eastern and southern Europe and Canada, brought a pool of surplus labor to the city. The coming of the immigrants coincided with new industrial methods so that Boston soon grew to be a major manufacturing center. This manufacturing prosperity of the city and its region around Boston endured until the 1921 collapse of prices after World War I. Thereafter Boston city and region experienced a long depression with the out-migration of its core textile and shoe industries. Only wartime orders brought relief. Then about 1960 a new regional economy of electronics and a city shift to finance and services restored prosperity and brought on a further remaking of the city.

COLONIAL BOSTON

During the first decade—the 1630s—hundreds of Puritan immigrants poured into the new colony bringing money and goods with them. By 1640, Boston's population was 1,200.⁴ This flow, however, stopped abruptly in 1641 with the outbreak of the Puritan Revolution in England Suddenly, clearing land and growing crops to supply newcomers would not suffice, and the little town was forced to fend for itself. Prosperity lay with the sea, not the farms. The fishermen of nearby Dorchester came with the necessary skills, and soon the farmboys of Massachusetts Bay towns became the sailors of an Atlantic fleet that traded to the West Indies, Europe, and along the continental coast from Newfoundland to South Carolina. Shipyards sprang up along the Mystic River while lumber, barrel staves, codfish, and hard tack served as the local staples to feed a complex trading web of rum, molasses, wine, iron, gold, grapes, and oranges. Boston soon became the wholesaler and shopping mall for the West Indies.⁵

For the next century the town of Boston prospered as a seaport. Its population of 7,000 in 1690 grew to 17,000 in 1740, thereby making it the largest city in England's American colonies. Small wooden houses lined the narrow portside streets that traced the water's edge and ran down Fort Hill on the south and Cops Hill on the north. These early pathways continue today as the downtown streets of the city.⁶

Imperial wars and high taxes later brought on a half-century of depression and stagnation. Boston and the Bay colony took an active role in the wars with France in 1744–1748 (King George's War), 1754–1763 (French and Indian War), and 1775–1783 (Revolution). As they did so the advantage in ship building, trading, and smuggling shifted to scattered small ports along the coast from Salem to Newport, Rhode Island, where regulations could be more easily avoided The costs of continuous war, in turn, led the mother country to adopt a policy of increased taxes, to regulate international trade to its own advantage, and to use the colonies as a farm for political patronage (figure 3).

Although Boston is famous for its eloquent Revolutionary leaders, Otis, Warren, Adams, and the like, the idea of revolution divided the town. Most of the steadfast soldiers and high revolutionary fervor came from the farmers outside the port. While the revolutionaries besieged the town, two-thirds of its residents fled. Then, when the British fleet abandoned the city on March 17, 1776, three thousand Boston Tories sailed away with them. Merchants from the small ports, like Salem and Marblehead, transferred their businesses to Boston to fill the vacuum left by the fleeing Tories. They formed the core of a new merchant aristocracy: the Cabots, the Lowells, the Higginsons, and the Jacksons. John Lowell of Newburyport (1743–1802) began a particularly active clan whose descendants included, among others, Francis Cabot Lowell (1775–1817), the textile pioneer, James Russell Lowell (1819–1891), the poet, Josephine Shaw Lowell (1843–1905), the city charity reformer, Amy Lowell (1874–1925), the poet, and Ralph Lowell (1890–1978), the banker and founder of Boston's public radio and public television enterprises. The first national census was taken in 1790; it showed that Boston had only just recovered its colonial size with 18,000 inhabitants, 761 of whom were free African Americans.⁷

INDUSTRIAL CITY

The long period of growth and prosperity that began during the 1790s and extended, despite sharp panics and depressions, until 1921, could be called Boston's best and worst times. It was its best time because a kind of merchant-shopowner-craftsman coalition allowed the city to reach its civic peak. Local taxpayers and local wealthy donors paid for the city projects whose programs, in turn, were based on local initiatives. The public undertakings were those that made the city modern: everything from libraries, schools, and hospitals to water, sewers, and parks. At the same time private citizens established a series of institutions that enabled the city to become a leading innovator of modern world culture: the Boston Public Library, the Museum of Fine Arts, Massachusetts General Hospital, Brigham and Women's Hospital, Beth Israel Hospital, Harvard Medical School, Massachusetts Institute of Technology, Boston University, Boston College, Simmons College, the settlement houses, and many more institutions were all creations of the Boston imaginations and Boston wealth in this era.

This long century was also a time of intense and unrelieved suffering. Sick and starving immigrants arrived in Boston with little to help them, disease carried off children and women in extraordinary numbers, the poor lived in mean cellars and makeshift tenements of the worst kinds, many trades were dangerous and there was no medical insurance, long hours and unpaid overtime were the norm, and drug addiction and family violence were commonplace. Fortunately most foreign immigrants and newcomers from the country were young people. They had much to endure. Fortunately for us all, their youth helped them to survive.

The English wars against revolutionary France and Napoleon inaugurated the long wave of prosperity. Blockade running, smuggling, and world trading carried Boston to its Pre-Civil War mercantile peak. The merchants' ships grew ever larger and better designed until they reached their peak in the clipper ships that Donald McKay built in his East Boston yards (1845–1869) (see plate 37 vignette). The old East Cove was filled to make Commercial Street and a line of new wharves, warehouses, and auction rooms opened. One was significantly named India Wharf (1803–1807) to celebrate the reach of Boston traders to India, China, and the Pacific. It might be well for the current generation, which is struggling with the importation of narcotics from overseas, to remember John Perkins Cushing (1787–1862), China trader and opium dealer, who served as agent for respectable Boston families and firms from 1816 to 1831 (see plate 21 vignette). He returned to Boston a millionaire, kept a grand house on Summer Street, complete with Chinese servants, and built a beautiful summer estate and gardens on top of a hill in what is now Belmont. Cushing Square in that town is named after this local nabob.[8]

The new mercantile wealth transformed the city in a rush of public works: a new state house for the Commonwealth on top of Beacon Hill (1798), the Quincy Market (1826), a new Customs House (1837–1847),

Figure 4 Photograph of Atlantic Avenue, Long, T, and Commercial wharves (ca. 1872). This photograph must have been taken about 1872, for it shows the newly completed Atlantic Avenue cutting across the waterfront before the railroad track was laid on it (see plate 41 vignette). The photograph, undoubtedly taken from the State Street Block (see figure 10 in chapter 7), shows the Long Wharf buildings in the foreground and Commercial Wharf in the background.

a Merchant's Exchange (1843), and the introduction of a public water supply (1848). Everywhere the city pushed outward, first by filling its edges at the North and South Ends, and then by expansion into Charlestown, East Boston, South Boston, and Roxbury. The filling of the Back Bay, begun in 1855, followed decades of land making that doubled the city's area (see plate 39 vignette). The population during the fifty years from 1790 grew five times over to a total of 93,000 by 1840.

Then in the next few decades the mercantile city commenced its transformation into an industrial manufacturing center (figure 4). The same money that financed the building of wharves and ships also funded the building of modern textile mills at river sites beyond Boston. The famous Lowell mill complex lay at the end of a twenty-eight mile canal (operated 1803–1852) that began in Haymarket Square of central Boston. These regional factories with their demand for thousands of mill hands, their need for large-scale supply of coal, cotton, wool, and leather remade Boston into a nest of portside warehouses and rail yards, remnants of which survive behind South Station along lower Summer Street.

Figure 3 Cartoon engraving, *The Able Doctor, or America Swallowing the Bitter Draught* (1774). Paul Revere "borrowed" this cartoon from one published in London earlier in the same year and made it famous throughout the American colonies. It is a depiction of the Boston Tea Party, showing a helpless female (the colonies) being given the tea treatment by authoritative males (representing the British crown).

Most immediately the city's transformation began with the coming of the packets of the Cunard Line, which made regular sailings from Liverpool to Boston in 1840, and the subsequent enlargement of that service by other companies. Eastbound sailing ships took two weeks; westbound, tacking against the prevailing winds, the journey took forty days and longer.[9] The opening of this service coincided with the repeal of the Corn Laws and the destruction of grain farming in Ireland (1846). The previous year a potato rot had begun a terrible famine that lasted for several years. Irish landlords cleared their lands of tenants, and the starving Irish made their way as best they could to England, Canada, and the United States. By 1850 Boston had 35,000 Irish, by 1860 50,000, almost a third of the city's population of 178,000.

Two men stand out as the first civic flowerings of this migration: John Boyle O'Reilly (1844–1890), the Irish revolutionary, poet, and journalist, and Patrick Collins (1844–1905), union leader and lawyer politician. O'Reilly was condemned to death as a young man for treason against the British but his sentence was commuted to deportation to Australia. With the aid of an American whaling ship he escaped and made his way to Boston. Here he edited the *Boston Pilot,* then a leading Irish newspaper, and later he and the bishop of Boston purchased the paper together. Collins came to Chelsea as an immigrant child where he faced the anger of the local Know-Nothings and their children. He made his way first as an upholsterer to become a leader in the union local, then to Harvard Law School, years in Congress (1882–1888), and, finally, as a leading Democrat, he was elected mayor of Boston (1901–1903).

It was the mix of new industrial methods and a pool of cheap labor that transformed Boston into the region's largest manufacturing center. The process began in the 1850s with clothing, iron and brass foundries, locomotive and machinery building, and piano and organ manufacture. It continued after the Civil War in every line of manufacture as Irish immigrants were joined by Italians and eastern European Jews.[10]

Now the social geography of the city assumed its modern form. The first immigrants settled in the old port-side neighborhoods, first in a band along the harbor from the North End to what is now Chinatown. The North End itself became a sort of nineteenth century immigrant registry, Irish until the 1880s, then Jewish and Italian. Both the West and South Ends of the city served as railroad terminals; factory work lay near at hand because Boston manufacturing settled next to the port and along the railroad tracks leading into the city. The well-to-do moved west, to the slopes of Beacon Hill and then out along the new Back Bay. The African-American community, first settled on the north slope of Beacon Hill in modest wooden houses, was displaced by speculators who built five-story brick tenements for the new immigrants pushing up from the West End flats. The African Americans then removed to the South End to live among immigrants and to follow the path of Yankees, Irish, and Jews out into the suburbs of Roxbury and Dorchester.

Figure 5 Photograph of Alexander Graham Bell.

The second half of the nineteenth century was a time of conservative business views but very aggressive business advances. Bostonians made fortunes building shoe machinery and looms, managing railroads in the West, exploiting copper mines in Michigan, contributing to the new industry of electricity. They even invented a whole new industry—telephones—and introduced a brand-new grocery item—the banana. Today Bostonians recall Alexander Graham Bell as one of a line of inventor-engineers and scientists who have made the region prosper (figure 5). The seafaring tradition, however, is almost forgotten. It was Lorenzo D. Baker (1840–1908), a sea captain from Wellfleet, who introduced bananas to Boston in 1870. His pioneering Boston Fruit Company in time joined the later Costa Rican organization of railroad builder Minor C. Keith (1848–1929) to form the United Fruit Company.

The business attitude, however, did not forbid active local government. The principal failure of government after the Civil War came after the fire of 1872. When much of the downtown burned, city government lacked the support it needed to reassemble parcels of private land and to substantially rework the old pattern of narrow streets. Like London after its great fire, there was neither public patience nor power to engage in large scale land reapportionment. The old Puritan belief that government was necessary continued with both Yankee and Irish businessmen mayors. The city's budget routinely exceeded that of the commonwealth itself. The city hospital, the schools, the library were objects of public pride. The great public works of these times were essentially suburbs, the building of infrastructure and amenities for the new suburban lands annexed to the city. Indeed, the towns of Roxbury (1868), Dorchester (1870), West Roxbury (1874), Brighton (1874), Charlestown (1874), and Hyde Park (1912) joined the city to get access to its fine services. A modern sewer system was begun in 1878 and public water extended out to all the new building sites. The most visible achievement was the miles of new suburban streets of small apartments, three deckers, and two-family and single-frame houses.

A new park system was laid down alongside the new developments. The Back Bay was finished off by having its marshes converted into a handsome park (the Fenway), a narrow park was extended from that base to a new Arboretum planted by Harvard University, and a large country park, Franklin Park, was created on the uplands of West Roxbury and Dorchester (figure 6; see also plate 43 vignette). In the inner city the park construction took the form of making a freshwater lake out of the estuarial Charles River in imitation of the Alster Park in Hamburg, Germany

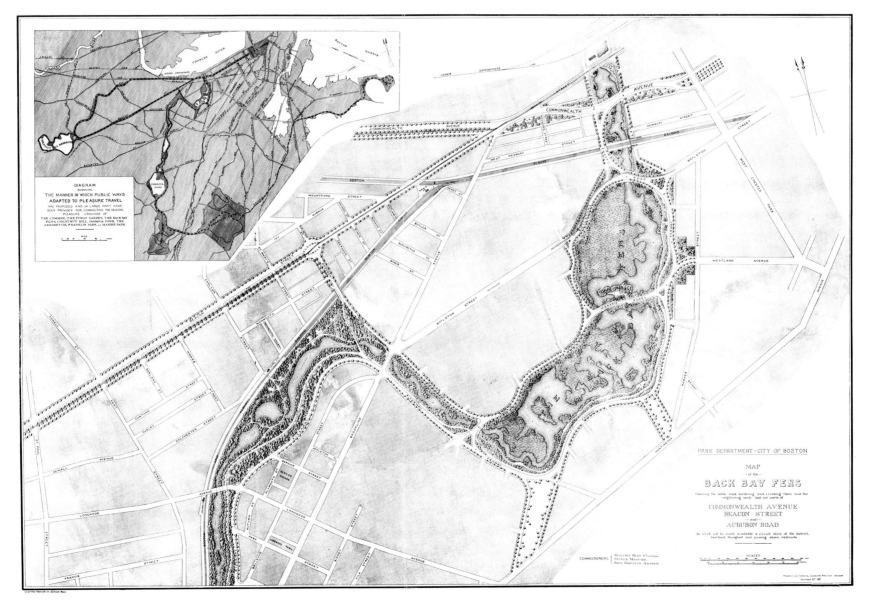

Figure 6 City of Boston Park Department, *Map of the Back Bay Fens* (1887). This plan of the Back Bay Fens, published by the city Park Department in 1887, shows the Fens as it was originally constructed and its proposed connection with the Muddy River Improvement, now Riverway. The smaller plan at the top left of the drawing is even more significant, for it shows Olmsted's plan for extending the park system all the way to the South Boston waterfront via Columbia Road. The title of this drawing is even clearer; it reads: "Diagram Showing the Manner in Which Public Ways Adapted to Pleasure Travel are proposed and in large part have been provided for, connecting the several pleasure grounds of The Common, The Public Garden, The Back Bay Fens, Chestnut Hill, Jamaica Pond, The Arboretum, Franklin Park and Marine Park."

(see figure 20 in chapter 8). The green edge of this lake was shared by the immigrants of the West End and the residents of the wealthy Beacon Hill and Back Bay.[11] All this park construction reached a civic peak in the ambitious gathering of new cultural institutions along the Fenway at the turn of the twentieth century: the Massachusetts Historical Society, the Massachusetts Horticultural Society, Symphony Hall, the New England Conservatory of Music, the YMCA, the Opera House (now demolished), and the Museum of Fine Arts.

THE TWENTIETH-CENTURY DEPRESSION

The long New England and Boston depression that came in 1921 with the collapse of wartime prices and demand is a time that might well be called the years of abandonment or the years of the "grandparents" (see plate 47 vignette). It was a time when the old Boston families left the city for the suburbs and when the new immigrants made a settled place for themselves in the city. It was a time of severe hardships and substantial gains, as people struggled to make their lives secure and to harvest some of the benefits of the modern world.[12] These are the times the grandparents, often immigrants or country people or their children, tell and retell. There are tales of strikes and goons, of honest and dishonest unions, of a relative who helped, of a decent employer, of trying to make ends meet, the big break, of successful saving to finally own a home. A few grew rich, but most made small gains and lived within the bounds of city, neighborhood, shops on the car lines, and seasonal adventures to the big downtown department stores.

One Jamaica Plain Bostonian began her career in the discovery of the slums of the North End and followed her sense of justice to the problems of international peace. In 1946 Emily Greene Balch (1867–1961) was awarded the Nobel Prize for Peace. But for most, these are the years of Edward O'Connor's settled Dorchester parishes, and painter Jack Levine and Nat Hentoff's Jewish neighborhoods, and Martin Luther King and Malcolm X's South End. It is characteristic of the times that the major land planning effort was the enactment of zoning in 1924, a law that attempted to nail things down as they were. Perhaps the most fitting symbol of the era would be Fred Allen (1894–1956), an extremely hard-working and quick-witted comedian who rose from poverty in Allston and Dorchester to national radio stardom. Allen built his Sunday night comedies on the ethnic stereotypes of the day, and used these figures to reveal the absurdities of the times.[13]

Slow change and economic depression did not mean no change. A multistory garage, the Motor Mart, was built on the site of the old Boston & Providence Railroad Station, and a few hotels and office buildings were built during the twenties. The North Station-Boston Garden-Hotel Manger (1928) was a kind of megaplex that gave a foretaste of the big pro-

jects that would characterize the urban renewal era of the 1960s and 1970s. Within the bounds of the municipality, its southern edges continued to fill up in the suburban style now more and more with small single-family homes. In 1920 Boston's population was 750,000; by 1960 it had fallen to 697,000.

Within the center city, the well-to-do abandoned their houses in the Back Bay, the Fenway, and Beacon Hill, some moving to old summer homes in the nearby suburbs. Their places in the city were taken by physicians offices, small efficiency apartments, and student digs. Immigrant names began to appear more and more on the names of businesses, skilled and white collar jobs opened to their children, and their children's names appeared on college graduation lists.[14] Chain stores began to move into the neighborhoods; First National was the creation of Irish butchers, Stop and Shop of Jewish grocers, and Star Market of an Armenian family.

These decades of depression were also decades of national corporate growth, of the gathering in of local firms and capital into large corporate organizations. Some Bostonians took an active role in this new phase of American business. For example, James Jackson Storrow (1864–1926), a partner in Lee Higginson and Company, investment bankers, reorganized the General Motors Corporation, and Ernest Henderson (1897–1967) consolidated strings of hotels into the successful Sheraton chain. But more and more the CEOs of Boston's big banks and insurance companies and many of the manufacturing firms were not local people. Or, if they were local, the headquarters and the major decisions lay elsewhere. Thus, unlike earlier periods, neither the merchant nor his money lived in the city. Perhaps the most notable exception to this trend was James Jackson Storrow, an unsuccessful candidate for mayor in 1912 against John F. Kennedy's grandfather. The localism of his political opponent meant that when prosperity returned and the city wished to rebuild itself, these new corporate sources of money and power lay beyond City Hall ways. A new form of civic management would be required to connect to this new wealth.

For the moment Boston's politics were squeezed by economic depression to those of anger, retreat, and frustration because no one in the twenties, in government or business, knew what to do to offset the economic losses stemming from the out migration of the textile and shoe industries. Boston's brilliant and ever-popular Mayor Curley (1874–1958) played upon public fear and ethnic animosities, but he could do little but pass out small jobs (figure 7). He widened many streets, laid out many playgrounds, built schools, Sumner Tunnel, and the Huntington Avenue subway extension, but could undertake no major projects because he lacked the trust of Washington and Boston businessmen (see plate 46 vignette). The civic consensus of the previous century collapsed under the weight of the Great Depression.[15]

Figure 7 Depression-era photograph, ca. 1933, showing a work crew of unemployed men clearing snow at Tremont Street.

The automobile was not the only transforming change. The rise in affluence and mobility of Americans called for a thorough reorganization of retailing. National branded products, national lines of goods, and national franchises moved in upon local retailers who suddenly found themselves disadvantaged. The old wars between the department stores and the specialty stores, the chains, and the locals resumed. Giant retail malls and huge food stores opened around the metropolitan region while specialty stores of all kinds lined the new automobile suburban shopping strips. In Boston this conflict took the form of the opening of the nation's first "festival mall," Faneuil Hall (figure 8) and later the Copley Place–Prudential Mall in the Back Bay (1984, and Prudential remodeling, 1995). The specialty stores have countered with the immensely popular Newbury Street promenade of shops and shoppers, and in the outer areas of the city Harvard Street in Brighton and Centre Street in Jamaica Plain are flourishing with blocks of small neighborhood specialty and ethnic stores and restaurants.

National retailing, from McDonald's to Tiffany's, was but the consumer side of a new nationalization and internationalization of the Boston economy. Local institutions had either to grow to national proportions or

PROSPERITY AND URBAN RECONSTRUCTION

The long postwar prosperity that began after the Korean War started a process of fashioning yet another new Boston. Many novel forces were at work. This new Boston was very much the product of the automobile, and it had to alter its old ways and forms to accommodate to a new role as a center in a dispersed American automobile metropolis. The city's population had peaked in 1950 in the days of the post–World War II housing shortage. By 1990 it had fallen from 801,000 to 574,000, a loss in forty years time equivalent to the population peak of 250,000 first attained in 1870 after two hundred and forty years of settlement.

This emptying out of the city accompanied the attempts to remake the city in the contemporary superhighway manner. The center of the city was cleared in one large gash to build the elevated Central Artery in the 1950s. In 1961 the Callahan Tunnel to East Boston opened and was joined to the Massachusetts Turnpike in 1965. The process of clearing the city out for highways halted in 1970 when a coalition of citizens from Roxbury, the Fenway, and Cambridge persuaded the mayor and the governor to stop the construction of a new inner-belt highway. In time the highway funds were diverted to build the new Orange Line transit from the Back Bay to Forest Hills and its lineal park.[16] The federal government, the state, and the city are now busy at work trying to bury the Central Artery and undo this 1950s error (see plate 50 vignette).

Figure 8 Photograph, ca. 1980, of the then recently restored and reopened Quincy Markets with Faneuil Hall in the background along with a portion of Boston's new City Hall. In the foreground is a parking lot that soon would be filled by a modern expansion of the markets.

be absorbed by out-of-town giants. Raytheon, Polaroid, Sheraton, Gillette, and John Hancock all grew to giant proportions. At the same time Boston's financiers invented new institutions of venture capital and mutual funds that revived the beleaguered financial district. But local innovation went forward within a context of national power so that old firms like the Boston Safe Deposit and Trust, Stride-Rite Shoes, Star Market, and New England Mutual Life Insurance were absorbed by nationals, just as the Jordan Marsh and the Filene's department stores had been years before.

With every decade after World War II Boston became more and more sharply divided into actors with different ranges of responsibility: nationally and internationally oriented chief executives, metropolitan real estate and businesses, and local storekeepers and professionals. These levels came to be mirrored in politics. The new political player was the federal government, so that to affect any major change in the city required the cooperation and assistance of congressmen and senators, Washington and state bureaucrats, as well as elected city officials and local citizens.

It took the city of Boston some time to learn to adjust to the new ways. Although the city had built public housing with federal funds since 1938, not until 1954 did it turn to the possibilities of the new urban renewal legislation (1949, 1954) that offered federal funds for parcel assembly, land clearance, loans to private developers, and later for infrastructure modernization. Boston, like other American cities, started out on the wrong foot, clearing whole neighborhoods in the West End and South End (figure 9; see also figure 24 in chapter 8). Long-time tenants and residents were suddenly displaced for the more affluent and for businesses like the *Boston Herald* (1958). The injustice brought increasing protests.[17]

By 1960 the city government had begun to learn. It brought a new administrator, Edward Logue, from New Haven to build a strong redevelopment agency in city hall (see plate 49 vignette). After some stormy meetings in Charlestown and the South End, the clearance strategy was abandoned in favor of preservation and infrastructure rebuilding in residential areas. Today the class mixing of Charlestown and the class and racial mixing of the South End testify to the success of this policy. Here the process of endless neighborhood meetings and piecemeal reconstruction have successfully modernized the two neighborhoods without tearing their social fabric apart.

Most of the redevelopment took place in the center of the city, where the new national scale of business and the new national presence of government took the form of an office building boom. The remaking began in 1961 with the building of the Prudential Insurance Company tower, which looms over the old Boston & Albany Railroad yards, and reached its apogee with the construction of the domineering and controversial John Hancock Tower in 1973 (figure 10).

Figure 9 A father and daughter watch a portion of the demolition of the West End in a November 2, 1958, *Boston Herald* photo. See also figures 26 and 27 in chapter 8.

Figure 10 Contemporary photograph of the John Hancock and Prudential Insurance Company towers forming the most conspicuous parts of the "Tall Spine." See also figures 29 and 30 in chapter 8.

The new giant office buildings and their plazas stand as signs of the new role of the city of Boston as the center of an enlarged multicity region (figure 11). It has inherited from the past its place next to the harbor and rivers of the Boston Basin. From that location came the building of a spiderweb of roads and railroads and transit with a hub at the Atlantic port side. To this it has added the land making in East Boston to make a downtown international airport. Thanks to this cumulative history the city remains the transportation hub of the region. Manufacturing has fled the

Figure 11 Contemporary aerial view of Boston with the inner harbor "pointing" toward the downtown at the center of the photograph. East Boston and Logan Airport are at the right and South Boston is at the left with the recognizable figures of Marine Park and Castle Island at the bottom.

city, as it has in all American cities, for cheap land and nonunion suburban labor. By 1970 three-fifths of Boston's workforce were engaged in service occupations, whereas only two-fifths of the suburbanites were working in such businesses. The city's business has become government, finance, services of all kinds, medicine, and education. Hospitals and dormitories spill out over their old neighborhoods, and the old downtown is now welcoming Suffolk University and Emerson College to its former busy retail locations.

The city is also once again becoming an immigrant center as new migrants from the Caribbean and Asia fill the old South End, Roxbury and Dorchester, and East Boston and Brighton. The African-American community has suburbanized and followed the southward march of Boston residences. Much of Dorchester, South Boston, Jamaica Plain, and West Roxbury remain the homes of the city's working people, but the city's working people have a very different life than they did fifty years ago. Now Boston is more of a residential center than it has ever been. Ninety-eight thousand of its residents commute outward to jobs in the region each day, while their places in town are taken by 292,000 coming in for work. These flows of Bostonians are a significant alteration of three centuries of regional employment dominance. Yet, ever since 1630 Boston has been a city in a larger world. Today, as the center of a new and prosperous multicity region, this newest Boston is once again striving to keep up with the changes and opportunities of the national economy and world events.

NOTES

1. Clifford A. Kaye, *The Geology and Early History of the Boston Area of Massachusetts, a Bicentennial Approach, Geological Survey Bulletin #1476* (Washington: U.S. Government Printing Office, 1976), figure 1.

2. E. Digby Baltzell, *Puritan Boston and Quaker Philadelphia* (New York: Free Press, 1979), 11.

3. David Fischer, *Paul Revere's Ride* (New York: Oxford University Press, 1994).

4. Darrett Rutman, *Winthrop's Boston: Portrait of a Puritan Town* (Chapel Hill: University of North Carolina Press, 1965).

5. Samuel Eliot Morison, *Maritime History of Massachusetts* (1921; reprint, Boston: Northeastern University Press, 1980), 11–22.

6. Michael P. Conzen and George K. Lewis, *Boston, a Geographical Portrait* (Cambridge: Ballinger, 1976), figure 6.

7. David T. Gilchrist et al., *The Growth of Seaport Cities* (Charlottesville: University of Virginia Press, 1967), 28–29, 34.

8. Russell B. Adams, Jr., *The Boston Money Tree* (New York: Crowell, 1977).

9. Morison, *Maritime History,* 230–236.

10. Oscar Handlin, *Boston's Immigrants,* rev. ed. (Cambridge: Harvard University Press, 1959), table 2, and 44–52.

11. Lawrence W. Kennedy, *Planning the City upon a Hill* (Amherst: University of Massachusetts Press, 1992); Cynthia Zaitzevsky, *Frederick Law Olmsted and the Boston Park System* (Cambridge: Harvard University Press, 1982).

12. Mary Antin, *The Promised Land* (1912; reprint, with a foreword by Oscar Handlin, Princeton: Princeton University Press, 1985).

13. Sam Bass Warner, Jr., *Province of Reason* (Cambridge: Harvard University Press, 1984).

14. Conzen and Lewis, *Geographical Portrait,* 26.

15. Jack Beatty, *The Rascal King* (Reading, Mass.: Addison-Wesley, 1992).

16. Alan Lupo, Frank Colcord, and Edmund P. Fowler, *Rites of Way: The Politics of Transportation in Boston and the U.S. City* (Boston: Little Brown, 1971).

17. John Mollenkopf, *The Contested City* (Princeton: Princeton Unversity Press, 1983).

Diagramming the Growth of Boston

Nancy S. Seasholes and Amy Turner

The following series of outline maps shows the enormous growth of Boston's land area and change in its shoreline from 1630, when Boston was founded, to the present, a transformation that was brought about by filling in the tidal flats that once surrounded the city.

The maps were produced by Herb Heidt and Eliza McClennen of MapWorks using a computer program in which the shorelines of selected historical maps were digitized and then overlaid on a digital version of a 1995 aerial photograph of the city. The dates of the outline maps correspond to the historical maps on which they were based, the intervals chosen to illustrate significant periods of Boston's land making. Chapter 7 discusses these topographic changes in detail.

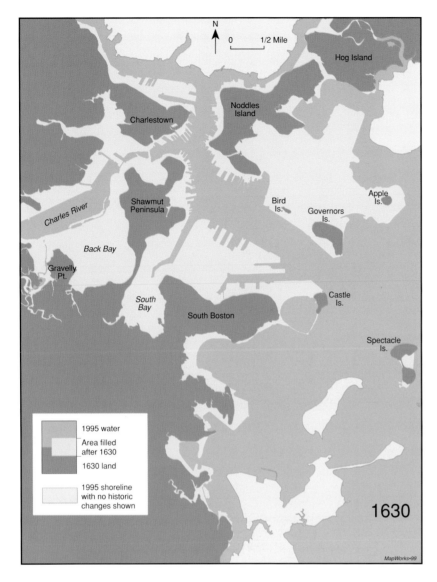

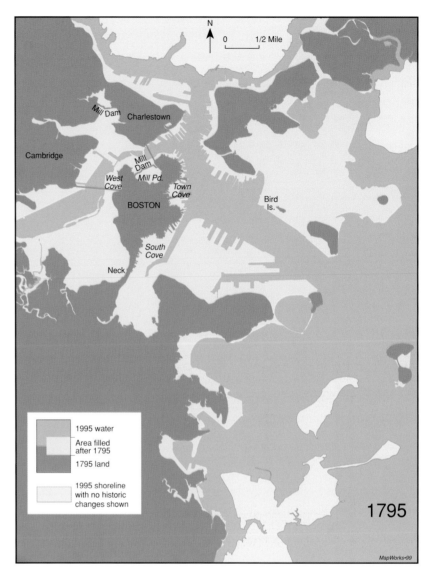

In 1630 the Shawmut Peninsula, on which Boston was established, was a small landform extending into the harbor and connected to the mainland by a narrow neck. On one side of the neck lay the back bay of the Charles River, divided into two unequal parts by Gravelly Point, and on the other was South Bay. Charlestown and South Boston were also peninsulas and what became East Boston was then two large islands and three small ones. In the harbor Spectacle Island was composed of two drumlins connected by a narrow neck.

The 1630 shoreline is largely based on Chesbrough's 1852 reconstruction (plate 37) with refinements from other maps including the 1781 Des Barres (plate 19), the 1777 Page of Charlestown (plate 17 vignette), the 1847 U.S. Coast Survey of the north shore of South Boston (plate 22), and an 1850 map of Dorchester by Elbridge Whiting and S. Dwight Eaton.

By 1795 the area of the Boston peninsula had been increased, primarily by "wharfing out"—the process of constructing wharves outward from the shore and later filling the slips between them. Wharfing out also added land to the southwestern shore of the Charlestown peninsula. Mill dams had been built across the North, or Mill, Cove on the Boston peninsula and the head of the cove between Charlestown and what is now Somerville. Two new bridges connected the Boston peninsula to Charlestown and to Cambridge. In the harbor, erosion had claimed most of Bird Island.

The 1795 shoreline of Boston is taken from the 1796 Carleton (plate 31) and of Charlestown from the 1777 Page (plate 17 vignette).

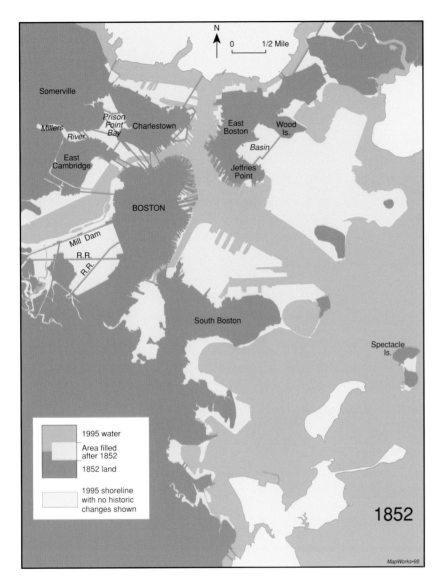

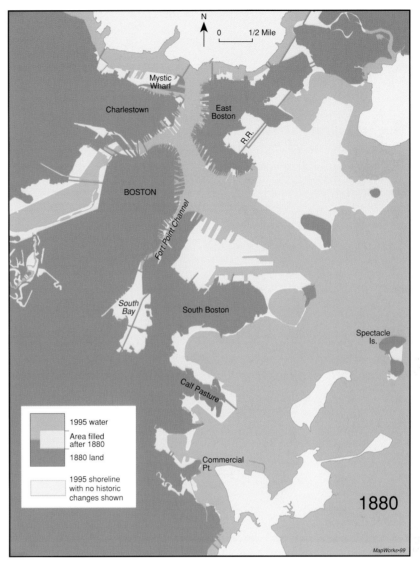

By 1852 South Cove, the Mill Pond, and much of the Town (East) and West Coves on the Boston peninsula had been filled in. Both sides of the Neck had been filled, too—the southeast side to create Harrison Avenue and some of Albany Street; the northwest side for Tremont Street. The Back Bay had been cut off by a Mill Dam and further obstructed by railroad tracks. New passenger bridges linked Boston, East Cambridge, Charlestown, and Somerville, but even more striking was the proliferation of railroad bridges. In East Boston, after only twenty years of development, the Marginal and Border Street water-fronts had been augmented by wharfing out, passenger and rail bridges connected the island with the mainland, and a seawall had been built across the Basin between Jeffries Point and Wood Island. Land had also been made on the north and northwest shores of South Boston. On Spectacle Island, however, the narrow neck connecting the two drum-lins had eroded away completely.

The 1852 shoreline is largely based on the 1852 Chesbrough (plate 37) with refine-ments from other maps including the 1848 Felton and Parker of Charlestown (figure 6 in chapter 7), the 1847 U. S. Coast Survey of the Boston Wharf Company wharf (plate 22), and the 1850 Whiting and Eaton of Dorchester.

By 1880 filling of Back Bay, the Massachusetts General Hospital flats in the West Cove, Atlantic Avenue across the Town Cove, and Albany Street in South Bay had extended the shoreline of Boston proper almost to its present limit. The southern shore of Charlestown had also been increased almost to the present line by the filling of Prison Point Bay and most of the Millers River, and, on the northern shore, filling of Mystic Wharf had begun. Wharfing out had added more land to East Boston and a railroad had been constructed across the Basin just northwest of the seawall. One of the most dramatic changes had occurred in South Boston, where the state's South Boston Flats project had created a mile-long lobster-claw-shaped area of made land that defined the eastern side of the Fort Point Channel. Further south, a long pier had been built out from the end of the Calf Pasture, now Columbia Point, as part of the city's Main Drainage sewage works, and the end of Commercial Point was being filled for the gas tanks of a predecessor of today's Boston Gas Company. In the harbor, a horse rendering plant was operating on Spectacle Island and the two halves of the island had been rejoined.

The 1880 shoreline is based on the Boston Map Company map (plate 43) with addi-tions from the 1881 Fuller and Whitney of Back Bay (figure 9 in chapter 7), an 1885 Bromley atlas index map of Charlestown, and an 1882 East Boston Company map of East Boston.

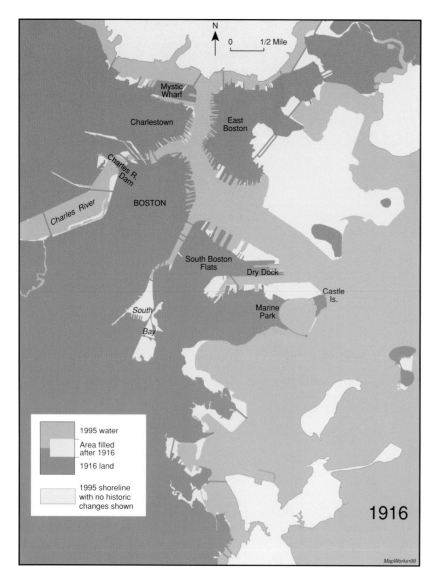

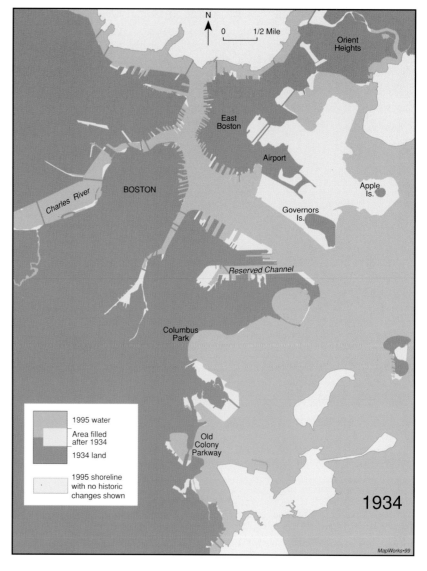

By 1916 the state had filled hundreds of acres of the South Boston, or Commonwealth, Flats and begun constructing a huge dry dock at its eastern end. At the eastern tip of the original South Boston peninsula, land had been created for Marine Park and connected to Castle Island by a bridge. The southwestern part of South Bay had been filled to create new wharves and, on the Charles River, the first strip of the Esplanade had been filled and the first Charles River Dam constructed. In Charlestown the Mystic Wharf had been completed, and in East Boston some of the Basin filled.

The 1916 shoreline is essentially based on the 1916 Coast and Geodetic Survey chart no. 246 (figure 18 in chapter 7).

By 1934 filling of the East Boston Flats, begun as a port development, was creating land for Boston's airport. New land at the north end of the main East Boston island joined it with Orient Heights. In South Boston filling the flats on the south side of the Reserved Channel had finally connected Castle Island with the mainland, and the area now called Columbus Park and Carson Beach had been filled. Further south, made land carried Old Colony Parkway, now Morrissey Boulevard, across Patten's Cove and the mouth of Savin Hill Bay. Most of South Bay had been filled in except for a channel and turning basin to serve the remaining wharf. And on the Charles River, filling had widened the Esplanade and created a lagoon and the "Make Way for Ducklings" islands.

The 1934 shoreline is based on the 1934 Coast and Geodetic Survey chart no. 246 (plate 47).

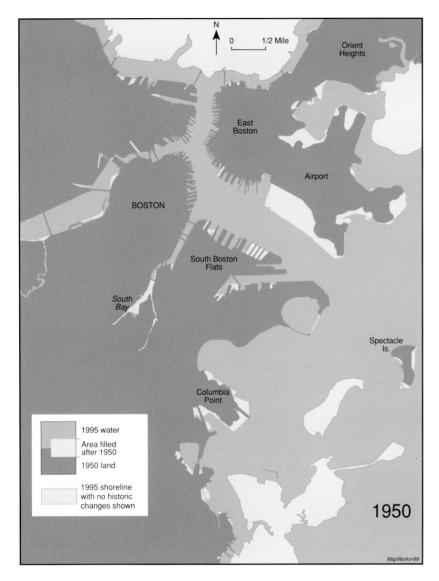

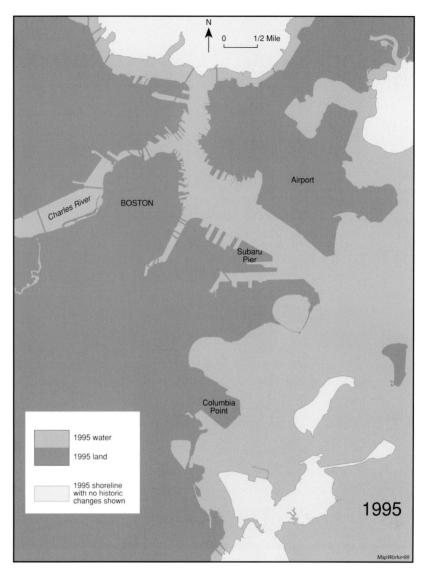

By 1950 hundreds of acres had been filled on the East Boston Flats for the airport, swallowing up Governors and Apple Islands. The inlet that had separated East Boston and Orient Heights had also been filled, merging the two former islands. On the South Boston Flats the U.S. Navy had created new land and piers north of the dry dock and filled the end of the Reserved Channel. Columbia Point had been greatly enlarged after years of being used as a trash dump, and trash fill and erosion had also transformed the shape of Spectacle Island.

The 1950 shoreline is based on the 1948 City Planning Board map (plate 48).

By 1995 the shoreline of Boston had reached its present extent. Since 1950 more land had been made for the airport; the navy's piers on the South Boston Flats had been filled in to create Subaru Pier; the edges of Columbia Point had been filled in for the Columbia Point housing project, JFK Library, UMass/Boston, and Boston College High School; South Bay had finally been completely filled; new land had been created on the Charles River to compensate for that taken for the construction of Storrow Drive; and Spectacle Island was being filled with dirt from the "Big Dig" (see figure 35 in chapter 8).

The 1995 shoreline is taken from a 1995 aerial photograph.

II

Mapping New England: A Region and City Come into Focus

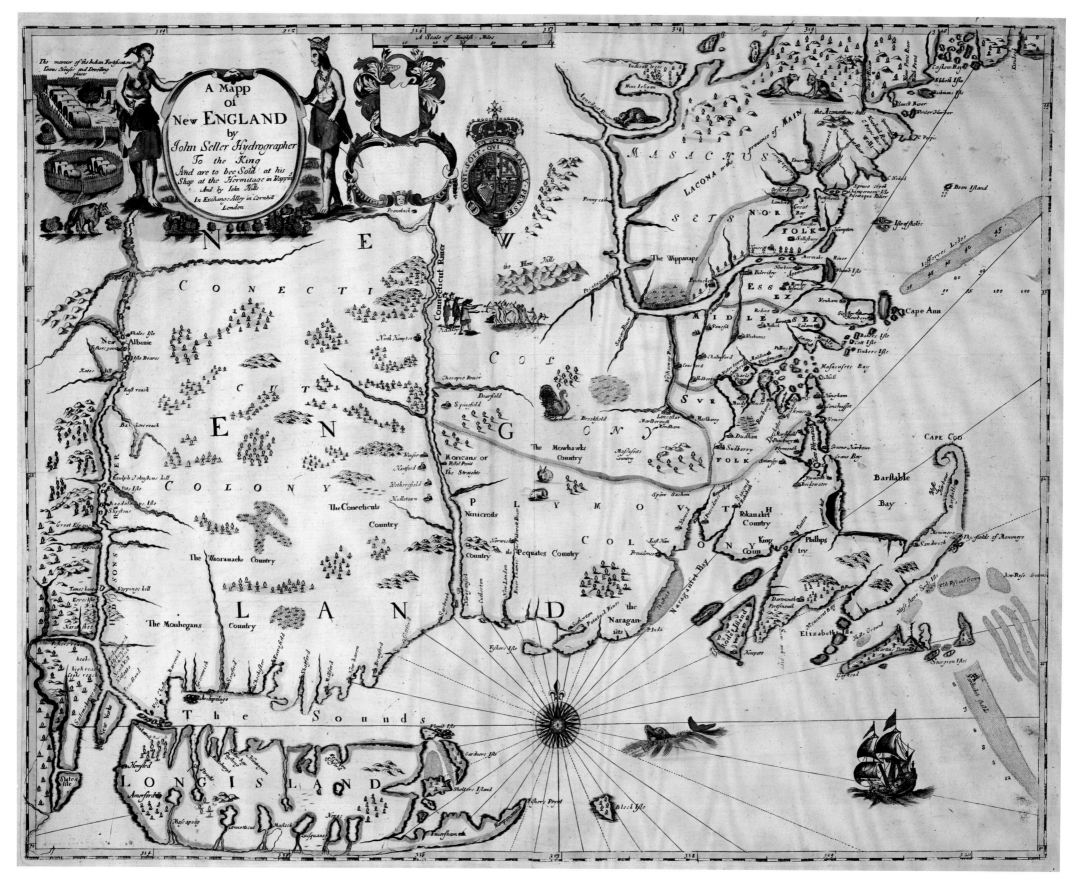

Frontispiece John Seller, *A Mapp of New England* (London, 1675). John Seller's *Mapp* is the first large, detailed map devoted solely to New England. While some of the figures on the map still hark back a century with images drawn from Theodore de Bry's great *Grand Voyages,* this map is more complete in its geographic coverage than the maps of John Smith (1616) (see plate 7) or William Wood (1634) (see plate 9), extending New England to almost its present boundaries.

3

The Mapping of New England before 1800

Barbara McCorkle

The story of the mapping of New England is not unlike the story of the mapping of other parts of North America—configuration based on conjecture from early explorers' reports was slowly replaced as more accurate information accumulated, and eventually scientific surveys resulted in a thoroughly modern representation. Adopting a scheme used in *The Southeast in Early Maps* by W. P. Cumming, this brief history of New England mapping is divided into three parts: Primary, or the period of European discovery; Transitional or descriptive; and Modern, the results of scientific surveys. It is a useful division, and a similar scheme is used here. Into the first, or Primary, division fall maps produced before 1634; into the second, which I call Developmental, fall the maps produced from 1634 to 1754; and into the last, the Modern, the maps of 1755–1850. The dates chosen are arbitrary, but are marked by developments that bring some logic to the plan. In 1634 William Wood published a map of New England that was clearly based on the results of local surveys (see plate 9). Maps produced in the second period reflect an increasing awareness of the size, dimensions, and physical characteristics of the land. And the third period begins in 1754 with the onset of the French and Indian War. The power struggle between France and England, as waged on the North American continent, brought on a cartographic deluge—as many maps showing the area of New England were published in 1755–1800 as had been published between 1513 and 1754. Several additional factors also came into play at this time: The English had become prolific mapmakers; increased literacy had created a large reading public; and an active English popular press began to include maps in their magazines, unlike the popular press in other European countries.

    In considering the cartographic history of the mapping of New England it is also necessary to think of its representation on two types of maps: small-scale representations of the world, the hemisphere, or the continents; and large-scale or regional maps. In this discussion world maps are excluded as their coverage of New England is too small to be useful. Generally, maps of the Western Hemisphere and North America are included only for the period of European exploration and discovery. It is the appearance of New England on maps of more limited scope that is most important for studying the history of New England cartography. At

the same time it is necessary to remember that many early regional maps focusing on Canada—"La Nouvelle France" or "Le Canada"—included either all or part of New England.

PRIMARY PERIOD

But when did New England first appear on a map? In the late fifteenth and early sixteenth centuries the English and French, seeking likely locations for a passage across the unexpected bulk of North America beyond the territories already claimed by Spain and Portugal, sent adventurous explorers north of the 40th parallel. New England, with its extensive east-facing coastline, became an early target. Although John Cabot's route is unknown, at least one authority would have New England, in embryonic form, appearing on the Juan de la Cosa manuscript map of ca. 1500–1507, which records his voyage of 1497.[1] Most historians agree on a course along the east coast of Newfoundland, but it could possibly have gone as far south as to skirt Maine's northeast coast. Giovanni da Verrazano, who sailed for Francis I of France in 1524, wrote the first report of New England in his letter to the king, telling of hospitable natives in a spot he considered so idyllic he called it "Refugio," in present-day Rhode Island, and unfriendly ones in a land now identified as Maine.

    The discoveries of Cabot and Verrazano were at first recorded only on manuscript maps. Perhaps the first printed map appeared in Benedetto Bordone's *Isolario,* published in Venice in 1528 and appearing in several editions to 1547. If "Terra de lavoratore," lettered across a large island mass on a small, 8.5 × 14.5 cm. untitled woodcut in that work is indeed North America, as has been argued, its northeast corner would be New England (see plate 3 vignette).

    European exploration of the northeast coast then lapsed, as Jacques Cartier drew the attention of the French to Canada, and the English turned to the far north in search of the elusive Northwest Passage. Nearly a century passed before Samuel de Champlain, Bartholomew Gosnold, Martin Pring, and George Weymouth coasted the Gulf of Maine and rounded Cape Cod.

    Until Giacomo Gastaldi's "Tierra Nueva," in the Venice 1548 edition of Ptolemy's *Geografia* (see plate 5), New England remained a small, undifferentiated area on maps of the world or the western hemisphere. The maps Gastaldi engraved for this edition of Ptolemy included the first regional maps of North America. The New England area bears the designation "Tierra de Nurumberg," the first appearance of this name on a printed map. In its various permutations Norumbega became the term for the lands of New England (see plate 5 vignette). The term is found as late as 1677 on Duval's issue of Champlain's 1616 plate, where it is shown northeast of "N. Angleterre," approximately in present-day New Brunswick. Gastaldi obviously based the geography of his map on Verrazano's report, for it places "Arcadia" (New Jersey), "Angoulesme" (New York), and "Refugio" (Narragansett Bay) in their correct west-east alignment. The area came under closer scrutiny in Giovanni Ramusio's *Navigatione et Viaggi* in 1556, which contained an untitled woodcut map based in part on the northern section of Gastaldi's 1548 map. It clearly designates, along the southern coast, "Terra de Nurumbega" and "Port du Refuge." New England is beginning to come into focus.

Gastaldi's 1548 map had a further offspring in Girolamo Ruscelli's 1561 edition of the *Geografia,* this time in a copper engraving, "Tierra Nueva," slightly larger than Gastaldi's original but otherwise a direct copy. An indication of how little the region was known in the late sixteenth century—understandable in the light of the long hiatus between the explorations of Verrazano and those of Champlain—can be seen on Michael Lok's untitled map of 1582.[2] "Norombega" here is the name given to a large island south of a great embayment labelled "Jac. Cartier," which leads to Hochelaga, present-day Montreal. The south shore of the island has a great harbor, obviously Verrazano's "Refugio," our Narragansett Bay.

The New England area continued to be depicted on many maps of the Western Hemisphere and North America but is not seen again in a regional map until Cornelis Wytfliet's *Descriptionis Ptolemaicae Augmentum,* first published in 1597. His map "Norumbega et Virginia" (see plate 6) clearly shows the Penobscot River and the area eastward, but compresses the land between Chesapeake Bay and the Penobscot, eliminating Verrazano's Angoulesme and Refugio and the entire southern part of New England. Wytfliet's map was closely copied by Jean Matal in 1598.

The seventeenth century saw renewed interest in the lands explored by Cartier, 1534–1535, and resulted in more accurate, more regional mapping. Marc Lescarbot based the map included in his 1609 *Histoire de la Nouvelle France* on a manuscript map of Champlain's, thus preceding the latter's own publication by four years. The Lescarbot map, limited to the coast north of Cape Cod, was the first to show that cape, which he named Malebarre. When Champlain's *Voyages* was published in 1613 it included two maps important for the development of the mapping of New England. Both extended inland from the coast and put Lake Champlain on the map, although apparently Champlain had not yet decided on the name; on one of the maps it is Lac des Irocois, on the other Lac de Champlain.

Perhaps the foundation map for New England is that of Captain John Smith, boldly titled "New England," and first published in his *A Description of New England,* 1616 (see plate 7). With this map Smith put his lasting stamp on the area. Although Smith's map included only the shores of Maine, New Hampshire, and Massachusetts as far as Cape Cod, the name he gave the area was quickly extended to include the hinterlands and the areas of present-day Connecticut and Rhode Island, and has defined the character of this northeastern corner of the United States ever since. Smith had requested the young Prince Charles to give proper English names to replace the "barbarous" native names, and a few of the prince's designations survive today. The Charles River runs with its correct course into an unnamed bay, New Plimouth is in an approximately correct location, as is Cape Anne, but such towns as Boston, Ipswich, and Cambridge are scattered somewhat randomly on Smith's map—not surprising, since none of them had yet been founded; but the prince's legacy was preserved when the names were eventually assigned to actual settlements. The map was very popular; it went through many states and editions and was extensively copied. It is interesting to note how quickly Smith's term *New England* was adopted. It is found on the untitled map by Sir William Alexander Stirling (see plate 8) which was used in his *Encouragement to Colonies* and in volume 4 of Samuel Purchas's *Pilgrimes,* both published in 1624; on Abraham Goos's "t Noorder deel van West-Indien," also in 1624; on Henry Briggs's "The North Part of America," 1625; on the western hemisphere map in John Speed's *Prospect of the Most Famous Parts of the World,* 1625; as Nieuw Engeland on Johannes de Laet's "Nova Anglia, Novum Belgium et Virginia," 1630 (figure 1); as Nova Anglia on Hondius's "America Septentrionalis" in 1636; as Inghiltera nuoua on Robert Dudley's "Carta seconda generale," 1646; and as N. Angleterre on Duval's "Le Canada," 1653. Thus, by mid-century, in the various languages of Europe, New England had become the accepted name.

DEVELOPMENTAL PERIOD

A map very important in the history of New England's cartography, and particularly for Boston's, is William Wood's "The South part of New England, as it is Planted this yeare, 1634" (see plate 9), published in his *New Englands Prospect,* 1634. Wood's New England reaches only from Narragansett Bay to the "Pascataque" river, but it includes the first geographically accurate appearance of Boston and Massachusetts Bay on a map. ("Massachusets" as an area was first seen on an otherwise blank space in the interior of "Nieuw Engeland" on DeLaet's "Nova Anglia, Novum Belgium et Virginia," 1630.) The map itself is a rather crude woodcut, but in its attention to local detail it is of great value.

Connecticut makes its appearance twelve years later on Robert Dudley's "Carta seconda Generale de America" in his *Arcano del Mare,* the

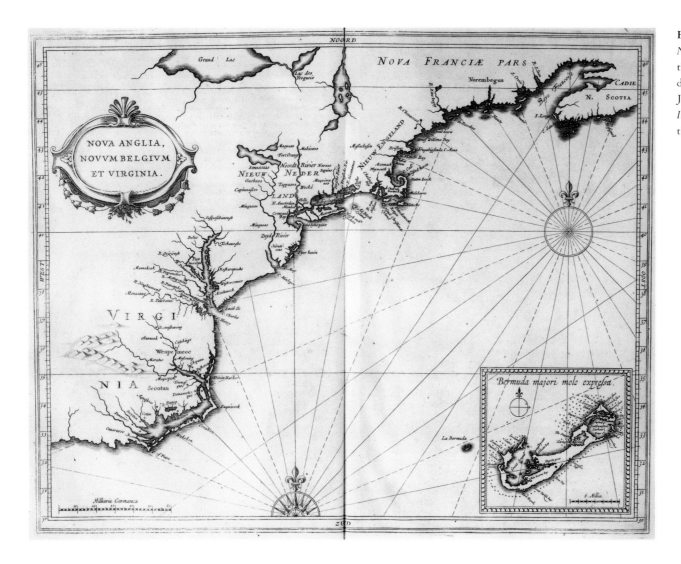

Figure 1 [Hessel Gerritsz], *Nova Anglia, Novvm Belgivm et Virginia* (1630). Detail of the New England area on a map, probably drawn by Hessel Gerritsz and appearing in Johannes de Laet's *Beschryvinghe van West-Indian,* shows "Massachusets" for the first time on a map.

earliest nautical atlas to show the coastline of the Americas, as "R. Conoknoot." More charts for Dudley's *Arcano* were published the following year, 1647, and on a regional chart, "Carta particolare della Nuoua Belgia è parte della nuoua Anglia" the name of the river takes a bit more recognizable form, "R. Conokteeok."

In about 1651 "Belgii Novi, Angliae Novae, et partis Virginiae Novissima Delineatio" (see plate 10), by Jan Jansson, made its appearance, and with it "Roode Eylant" in Narragansett Bay, the first cartographic reference to Rhode Island. This regional map is the first of a score of maps known as the Jansson-Visscher series. Covering the area from the St. Lawrence River to Chesapeake Bay, and handsomely adorned with scenes borrowed from de Bry's collection of voyages (transferred far from their original southern locations to the frigid north), the map and its derivatives continued to appear for more than 100 years. Its popularity undoubtedly helped form an image of New England as a discrete geographic entity.

While New England, now firmly on the map, continued to be represented on maps of the hemisphere and continent, its depiction on regional maps became more frequent. On "A Map of New England, New Yorke, New Jersey . . ." by Robert Morden and William Berry, published ca. 1675, the words "Laconia or the Province of Main" stretch across the area of the present state, the first use of this designation on a map. A curious, little-known map, it follows in general the shape of maps in the Jansson-Visscher series, and its cartouche is a direct copy of the one in "Novi Belgii Quod nunc Novi Jorck vocatur," a version of the series found in John Ogilby's *America,* 1671, yet its depiction of geography is far superior to that found in the Ogilby map. Also notable is John Seller's "A Mapp of New England," 1675 (frontispiece), which might be considered the first true map of New England as it includes the Conecticut Colony [sic], the Plymouth Colony, the Masachussets [sic] Colony, and Lacona or the province of Main, and thus is much more inclusive than either the Smith or Wood maps.

The last quarter of the seventeenth century saw the publication of small, inexpensive atlases and geography books, making maps available to a wider market than that for the large, expensive atlases. Five small maps of New England were published at this time: "New-England and New York" in a miniature edition of John Speed's *Prospect of the Most Famous Parts of the World,* 1675 (figure 2); "New England and New York by Robt. Morden" in his *Geography Rectified,* 1680; "New England and New York by John Seller" in the miniature edition of his *Atlas Maritimus,* 1682; "A new map of New England and New York by Robt. Morden," which in 1683 replaced the earlier map; and "Nouvelle Angleterre et Nouvel York," a French version of Morden's map published in Richard Blome's *L'Amerique angloise,* 1688. These small maps—the largest measures only 16 x 17.5 cm. and is the French enlargement of Morden's 8.5 x 12.5 cm. original—make an interesting study. Nomenclature and geography vary in all five. It is obvious that no single model representing New England was yet accepted as a norm. Speed's 1675 map has the most archaic geography, and considering that Speed himself had been dead for forty-four years reflects the sources used by the publisher of this posthumously published atlas. The map still shows the conflation of Lakes Champlain and Winnepesauke as one large lake. Morden's map of 1680 corrects this error by showing two separate lakes, one named Lake Irocoso, the other nameless. His map is followed in many details by the Sellers map of 1682,

although the nomenclature varies. Morden's "new map," 1683, makes further correction in the shape of Lake Winnepesauke and recognizes a more correct location of Lake Champlain by eliminating it entirely, since it lies beyond the area of the map. The French version of Morden's map of 1688 is a curious mixture of geographical elements but does show the eastern ends of Lakes Ontario and Erie. What could a seventeenth-century gentleman who had access to this handful of maps published within thirteen years make of it all?

Herman Moll, a Dutchman who moved to England late in the seventeenth century, became one of the most prolific English cartographers. He made a number of maps of North America, three of which, dated 1708–1730, are regional maps of the northeast. The best known of these, "New England, New York, New Jersey and Pensilvania. By H. Moll Geographer" (see plate 14), is the so-called "Post Road" map, first appearing in his *Atlas Minor,* 1729. The Post Road—still called today the Boston Post Road—snakes along the coast from Boston to New York, then on to Philadelphia (see plate 14 vignette). A sixteen-line legend, "An account of ye Post of ye Continent of Nth. America," details the schedule and routes. This map is sometimes confused with two others that have almost identical titles. "New England, New York, New Jersey, and Pensilvania &c. By H. Moll Geographer" preceded the Post Road map, as it was published in 1708 in John Oldmixon's *The British Empire in America.* Only the "&c."

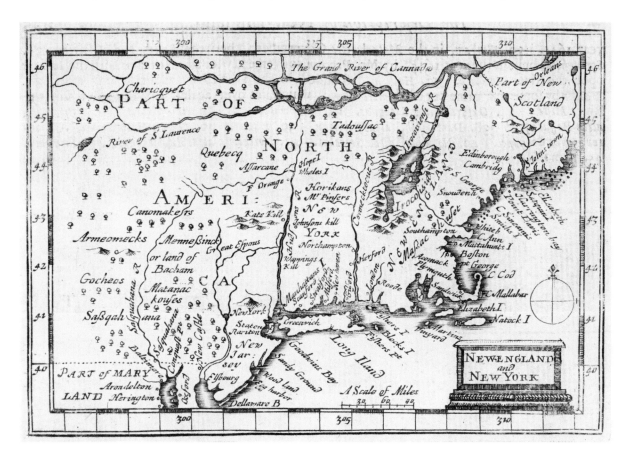

Figure 2 John Speed, *New-England and New York* (London, 1675). One of five small maps of New England published between 1675 and 1688, this one appeared in the small edition of Speed's *A Prospect of the most famous parts of the World.* It includes a large "Irocois" lake, the conflation of Lakes Champlain and Winnepesauke often found on maps of the period, and assigns much of western New England to New York, indicative of the still sketchy knowledge of inland New England.

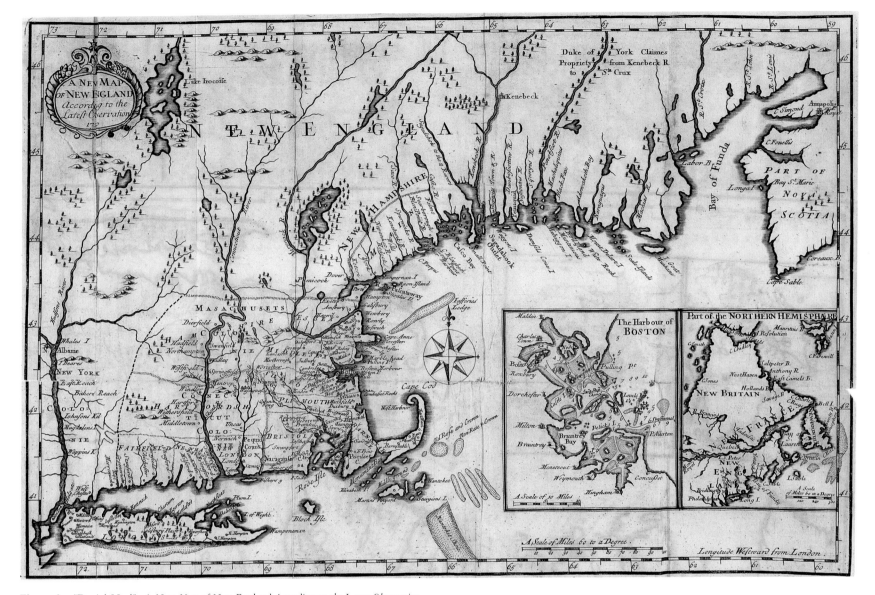

Figure 3 [Daniel Neal], *A New Map of New England According to the Latest Observation, 1720.* New Hampshire makes its first appearance on this map. While information on the area west of the Connecticut River and north of Massachusetts is still scanty, the population growth of eastern New England is clearly shown by the proliferation of town names.

distinguishes the titles. This slightly smaller map was later used in the *Atlas Geographus,* 1717, and in editions of Moll's atlases for many years. It lacks the Post Road. The third Moll map of New England appeared in David Humphrey's *An Historical Account of the Incorporated Society for the Propagation of the Gospel,* 1730, titled "A Map of New England, New York, New Jersey and Pensilvania By H. Moll Geographer. Note. the Towns to which Missionaries are sent are marked thus [church symbol] 1730." The Post Road is also marked on this map, but the explanatory legend is omit-

ted and the engraving lacks the "look" of most Moll maps. Moll's maps were popular and were copied abroad. The 1708 map was closely copied in a Dutch edition of Oldmixon, 1721, as "Nieu Engeland Nieu York Nieu Jersey en Pensilvania door H. Mol." Particularly interesting for the history of the mapping of Boston is the addition of an insert, "De Haven van Boston int Groot." The Post Road map was copied by the firm Homannischen Erben ca. 1740 as "New Engelland New York New Yersey und Pensilvania" as one of four maps of America, while a nearly indistinguishable, line-for-line copy of it appeared in the Dublin edition of Salmon's *Modern History* in 1755.

We have seen Connecticut, Massachusetts, Rhode Island, and Maine make their cartographic debuts. New Hampshire's turn came in 1720, in Daniel Neal's *History of New-England.* Its accompanying map, "A New Map of New England According to the Latest Observation 1720" (figure 3), not only has "New Hampshire" lettered above the east coast of Maine, it also has a small inset: "The Harbour of Boston." As the interior between the Gulf of Maine and the Great Lakes began to shed its secrets, the confusion over one large lake located somewhere inland, or two lakes, gradually yielded to a distinction between Lake Champlain (or Iroquois) and a large unnamed lake. At length, on his "Carte de la Partie Orientale de la Nouvelle France ou du Canada," 1744, Jacques Nicolas Bellin named both: "Lac Champlain" and "Lac Winipisioke."

The last map to be considered paints one of the most delightful, fantastical images of New England. But first, a bit of background. In 1749 the American cartographer Lewis Evans published a now very rare map, "A Map of Pensilvania, New-Jersey, New-York, and the three Delaware Counties. 1749." Evans's map covered exactly that area, showing nothing east of the Hudson River. Matthaeus Seutter, a leading eighteenth-century German map publisher, did little original work but was a great compiler. Probably shortly after the publication of the Evans map, ca. 1750, Seutter copied it. While his "Pensylvania Nova Jersey et Nova York . . ." follows quite faithfully the geography of the original, the map bears typical Seutter touches—an elaborate cartouche, jagged mountains rearing like up-ended scallop shells. But Seutter was evidently unwilling to leave a little blank area beyond the Hudson River. Into the small space between that river and the border of the map he squeezed New England, but a New England never seen before or since. Connecticut's border is drawn north of Boston, and wraps around a small Rhode Island to include Cape Cod; a chunky Massachusetts stops at Northfield, and New Hampshire is a narrow wedge between New York and the sea. When Seutter's son-in-law Tobias Conrad Lotter took over the business he put his name on the map, but changed nothing else.

MODERN PERIOD

The year 1755 ushers in a fateful period, five decades marked by two major wars and rapid expansion of settlement in New England. By the end of the century we find individual maps existing for each state, where none had been known before. The year itself was notable. Publishers brought out more than thirty maps in 1755 alone, an explosive change at the time. The year saw not just many maps, but the publication of some of the most important. The first edition of John Mitchell's "A Map of the British and French Dominions in North America" came out early that

year, on February 13th. It is by no means a regional map, but it must be considered here not only because it has been called the most important map in United States history, but also because of its size—53 × 76.5 inches or 134.5 × 194.5 cm., printed on eight sheets. The New England area is therefore large, and since the map was widely copied and the 1775 edition was used in setting the boundary between the new United States and the remaining British colonies, it greatly influenced perceptions of New England. The map went through four English editions with numerous states as well as editions published in Amsterdam, Paris, and Venice.

Seventeen fifty-five was also the year in which Lewis Evans's "A General Map of the Middle British Colonies in America . . ." and Thomas Jefferys's "A Map of the Most Inhabited Part of New England" (figure 4; see also plate 16) were published. New England as shown in the first edition of Evans's map included only Connecticut, Rhode Island, part of Massachusetts, and New Hampshire but later, in 1776, Thomas Pownall added to the original plate an extension covering all of New England. The Jefferys map is the first truly large scale map of New England. It seems to have been based on the very rare map of the British Dominions by William Douglass, published circa 1753 (see figure 2 in chapter 4). On four sheets, Jefferys's map was ample enough to include many small communities. The map was updated through the end of the century with many geographical additions and changes. The development of New

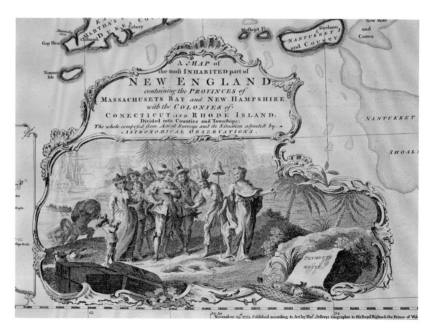

Figure 4 Thomas Jefferys, *A Map of the most Inhabited part of New England* (London, 1774). The cartouche of Jefferys's large and influential map of New England, here shown in a later edition (see plate 16), illustrates the typical contemporary view of civilized Europe meeting barbaric America.

Hampshire, which included Vermont, is strikingly shown both in corrections of the shape of its lakes and in delineation of the rectangular township pattern, unique to that part of the country. By 1777 several French and German editions of the map had appeared.

The dispute between England and France known as the French and Indian War spawned a spate of new maps. Readers following the war could find French, English, Dutch, German, Italian, and Spanish versions of one particular map covering Acadia and northern New England that, depending on the cartographer's point of view, showed either the "French Encroachments" or "les Prétentions des Anglois." Several of these maps emphasize their political position by a complicated system of dotted lines, crosses, and hatching. A Society of Anti-Gallicans brought out one of the most overtly propagandistic maps of the year, "A New and Accurate Map of the English Empire in North America: Representing their Rightful Claim as confirm'd by Charters and the formal Surrender of their Indian Friends; Likewise the Encroachments of the French, with the several Forts they have unjustly erected therein. By a Society of Anti-Gallicans." The hand behind this Society has not yet been discovered.

The French and Indian War dominated map titles during its waging, 1754–1763. Titles, often lengthy in the eighteenth-century manner, included such phrases as "the principal seat of war," "les pays contestez," "Map of the present war in North America," and "Theatrum Belli in America Septentrionali." The period of calm between the Peace of Paris, 1763, which ended the war, and the beginning of new hostilities in 1775 with the outbreak of the Revolutionary War produced fewer maps showing New England than in the one year 1755. These few included six that concentrated on New England: "Carte de la Nouvelle Angleterre, Nouvelle Jorck, et Pensilvanie," one of the maps Jacques Nicolas Bellin prepared to illustrate an edition of Prévost's *Voyages,* 1757 (figure 5); "New England," a small map John Gibson included in editions of his *Atlas Minimus,* 1758–1792; "Carte de la Nouvelle Angleterre, Nouvelle Iork, Nouvelle Jersey, et Pensilvanie" in *Nouvel Atlas Portatif,* a small atlas for children, by Robert de Vaugondy, 1762; "Carta della Nuova Inghilterra Nuova Iork, e Pensilvania," an Italian copy of the Bellin map of 1757, in *Il Gazzettiere Americana,* 1763; "Carte de la Nouvelle Angleterre New York Pensilvanie et Nouveau Jersay suivant les cartes Angloises," another Bellin map, this one from his *Petit Atlas Maritime,* 1764; and Carington Bowles's one-sheet adaptation of the great Jefferys map of New England, "A Map of the Most Inhabited Part of New England . . . ," 1765. Several of these maps had long lives, and in their later states were corrected to agree with the establishment of the United States. Bowles's map, additionally, went through several title changes, becoming successively "Bowles's Map of the Seat of War in New England," "Bowles's New Pocket-Map of the Most Inhabited Part of New England," and finally "Bowles's New One-Sheet Map of New England."

To the later editions of the map Bowles added an inset of Boston and Boston Harbor. Perhaps in challenge to the Bowles map, which had given no recognition to its basis in the Jefferys map, the firm of Sayer and Bennett, which had acquired some of Jefferys's stock after his death in 1771, brought out their own one-sheet map, "A Map of New England . . . Being an Abridgement of the Large Map Published by Thomas Jefferys . . . ," ca. 1775. The Bowles and the Sayer and Bennett maps are very similar, but are from quite different plates.

New England, of course, as the focus of the early battles of the Revolution, was well represented on maps. The title of one, "The Seat of War in New England, by an American Volunteer, with the Marches of the Several Corps sent by the Colonies, toward Boston, with the Attack on Bunkers-Hill," is a good example (see plate 17). Published by Sayer and Bennett in September 1775, the map covers parts of New Hampshire, Massachusetts, Connecticut, and Rhode Island, with insets of Boston Harbor and the town of Boston and Bunkers Hill added on a separate, adjoining plate. The unknown American Volunteer has drawn lines indicating opposing armies and the march routes of various forces, enabling armchair generals to visualize the conflict. As the war raged in the northern colonies, leading British periodicals supplemented their reports with maps. In October 1775, only six months after "the shot heard 'round the world" was fired, the *Universal Magazine* presented "A New and Accurate Map of the present Seat of War in North America, from a late Survey" to its readers. Over the following five years, until the action had moved well south, the *Universal Magazine, Lottery Magazine, Westminster Magazine, London Magazine,* and *Political Magazine* (figure 6) all included maps in which New England played a part. Histories of America naturally covered the war. "A Map of 100 Miles round Boston," from *Concise Historical Account of all the British Colonies in North-America,* Dublin, 1776, actually encompassed parts of New Hampshire, Connecticut, and Rhode Island, as well as Massachusetts. William Russell's *The History of America,* 1778, used a map by John Lodge, "An Exact Map of New England, New York, Pensylvania & New Jersey, from the latest surveys" as an illustration. The eighteenth-century penchant for such phrases as "from the latest surveys," "from the best authorities," or "from the latest astronomical observations" was often exercised. Intense French interest in the war resulted in large, separately published maps covering the northeastern battle areas. They often began "Carte du Théâtre de la Guerre . . . ," for example, "Carte du Théâtre de la Guerre entre les Anglais et les Américains," by Louis Brion de la Tour, first published in 1777 and reissued several times; the 1778 "Carte du Théátre de la Guerre actuel Entre les Anglais et les Treize Colonies Unies de l'Amerique Septentrionale . . ." by J. B. Eliot, who styled himself "Ingénieurs [!] des Etats Unis"; and "Carte du Théâtre de la Guerre dans l'Amerique Septentrionale" of 1779 by Capitaine de Chesnoy, an Aide-de-Camp of Lafayette.

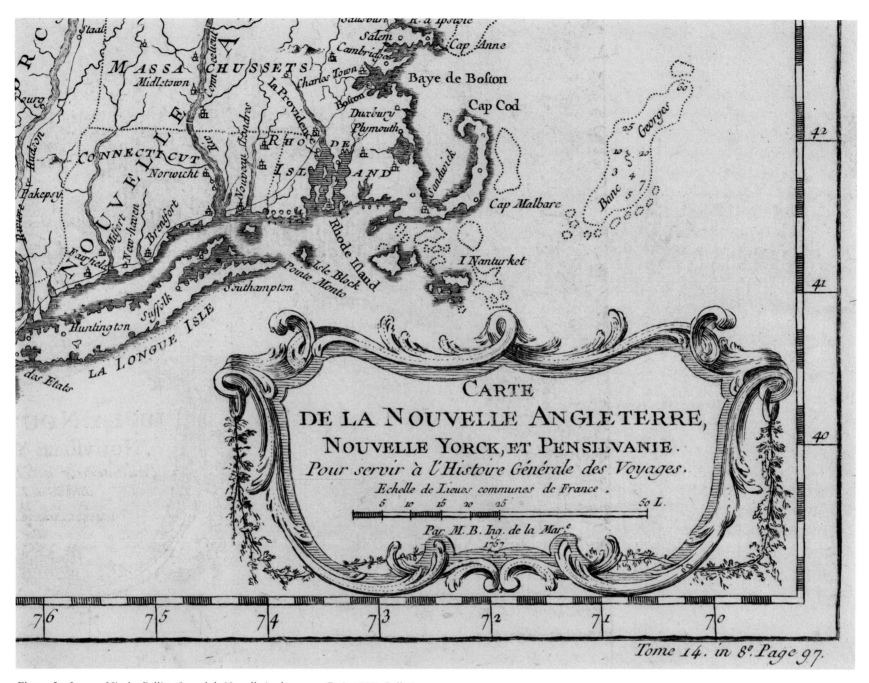

Figure 5a Jacques Nicolas Bellin, *Carte de la Nouvelle Angleterre . . .* (Paris 1757). Bellin's map and close copies appeared in French, Italian, and German publications for more than a quarter of a century.

Not all maps published during the war years, however, were war maps. Bernard Romans, whose most well-known maps were of Florida and the Gulf Coast done while he was surveyor general of the Southern District, made at least two maps of New England. Copies of his "Connecticut and Parts adjacent" and "A Chorographical Map of the "Northern Department of North America . . .", both printed in New Haven in 1778, are very rare but were republished in 1780 in Amsterdam by Covens and Mortier, making them more widely available. The "Chorographical Map" is oddly angled, as though viewed from the northwest. Townships in New York, Vermont, and New Hampshire are demarcated, and the name Vermont first appears on a map. An exceedingly rare, unusual little map of New England appeared on a playing card in 1779,

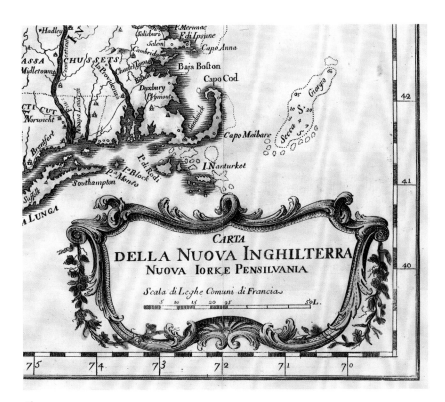

5b

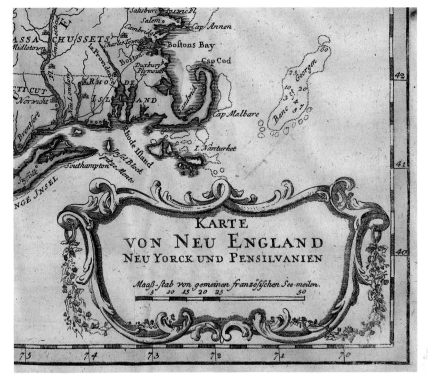

5c

5d

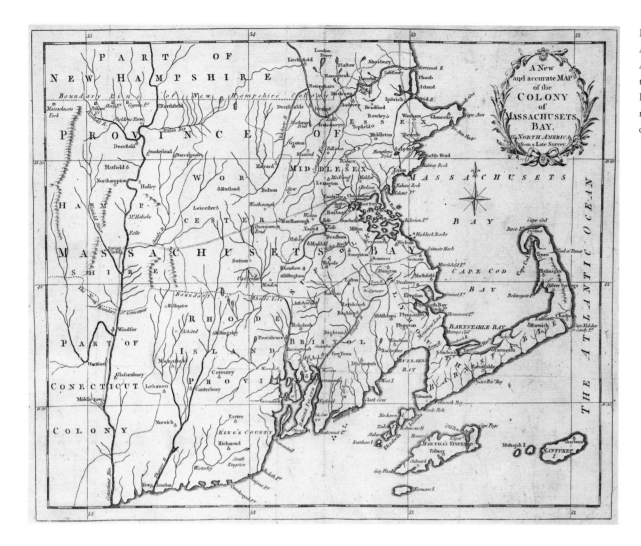

Figure 6 *A New and accurate Map of the Colony of Massachusetts Bay, in North America,* from *Universal Magazine* (December 1780). Interest in events in the rebellious American colonies ran high in England, and many British periodicals carried maps of areas of conflict, enabling armchair tacticians to follow the progress of the war.

one of a Minchiate pack of ninety-seven cards, printed in Florence. The "Colonie Inglesi" measures only 3.5 × 5.5 cm.

Travelers' accounts, too, furnished an outlet for maps. Several were drawn to illustrate the travels of Peter Kalm, and "Carte pour servir au Journal de Mr. Le Mquis. de Chastellux," from his *Voyages de M. le Marquis de Chastellux dans l'Amerique Septentrionalis,* 1786, traces his route through New England to Philadelphia, yielding evidence of a network of roads not otherwise mapped at this time.

The Treaty of Paris, 1783, ended the Revolutionary War and recognized the existence of a new country, the United States of America. Among some 150 maps that include New England published between 1783–1800, fully two-thirds had the United States—whether as Etats-Unis, Vereinigten Staaten, or Gli Stati Uniti—specifically mentioned in the title. The New England area was subsumed into maps of the country or fractured into maps of individual states. But not entirely. John Norman's large "An Accurate Map of the Four New England States," pub-

lished in Boston in 1783 and now known in only a few copies, is an outstanding example that affords many details of the area as it was late in the eighteenth century. Christopher Colles's attempt at producing a serial atlas in a publication to be called *The Geographical Ledger and Systematized Atlas* foundered. He produced only five untitled sheets which covered much of New England and eastern New York. The Library of Congress holds the only complete set. These maps, never disseminated to the public, are nevertheless important because they were, at least in part, engraved by a woman. Elizabeth Colles, the daughter of Christopher Colles, signed her name to several of the plates (figure 7). The active London engraver-publisher John Russell published "Map of the Northern, or New England States of America, comprehending Vermont, New-Hampshire, District of Main, Massachusetts, Rhode-Island, and Connecticut" in his *American Atlas.* The map was also used to illustrate Winterbotham's *Historical, Geographical . . . View of the American United States.* Both works were published in 1795.

Maps of the individual states proliferated. David Cobb documented the maps of New Hampshire and Vermont[3] and Edmund Thompson the maps of Connecticut,[4] but we lack cartobibliographies of the remaining New England states. Although most state maps postdate 1783, three each for New Hampshire and Rhode Island and six for Connecticut are earlier. The earliest individual "state" map even predates the Revolution, the "Correct Plan of the Province of New Hampshire together with part of Hudsons River from Albany to Lake George," 1756. Two states made

their map debut together two years later, "A Map of the Colonies of Connecticut and Rhode Island, Divided into Counties & Townships from the best Authorities," which Thomas Kitchin engraved for the April 1758 issue of the *London Magazine*. It was a small map, but Connecticut and Rhode Island are small states, and the map's scale was sufficient to allow inclusion of township lines, roads, and counties for the first time. Several other early state maps deserve to be singled out. "An Accurate Map of His Majesty's Province of New-Hampshire in New-England" is a very large,

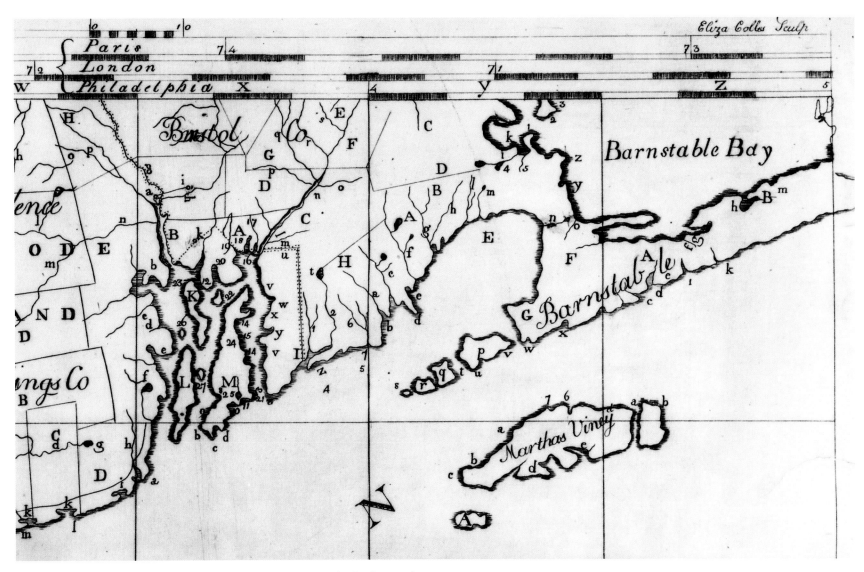

Figure 7 Christopher Colles, untitled sheet from unpublished *Geographical Ledger* (1794). Publisher Christopher Colles outreached himself. His plans for an atlas to cover the new United States never reached fruition, leaving an unfinished set of only five maps. Place names on the maps were indicated by letters, keyed to an accompanying index. Colles's daughter Eliza, whose name is found on several of the sheets, may have been the first female engraver in the United States.

handsome, detailed map by Thomas Jefferys. In 1784 the original plate was taken to Boston, where Abel Sawyer made corrections and additions to reflect New Hampshire's new status and the title was revised, becoming "An Accurate Map of the State and Province of New-Hampshire in New England." In addition to Bernard Roman's map of Connecticut, already mentioned, a second noteworthy large map of Connecticut is Moses Park's ". . . this plan of the Colony of Connecticut . . . ," 1766.

The hey day of state maps, however, came after the Treaty of Paris. In the following years eleven maps of Maine, thirteen each of Vermont, New Hampshire, and Massachusetts, nine of Rhode Island, and ten of Connecticut were published, most in England or the United States where there was avid interest in the development of the new republic. An exception is the work of a German cartographer, Daniel Sotzmann, who was commissioned to produce an atlas of maps of the United States to accompany the *Erdbeschreibung und Geschichte von Amerika,* an ambitious multivolume work by Christoph Ebeling, a professor of history and classics in Hamburg. The entire project envisioned by Ebeling was never completed, as only ten of the eighteen maps planned for the atlas were published, but among them were those for the six New England states. The Sotzmann-Ebeling maps, executed at a fairly large scale, were finely detailed. Their exactness is due to Ebeling's use of the latest and most up-to-date American maps and surveys.

With few exceptions the maps so far discussed were printed abroad. Not until after the American Revolution did a flourishing map trade develop on this side of the Atlantic. By the nineteenth century Philadelphia had become the center of the American map publishing trade, but until that center was well established publishing houses in Boston and New York were also active (see chapter 4). The bulk of state maps published before 1800 came from the last decade of the eighteenth century, and from works of American authors. Mathew Carey, an entrepreneurial Irish immigrant, settled in Philadelphia and was responsible for the first American atlas and the first American edition (1794/95) of William Guthrie's popular *New System of Modern Geography,* first published in London in 1780. Carey addressed what he rightly considered Guthrie's scant treatment of America by adding a lengthy text to correct those deficiencies. He illustrated the whole with a set of state maps, all executed by American cartographers and engravers. These maps appeared again in Carey's *American Atlas* and in his *General Atlas.* New England native Jedidiah Morse illustrated his *American Geography,* printed in Elizabeth Town, New Jersey, in 1789 not with individual state maps, but with two regional maps, one of which, "A Map of the Northern and Middle States, Comprehending the Western Territory" included New England. Morse's work was quickly adopted by British publishers to answer the need for information on the United States, and the edition published by John Stockdale in London, 1794, included state

maps. American editions followed suit. The edition published in Boston, 1796, included a set of state maps.

By 1800 maps of the individual states were no longer scarce, having been published in Boston in several editions of Morse's *Geography,* in Philadelphia in Joseph Scott's *United States Gazetteer,* his *Atlas of the United States,* and *New and Universal Gazetteer,* and in New York in John Payne's *New and Complete System of Universal Geography.* The stage was now set for the introduction of new technologies and mass production, which would change map publishing forever.

During the first decades of the nineteenth century map publishing in the United States burgeoned. Maps were needed not just to satisfy the desire of Americans to learn more about their new country, but also for the proper functioning of state governments. To support these new demands surveyors, cartographers, engravers, and others working in the publishing centers of the time had to be recruited and trained. New names appeared among the lists of publishers. Among the first to join Mathew Carey in Philadelphia was Henry Schenk Tanner. Tanner's *New American Atlas,* published serially from 1818 to 1823, contained a splendid "Map of the States of Maine New Hampshire Vermont Massachusetts Connecticut & Rhode Island." This large, two-sheet, elegantly engraved map demonstrates that American engravers had mastered their art. Samuel Augustus Mitchell was another notable Philadelphia map publisher. Between 1831 and 1887 maps and atlases bearing the Mitchell name, together with those of Joseph H. Colton of New York, dominated the domestic market and produced dozens of maps of the New England states. The careers of both of these publishers overlapped the introduction of a revolutionary new technology—lithography. Earlier atlases were produced from copperplate engravings, an expensive and labor-intensive process. In the lithographic process maps were drawn on fine-grained stones, an easier, faster, and hence cheaper method. The lithographic shop of William and John Pendleton was founded in Boston in 1826, and from it issued the earliest lithographed maps published in the United States. Lithography opened the way for the explosion of maps that characterized the latter half of the century.

These Mitchell and Colton maps, along with those of other contemporary map makers, appeared not only in atlases but also in popular "pocket" editions, single sheets of individual states printed on thin paper and folded into leather or, more commonly, embossed cloth-covered cardboard covers, a very handy way for travelers to carry maps. Convenient as they were, the quality of the paper on which they were printed together with the strains occasioned by unfolding and refolding has made these maps very fragile, far less durable than their counterparts protected within the stout covers of atlases. Nevertheless they are important as they are indicative of an increasingly mobile population. New Englanders were on the move, and maps marked the way with roads, canal routes, and railroad lines.

NOTES

1. James A. Williamson, *The Cabot Voyages and Bristol Discovery under Henry VII* (Cambridge, England: Hakluyt Society, 1962), 2d series, no. 120, 71–72.

2. Richard Hakluyt, *Divers Voyages* (London, 1582).

3. David Cobb, *New Hampshire Maps Prior to 1900: An Annotated Checklist* (Hanover: New Hampshire Historical Society, 1981); David Cobb, *Vermont Maps Prior to 1900: An Annotated Cartobibliography* (Burlington: Vermont Historical Society, 1971).

4. Edmund Thompson, *Maps of Connecticut before the Year 1800 (*Wyndham, Conn.: Hawthorn House, 1940; reprint, G. B. Manasek: Norwich, Vt., 1995).

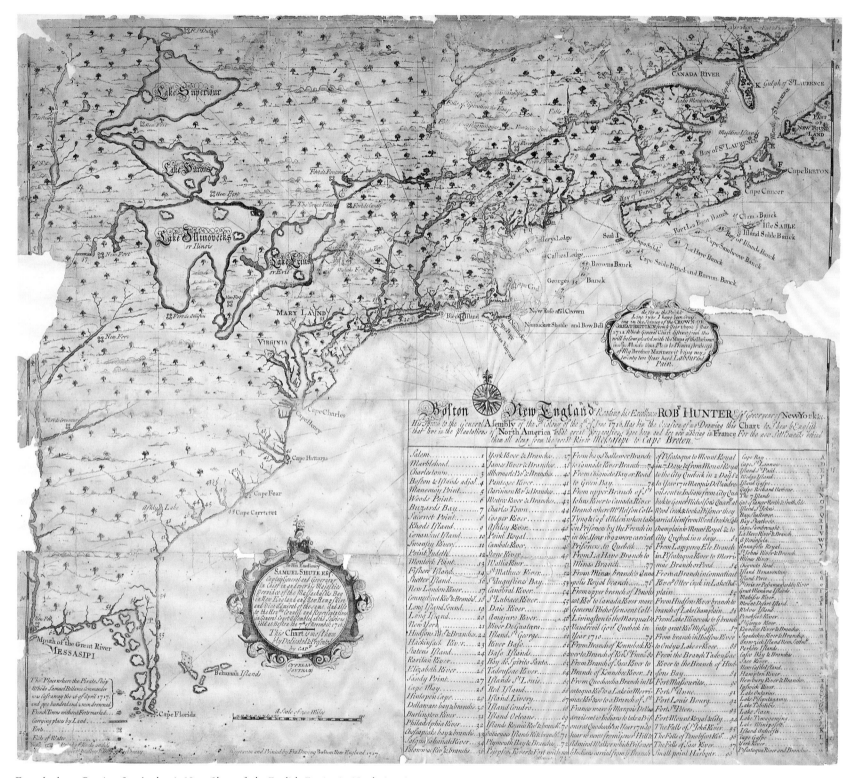

Frontispiece Cyprian Southack, *A New Chart of the English Empire in North America* (Boston, 1717). A redoubtable navigator, Southack was out of his element when he prepared this chart. Notes on the chart indicate that its ultimate purpose may have been as much political as cartographic. William Douglass, whose map of New England appeared in 1755, described Southack's effort as "one continued error," and suggested that it might actually inhibit navigation. Despite the many inaccuracies south of Long Island and in the interior, the chart was reissued on four separate occasions, the last in 1754.

The Boston Map Trade of the Eighteenth Century

David Bosse

When London merchant John Dunton arrived in Boston in March 1686 with a consignment of books, he visited several of the town's principal figures. After calling on Increase Mather and his son, Cotton, Dunton declared their personal library the best of his acquaintance, and "the glory of New England, if not all of America."[1] Dunton went on to describe John Usher, who "got his estate by book selling," as one of the richest men in Boston. While hardly typical of their contemporaries, the Mathers' extensive library and Usher's success attest to an abiding interest in books and a corresponding market for them in Boston at the end of the seventeenth century. From its beginnings, a literary culture permeated New England. Most Plymouth Colony householders counted books among their possessions, and in neighboring Boston, books and libraries were even more common.[2] Many of these first colonists brought whatever books and maps they owned with them. As early as 1653, probate inventories include maps among the possessions listed.[3] Records of atlas ownership, such as Plymouth Colony governor William Bradford's copy of John Speed's *A Prospect of the Most Famous Parts of the World* (London, 1631) also survive from an early date.[4]

Within a generation of the arrival of colonists, a thriving trade in printed materials including maps had developed in the Boston area, and with it the growth of personal libraries. England furnished the bulk of printed items that circulated in early Boston, and continued to do so throughout much of the eighteenth century. The letters of prominent Bostonians reveal that they received shipments of English books with some regularity.[5] Maps and atlases arrived from London in this manner as well; in August 1683, Chief Justice Samuel Sewall, a celebrated diarist, recorded that his cousin had just arrived from London with "a barrel of books" for him, and "a map of England and London."[6] Failing a direct London connection of their own, Bostonians could purchase printed matter from local retailers.

Boston's first book shop opened in 1647, and by 1711 the number had grown to thirty.[7] Booksellers frequently offered atlases, maps, and prints, although none of these accounted for a significant portion of their trade in the seventeenth century. Like his father Hezekiah, Boston's first bookseller, John Usher published books and imported them for resale. In 1683, his London agent, John Ive, supplied him with six copies of the *Atlas Coelestis* (London, 1677) by John Seller, and would have been the source of other cartographic titles.[8] That Usher took six copies suggests a ready market for a somewhat expensive collection of small celestial maps and diagrams. Ive's invoice provides a relative measure of the duodecimo atlas's cost. For the price of a single copy of the *Atlas Coelestis,* Usher could purchase three copies of Milton's *Paradise Lost* (London, 1678), or five copies of Richard Norwood's *An Application of the Doctrine of Triangles in the Use of the Plain Sea Chart* (London, 1678), or seventeen copies of *The Psalms of the Old and New Testament* (London, 1671).

By the eighteenth century, greater evidence of maps and atlases, as both commodities and possessions, appears in the Boston area. The estates of men like William Tailer of Dorchester, who owned more than a dozen maps at the time of his death in 1732, reflect an increase in map ownership.[9] As modest as it may seem, a collection of that size would have been remarkable just a few decades earlier. A greater availability of maps in Boston can, in part, be traced to a local event. In 1711, a fire destroyed the Town House, the center of Boston commerce, and all but one of the book shops clustered around it. Following this disaster merchants other than booksellers began to deal in print material, and many continued to do so even after booksellers re-established their shops.[10] Any shopkeeper importing goods from England might now find himself in the book or map trade, at least temporarily.

Sales held at public venues became an increasingly important means of marketing maps and atlases. Auctions such as that held by Stephen Labbe at the Crown Coffee House on March 1, 1714, frequently included cartographic material. Along with an assortment of general merchandise Labbe offered "maps and prints in gilt frames," suggesting an intended use as decorative wall hangings.[11] Similarly, the *New England Weekly Journal* of May 29, 1727, advertised an auction at the Royal Exchange that featured "a large parcel of fine maps and prints lately imported from London in frames or without." Such announcements confirm the existence of public sales of maps, but rarely do they identify the individual items for sale. Even catalogs of booksellers generally failed to specify cartographic titles. Of the fifty-five known catalogs printed in Boston between 1693 and 1800, only eight include maps and charts.[12] All but three of these date from after the American Revolution, making it difficult to evaluate the nature of Boston's early cartographic market.

Philip Freeman's broadside of September 30, 1766, is only the second Boston bookseller's catalog to list maps, and the first to provide some clue as to titles.[13] The inclusion of prices also distinguishes his catalog from that of most booksellers and from newspaper notices. Books comprise three-quarters of the catalog's more than 200 items, with maps, prints, globes, and optical and surveying instruments forming the remainder (figure 1). Certain maps among the catalog's cartographic offerings can be identified as follows:

four-sheet map of the world—7 shillings, 6 pence; 13 shillings on cloth
four-sheet map of Europe—7s 6d; 13s on cloth
four-sheet map of Africa—3s 8d; 10s 4d on cloth
four-sheet map of Asia—3s 8d; 10s 4d on cloth
four-sheet map of North America—5s; 10s 4d on cloth
chart of the West Indies—2s 5d
chart of the Mediterranean—6s
"Coast of New-England"—2s 2d
"Land of Canaan" on 13 sheets (i.e., John More, *The Land of Canaan Described with the City of Jerusalem,* London, 1683; reprinted by Carrington Bowles, ca. 1763)— £1 7s 8d
"Antigallican North-America" (i.e., *A New and Accurate Map of the English Empire in North America,* London, 1755)—2s 6d
"Plan of London"—8d
"Plan of London by Gibson" (i.e., *A New and Correct Plan of the Cities and Suburbs of London and Westminster,* London, 1766)—1s 4d
"Senex's Atlas, 34 maps" (i.e., *A New General Atlas,* London, 1721)— £3 6s 8d

This miscellany of predominantly (and perhaps exclusively) English cartography offers a narrow view into the Boston market at mid-century. An emphasis on maps of the continents may reflect the proclivity of Philip Freeman's London sources, or the tastes of his clientele, or both. The catalog printed in Boston by John Mein four months earlier also featured continental maps and maps of European countries, a selection that resembles the maps that one might expect to find in a general bookstore today.[14] Freeman's inclusion of charts of the West Indies and coast of New England would predictably appeal to Bostonians interested in trade and navigation. Whether his offering of a wall map of the Holy Land and a chart of the Mediterranean largely reflected his own interests (as a publisher Freeman specialized in religious tracts) or those of his clientele remains unknown.

The presence of both recent and older maps in Freeman's catalog again speaks to supply and market. John Gibson's map of London was the latest depiction of that city, and would have been of use to Boston mer-

chants and others. In selling the *Map of the English Empire,* Freeman may have counted upon the anti-French sympathies of fellow British Americans who had suffered the effects of colonial wars. Published over a decade earlier in 1755, the map had served as an instrument of propaganda on the eve of the French and Indian War, not long concluded at the time of Freeman's sale. By 1766, the Senex atlas was obviously rather dated, but colonial readers may have considered the atlas valuable for any number of reasons. Although a traffic in antiquarian materials existed in the eighteenth century, a forty-five-year-old atlas would probably not have been viewed as collectable on those grounds.

A reliance on English cartography throughout much of the eighteenth century encouraged the sale of out-of-date maps and atlases in Boston. In some ways this paralleled the situation of the book trade wherein London suppliers tried to dump titles no longer in vogue on the colonial market.[15] Judging the currency of maps and charts advertised only by short titles or vague descriptions can be problematical. The map of the "Four provinces of Massachusetts, New Hampshire, Rhode Island and Connecticut" advertised in the *Boston News-Letter* of May 16, 1771, may have referred to Thomas Jefferys's *A Map of the Most Inhabited Part of New England* (London, 1755) (see plate 16). It may just as well have indicated one of the reissues of the map, such as that published by Carrington Bowles in January 1771, or another map altogether. Even when the identity of the map is certain, questions arise regarding the copy offered for sale. In their *Catalogue of a Large Assortment of the Most Esteemed Books* (Boston, 1772) the firm of Cox and Berry listed "Popple's Map of America," being Henry Popple's *A Map of the British Empire in America.* Originally published in London in 1733 and again in 1734 as a twenty-sheet wall map, the copies sold by Cox and Berry may have been the single-sheet London printings of the map issued in 1735, 1738, and 1740, or possibly the wall map itself. Regardless of the edition, Popple's map had long been superseded, and in all likelihood would not have been found on the shelves of a London map seller in 1772.

English cartographic productions typically reached the American market in a more timely manner. An announcement in the *Boston Gazette* of December 29, 1755, stated "Just imported from London, a Plan of the Four Governments of New England, on four sheets of Imperial Paper . . . composed from surveys by the late Dr. William Douglass." Actually titled *Plan of the British Dominions of New England in America,* the map was the work of a respected, if outspoken, Boston physician and political commentator, and would have commanded great interest in New England (figure 2). Recent research has established that the map's publication most likely occurred in the summer of 1755, rather than 1753 as has long been assumed.[16] As the exact date remains unknown, the map's initial appearance in Boston at the end of the year may indicate a lag of time beyond the average eight weeks required for an Atlantic crossing. Any number of

Figure 1 Printed broadside catalog of a book sale, issued by Philip Freeman (Boston, 1766). Freeman's catalog, like others of the time, demonstrates the availability and cost of titles, and is suggestive of the tastes of the reading public. Although maps did not frequently appear in book seller's catalogs, such listings are of great interest to bibliographers and historians.

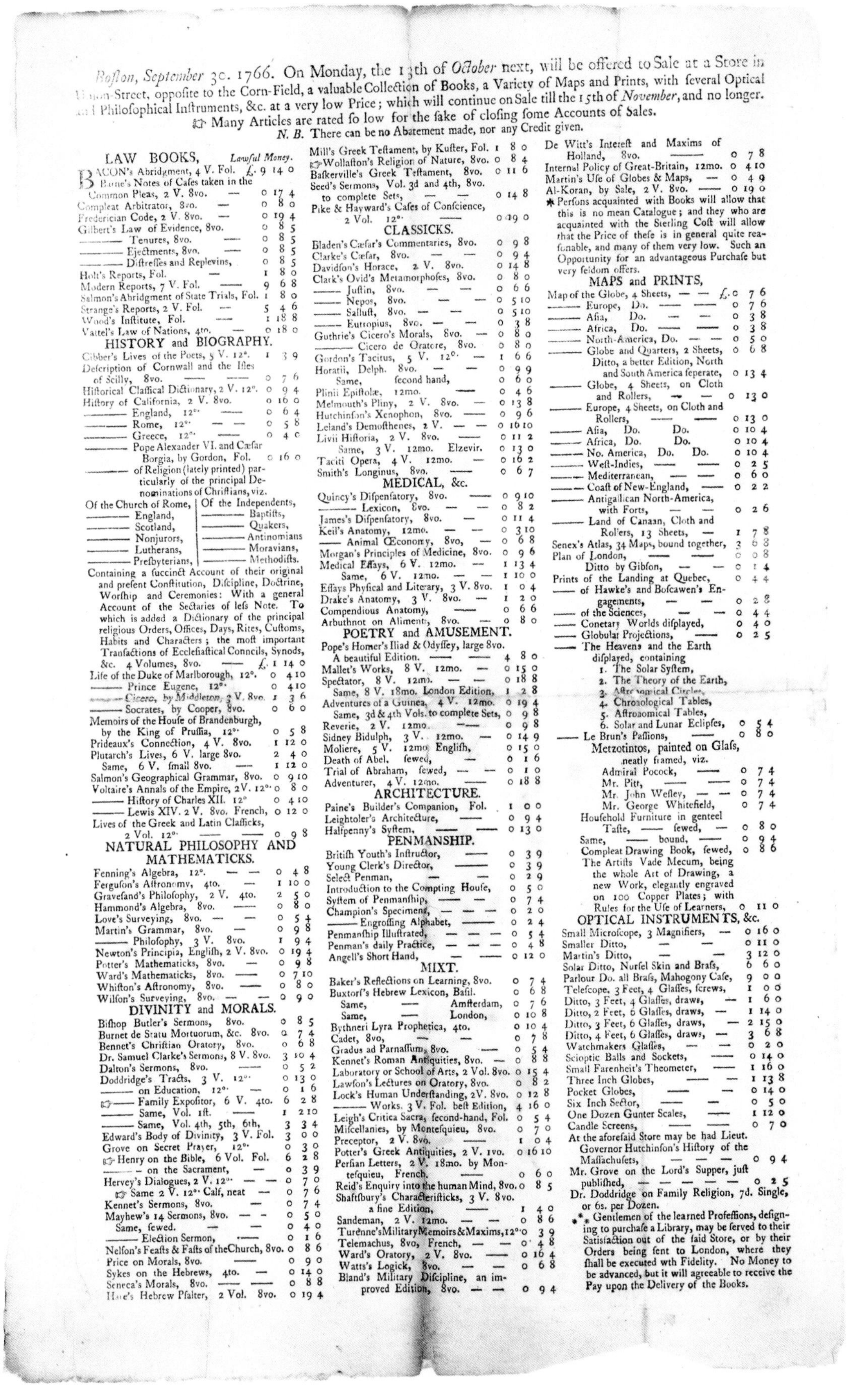

Boston, September 30. 1766. On Monday, the 13th of *October* next, will be offered to Sale at a Store in Union-Street, opposite to the Corn-Field, a valuable Collection of Books, a Variety of Maps and Prints, with several Optical and Philosophical Instruments, &c. at a very low Price; which will continue on Sale till the 15th of *November*, and no longer.

☞ Many Articles are rated so low for the sake of closing some Accounts of Sales.

N. B. There can be no Abatement made, nor any Credit given.

LAW BOOKS, *Lawful Money.*

	£ s d
BACON's Abridgment, 4 V. Fol.	£. 9 14 0
Barne's Notes of Cases taken in the Common Pleas, 2 V. 8vo. —	0 17 4
Compleat Arbitrator, 8vo. —	0 8 0
Frederician Code, 2 V. 8vo. —	0 19 4
Gilbert's Law of Evidence, 8vo.	0 8 5
——— Tenures, 8vo. —	0 8 5
——— Ejectments, 8vo. —	0 8 5
——— Distresses and Replevins,	0 8 5
Holt's Reports, Fol. —	1 8 0
Modern Reports, 7 V. Fol. —	9 6 8
Salmon's Abridgment of State Trials, Fol.	1 8 0
Strange's Reports, 2 V. Fol. —	5 4 6
Wood's Institute, Fol. —	1 18 8
Vattel's Law of Nations, 4to. —	0 18 0

HISTORY and BIOGRAPHY.

	£ s d
Cibber's Lives of the Poets, 5 V. 12°.	1 3 9
Description of Cornwall and the Isles of Scilly, 8vo. — —	0 7 6
Historical Classical Dictionary, 2 V. 12°.	0 9 4
History of California, 2 V. 8vo.	0 16 0
——— England, 12°. —	0 6 4
——— Rome, 12°. — —	0 5 8
——— Greece, 12°. —	0 4 0
——— Pope Alexander VI. and Cæsar Borgia, by Gordon, Fol.	0 16 0

——— of Religion (lately printed) particularly of the principal Denominations of Christians, viz.

Of the Church of Rome,	Of the Independents,
——— England,	——— Baptists,
——— Scotland,	——— Quakers,
——— Nonjurors,	——— Antinomians
——— Lutherans,	——— Moravians,
——— Presbyterians,	——— Methodists.

	£ s d
Containing a succinct Account of their original and present Constitution, Discipline, Doctrine, Worship and Ceremonies: With a general Account of the Sectaries of less Note. To which is added a Dictionary of the principal religious Orders, Offices, Days, Rites, Customs, Habits and Characters; the most important Transactions of Ecclesiastical Conncils, Synods, &c. 4 Volumes, 8vo. —	£. 1 14 0
Life of the Duke of Marlborough, 12°.	0 4 10
——— Prince Eugene, 12°.	0 4 10
——— Cicero, by Middleton, 3 V. 8vo.	1 3 6
——— Socrates, by Cooper, 8vo.	0 6 0
Memoirs of the House of Brandenburgh, by the King of Prussia, 12°.	0 5 8
Prideaux's Connection, 4 V. 8vo.	1 12 0
Plutarch's Lives, 6 V. large 8vo.	2 4 0
Same, 6 V. small 8vo. —	1 12 0
Salmon's Geographical Grammar, 8vo.	0 9 10
Voltaire's Annals of the Empire, 2 V. 12°.	0 8 0
——— History of Charles XII. 12°	0 4 10
——— Lewis XIV. 2 V. 8vo. French,	0 12 0
Lives of the Greek and Latin Classicks, 2 Vol. 12°. — —	0 9 8

NATURAL PHILOSOPHY AND MATHEMATICKS.

	£ s d
Fenning's Algebra, 12°. — —	0 4 8
Ferguson's Astronomy, 4to. —	1 10 0
Gravesand's Philosophy, 2 V. 4to.	2 5 0
Hammond's Algebra, 8vo. —	0 8 0
Love's Surveying, 8vo. — —	0 5 4
Martin's Grammar, 8vo. —	0 9 8
——— Philosophy, 3 V. 8vo.	1 9 4
Newton's Principia, English, 2 V. 8vo.	0 19 4
Potter's Mathematicks, 8vo. —	0 9 8
Ward's Mathematicks, 8vo. —	0 7 10
Whiston's Astronomy, 8vo. —	0 8 0
Wilson's Surveying, 8vo. — —	0 9 0

DIVINITY and MORALS.

	£ s d
Bishop Butler's Sermons, 8vo.	0 8 5
Burnet de Statu Mortuorum, &c. 8vo.	0 7 4
Bennet's Christian Oratory, 8vo.	0 6 8
Dr. Samuel Clarke's Sermons, 8 V. 8vo.	3 10 4
Dalton's Sermons, 8vo. —	0 5 2
Doddridge's Tracts, 3 V. 12°.	0 13 0
——— on Education, 12°. —	0 1 6
☞ ——— Family Expositor, 6 V. 4to.	6 2 8
——— Same, Vol. 1st. —	1 2 10
——— Same, Vol. 4th, 5th, 6th,	3 3 4
Edward's Body of Divinity, 3 V. Fol.	3 0 0
Grove on Secret Prayer, 12°.	0 3 0
☞ Henry on the Bible, 6 Vol. Fol.	6 2 8
——— on the Sacrament, —	0 3 9
Hervey's Dialogues, 2 V. 12°. — —	0 7 0
☞ Same 2 V. 12°. Calf, neat —	0 7 6
Kennet's Sermons, 8vo. —	0 7 4
Mayhew's 14 Sermons, 8vo. — —	0 5 0
Same, sewed. — —	0 4 0
——— Election Sermon, —	0 1 6
Nelson's Feasts & Fasts of the Church, 8vo.	0 8 6
Price on Morals, 8vo. —	0 9 0
Sykes on the Hebrews, 4to. —	0 14 0
Seneca's Morals, 8vo. — —	0 8 8
Hare's Hebrew Psalter, 2 Vol. 8vo.	0 19 4

	£ s d
Mill's Greek Testament, by Kuster, Fol.	1 8 0
☞ Wollaston's Religion of Nature, 8vo.	0 8 4
Baskerville's Greek Testament, 8vo.	0 11 6
Seed's Sermons, Vol. 3d and 4th, 8vo. to complete Sets, — —	0 14 8
Pike & Hayward's Cases of Conscience, 2 Vol. 12°. —	0 19 0

CLASSICKS.

	£ s d
Bladen's Cæsar's Commentaries, 8vo.	0 9 8
Clarke's Cæsar, 8vo. — —	0 9 4
Davidson's Horace, 2 V. 8vo.	0 14 8
Clark's Ovid's Metamorphoses, 8vo.	0 8 0
——— Justin, 8vo. — —	0 6 6
——— Nepos, 8vo. — —	0 5 10
——— Sallust, 8vo. — —	0 5 10
——— Eutropius, 8vo. — —	0 3 8
Guthrie's Cicero's Morals, 8vo. —	0 8 0
——— Cicero de Oratore, 8vo.	0 8 0
Gordon's Tacitus, 5 V. 12°. —	1 6 6
Horatii, Delph. 8vo. — —	0 9 9
Same, second hand,	0 6 0
Plinii Epistolæ, 12mo. —	0 4 6
Melmouth's Pliny, 2 V. 8vo. —	0 13 8
Hutchinson's Xenophon, 8vo. —	0 9 6
Leland's Demosthenes, 2 V. — —	0 16 10
Livii Historia, 2 V. 8vo. —	0 11 2
Same, 3 V. 12mo. Elzevir.	0 13 0
Taciti Opera, 4 V. 12mo. —	0 16 2
Smith's Longinus, 8vo. —	0 6 7

MEDICAL, &c.

	£ s d
Quincy's Dispensatory, 8vo. —	0 9 10
——— Lexicon, 8vo. — —	0 8 2
James's Dispensatory, 8vo. —	0 11 4
Keil's Anatomy, 12mo. — —	0 3 10
——— Animal Œconomy, 8vo, —	0 6 8
Morgan's Principles of Medicine, 8vo.	0 9 6
Medical Essays, 6 V. 12mo. —	1 13 4
Same, 6 V. 12mo. — —	1 10 0
Essays Physical and Literary, 3 V. 8vo.	1 0 4
Drake's Anatomy, 3 V. 8vo. —	1 2 0
Compendious Anatomy, —	0 6 6
Arbuthnot on Aliments, 8vo. —	0 8 0

POETRY and AMUSEMENT.

	£ s d
Pope's Homer's Iliad & Odyssey, large 8vo. A beautiful Edition. — —	4 8 0
Mallet's Works, 8 V. 12mo. —	0 15 0
Spectator, 8 V. 12mo. — —	0 18 8
Same, 8 V. 18mo. London Edition,	1 2 8
Adventures of a Guinea, 4 V. 12mo.	0 19 4
Same, 3d & 4th Vols. to complete Sets,	0 9 8
Reverie, 2 V. 12mo. —	0 9 8
Sidney Bidulph, 3 V. 12mo. —	0 14 9
Moliere, 5 V. 12mo English,	0 15 0
Death of Abel. sewed, —	0 1 6
Trial of Abraham, sewed, — —	0 1 0
Adventurer, 4 V. 12mo. —	0 18 8

ARCHITECTURE.

	£ s d
Paine's Builder's Companion, Fol.	1 0 0
Leightoler's Architecture, —	0 9 4
Halfpenny's System, — —	0 13 0

PENMANSHIP.

	£ s d
British Youth's Instructor, —	0 3 9
Young Clerk's Director, —	0 3 9
Select Penman, — —	0 2 9
Introduction to the Compting House,	0 5 0
System of Penmanship, — —	0 7 4
Champion's Specimens, — — —	0 2 0
——— Engrossing Alphabet, —	0 2 4
Penmanship Illustrated, — — —	0 5 4
Penman's daily Practice, — — —	0 4 8
Angell's Short Hand, — —	0 12 0

MIXT.

	£ s d
Baker's Reflections on Learning, 8vo.	0 7 4
Buxtorf's Hebrew Lexicon, Basil.	0 6 8
Same, — Amsterdam,	0 7 6
Same, — London,	0 10 8
Bythneri Lyra Prophetica, 4to.	0 10 4
Cadet, 8vo, — —	0 7 8
Gradus ad Parnassum, 8vo. —	0 5 4
Kennet's Roman Antiquities, 8vo. —	0 8 8
Laboratory or School of Arts, 2 Vol. 8vo.	0 15 4
Lawson's Lectures on Oratory, 8vo.	0 8 2
Lock's Human Understanding, 2 V. 8vo.	0 12 8
——— Works. 3 V. Fol. best Edition,	4 16 0
Leigh's Critica Sacra, second-hand, Fol.	0 5 4
Miscellanies, by Montesquieu, 8vo.	0 7 0
Preceptor, 2 V. 8vo. —	1 0 4
Potter's Greek Antiquities, 2 V. 1vo.	0 16 10
Persian Letters, 2 V. 18mo. by Montesquieu, French.	0 6 0
Reid's Enquiry into the human Mind, 8vo.	0 8 5
Shaftsbury's Characteristicks, 3 V. 8vo. a fine Edition, —	1 4 0
Sandeman, 2 V. 12mo. — —	0 8 6
Turenne's Military Memoirs & Maxims, 12°.	0 3 9
Telemachus, 8vo, French, — —	0 4 8
Ward's Oratory, 2 V. 8vo. —	0 16 4
Watts's Logick, 8vo. — —	0 6 8
Bland's Military Discipline, an improved Edition, 8vo. — —	0 9 4

	£ s d
De Witt's Interest and Maxims of Holland, 8vo. —	0 7 8
Internal Policy of Great-Britain, 12mo.	0 4 10
Martin's Use of Globes & Maps, —	0 4 9
Al-Koran, by Sale, 2 V. 8vo. —	0 19 0

✱ Persons acquainted with Books will allow that this is no mean Catalogue; and they who are acquainted with the Sterling Cost will allow that the Price of these is in general quite reasonable, and many of them very low. Such an Opportunity for an advantageous Purchase but very seldom offers.

MAPS and PRINTS,

	£ s d
Map of the Globe, 4 Sheets, — —	£. 0 7 6
——— Europe, Do. — —	0 7 6
——— Asia, Do. — —	0 3 8
——— Africa, Do. — —	0 3 8
——— North-America, Do. — —	0 5 0
——— Globe and Quarters, 2 Sheets,	0 6 8
Ditto, a better Edition, North and South America seperate,	0 13 4
——— Globe, 4 Sheets, on Cloth and Rollers, — —	0 13 0
——— Europe, 4 Sheets, on Cloth and Rollers, — —	0 13 0
——— Asia, Do. Do.	0 10 4
——— Africa, Do. Do.	0 10 4
——— No. America, Do. Do.	0 10 4
——— West-Indies, — —	0 2 5
——— Mediterranean, — —	0 6 0
——— Coast of New-England, —	0 2 2
——— Antigallican North-America, with Forts, — —	0 2 6
——— Land of Canaan, Cloth and Rollers, 13 Sheets, —	1 7 8
Senex's Atlas, 34 Maps, bound together,	3 6 8
Plan of London, — —	0 0 8
Ditto by Gibson, — —	0 1 4
Prints of the Landing at Quebec,	0 4 4
——— of Hawke's and Boscawen's Engagements, — —	0 2 8
——— of the Sciences, — —	0 4 4
——— Conetary Worlds displayed,	0 4 0
——— Globular Projections, —	0 2 5
——— The Heavens and the Earth displayed, containing 1. The Solar System, 2. The Theory of the Earth, 3. Astronomical Circles, 4. Chronological Tables, 5. Astronomical Tables, 6. Solar and Lunar Eclipses,	0 5 4
——— Le Brun's Passions, —	0 8 0

Metzotintos, painted on Glass, neatly framed, viz.

	£ s d
Admiral Pocock, —	0 7 4
Mr. Pitt, — —	0 7 4
Mr. John Wesley, — —	0 7 4
Mr. George Whitefield,	0 7 4
Household Furniture in genteel Taste, — sewed, —	0 8 0
Same, — bound, —	0 9 4
Compleat Drawing Book, sewed,	0 8 6
The Artists Vade Mecum, being the whole Art of Drawing, a new Work, elegantly engraved on 100 Copper Plates; with Rules for the Use of Learners,	0 11 0

OPTICAL INSTRUMENTS, &c.

	£ s d
Small Microscope, 3 Magnifiers, —	0 16 0
Smaller Ditto, — —	0 11 0
Martin's Ditto, — —	3 12 0
Solar Ditto, Nursel Skin and Brass,	6 6 0
Parlour Do. all Brass, Mahogony Case,	9 0 0
Telescope, 3 Feet, 4 Glasses, screws,	1 0 0
Ditto, 3 Feet, 4 Glasses, draws, —	1 6 0
Ditto, 2 Feet, 6 Glasses, draws, —	1 14 0
Ditto, 3 Feet, 6 Glasses, draws, —	2 15 0
Ditto, 4 Feet, 6 Glasses, draws, —	3 6 8
Watchmakers Glasses, — —	0 2 0
Scioptic Balls and Sockets, —	0 14 0
Small Farenheit's Theometer, —	1 16 0
Three Inch Globes, — —	1 13 8
Pocket Globes, — —	0 14 0
Six Inch Sector, — —	0 5 0
One Dozen Gunter Scales, —	1 12 0
Candle Screens, — —	0 7 0
At the aforesaid Store may be had Lieut. Governor Hutchinson's History of the Massachusets, — — —	0 9 4
Mr. Grove on the Lord's Supper, just published, — — — — —	0 2 5

Dr. Doddridge on Family Religion, 7d. Single, or 6s. per Dozen.

*** Gentlemen of the learned Professions, designing to purchase a Library, may be served to their Satisfaction out of the said Store, or by their Orders being sent to London, where they shall be executed wth Fidelity. No Money to be advanced, but it will agreeable to receive the Pay upon the Delivery of the Books.

factors may have contributed to a delay, including economic uncertainties caused by the war with France, or the apparent involvement of four retailers (two map and print dealers, the printers of the Gazette, and an innkeeper) in the map's importation.

A lapse of a matter of months between publication in London and sale in Boston in no way diminished a map's marketability. James Buck, publisher of architectural views engraved by Thomas Johnston and Nathaniel Hurd, sold books and other merchandise at a shop called The Spectacles in Queen Street. In the *Boston News-Letter* of August 23, 1750, he advertised "imported in the last ship from London a New and Correct Map of Nova Scotia . . . together with the Harbour of Chebucto and Town of Hallifax [sic] as surveyed by Mr. Harris." The map sold by Buck actually consisted of three images: *A Map of the South Part of Nova Scotia* by Thomas Jefferys, *A Plan of Halifax* by Moses Harris, and a view of Halifax. Jefferys published the sheet in London on January 25, 1750, and sold it retail for 1s 3d as stated on the map itself. In Boston, James Buck charged 15 shillings "old tenor" Massachusetts currency, or 7s 10d sterling.[17] Assuming a discount of 5 to 15 percent from a London wholesaler as was commonly practiced in the book trade, Buck made a considerable profit on the map.[18]

Although London supplied most of the imported cartographic merchandise sold in Boston, maps published in American cities were distributed as well. Two months after the publication of Lewis Evans's *A General Map of the Middle British Colonies in America* in Philadelphia, John Franklin, older brother of Benjamin, advertised it as "just published" and for sale at the Post Office in Cornhill. Franklin's notice in the *Boston Gazette* of September 22, 1755, included a lengthy description of the map, and a statement that declared it "engraved in a manner perfectly neat and correct" (figure 3). James Turner, who had recently moved from Boston to Philadelphia, executed the engraving and Benjamin Franklin printed the thirty-two-page *Analysis* that accompanied the map. It took slightly longer for Abel Buell's *A New and Correct Map of the United States* to reach Boston. Published in New Haven on March 31, 1784, it was first advertised in the *Boston Gazette* on September 6th and sold by a group of booksellers, printers, and publishers.

Maritime commerce and navigation assumed a singular importance in the economic life of colonial Boston, and it follows that much of the map trade entailed charts. A trade in foreign, particularly English, charts existed before Bostonians began to produce printed charts of their own, and continued long after American products became available. Initially the Dutch established an influential cartographic precedent, but by the end of the seventeenth century English mapmakers had begun to print charts and maps of North America incorporating new information.[19] One such mapmaker was John Seller (d. 1697), hydrographer to the king, who became the first publisher of sea charts in England (see plate 11). *The English Pilot* (London, 1671), Seller's most enduring collection of charts, went through thirty-seven editions in the span of 105 years (see plate 13 vignette).

English chartmakers established an unrivaled presence in the colonial chart trade with the 1689 publication of the *Fourth Book* of *The English Pilot* devoted to American waters (see plate 13). The *Fourth Book,* published by John Thornton and William Fisher, who succeeded Seller, quickly became standard fare in America and appeared in booksellers' catalogs until the end of the eighteenth century. Captain Cyprian Southack's well-used copy of the atlas, now in the collection of the Massachusetts Historical Society, attests to its esteem among Boston navigators. The "mariner's book in folio" listed in John Bankes's probate inventory of 1698 may also refer to one of John Seller's works, or possibly a Dutch sea atlas.[20] Other examples of foreign charts either owned locally or purchased in Boston can be found in the 1723 catalog of the Harvard College library. These include Jacobus Robijn's atlas of sea charts prepared for the English market, *The New Enlarged Lightning Sea Colom* (Amsterdam, 1669), and John Seller's *Atlas Maritimus* (London, 1675) (see plate 11).

The inventory of the estate of Michael Perry, dated January 23, 1700, clearly demonstrates a market for charts in Boston. Perry's bookstore carried works on geography, navigation, and maps, as early as 1694. Among the titles listed as part of his stock are John Seller's *Practical Navigation* (London, 1680), and "13 sea charts" valued at £1 19s.[21] The chart trade grew over time as more Boston vendors began importing cartographic products, and notices of "sea books," pilots, and unidentified charts periodically appeared in newspapers. Yet chart advertisements occurred less often than did those for maps, particularly before 1790, the year when locally printed charts began to proliferate. A comparable situation existed in London. There less than 7 percent of cartographic advertisements between 1660 and 1720 publicized navigational aids, leading one historian to conclude that the understood source of charts was the ship chandler.[22] Those Boston merchants and booksellers who did advertise sold copies of Henry Barnsley's *New and Correct Chart of the Sea Coast of New-England* (London, 1751), Daniel Dunbibin's *Chart of the Coast of America from Cape Hatteras to Cape Roman* (Wilmington, N.C., 1761), numerous Boston-made charts, and the ubiquitous *Fourth Book* of *The English Pilot.*[23]

In addition to *The English Pilot,* British Admiralty charts depicting the waters from Nova Scotia to the Gulf of Mexico became a staple of the Boston map trade. More than 200 charts published between 1774 and 1784 represent the period's greatest achievement in the hydrographic mapping of the North American coast. Many of these were issued together as *The Atlantic Neptune,* a three-volume collection that beautifully reproduced the painstaking efforts of British naval surveyors, chiefly Joseph Des Barres and Samuel Holland (figure 4). Newspaper advertisements typically identified these charts simply as "Des Barres's" or "Holland's." In

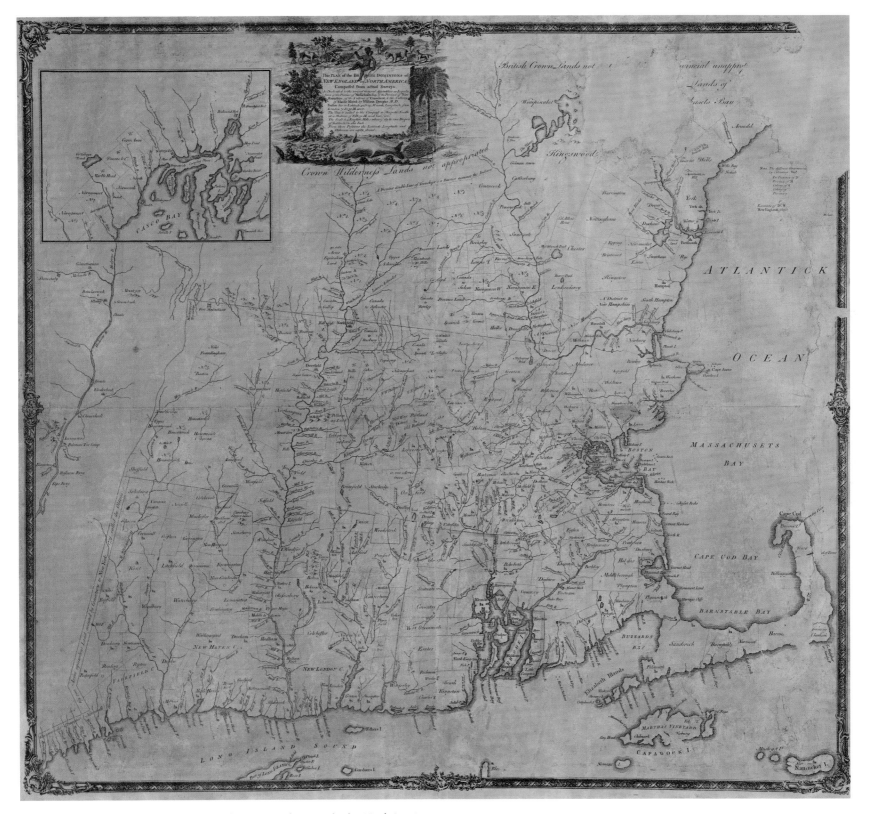

Figure 2 William Douglass, *Plan of the British Dominions of New England in North America* (London, 1753). Published by his executors after Douglass's death in 1752, the map was engraved in London from an "original draught" by Douglass. This landmark map includes information on townships, grants, and topography reflecting the twenty years of effort Douglass put into his cartographic creation.

Figure 3 Advertisement for Lewis Evans' *A General Map of the middle British Colonies,* from the *Boston Gazette,* September 22, 1755. John Franklin's notice of Evans's map quickly establishes the location of the vendor then goes on to describe the map's attributes in great detail. Drawn from actual surveys, Evans's observations, and the journals of travelers, the map includes a wide variety of topographical, geological, and ethnographical information. Unlike most cartographic advertisements of the time, Franklin provides the map's size, but fails to state its price.

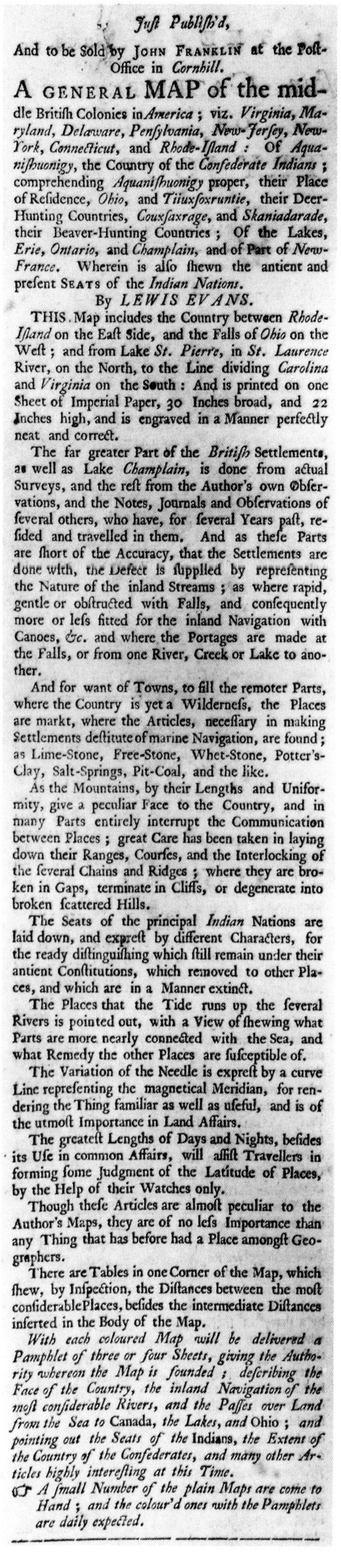

Juſt Publiſh'd,

And to be Sold by JOHN FRANKLIN at the Poſt-Office in *Cornhill.*

A GENERAL MAP of the middle Britiſh Colonies in *America* ; viz. *Virginia, Maryland, Delaware, Penſylvania, New-Jerſey, New-York, Connecticut,* and *Rhode-Iſland :* Of *Aquaniſhuonigy,* the Country of the *Confederate Indians* ; comprehending *Aquaniſhuonigy* proper, their Place of Reſidence, *Ohio,* and *Tiiuxſoxruntie,* their Deer-Hunting Countries, *Couxſaxrage,* and *Skaniadarade,* their Beaver-Hunting Countries ; Of the Lakes, *Erie, Ontario,* and *Champlain,* and of Part of *New-France.* Wherein is alſo ſhewn the antient and preſent SEATS of the *Indian Nations.*

By *LEWIS EVANS.*

THIS Map includes the Country between *Rhode-Iſland* on the Eaſt Side, and the Falls of *Ohio* on the Weſt ; and from Lake *St. Pierre,* in *St. Laurence* River, on the North, to the Line dividing *Carolina* and *Virginia* on the South : And is printed on one Sheet of Imperial Paper, 30 Inches broad, and 22 Inches high, and is engraved in a Manner perfectly neat and correct.

The far greater Part of the *Britiſh* Settlements, as well as Lake *Champlain,* is done from actual Surveys, and the reſt from the Author's own Obſervations, and the Notes, Journals and Obſervations of ſeveral others, who have, for ſeveral Years paſt, reſided and travelled in them. And as theſe Parts are ſhort of the Accuracy, that the Settlements are done with, the Defect is ſupplied by repreſenting the Nature of the inland Streams ; as where rapid, gentle or obſtructed with Falls, and conſequently more or leſs fitted for the inland Navigation with Canoes, &c. and where the Portages are made at the Falls, or from one River, Creek or Lake to another.

And for want of Towns, to fill the remoter Parts, where the Country is yet a Wilderneſs, the Places are markt, where the Articles, neceſſary in making Settlements deſtitute of marine Navigation, are found ; as Lime-Stone, Free-Stone, Whet-Stone, Potter's-Clay, Salt-Springs, Pit-Coal, and the like.

As the Mountains, by their Lengths and Uniformity, give a peculiar Face to the Country, and in many Parts entirely interrupt the Communication between Places ; great Care has been taken in laying down their Ranges, Courſes, and the Interlocking of the ſeveral Chains and Ridges ; where they are broken in Gaps, terminate in Cliffs, or degenerate into broken ſcattered Hills.

The Seats of the principal *Indian* Nations are laid down, and expreſt by different Characters, for the ready diſtinguiſhing which ſtill remain under their antient Conſtitutions, which removed to other Places, and which are in a Manner extinct.

The Places that the Tide runs up the ſeveral Rivers is pointed out, with a View of ſhewing what Parts are more nearly connected with the Sea, and what Remedy the other Places are ſuſceptible of.

The Variation of the Needle is expreſt by a curve Line repreſenting the magnetical Meridian, for rendering the Thing familiar as well as uſeful, and is of the utmoſt Importance in Land Affairs.

The greateſt Lengths of Days and Nights, beſides its Uſe in common Affairs, will aſſiſt Travellers in forming ſome Judgment of the Latitude of Places, by the Help of their Watches only.

Though theſe Articles are almoſt peculiar to the Author's Maps, they are of no leſs Importance than any Thing that has before had a Place amongſt Geographers.

There are Tables in one Corner of the Map, which ſhew, by Inſpection, the Diſtances between the moſt conſiderable Places, beſides the intermediate Diſtances inſerted in the Body of the Map.

With each coloured Map will be delivered a Pamphlet of three or four Sheets, giving the Authority whereon the Map is founded ; deſcribing the Face of the Country, the inland Navigation of the moſt conſiderable Rivers, and the Paſſes over Land from the Sea to Canada, the Lakes, and Ohio ; and pointing out the Seats of the Indians, *the Extent of the Country of the Confederates, and many other Articles highly intereſting at this Time.*

☞ *A ſmall Number of the plain Maps are come to Hand ; and the colour'd ones with the Pamphlets are daily expected.*

his *Catalogue of a Large Assortment of Books Consisting of the Most Celebrated Authors* (Boston, 1787) Benjamin Guild listed seventeen charts from the *Atlantic Neptune* by geographic location, noting the number of sheets per chart. Guild failed to include prices, but a contemporary newspaper notice indicated that the *Neptune's* charts sold for 6 shillings per sheet.[24]

Spurred on by the lucrative China trade initiated in the 1780s, the market for charts in Boston expanded at the end of the century. The demand for navigational aids induced individuals like William T. Clapp, publisher, bookseller, and general merchandiser, to embrace the map trade. In the spring and summer of 1797, Clapp advertised "seaman's books, charts, &c.," adding that "masters of vessels and others supplied with every article necessary for long or short voyages."[25] In the same year, James White's *Catalogue of Books, Consisting of a Large Collection of the Various Branches of Literature,* contained the longest list of charts advertised in Boston to date. Nearly half of the thirty-one items sold by White depicted non-American waters, including "Moore's Chart of the Indian Seas, &c." and "Indian Ocean, from Cape of Good Hope to Canton, with the Western Part of the Pacific Ocean, etc."

Boston chartmaking began to resemble an organized enterprise in the last decade of the eighteenth century. Publishers like John and William Norman, whose work is discussed below, issued charts and atlases that achieved a market well beyond Boston. Lacking original surveys to draw upon, they pirated the publications of others. William Norman's broadside advertisement (Boston, ca. 1798) featured pilots composed largely of derivative charts, and reengraved copies of individual British charts. In addition to relying on the contents of *The Atlantic Neptune,* the Normans frequently reproduced the work of London publishers Sayer and Bennett, whose *Bay of Chesapeak* [sic] they advertised (figure 5). The Normans made no attempt to represent the charts as their own work, for English products still carried the weight of cartographic authority. They did, however, claim in many instances to have "revised and corrected" the originals.

A later broadside (ca. 1804) reveals the Normans' prodigious industry as engravers and publishers.[26] In addition to nine maritime atlases, some of which have never been bibliographically recorded, it includes forty single charts, all reengraved from the original British publications. Prices ranged from a staggering fifty dollars for the *Marine Atlas or Seaman's Complete Pilot,* apparently a compilation of all the Norman charts, to thirty-seven and one-half cents for a *Plan of the River Missisippi* [sic]. Individuals who sold Norman's publications are identified on the broadside and grouped by vocation. The list of Boston vendors consists of Nathaniel Thayer, Joseph Newell, and Samuel Browning (ship chandlers), Samuel Thaxter (mathematical instrument maker), and Ebenezer Larkin, Manning and Loring, William Pelham, and William T. Clapp (booksellers).

A diversity of suppliers characterized Boston's map trade for the entirety of the eighteenth century. Similarly, individuals from a number

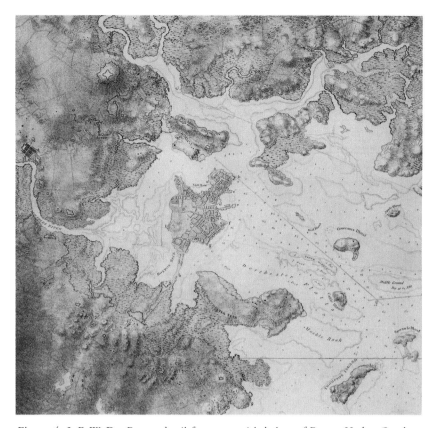

Figure 4 J. F. W. Des Barres, detail from an untitled chart of Boston Harbor (London, 1781). The charts gathered together in Des Barres's *Atlantic Neptune* are the result of the highly successful marriage of science and art. Although designed for use by the British Admiralty, the maps delineate roads, buildings, topography as carefully as shoals and shorelines. Not surprisingly, the *Neptune's* charts found a wide audience in the colonies and served as a model for derivative American efforts.

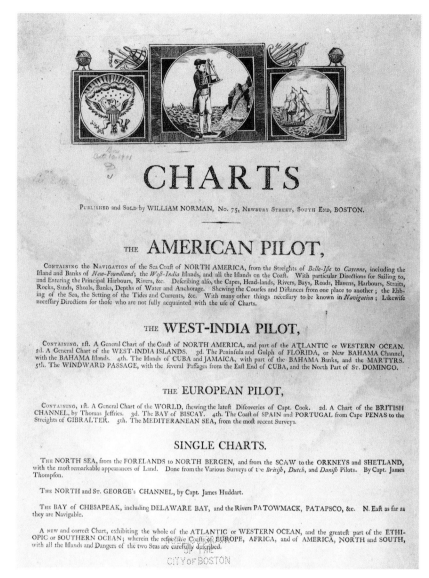

Figure 5 William Norman, printed broadside advertisement (Boston, ca. 1798). Norman's broadside displays the variety of cartographic products that he and his father, John Norman, had available at their shop in Newbury (now Washington) Street. In addition to their own atlases, they offered a variety of English charts. The illustration of a mariner taking an astronomical reading symbolizes the common nautical address, "at the sign of the quadrant."

of occupations became involved in cartography. During the course of the eighteenth century, Bostonians produced a wide range of printed maps and charts. A common goal, financial gain, inspired nearly all of these endeavors. Some cartographic ventures also sought official recognition and its attendant rewards. If economics and patronage played fundamental roles in Boston cartography, so too did the concerns and interests of Bostonians. Civic consciousness, trade, warfare, and political administration find expression in these maps. Beginning with John Foster, whose 1677 *A Map of New-England* (see plate 12) marks the commencement of cartographic printing in British America, an assortment of enterprising Bostonians tried their hand at mapmaking with varying degrees of success. Foster's cartographic heirs included Cyprian Southack, John Bonner, William Price, William Burgis, Thomas Johnston, Peter Pelham, John Smibert, James Turner, John and William Norman, Osgood Carleton, and Matthew Clark. The activities of these individuals, as both creators and vendors, embody the greater part of Boston's map trade before 1800.

CYPRIAN SOUTHACK

New Englanders began drawing manuscript charts practically from the moment they arrived in the New World. One such chartmaker was Cyprian Southack (1662–1745), commander of a galley in the service of the Province of Massachusetts and one of the most knowledgeable of New England's pilots (see plate 15 vignette). Southack's "Draught of Boston Harbour" became one of the earliest local charts to achieve distribution to a wider audience when an engraved version of it appeared in *The English Pilot, the Fourth Book.* The distinction of producing the first chart printed from a copperplate in Britain's North American colonies also belongs to Southack. Published in 1717, *A New Chart of the English Empire in North America* depicts the entire coast from Newfoundland to the mouth of the Mississippi (see frontispiece). Given its vast scope, the chart had limited utility for navigation. An explanation for the subject of this New England pilot's chart appears in the printed dedication. There Southack revealed that his motive had more to do with exposing the French threat to Britain's colonies than with aiding navigators.

An advertisement in the *Boston News-Letter* of June 17, 1717, described Southack's chart as "the like never yet extant, of great use to all, but especially mariners." Joanna Perry, the author of this hyperbole, informed the public that she had copies of the chart for sale in her bookshop on King Street. In November 1716, Southack had successfully petitioned the Massachusetts General Court for aid in engraving the chart.[26] Francis Dewing, a recent arrival from London, executed the engraving and printing, and after 150 copies had been struck for the use of the Court, the plate became Southack's property.

The fact that Perry, rather than Southack, first advertised the chart suggests her involvement in its production. As a publisher and owner of a successful bookstore, Joanna Perry could have assumed the cost of paper (typically the most expensive component of publishing at this time in America) and printing copies of the chart for public consumption. Like her husband Michael before her, Perry had published the writings of Cotton Mather, Benjamin Colman, and other Boston luminaries, and may have, in effect, published America's first printed chart. By 1721, it was Southack who advertised copies of *A New Chart of the English Empire* for sale at his home for five shillings. The plates later passed to William Price who advertised the map in the August 25, 1746, issue of the *Boston News-Letter,* noting the addition of an account of the fall of Louisbourg to the plate.

In an engraved cartouche on his 1717 chart, Southack stated that in six months he intended to complete a chart "distinct from this" with added harbor maps. This note refers to his most ambitious, and problematical, venture, *The New England Coasting Pilot.* Questions still surround the history of *The Pilot,* to the extent that even the publication date remains in doubt. An announcement in the *Boston News-Letter* of May 19, 1718, establishes that Southack had by then completed the manuscript draft of a "general chart" depicting the coast from New York to Cape Canso, Nova Scotia. Southack called upon his fellow Boston mariners to inspect his work so that he might correct any errors before having it engraved. This general chart encompassed the eight sheets comprising *The New England Coasting Pilot.*

To finance the engraving and printing of *The Pilot,* Southack offered the atlas by subscription. This procedure, in which a number of individu-

als agree to purchase one or more copies of a book or map upon publication or in advance, had been practiced in England since the early seventeenth century. Southack chose not to have the plates for *The Pilot* engraved in Boston, a decision that seemingly addressed two concerns. Competition in the London printing trades tended to keep prices below those found in the colonies, allowing Southack to reduce his expenses as publisher of the atlas.[28] Equally important, by basing the work in London, English subscribers could be assured of its quality. In all, eighty-one individuals contributed one guinea (21 shillings) each toward the cost of *The Pilot,* with English subscribers accounting for nearly three-quarters of the total.

As of the end of February 1723, the plates for Southack's atlas had yet to be completed due to a lack of funds.[29] During the time *The New England Coasting Pilot* inched toward publication, Southack produced another chart, *The Harbor and Islands of Canso,* illustrating the proximity of the vital Nova Scotia fisheries to French forts and settlements. Opposite the map's title cartouche a vignette of fishermen hauling in a catch emphasizes the commercial value of Canso. Southack, who had considerable experience in these waters and owned a number of fishing vessels operating in the area, had drawn the chart in 1718.[30] Francis Dewing engraved and printed the chart, and Samuel Phillips, cousin of Joanna Perry, published it in Boston in April 1720. Perhaps coincidentally, Southack received an appointment to the Council of Nova Scotia the following week.

Publication of *The New England Coasting Pilot* eventually occurred sometime before June 30, 1729, for on that date the *Boston Gazette* announced the arrival from London of fifty unbound copies. Those copies not intended for subscribers were made available to the general public, who could purchase the charts from Southack at his home. The list of subscribers shows that nearly two dozen Bostonians, including the governor and lieutenant governor of Massachusetts, the publisher of the *Boston Gazette,* the postmaster, the collector of customs, a Harvard tutor, and a group of prominent merchants, helped underwrite *The Pilot.*

On October 28, 1734, an advertisement in the *New England Weekly Journal* stated that Southack had just imported from London a large-scale map of Cape Breton and the port of Louisbourg. Although not identified as such, the map was in fact his own work, and forms the eighth sheet of *The New England Coasting Pilot* (see plate 15). Southack had added a lengthy note to the chart dated October 30, 1733, indicating either a new printing of *The Pilot* or at least of this plate. In the same advertisement he offered "books of the coast from New York to Cape Canso" for sale, clearly a reference to copies of his atlas of sea charts. Although this revision to *The Pilot* proved to be his last cartographic effort, Southack's name continued to appear before the public as London publishers issued versions of his charts either as single sheets or in later editions of *The English Pilot.*

The first printed plan of Boston, titled *The Town of Boston in New England,* came from the hand of Captain John Bonner (1643–1726), a navigator and shipwright (see plate 24). The *Boston News-Letter* of May 14, 1722, advertised it as "A Curious Ingraven Map of the Town of Boston, with all of the Streets, Lanes, Alleys, Wharffs & Houses, the Like never done before. . . ." The plan indicates key structures, shows the town's buildings in perspective, and records fires and epidemics. The nine reissues of the map over a period of nearly half a century have secured for it a place in the town's early cartographic history, its topographical and design faults notwithstanding.[31] Francis Dewing, whose work with Cyprian Southack has been noted, engraved and printed the plan. Bonner drew and published the map, and also sold it from his dwelling on Common Street. Others who stocked the map included Bartholomew Green, Samuel Gerrish, and Daniel Henchman, three of the most prolific and successful Boston publishers and booksellers.

Curiously, the name of William Price (ca. 1685–1771) does not initially appear among the retailers of Bonner's map. He would, however, play a significant role in its history. Price, a cabinetmaker and merchant, has been described as America's first art dealer.[32] His shop, the King's Head and Looking Glass, carried musical instruments, toys, cutlery, and other merchandise. As early as 1721, Price advertised maps for sale, and for the next fifty years he remained one of the chief map importers and retailers in Boston. In 1725, he became a cartographic publisher, reprinting Bonner's map.

Less than a year later John Bonner died and the plate of *The Town of Boston in New England* became the property of William Price. Although Francis Dewing's name remains on the 1725 printing of the Bonner plan, his association with the map had ended. Records of the town council, dated July 9, 1722, show that Dewing's rooms had been searched and his tools confiscated under a warrant for his arrest under suspicion of counterfeiting.[33] As no further mention of him appears in the records, Dewing seemingly hastened to London where he continued to work until 1745.

William Price next issued Bonner's map in 1732 with the title changed to *A New Plan of ye Great Town of Boston in New England,* and Bonner's name removed. Thomas Johnston engraved the considerable changes to the plate that included a dedication to then-governor Jonathan Belcher contained within an ornate, if somewhat crudely executed, cartouche. In revising the plate Price took the opportunity to insert a lengthy advertisement for his shop in Cornhill, with a disembodied hand pointing out its location (figure 6). The Bonner/Price plan made its final appearance in a 1769 edition, which graphically and textually recorded some of the changes to the town that had occurred since the 1732 publication. Price also updated the list of goods available at his shop.

Figure 6 John Bonner/William Price, detail from *A New Plan of ye Great Town of Boston in New England* (Boston, 1733). Ever the entrepreneur, Price took full advantage of the opportunity to publicize his shop. This re-engraved version of Bonner's *The Town of Boston in New England* would be revised and reissued by Price for the next thirty years, with the goods at the King's Head and Looking Glass periodically updated (see the 1743 edition, plate 26).

Figure 7 William Burgis, *A South East View of ye Great Town of Boston in New England in America* (Boston, 1725). This large, three-sheet view was engraved in London by John Harris, but printed and published in Boston by William Price. Below the array of ships in the harbor are fifty numbered references to buildings and locales in the town. Burgis went on to produce other views of Boston and its buildings in collaboration with Price.

William Burgis (fl. 1716–1731) briefly entered the map trade while working as an artist and draftsman. In 1722, he arrived in Boston from New York where he had published a large view of that city, and began preparing a prospect of his new residence.[34] Upon its completion he enlisted the aid of William Price, who displayed the drawing at his shop to encourage subscriptions for its publication.[35] The imprint of *A South East View of ye Great Town of Boston in New England in America* (Boston, ca. 1725) identifies William Price as the printer, colorist, and retailer, and Price and Thomas Selby as the publishers (figure 7).

In 1728, the former collaborators seemingly became competitors, if only briefly, when Burgis published his own map of Boston. Essentially a reduced copy of the 1725 Bonner/Price map, Burgis's *Plan of Boston in New England* demonstrates greater artistic ability on the part of its engraver, Thomas Johnston (see plate 25). The statement "Sold at the Crown Coffee House" found below the map's lower border refers to Burgis's establishment, as he had by then married the widow of Thomas Selby, the previ-

ous landlord.[36] The *Plan of Boston* did not, however, achieve the stature of its less attractive precursor and exists only in a single edition.

William Burgis went on to produce additional architectural and topographical prints, but made no other maps. William Price maintained a working relationship with Burgis, selling copies of Burgis's views and even his rival map of Boston. Price eventually gained possession of the plate for Burgis's view of Harvard (see figure 2 in chapter 1) from which he issued a second printing in 1743, after Burgis had left Boston, and the former Mrs. Selby, for New York.

PETER PELHAM AND JOHN SMIBERT

During King George's War (1744–1748) the French and British dispute over fishing rights in the North Atlantic directly affected the livelihood of many Bostonians. In the spring of 1745, men and ships assembled at Boston in preparation for an assault on the French fortress of Louisbourg,

Nova Scotia. Some three thousand Massachusetts militia volunteers participated in the siege, and Boston publishers responded to public interest with a number of maps. On September 9, 1746, the *Boston Gazette* announced the publication of *A Plan of the City and Fortress of Louisbourg*, drawn on the scene by Lieutenant-Colonel Richard Gridley, commander of the expedition's artillery. Consisting of a chart of the harbor and a detailed map of the town, Gridley's plan features a considerable amount of text, including his lengthy dedication to Massachusetts governor and joint commander of the expedition, William Shirley (figure 8).

Peter Pelham (1697–1751), the map's engraver and probably also its printer, and John Smibert (1688–1751), its publisher, had worked together in the past, but never on a map. Pelham had achieved a reputation as a print portraitist whose use of mezzotint preceded that of any other artist in America.[37] When not capturing the likeness of Boston clergymen, he ran a dancing school and offered public concerts. Pelham's third marriage brought John Singleton Copley, one of colonial America's greatest artists, into his household as his stepson (see plate 29 vignette). Smibert, Pelham's friend and business associate, also specialized in portraits but worked primarily in oils. Among his subjects were Samuel Sewall, Thomas Hancock, and Paul Mascarene, a military officer and subscriber to Cyprian Southack's *New England Coasting Pilot.* Perhaps more than his glorification of Boston contemporaries, the design of the original Faneuil Hall stands as Smibert's greatest contribution to his adopted home.

Why two portraitists received the commission to produce Gridley's map of Louisbourg is not readily apparent. Possibly Smibert's painting of a victorious William Shirley done shortly after the fall of Louisbourg inspired Gridley to entrust his plan with him. Gridley's effusive dedication to Shirley suggests that he hoped to gain the governor's political favor, and perhaps he thought to capitalize on whatever good will Smibert enjoyed. A more compelling factor, however, probably decided the matter. Thomas Johnston and James Turner, Boston's principal engravers at the time, were each engaged on other maps, leaving Gridley with little choice.[38] Gridley, Pelham, and Smibert count a single cartographic imprint to their credit. Printed on "Royal Paper," the plan sold for 20 shillings "old tenor" at Smibert's shop where he dealt in prints, paint, and art supplies. Because Louisbourg remained a point of contention between England and France, Gridley's plan found a ready market abroad. London engraver and publisher Thomas Jefferys issued his own versions of the map in 1758, 1760, and again in 1768.

THOMAS JOHNSTON

Like other artisans in eighteenth-century Boston, Thomas Johnston (1708–1767) practiced several vocations. Among his skills he counted organ building, painting, furniture decorating (japanning), and engrav-

Figure 8 Peter Pelham, mezzotint portrait of William Shirley (Boston, 1747). Gov. Shirley proudly points toward the French fortress of Louisbourg, Nova Scotia, which fell to an expedition jointly commanded by him in 1745. Partially visible on a table behind him lie two maps of the operation. Pelham's print, based on a lost oil portrait by John Smibert, was published nearly a year after they prepared and published Richard Gridley's map of the siege of Louisbourg (see Pelham's son's map, plate 29).

ing. In pursuing multiple crafts he signed his work both Johnston and Johnson, creating some confusion among historians, if not contemporaries, as to his identity. What is certain is that he performed his first cartographic engraving in 1728 for William Burgis, and inscribed the plate of *Plan of Boston in New England,* "Thomas Johnson" (see plate 25). In 1732 he revised William Price's *A New Plan of ye Great Town of Boston in New England* (figure 6), but his next effort at mapmaking did not come for over a decade. In July of 1745, Johnston engraved *A Plan of Cape Breton & Fort Louisbourgh, &c.* to mark the French surrender. Although the map bears the statement "engraved by authority," there is no evidence of it being commissioned by Governor William Shirley or the Massachusetts House of Representatives, and no information on the map appears in Boston newspapers.

The *Boston News-Letter* of August 8, 1746, announced the publication of Johnston's next map. Titled *A Chart of Canada River From ye Island of Anticosty as Far Up as Quebeck,* its description in the advertisement as a copy of a "Correct French Draft of the River of Canada" provides the only information on the chart's cartographic origins. Done in a style reminiscent of that of a portolan chart, the banks of Johnston's depiction of the St. Lawrence bristle with placenames (figure 9). Johnston sold the chart from his shop in Brattle Street for 15 shillings "old tenor," and William Price advertised that he, too, carried the chart at the King's Head and Looking Glass. When the St. Lawrence became the scene of warfare during the French and Indian War, Johnston capitalized on local interest in Canadian geography by reissuing the chart in July 1759. He also engraved and printed a view of Quebec City that Stephen Whiting published and sold in August 1759, just weeks before the decisive battle on the Plains of Abraham.

Far from Quebec, but part of the same conflict, British troops and colonial militia defeated the French and their Indian allies near Lake George, New York, on September 8, 1755. Two participants in the battle each produced a map reflecting their experience and commemorating the event. *A Prospective Plan of the Battle Fought Near Lake George,* by Samuel Blodgett, and *A Plan of Hudsons River From Albany to Fort Edward,* by Timothy Clement, share more than a common historical episode. Both were engraved and printed in Boston by Thomas Johnston, Blodgett's in December of 1755, and Clement's in April of the following year. Johnston appears to have published as well as engraved Clement's *Plan of Hudsons River,* and in an advertisement in the *Boston Weekly News-Letter* of May 13, 1756, he, Jacob Griggs, a merchant in King Street, and Timothy Clements are each noted as selling copies. Blodgett, a sutler at the time of the battle who would later become a substantial merchant and manufacturer, advertised in the *Boston Weekly News-Letter* of January 9, 1756, as the map's publisher and purveyor without mention of Johnston. Blodgett's plan attracted notice in England, and shortly after its American publication Thomas Jefferys issued a re-engraved version in London.

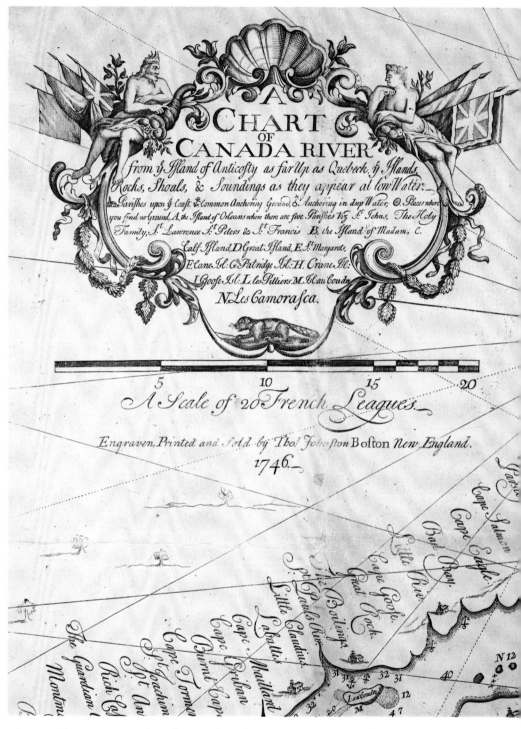

Figure 9 Thomas Johnston, detail from *A Chart of Canada River* (Boston, 1746). Much like the portolan charts of an earlier age, Johnston's *Canada River* focuses on the shoreline to the exclusion of the interior, and greatly emphasizes place names. The unknown, and apparently manuscript, French chart on which Johnston based his chart may have been captured at the fall of the French fortress at Louisbourg in 1745.

Johnston's maps of a martial nature put him in no danger, but his indirect involvement with land speculation nearly proved disastrous. In 1753, he engraved and printed a small plan of southeastern Maine for the proprietors of the Town of Brunswick, who issued it with letterpress text as a broadside. Framed as a resolution, it attacked the land claims of the Plymouth Company, proprietors of the Kennebeck Purchase. The engraver later admitted he had cobbled the map from several sources under instructions from the Brunswick proprietors.[38] Johnston's "confession" became part of a pamphlet war that brought upon him the enmity of his former employers and pulled him into the center of a controversy between competing land speculators. Nearly two years later, he engraved and printed a *Plan of Kennebeck & Sagadahock Rivers & Country Adjacent,* cartographically contradicting the boundaries set forth in the first map. Dated November 20, 1754, the two-sheet Kennebeck map was commissioned by the Plymouth Company to press their claim to the disputed land. Johnston retained the plates, and on June 16, 1755, announced in the *Boston Gazette,* "Just Published, a Map of Kennebeck and Shadahock Rivers . . . sold by Thomas Johnston, in Brattle Street, at half a Dollar." Later that year Thomas Kitchin re-engraved the map in London where Andrew Millar published it.

Johnston's work also includes two largely unknown titles. No copy survives of the first, "A Plan of Part of Lake Champlain and the Large New Forts at Crown Point"; an advertisement in the *Boston Gazette* of June 7, 1762, comprises the only reference to the map. The second, *Plan of ye Town of Pownall by Order of ye Proprietors of ye Kenebeck Purchase,* dated November 12, 1763, exists in a single example discovered in England. Along with the final reissue of the Bonner/Price plan of Boston in 1769, these two elusive Johnston engravings represent the only separate maps published in Boston during the decade of the 1760s, and the last to be published there until the American Revolution.

JAMES TURNER

While Boston can claim James Turner (1722–1759) as one of its own, his greatest contributions to American cartography occurred in Philadelphia. A silversmith, printer, and engraver, Turner produced a variety of wood and copper engravings ranging from trade cards and portraits to topographical views. Revisions to the 1743 state of William Price's map of Boston done in a style identified as Turner's may constitute his initial cartographic work, although he received no credit on the map itself (see plate 26).[40] Two years later his name did appear on a map, leaving no question as to his involvement. Along with several other Boston publishers, Thomas Fleet commemorated the fall of the French fortress of Louisbourg in the summer of 1745 with a broadside of the "Song of the Victorious Sailors," accompanied by Turner's *A Plan of the City and Harbour of*

Louisbourg. &c. The plan also appeared in the *American Magazine and Historical Chronicle.*

Turner's most ambitious cartographic project while in Boston, *A Chart of the Coasts of Nova Scotia and Parts Adjacent,* cannot be dated with certainty (figure 10). Dedicated to Edward Cornwallis, founder of Halifax in 1749, most sources ascribe to it a date of ca. 1750. In constructing the coastal portion of the chart, Turner closely followed Thomas Jefferys's version of a 1744 French map by Jacques Bellin. To this Turner added inset plans of Halifax, Quebec, and Louisbourg, drawn from a variety of sources. Turner also included a view of Boston that greatly resembles his own view of the town first published in the *American Magazine and Historical Chronicle* in 1744.

A close relationship developed between Turner and Benjamin Franklin. In 1744, Turner engraved illustrations for a book on fireplaces published by Franklin, and would receive other engraving commissions through the Philadelphia printer, including cartographic work. Franklin seemingly influenced Turner's decision to leave Boston for Philadelphia in 1754. Once there, James Turner went on to engrave landmark maps for Lewis Evans, Nicholas Scull, and Joshua Fisher.

JOHN AND WILLIAM NORMAN AND OSGOOD CARLETON

Immediately following the cessation of the Revolutionary War, British, French, and American mapmakers rushed to produce depictions of the newly recognized United States. Yet with the exception of small national maps printed in almanacs and geographies, Boston map publishers turned their attention elsewhere. The first significant mapping venture entered upon in federal Boston focused closer to home. On February 17, 1785, the *Independent Chronicle* advertised the intention of John Norman (ca. 1748–1817) and John Coles (ca. 1749–1809) to take subscriptions for a wall map of New England reputedly based on "actual surveys" of Samuel Holland, Lewis Evans, and Thomas Jefferys, the London engraver and publisher. Norman, a prolific, albeit largely derivative, engraver and printer of books, maps, charts, music, and portraits, and Coles, a painter and printer, had previously collaborated when Coles published Norman's less-than-flattering portraits of George and Martha Washington.

Less than two months later Norman and Coles announced the publication of *An Accurate Map of the Four New England States,* describing it as "the greatest undertaking of the kind that has hitherto been published."[41] Printed from twelve plates and measuring just over five feet by five feet, the map depicts Massachusetts (including Maine), New Hampshire (including Vermont counties), Connecticut, and Rhode Island. Norman and Coles's *Four New England States* dwarfed any previous American map and exceeded Jefferys's *A Map of the most Inhabited part of New England* (London, 1755 with later editions; see plate 16), which served as its prin-

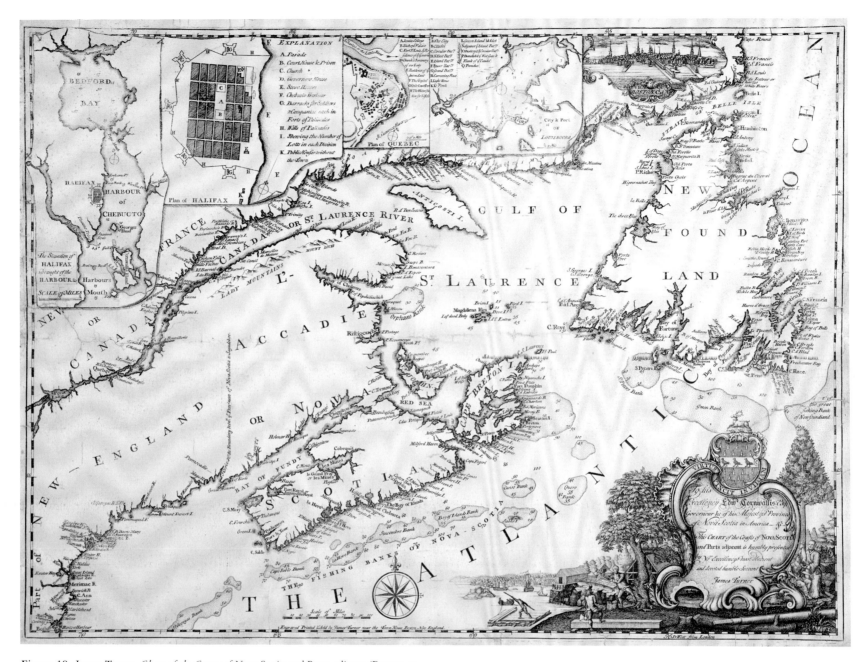

Figure 10 James Turner, *Chart of the Coasts of Nova Scotia and Parts adjacent* (Boston, ca. 1750). The treaty between Britain and France that concluded King George's War restored Louisbourg to the French. In order to protect New England and her maritime trade, the British established a settlement and garrison at Halifax, Nova Scotia. Turner dedicated his chart to Edward Cornwallis, a British officer who founded Halifax and championed New England's interests in the area. The inclusion of plans of Halifax and Louisbourg and a view of Boston underscores the interrelatedness of the locations.

cipal model. Subscribers paid 14 shillings for a colored copy, with the cost to others being 18 shillings. The list of subscribers preserved in the Bostonian Society totals 221, including such notables as John Hancock, the Marquis de Lafayette, Henry Knox, James Bowdoin (to whom the map is dedicated), and Samuel Adams.

In the fall of 1789, John Norman turned to chartmaking, copying and engraving sections of *The Atlantic Neptune* for Bartholomew Burges, and continuing the same work for Matthew Clark (see below). At the same time, he was engaged on a four-sheet chart of the West Indies, also derived from English sources. The *Boston Gazette* of December 30, 1789, announced the publication of *A New General Chart of the West Indies,* linking for the first time the names of Osgood Carleton and John Norman. Carleton (1742–1816) described himself as a teacher of mathematics and professor of astronomy. Beyond those attainments he was a surveyor, compiler of almanacs, and a cartographer. Both men kept shop at Oliver's Dock between 1788 and 1789 where they began a cartographic collaboration that extended into the next century.

Following their work with Matthew Clark, which terminated in the summer of 1790, Norman and Carleton completed a six-sheet map titled *The United States of America Laid Down From the Best Authorities.* Carleton may have compiled the map from various sources and drawn a fair copy from which Norman engraved the plates. Published by John Norman on February 28, 1791, the map found a wide audience with copies sold in such locations as New York and Baltimore.[42] Carleton revised the map in 1797, when John Norman's son, William (d. 1807), published it as *A New Map of the United States of America.* In 1791, John Norman also engraved and printed Paul Pinkham's *Chart of Nantucket Shoals,* the first printed chart of the Massachusetts coast done by an American since Cyprian Southack's much earlier efforts. According to Norman's advertisement in the *Boston Gazette* of April 11, the *Chart of Nantucket Shoals* sold for one dollar. More than a decade later the Normans still kept it in stock, but had reduced the price to 75 cents.

John Norman included Pinkham's chart in his most important cartographic accomplishment, an atlas titled *The American Pilot Containing the Navigation of the Sea Coast of North America,* first published in September 1791. He assembled the work from a variety of sources, among them Daniel Dunbibin's thirty-year-old chart of the Carolinas, Osgood Carleton's new chart of the coast of Surinam, a chart of the Newfoundland Banks first published in London by Robert Sayer in 1783, the 1789 chart of the West Indies produced with Carleton, and copies of charts in *The Atlantic Neptune* and *The North American Pilot* (London, 1776) (figure 11). The atlas went through four printings before 1800; extant copies contain between nine and twelve charts and a page of sailing directions copied almost verbatim from *The English Pilot.*

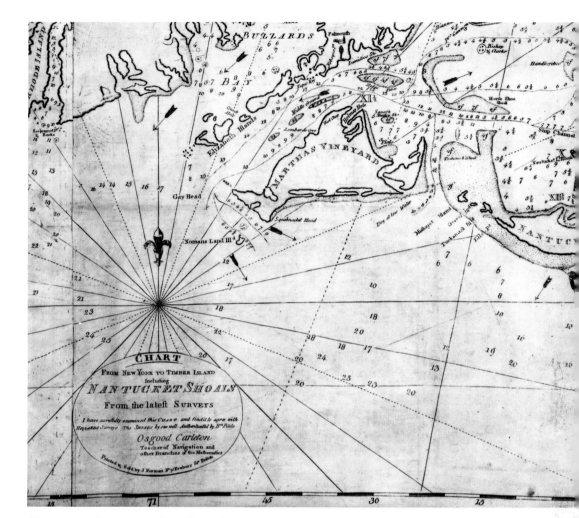

Figure 11 John Norman, detail from *Chart From New York to Timber Island Including Nantucket Shoals* published in *The American Pilot* (Boston, 1791). After engraving for Matthew Clark, Norman determined to publish his own atlas of sea charts. *The American Pilot* consisted of eleven sheets depicting the Atlantic coast from Maine to Georgia. While claiming to be based on the latest surveys, this chart bears a striking resemblance to his earlier effort for Clark (see plate 20).

The elder Norman did not deposit a federal copyright for *The American Pilot* until August 1794, coinciding with the third edition of the atlas. *The Pilot* was issued for a second time in 1794 on September 10, this time with William Norman listed as publisher. From then until William's death, the majority of the maps and charts produced by the Normans appeared under his imprint. Other marine atlases published by William Norman include *A Pilot for the West Indies* (1795), *The New West India Pilot* (1803), and *The New East India Pilot* (1804). Each of these publications involved Osgood Carleton, whose name appeared on the title pages attesting to the accuracy of the charts.

In addition to chartmaking, John Norman and Carleton pursued other cartographic opportunities. In 1794, Carleton petitioned the Massachusetts House of Representatives with a proposal for publishing an official map of the Commonwealth. The General Court legislature approved his plan and ordered each town in Massachusetts and Maine to prepare a survey from which to compile a general map. Three years later, Carleton and John Norman were awarded a contract to produce maps of Massachusetts and the District of Maine. While sanctioned by the Massachusetts government, the production costs of the map fell to Carleton and Norman, who solicited subscriptions to that end. Their proposal printed in the *Massachusetts Mercury* of July 18, 1797, promised maps "neatly engraved, printed on good paper, and coloured," costing subscribers three dollars, and all others four. The proposal concluded by stating that if the maps did not gain official approval, subscriptions would not be binding.

In June 1798, Carleton and Norman presented the legislature with copies of *An Accurate Map of the District of Maine,* and *An Accurate Map of the Commonwealth of Massachusetts.* The undated maps bear the imprint "Published and Sold by O. Carleton & J. Norman." Largely owing to the "inelegant" engraving, the legislature would not allow publication until Norman amended the plates.[43] Undeterred by this development, Carleton and Norman announced in the *Columbian Centinel* of July 14 that subscribers would receive their maps in three to four weeks. Norman never did correct the plates to the legislature's satisfaction, and was replaced by Samuel Hill and Benjamin Callendar, Jr., who engraved completely new plates. The resulting versions of Carleton's maps, sanctioned by the General Court, did not appear until 1801. In the meantime, Carleton and Norman had surreptitiously sold the copies of their "unofficial" maps of Maine and Massachusetts.

As Carleton and Norman labored on the state maps, the need for a detailed map of Boston had not escaped their attention. In 1796, John West published Carleton's *A Plan of Boston from actual Survey,* engraved by Samuel Hill (see plate 31). A relatively small map, it was bound into copies of West's *Boston Directory,* but sold also as a separate sheet. The following year Carleton and Norman embarked upon a more ambitious map of the town. On April 3, 1797, Carleton deposited the copyright for a map titled *An Accurate Plan of the Town of Boston, and its Vicinity* (figure 12). Published by Osgood Carleton on May 16, 1797, this large-scale plan engraved on two sheets by John Norman measures nearly three feet by four feet. It incorporates surveys by Carleton, Samuel Thompson, and Matthew Withington, and contains greater detail and considerably different information than that found on Carleton's city plan of the previous year. William Norman, who along with Carleton sold the map, reissued it with revisions in 1806 under the title *A New Plan of Boston Drawn from the Best Authorities.*

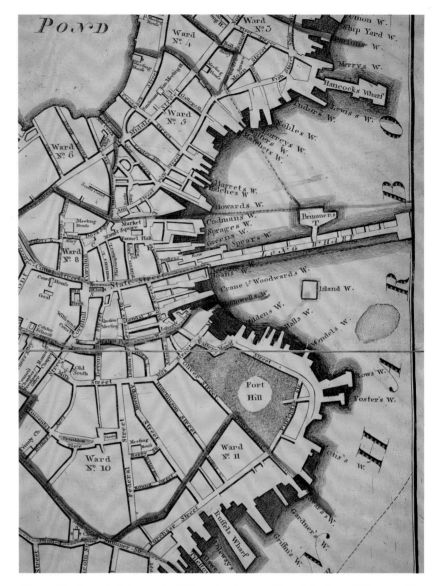

Figure 12 Osgood Carleton, detail from *An Accurate Plan of the Town of Boston and its Vicinity* (Boston, 1797). Engraved by John Norman, Carleton's map of Boston surpassed any previous effort in both size and accuracy. Perhaps because of its size only two copies are known to survive today. The map depicts the location of schools, churches and meeting houses, courthouses, theaters, and Boston's all-important wharves.

The atlas of sea charts published by Matthew Clark (1714–1798) has long been considered one of the landmarks of American cartographic history. But being largely derivative, the atlas offers little in the way of carto-graphic innovation and may more accurately be considered an achieve-ment of American publishing, rather than chartmaking. Bartholomew Burges (ca. 1740–1807) initiated the atlas project in July 1789, by solic-iting subscriptions for "Charts of the Coasts of America, in separate sec-tions, protracted from Holland's and Des Barres's last eminent Admiralty Charts."[44] Burges had published titles on navigation and astronomy, and now intended to selectively copy the contents of *The Atlantic Neptune.* His proposal offered twelve charts depicting the coast from Newfoundland to the Gulf of Mexico with accompanying nautical directions. Printing of the charts would begin once 100 subscribers had been secured, with sheets delivered weekly at a cost of two shillings apiece.

To encourage subscriptions, Burges declared that the Boston Marine Society would guarantee the accuracy of the charts. He neglected, howev-er, to request the society's consent before making this claim, and conse-quently lost favor with them. Burges apparently failed to secure adequate support to publish the charts, for by the end of the year his involvement in the publication had terminated (figure 13). At that time Matthew Clark, an auctioneer with no previous publishing experience, emerged as the principal figure behind the venture. The minutes of the Boston Marine Society show that in October 1789, Clark petitioned for the society's approval of the charts, and in January of 1790, he appeared before a com-mittee of local pilots chosen to determine the charts' accuracy. The society agreed to endorse the charts and Clark issued his own subscription pro-posal in the January 30 issue of the *Massachusetts Centinel.* He proposed to print fifteen charts, available individually, in groups of three, or bound as an atlas, claiming that each would bear an engraved certificate of accuracy signed by Osgood Carleton, acting on behalf of the Boston Marine Society.

Clark had greater success in attracting subscribers than had Burges, and on July 5, 1790, the *Boston Gazette* announced, "Just published (price thirty-six shillings) . . . a Complete Chart of the Coast of America, from Cape Breton into the Gulf of Mexico—upon a large scale—neatly bound. Subscribers will be waited upon with their books." The *Gazette* advertise-ment listed only Clark and Carleton as retailing the atlas, but in fact a number of Boston booksellers later sold copies. The atlas, which lacks a title page, ultimately numbered eighteen charts joined in nine pairs pro-gressing from south to north (see plate 20). Although only three plates bear his signature, John Norman did the majority of the engraving and may have printed the charts. Joseph Seymour engraved several plates that contrast noticeably with Norman's efforts. As promised, the charts includ-ed an engraved inscription signed by Carleton attesting to their accuracy.

Figure 13 Bartholomew Burges/John Norman, title cartouche of a chart published in Matthew Clark's untitled atlas of charts (Boston, 1790). Burges and Norman had previ-ously collaborated on a celestial diagram, and Burges selected Norman as the engraver of his proposed atlas of sea charts. Largely owing to financial reasons, Burges never saw the project to completion and Matthew Clark assumed the role of publisher. Before publica-tion, Burges's name was obliterated from the plates engraved by Norman, but one surviv-ing copy of this chart shows the original attribution dating from October 1789.

Although adapted primarily from *The Atlantic Neptune,* some of the charts in Clark's atlas incorporated new information. The sheet covering the Nantucket Shoals, for example, contains soundings and observations pro-vided by three local pilots. Unlike Des Barres's work, most of the harbor insets do not provide enough detail to be of utilitarian value.

The early history of the Boston map trade clearly illustrates the town's ties to England, evident in so many aspects of colonial life. Not only did a great deal of the cartographic supply originate in London, many of the individuals who became part of the map trade did so as well. But unlike London, where the majority of map sellers belonged to the print-ing or allied trades, the Boston map trade consisted of a more complex cast of characters.[45] Navigators, ship chandlers, cabinet makers, portraitists, postmasters, japanners, auctioneers, and school teachers participated in marketing cartographic products to one degree or another, although not all of them operated shops, and many would not have been identified as map dealers by their contemporaries. Colonial artisans and merchants typ-ically took advantage of likely entrepreneurial opportunities while pursu-ing more than one vocation. In such a climate an individual normally assumed multiple roles in the map trade, combining the functions of pub-lisher, engraver, vendor, cartographer, or printer.

Just as book and print sellers became Boston's chief merchandisers of maps, engravers and printers added commercial mapmaking to their repertoire. The presence of competent engravers made cartographic publishing possible and encouraged the creation of printed maps of local interest. Bostonians continued, however, to purchase English maps and charts, whose superior quality contributed to their lasting popularity. A ready supply of English maps, a limited number of local engravers, and a general lack of venture capital combined to restrict commercial mapmaking in colonial Boston. But by the early federal period engravers and capital had become more plentiful in Boston. In 1791, publisher Isaiah Thomas could compare prices and choose among three engravers to produce a map of New Hampshire.[46] Soon thereafter, Boston cartographic products and their English counterparts would be on an equal footing in the marketplace.

Matthew Clark's atlas signaled the beginning of Boston's ascendancy in American chartmaking. With an economy largely based on maritime commerce and a flourishing printing trade, eighteenth-century Boston was the logical seat of nautical cartography in the new republic. Despite enjoying renewed prosperity after the American Revolution, the town's tenure as a leading cartographic center would quickly be eclipsed by New York and Philadelphia. An equivalent situation developed in the book trade. Just before the Revolution, Boston could boast nearly twice the number of publishing firms as found in any other American city, but by 1798, Philadelphia and New York had surpassed Boston.[47] The close of the eighteenth century witnessed the transformation of the colonial printer into the American publisher, with Boston book publishing firms such as that of Isaiah Thomas and Ebenezer Andrews embracing new methods of production and marketing to great advantage. Not until the establishment of lithography in the nineteenth century would Boston cartographic publishers achieve a similar success.

NOTES

1. Quoted in Julius H. Tuttle, "The Libraries of the Mathers," *Proceedings of the American Antiquarian Society* 20 (1910): 294.

2. Thomas G. Wright, *Literary Culture in Early New England, 1620–1730* (New York, 1966), 27–29.

3. Inventory of William Bacon of Salem. *Probate Inventories of Essex County Massachusetts* (Salem, 1916), I: 162.

4. George Bowman, "Governor William Bradford's Will and Inventory," *Mayflower Descendant* 2 (1900): 232.

5. Numerous examples are found in Wright, *Literary Culture in Early New England*, 32–37.

6. *The Diary of Samuel Sewall, 1674–1729,* M. Halsey Thomas, ed. (New York, 1973), I: 235.

7. George Littlefield, *Early Boston Booksellers, 1642–1711* (reprint ed., New York, 1969), 12.

8. Worthington C. Ford, *The Boston Book Market, 1679–1700* (reprint ed., New York, 1972), 122.

9. Inventory dated August 29, 1732. Abbott Lowell Cummings, *Rural Household Inventories* (Boston, 1964), 114–118.

10. Carl Bridenbaugh, *Cities in the Wilderness, the First Century of Urban Life in America, 1625–1742* (New York, 1968), 291.

11. *Boston News-Letter,* March 1, 1714.

12. Based on information compiled by Robert Winans, *A Descriptive Checklist of Book Catalogues Separately Printed in America, 1693–1800* (Worcester, 1981), and the author's inspection of individual catalogs. These figures do not include catalogs of institutional or private circulating libraries.

13. Boston, September 30, 1766. "On Monday, the 13th of October next, will be offered for sale . . . a Valuable Collection of Books, a variety of Maps and Prints with several Optical and Philosophical Instruments, &c...." Copy in the American Antiquarian Society, Worcester. John Mein's *A Catalogue of Curious and Valuable Books* was advertised in the *Boston Evening Post* of May 19, 1766. It includes notices of 17 two- and four-sheet maps identified solely by geographical location (i.e., two-sheet map of Asia).

14. *A Catalogue of Curious and Valuable Books to be Sold at the London Bookstore* (Boston, 1766).

15. Stephen Botein, "The Anglo-American Book Trade Before 1776: Personnel and Strategies," in *Printing and Society in Early America* (Worcester, 1983), 72–73.

16. These figures are derived from John McCusker, *Money and Exchange in Europe and America, 1600–1775: A Handbook* (Chapel Hill, 1978).

17. Matthew H. Edney, *An Eighteenth Century Map of New England and the Intersecting Cultures of Print and Cartography* (forthcoming).

18. See Botein, "The Anglo-American Book Trade," 65–69.

19. William P. Cumming, "The Colonial Charting of the Massachusetts Coast," in *Seafaring in Colonial Massachusetts,* ed. Philip C. Smith (Charlottesville, Va., 1980), 81–84.

20. Suffolk County Probate 2459, March 2, 1698.

21. Littlefield, *Early Boston Booksellers,* 175–177.

22. Cornelis Koeman, "The Chart Trade in Europe from the Middle Ages to the Twentieth Century," in *Five Hundred Years of Nautical Science* (Greenwich, 1979), 139. Koeman's comment is based on information compiled by Sarah Tyacke, *London Map-Sellers, 1660–1720* (Tring, England, 1978).

23. Sold by Jarvis & Parker (*Boston Evening Post,* May 21, 1753); Edmund Quincy, Jr., (*Boston Gazette,* September 14, 1761); Thomas Rand (*Boston Weekly News-Letter,* June 24, 1756). Dunbibin's chart is known only as a copy published by John Norman in 1791. Quincy's advertisement provides one of the few contemporary references to the chart.

24. *Massachusetts Centinel,* July 29, 1789.

25. *Independent Chronicle,* May 22, 1797; August 10, 1797.

26. Yale University's copy of Norman's *The American Pilot* contains the broadside titled *Charts Published and Sold (wholesale) by William Norman, Pleasant-street, Boston.* The assigned date of ca.1804 is based on the publication dates of items sold by Norman.

27. Clara E. LeGear, "The New England Coasting Pilot of Cyprian Southack," *Imago Mundi* 11 (1954): 140–141.

28. See, for example, Lawrence C. Wroth, *The Colonial Printer* (reprint ed. New York, 1994), 185–188.

29. LeGear, "The New England Coasting Pilot of Cyprian Southack," 139.

30. Sinclair Hitchings, "Guarding the New England Coast: The Naval Career of Cyprian Southack," *Seafaring in Colonial Massachusetts,* 49, 60; William P. Cumming, *British Maps of Colonial America* (Chicago, 1974), 42.

31. For an analysis of the Bonner map see John Reps, "Boston by Bostonians: The Printed Plans and Views of the Colonial City by its Artists, Cartographers, Engravers, and Publishers," in *Boston Prints and Printmakers, 1670–1775* (Boston, 1973), 3–33.

32. Benjamin Franklin V, *Boston Printers, Publishers, and Booksellers: 1640–1800* (Boston, 1980), 417.

33. "Diary of Samuel Sewall, 1674–1729," *Massachusetts Historical Society Collections* 47 (1882): 188–189. The reference to Dewing appears in a note.

34. *A South Prospect of ye Flourishing City of New York in the Province of New York in America* (New York, ca. 1719–1722).

35. *New England Courant,* May 13, 1723.

36. Richard B. Holman, "William Burgis," *Boston Prints and Printmakers,* 69.

37. Frederick W. Coburn, "Peter Pelham," *Dictionary of American Biography* (New York, 1934), 7:409.

38. Johnston's *Chart of Canada River* was published in August, 1746; Turner was engraving and printing three maps for the General Proprietors of the Eastern Division of New Jersey, published by them in 1747.

39. Lawrence C. Wroth discusses the controversy in *The Walpole Society Notebook* (Portland, Me., 1950), 29–31.

40. See Reps, "Boston by Bostonians," 24–25.

41. *Independent Chronicle,* April 14, 1785.

42. Rita S. Gottesman, *The Arts and Crafts in New York, 1777–1799* (New York, 1954), 56; Alfred C. Prime, *The Arts and Crafts in Philadelphia, Maryland and South Carolina, 1786–1800* (Topsfield, Mass., 1932), 83

43. Susan Danforth, "The First Official Maps of Maine and Massachusetts," *Imago Mundi* 35 (1983): 38.

44. *Massachusetts Centinel,* July 29, 1789.

45. Tyacke, *London Map-Sellers*, xii.

46. Rollo Silver, *The American Printer, 1787–1825* (Charlottesville, 1967), 164.

47. Lawrence C. Wroth and Rollo Silver, "The Book Trade, 1784–1860," in *The Book in America* (New York, 1952), 120.

Frontispiece D. A. Sanborn, detail from *Insurance Map of Boston,* volume 1
(New York, 1867), title page.

Windows to Our Past: Mapping in the Nineteenth Century and Beyond

David Cobb

The nineteenth century, the first century of American mapmaking, represents the transition from a European-dominated map publishing industry for American maps to a flourishing American map industry in Boston, New York, Philadelphia, Washington, and beyond. It brings familiar names such as John Melish, Osgood Carleton, Henry Tanner, the Colton family, Samuel Augustus Mitchell, D. A. Sanborn, George Hopkins, Henry Francis Walling, George Bromley, and Frederick W. Beers, to name but a few. These firms dominated American mapmaking in the nineteenth century every bit as much as the previous centuries had been dominated by the Dutch, English, and French. This section will discuss some of the significant maps and series that were produced in the nineteenth century and their effect on the recorded history of Boston.

PRIVATE ENTERPRISE: THE LAND OWNERSHIP MAP AND EARLY ATLASES

Cadastral maps, or maps recording land ownership, represent one of the earliest forms of cartographic enterprise. The Babylonians were known to have mapped land holdings on clay tablets as early as 2000 B.C. It has also been reported that the Egyptians had planned a cadastral survey as early as the thirteenth century B.C., although this survey has not survived.

Early American cadastral surveys began in the eighteenth century and were usually maps of small land plats, necessary documentation in a land of new settlements and ownership claims. A manuscript survey of a small portion of the wharf area in Boston is an example of early cadastral mapping. Drawn in 1772, this survey was the result of a contest over property and shows in detail the owners of property in the vicinity of Doane's Wharf (figure 1).

State maps were required as the young country approached the end of the eighteenth century, and the advent of a growing commercial and transportation system in the nineteenth century made apparent the need for more detailed maps. Very few of these early cadastral maps of the late eighteenth and early nineteenth centuries ever reached the publication stage. Most exist today in manuscript form and are located in archives, such as the Massachusetts State Archives, and local county record offices.

Massachusetts was well prepared cartographically to enter the nineteenth century, for its General Court resolved on June 26, 1794:

Resolve requiring the inhabitants of the several towns and districts in the Commonwealth, to cause to be taken by their Selectmen, or some other desirable persons, accurate plans of their respective towns, and to lodge the same in the Secretary's Office. . . . Whereas an accurate Map of this Commonwealth will tend to facilitate and promote such information and improvements as will be favorable to its growth and prosperity, and will otherwise be highly useful and important, on many public and private occasions, for the procurement of the materials necessary for the accomplishment of an object so desirable, and by which the reputation and interest of the Commonwealth will be advanced. . . . [1]

Resolved, That the inhabitants of the several towns . . . are required to take or cause to be taken . . . accurate plans of their respective towns or districts, upon a scale of two hundred rods to an inch . . . and the same plans to lodge in the Secretary's office, free of expence to the Commonwealth, on or before the fifth day of June, 1795. [2]

Thus, as can be viewed at its State Archives, the Commonwealth of Massachusetts entered the nineteenth century with a complete set of town plans. This project had been petitioned to the House and Senate by both Osgood Carleton, on January 16, 1794, and William Blodgett, on February 6, 1794. The resulting surveys represent the existing knowledge of surveying throughout the Commonwealth; the manuscript maps sent to the secretary's office reveal exquisitely detailed surveys for a small number of towns and a general outline for the majority. Carleton had begun his own surveys for a state map but the scarcity of available information led him to appeal to the state for assistance in what could become an official survey. Carleton himself prepared the survey for Boston; while not showing detail for the city, it does attempt to show its geographical delineation at that time (see plate 30). The resulting surveys from the towns must have been a disappointment to Carleton, but they did not prevent him from advertising his 1801 map as an official survey.

The House of Representatives had refused to fund Carleton's initial survey on the basis of its disappointing data and, in 1829, appointed a committee to study the feasibility of producing another state map. While

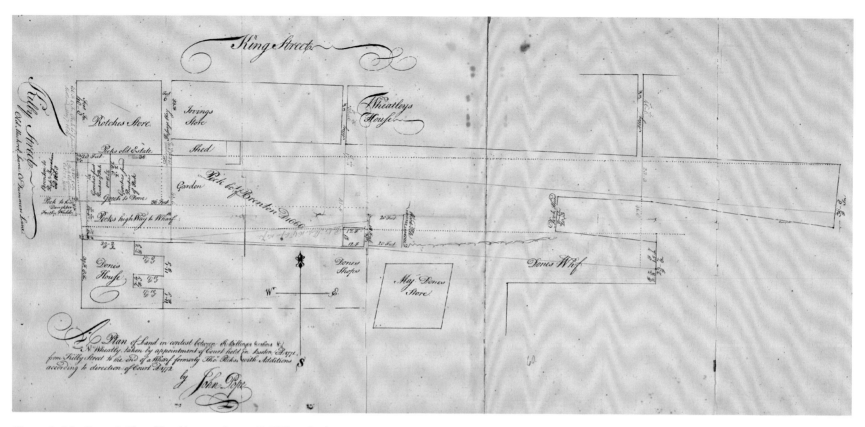

Figure 1 John Pope, *A Plan of Land in contest between R. Billings & others, . . .* (1772)

acknowledging that Carleton's map of 1801 represented the only map "of the State on a scale of any magnitude, which bears evidence of being made from authentic sources of information," the committee went on to report that because of "the want of a general survey of the Commonwealth upon the principles of triangulation, Mr. Carleton found himself unable to accomplish his undertaking to the satisfaction of the legislature under whose authority he acted." The legislature then wrote on February 12, 1830, a Resolve "requiring towns to make surveys of their territory . . . a scale of one hundred rods to an inch" and required specific cultural features to be mapped, such as mills, taverns, and roads. The committee report also suggested that "the expense to the towns of these surveys, would be remunerated, should the manuscript plans be lithographed."[3] This wording was adopted by many towns; although many of the manuscripts, such as Hales's 1830 map of Boston (see plate 34), are available in manuscript only, some of the town maps were published and can be found in numerous collections throughout Boston.

It was not until the 1850s that a market for large-scale county maps developed among the affluent rural residents in New England. This growth is evident in the number of county maps produced from 1851 to 1860.

Three hundred and twenty-seven county maps represent the decade of the 1850s, while only twenty-eight had been published during the 1840s.

One of the most prolific of these county mapmakers was Henry Francis Walling. He began his career in Providence, Rhode Island, and published his first cadastral map of Northbridge, Massachusetts, in 1848. He continued to produce maps of other towns and cities in Massachusetts and, in 1850, produced his first county map—of Newport County, Rhode Island. His success led him to produce maps of states from Alabama to Vermont. He produced maps for nearly 280 counties including those of thirteen in Massachusetts. It may be assumed that the existence of many maps of Boston, which comprised Suffolk County, prevented the production of a county map of Suffolk being produced at that time. Every other county in Massachusetts was mapped during the mid-nineteenth century. These maps evolved to a standard format that included political boundaries, roads, railroads, towns, churches, schools, post offices, land ownership, and physical features such as rivers and mountains. They often included insets of major towns with business directories and views of significant buildings.

County maps remained popular throughout New England and beyond until after the Civil War. By this time the market had become saturated. The desire to reveal an increasing amount of information also led to their demise. Their large size (approximately 5 to 6 feet square) required printing of multiple sheets, coloring, usually varnishing, and then mounting on rods so they might be easily displayed in the office or home parlor. Such characteristics soon led to the development of a county atlas as the preferred printing format. This was more conventional in size and allowed additional information to be presented on separate pages. Also, atlases could be sold to a new group of subscribers.

These county maps and atlases were sufficiently accurate for cadastral, lithographic views, and settlement information. They were made for a limited audience with limited resources. The publisher needed a staff that could expeditiously and cost-effectively map a county and then move on to the next. This required organizing a sales team and a surveying team, locating artists and biographical and history writers, finding a printing establishment, and establishing a collection team. Compilers regularly used local land records and offices containing the most up-to-date, if not the most accurate, information. The accuracy of additional fieldwork varied among individual publishers.

The atlas and map business was unique in that it depended almost exclusively on private enterprise, because state and federal governments had meager resources to devote to such ventures. It is extraordinary that entrepreneurs appeared who were willing to invest in this product with no certainty for profit. After the profits began to accumulate, however, so did the participants. There were few, if any, requirements to enter the business, no specialized training or certification; many learned from others in the business and then moved on to form their own enterprise. Traditionally, surveyors and civil engineers formed the nucleus of mapmakers, although lawyers, doctors, and professors in various fields also played a role.

Map sales forces, and even surveyors, were ridiculed for being hucksters and frauds, as exemplified by these quotes from an 1879 book:

> Most subscribers assumed a real surveyor with chains and compass would survey their property—imagine the reaction when he saw a man stop in front of his home in a buggy, make a dot on the map and drive on—knowing he had already signed and paid for his subscription.[4]

> Some classes of men have constant occasion to use books of reference . . . but they are professional men, who live by brainwork. The majority of people live by hard labor, or a combination of hand and brain which requires no special original literary research. Hence, we place volumes of reference under the heading of articles indispensable to a limited class; valuable to still another class who are rich and have leisure to gratify peculiar tastes; and almost valueless to the great mass of humanity.[5]

As the genre evolved it became evident that additional information could be included, and atlases soon contained more and larger views, detailed town plans, biographical sketches, town and county histories, distance tables, business directories, and lithographs of notable citizens. County mapmakers could reenter the market with a new format and sell updated maps with supplemental material. Conzen suggests that the publishers moved with the market: in the 1850s and 1860s it was the county map; in the 1870s and 1880s it became the county atlas; in the 1880s it was the county history; and in the 1890s it was biographies that brought the profits.[6] These publishers were not cartographers but rather managers and could therefore abandon one format for another with little concern. The following estimate of costs and sales for a county map show that there was indeed a potential profit in this mapmaking business:[7]

Sales

1,200 maps (average), at $6 each	$7,200
views, at $40 each	2000
	Total $9,200

Expenses

Commission on maps, 50 cents each	$600
Commissions on views, 10% each	200
Copying plats from tax lists, $3.50 each	56
Making township maps from observation & copying, $28/each	448
Making city and township plats	25
Engraving 16 townships, $15 each	240
Engraving plats	20
Printing 1,200 maps	140
Lithographing 50 views, $5.50 each	275
Heading and extras	20
Sketching view, 10% commission	200
Mounting & coloring, 90 cents each	1080
Paper	200
Freight and incidental expenses	300
Commissions for collecting on maps, 40 cents each	480
Commissions for collecting views, 3% each	60
	Total $4,344
	Profits $4,856

It was not long before Griffith M. Hopkins realized the potential profit of an atlas for Boston and published his *Atlas of the County of Suffolk* in Philadelphia in 1874 (see figure 2; see also plate 42 for a Hopkins map of Boston published concurrently with the atlas). This was not just one atlas, but seven, and the map scales varied in each volume from 1 inch = 100 feet to 1 inch = 300 feet. Each volume was divided geographically: 1. Boston proper; 2. Roxbury; 3. South Boston and Dorchester; 4. East Boston, Chelsea, Revere, and Winthrop; 5. West Roxbury; 6. Charlestown; and 7. Brighton. Hopkins's surveyors, unlike those of Sanborn, as we shall see, identified land ownership, the major advantage of this atlas.

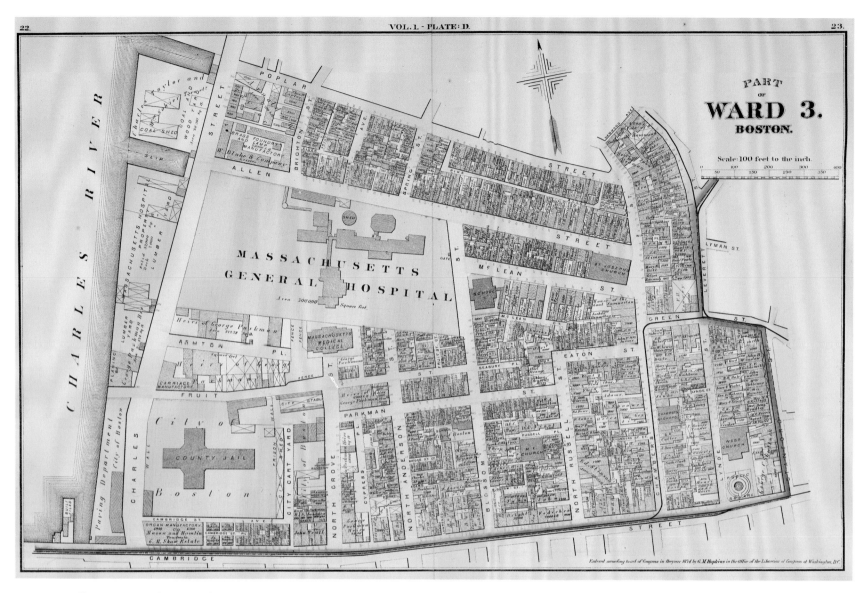

Figure 2 Griffith Morgan Hopkins, *Part of Ward 3. Boston,* volume 1 (Philadelphia, 1874),
Plate D.

Hopkins followed his obviously extravagant 1874 project with his 1882 one-volume *City Atlas of Boston,* on a smaller scale. This atlas was a direct reaction to the fire insurance atlases produced by Sanborn, for the buildings were coded by color to indicate brick or stone architecture, frame buildings, stables, sheds, and fire hydrants.

George Bromley, also of Philadelphia and a successful county atlas publisher, created his *Atlas of the City of Boston* in 1883. It also shows building construction materials for he, too, was trying to compete with the new fire insurance mapping companies.

County atlases continue to be produced today in many regions of the country and are especially prevalent in the Midwest. Their characteristics have become more utilitarian and the elaborate nineteenth-century deco-

ration has vanished. Nevertheless, land-ownership mapping in America represents an interesting web of connections between cartography, nineteenth-century technology, business entrepreneurship, and a popular culture that appreciated such local atlases.

FIRE INSURANCE MAPS AND ATLASES

The study of urban history has been made more difficult because many of the primary documents have been scattered among numerous archival collections and, far worse, needlessly destroyed. Early newspapers, city directories, photograph files, and genealogies can be studied by historians, but while these documents reveal valuable information about buildings and other landmarks, they inadequately establish spatial relationships. Maps provide investigators with this spatial dimension as well as with visible clues to changes in the landscape. The fire insurance map is beginning to unlock many secrets of nineteenth-century urban America.

While numerous companies engaged in the mapping of nineteenth-century cities, among the most valuable sources for monitoring and viewing urban change are the maps published by the Sanborn Map Company. Produced for the insurance industry to provide current information on the fire risks of a particular building, they are increasingly becoming primary resources for architects, preservationists, genealogists, urban planners, environmentalists, and others interested in the land use changes within our towns and cities.

The earliest known American fire insurance plan was of Charleston, South Carolina, surveyed in 1788 and published in 1790 by Edmund Petrie for the Phoenix Fire-Company of London. It was not until the mid-nineteenth century, however, that the insurance industry seemed willing to sponsor these highly detailed surveys in the United States. Fire was one of the most feared calamities that could occur in cities, which usually were ill equipped to deal with such catastrophes. Fire stations were not plentiful or geographically dispersed, firefighters were not adequately trained, and pumped water was unavailable in many regions. Boston suffered from these deficiencies; it survived numerous fires, but not without losses, as an 1873 map reveals (figure 3). It was important for fire insurance underwriters to learn more of the urban architecture and some of its land uses. The fire insurance mapping industry would begin to fill many of these information gaps.

Under the auspices of the Aetna Insurance Company, a young man from Somerville, Massachusetts, was commissioned to survey several towns and cities in Tennessee in 1866. Although never formally published, these surveys encouraged their author, D. A. Sanborn, to publish his own *Insurance Map of Boston* in 1867 (see frontispiece). In that same year, based on the success of these ventures, he formed the D. A. Sanborn National Insurance Diagram Bureau. This company grew rapidly and soon became the Sanborn Map Company. At one time they employed 300 surveyors in the field and another 400 in their offices in New York, Chicago, and San Francisco. Sanborn's mapmakers and surveyors worked anonymously—their names never appeared on the maps they worked so hard to compile. One surveyor, however, wrote of his experiences with the Sanborn Map Company:

> While working for [Sanborn] I not only saw all those places I had heard about but I made maps of them, made diagrams of all the houses in each town and city I visited. After four or five years of this work I knew a lot about our people, saints and sinners, rich and poor.[8]

Furthermore, he states,

> In Mobile, New Orleans and St. Louis I could hear them all night calling off the numbers for keno, the gambling game which today is

innocent bingo. When we finished a survey of a city we had more intimate knowledge of its occupants than even the police or detective department, for we could enter where they could not without use of force.[9]

To place their accomplishments in proper perspective, these surveyors mapped the built-up area, or central business district, and surrounding residential blocks for over 12,000 towns and cities nationwide by the 1950s. It is reported that the Sanborn Map Company had mapped every town in the United States with a population of 2,000 persons (in 1950). These maps were drawn at a scale of 1 inch = 50 feet. This large scale allowed specific details to be shown for each structure, such as type of construction (frame, brick, or stone, using carefully selected colors that are consistent within each edition), number of floors, roof composition, windows, elevators, wall construction, street addresses, general retail identifications, width of streets, location of water pipelines, fire hydrants, and many more characteristics.

These wonderfully detailed maps take us back in time and allow us to walk around the blocks of nineteenth-century America—be it a large city such as Boston or a small town such as Belchertown. They allow us to identify paint factories, grocers, butchers, and saloons, and to imagine where the railroad tracks go beyond the gates. Today, they are being recognized beyond the fire insurance industry as valuable documents that record variations in urban land use and structural change. They have proven to be excellent sources for revealing industrial locations and potential environmental hazards in whole blocks or specific areas of a town. As our concerns for environmental safety rise, the Sanborn fire insurance maps are proving to be an excellent resource for identifying potential and historical hazardous sites.

Although these maps are usually highly accurate, this incident from our earlier Sanborn surveyor will perhaps explain the few instances of error:

> At one chemical plant I noted that the old map indicated a shed marked "Retort House." I saw at a glance that the dimensions and distances were wrong on the old map, but when I started to measure them for myself and reached the shed, I discovered that it was full of chemical retorts. From each retort issued a hazy mist of poisonous gases. However, the wind was blowing in the right direction, and I got the correct measurements of the shed, counted the retorts and marked them all down, just as the wind changed and a cloud of that suffocating poison gas encompassed me. I threw myself on my face and rolled over the bank, down to the towpath of the canal, where I lay until I had cleared my lungs of the suffocating fume. I knew exactly why the other fellow who made the old map did not have the correct distances and dimensions. He had evidently worked at a safe distance.[10]

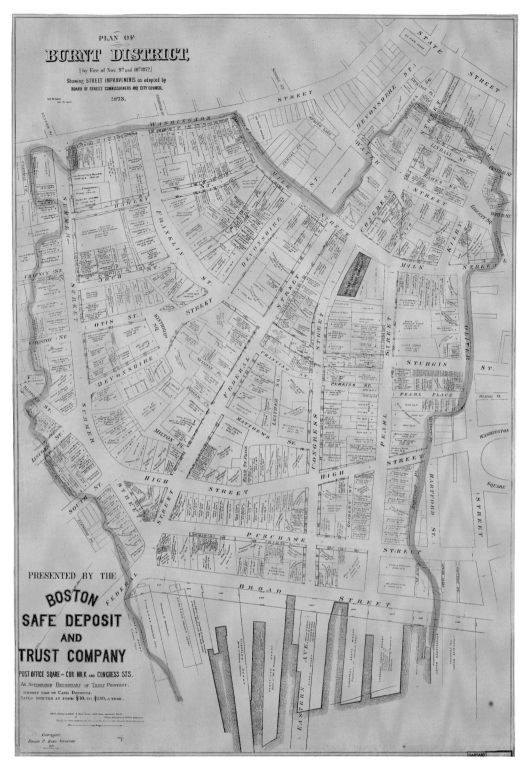

Figure 3 Thomas W. Davis, *Plan of Burnt District {by Fire of Nov. 9th and 10th 1872} Showing Street Improvements as adopted by Board of Street Commissioners and City Council* ([Boston], 1873).

Furthermore, these maps are excellent indicators of economic growth, urban change, and even decline within a city, block by block. Four maps illustrated here show the change in a small four-block area of downtown Boston bounded by India, Broad, Custom House and Wharf Streets.

In 1867, most of the buildings were brick (those shown in blue) and mainly warehouses (figure 4). Potential environmental hazards, with several paint shops and an alkali works, are also identifiable.

Only fifteen years later, in 1883, a competitor of Sanborn's, George Bromley of Philadelphia, produced a map of the area showing all of the property owners and one lone frame structure (in yellow) along Wharf Street (figure 5). The Bromley map provides land ownership information, but the land use information from the Sanborn is not included.

The 1909 Sanborn map shows further change (figure 6). The major addition was the Broad Exchange Building, which was built of fireproof construction. In addition, numerous stores had established residence and there was a coffee roaster, a paper box factory, and a printing firm, among others. Similarly, the "drugs, paints, & oil" firms remained, but by then they had automatic fire alarms.

The 1938 Sanborn map reveals the impact of the automobile, as nearly two blocks were devoted to parking (figure 7). The Broad Exchange remained and the adjoining block had fewer stores. The detail that these surveyors recorded shows, for example, in the blue line along Broad Street, which signifies new concrete facing on this building.

These maps continue to expose the changing urban fabric of our major cities and to reveal, from their many layers of time, a historical window on our towns and cities. The fire insurance maps are primary research documents for a diversity of users including historians, government officials, genealogists, preservationists, and anyone interested in urban land use change. While the major collection of these maps is with the Sanborn Company and, by copyright law, at the Library of Congress, the Harvard Map Collection has the greatest number of these maps for Boston and Massachusetts.

FEDERAL GOVERNMENT MAPPING IN THE NINETEENTH CENTURY

Boston's role as a transportation hub for New England attracted the attention of a new nation and of its new federal agencies. While responsible for charting the nation's coastlines and harbors, the U.S. Coast Survey's early directors performed tasks beyond what their official name might imply. In fact, only after the formation of the U.S. Geological Survey in 1879 did the Coast Survey actually begin to restrict itself to the surveying and production of nautical charts. Their interest in topographic mapping several miles inland from the coast produced intricate charts and topographic maps showing roads, settlements, names of homeowners, industries, vegetation types, and crop patterns.

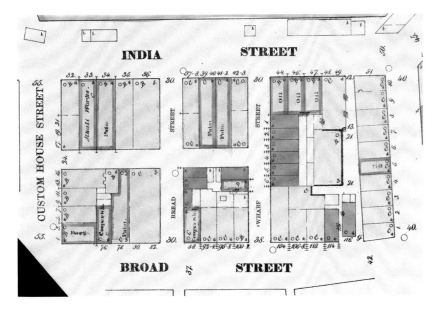

Figure 4 D. A. Sanborn, detail from *Insurance Map of Boston,* volume 1 (New York, 1867), Plate 13.

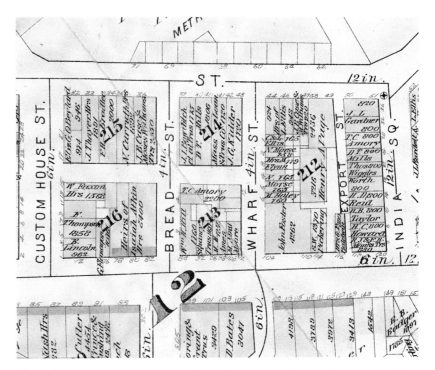

Figure 6 Sanborn Map Company, detail from *Boston, Massachusetts,* volume 1 (New York, 1909), Plate 36.

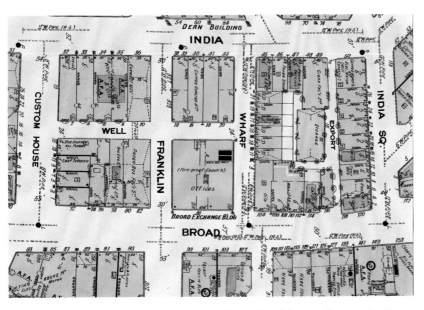

Figure 5 George Washington Bromley, detail from *Atlas of the City of Boston. City Proper,* volume 1 (Philadelphia, 1883), Plate C.

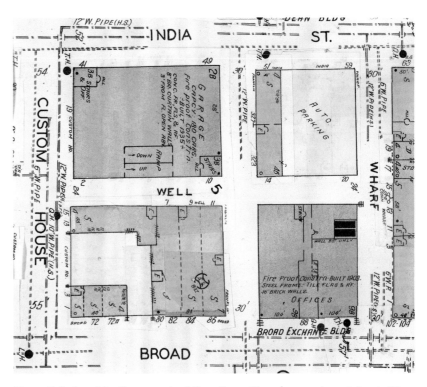

Figure 7 Sanborn Map Company, detail from *Boston, Massachusetts,* volume 1, South (New York, 1929, corrected December 1938), Plate 42.

Therefore, it was the Coast Survey that actually produced some of the first scientific topographic maps of the coastline since Des Barres's *Atlantic Neptune* was published in the eighteenth century. Boston received its fair share of attention; the first official naval chart of Boston Harbor was surveyed in 1817 by Alexander Wadsworth and published by John Melish in 1819 (see plate 21). It is the most detailed and accurate chart of the harbor in the early nineteenth century. The Coast Survey produced an 1847 survey of the Inner Harbor (see plate 22), but nautical information culminated in the publication of the accurate and stunning 1857 map of *Boston Harbor* at a scale of 1:40,000 (figure 8). This map, considered a nineteenth-century cartographic masterpiece, includes detail nearly three miles inland and extends far to the north and south of Boston.

Charts continued to be updated and published showing not only nautical information but also a revision of the changes along the coastline and changes on the harborside. A sequence of Boston charts reveals these subtle changes in 1875, 1889, and 1899 (figure 9). These maps typically show soundings, sailing directions, shoreline profiles, islands, mudflats, lighthouses, roads, railroads, dwellings, and vegetation, among other characteristics.

On March 3, 1879, the U.S. Congress established the U.S. Geological Survey (USGS), charging it with classification of the public lands and the geological structure, mineral resources, and products of the national domain. This charge included the mapping of a country whose fullest extent from east to west and north to south was now fully known but poorly mapped. Most maps were general in nature, concentrated on transportation features such as canals, railroads, and roads, and were of small scale, restricting their detail. The country needed to establish a national grid and create detailed topographic maps that would show settlements, transportation systems, drainage features, and the topography of the land.

Many of these early surveys had concentrated on the trans-Mississippi West, even prior to the formation of the survey, but in the 1880s a new focus on mapping the established eastern states began. Boston's first USGS map was surveyed in the years 1885–1886 and was produced at a scale of 1:62,500 (figure 10). This map shows an area from Stoneham in the north to Hyde Park in the south and from Waltham in the west to the Boston Harbor in the east. As a scientific survey, it accurately reveals not only the topographic features of this geographic area but also towns, roads, and railroads. A second survey, in 1898–1900, closes the nineteenth century and provides a detailed view of the city at this critical time (see plate 23). Comparing the two maps, it is striking to view the significant urban development growth, changing railroad and road patterns, and extensive land making. Furthermore, it is possible to compare the U.S. Coast Survey charts and the U.S. Geological Survey topographic quadrangles, for their scales are similar; they reveal urban and

landscape changes from 1857. The second edition of the U.S. Geological Survey topographic quadrangle closes a century characterized by the development of American commercial mapmakers and the later development of the federal mapping agencies.

The twentieth century would witness the further growth of these federal mapping agencies and the development of such commercial mapping firms as Rand McNally to meet the needs of the growing road network. The nineteenth century, however, will be able to stand proud as the first century of American mapmaking.

CURRENT MAPPING TRENDS—THOSE MYSTERIOUS ELECTRONIC MAPS

A speaker at a recent Boston Map Society meeting suggested that there had been few changes in cartographic production methods from the mid–nineteenth century through the mid–twentieth century.[11] The speaker went on to suggest, however, that there had been a remarkable change in mapmaking since 1980 that was related to computing and geographic information system technologies. This trend will intensify in the years to come as computing power increases, speed improves, and output devices approach print quality.

Mapmakers are now able to store data electronically, update it with the click of a mouse, create maps in minutes rather than in weeks or months, and create maps on demand with only the features desired. In the past, map users were dependent upon government or commercial mapmakers to publish a map showing thematic data from the U.S. census, for example. Today, users are able to visit libraries, request certain types of data, match those with specific geographic boundary files, and then print out a map.

The development of geographic information services (GIS) allows users to access data from a Web site and create maps based on their own criteria. It is now possible to purchase a CD-ROM that includes all of the streets in the United States and use it to build maps of Boston, Chicago, or Massachusetts, all within minutes. The entire U.S. census is available on one CD-ROM, which also includes mapping software. In the past, demographers, planners, and librarians were dependent upon paper maps produced by the census to show demographic changes, population shifts, ethnic population, and so forth. Today, these data are readily available and, when matched with geographic boundary files, can produce informative maps at the country, state, county, town, census tract, or block level. All of these electronic mapping programs, whether on CDs or the Web, use TIGER (Topographically Integrated Geographic Encoding and Referencing system) as their general reference file. This system, developed for the 1990 U.S. census, includes streets and addresses across the United States in its database and all new census and planning studies will be keyed to this file.

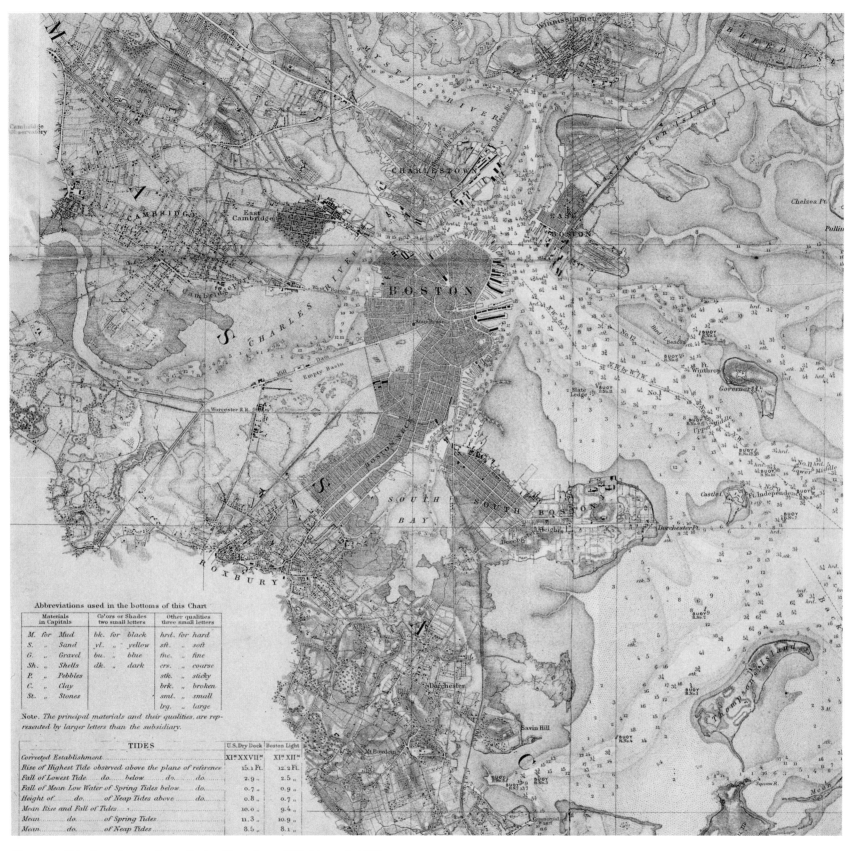

Abbreviations used in the bottoms of this Chart

Materials in Capitals	Co'ors or Shades two small letters	Other qualities three small letters
M. for Mud	bk. for black	hrd. for hard
S. „ Sand	yl. „ yellow	sft. „ soft
G. „ Gravel	bu. „ blue	fne. „ fine
Sh. „ Shells	dk. „ dark	crs. „ course
P. „ Pebbles		stk. „ sticky
C. „ Clay		brk. „ broken
St. „ Stones		sml. „ small
		lrg. „ large

Note. The principal materials and their qualities, are represented by larger letters than the subsidiary.

TIDES	U.S. Dry Dock	Boston Light
Corrected Establishment	XIᴴ XXVIIᴹ	XIᴴ XIIᴹ
Rise of Highest Tide observed above the plane of reference	15.1 Ft.	12.3 Ft.
Fall of Lowest Tide do. below do. do.	2.9 „	2.5 „
Fall of Mean Low Water of Spring Tides below do.	0.7 „	0.9 „
Height of do. of Neap Tides above do.	0.8 „	0.7 „
Mean Rise and Fall of Tides	10.0 „	9.4 „
Mean do. of Spring Tides	11.3 „	10.9 „
Mean do. of Neap Tides	8.5 „	8.1 „

Figure 8 U.S. Coast Survey, *Boston Harbor, Massachusetts* ([Washington], 1857), Chart 0.337.

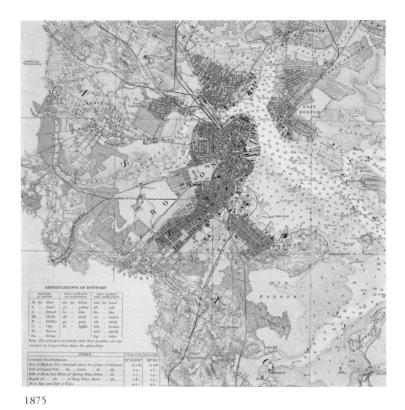

1875

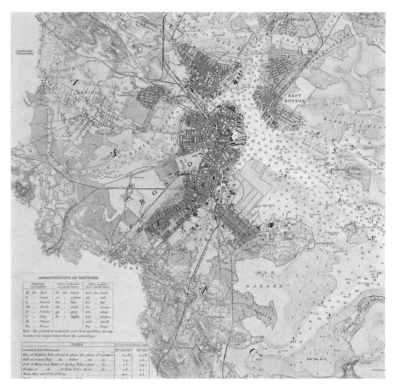

1889

Figure 9 U.S. Coast and Geodetic Survey, details from *Boston Harbor, Massachusetts* ([Washington], 1875, 1889, and 1899).

1899

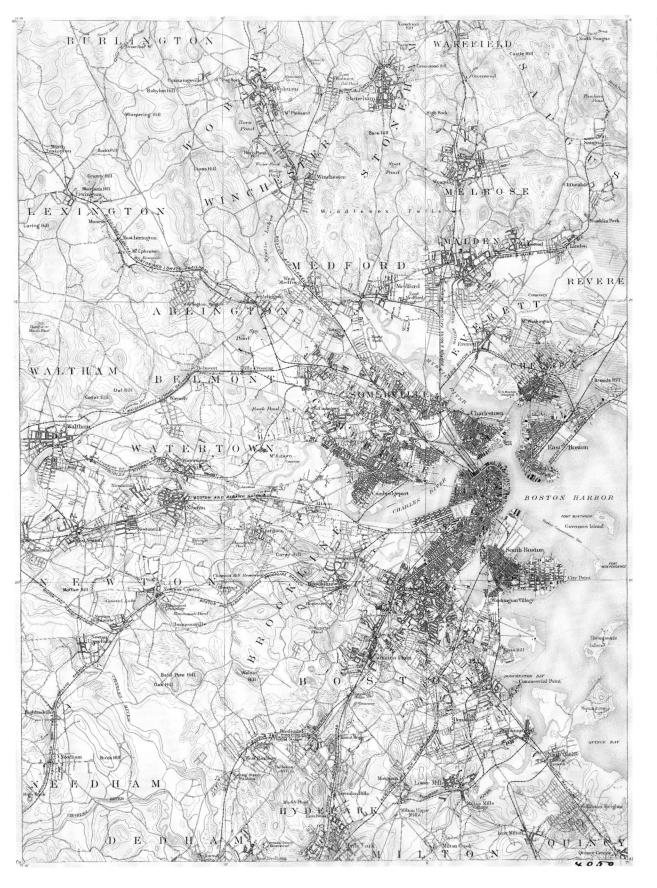

Figure 10 U.S. Geological Survey, *Massachusetts, Boston* quadrangle ([Washington], surveyed in 1885–1886).

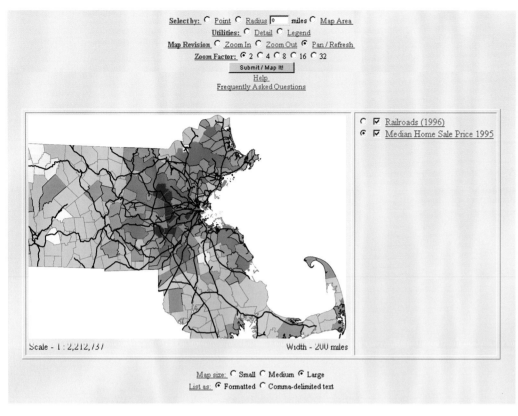

Figure 11 Massachusetts Electronic Atlas, *Railroads and Median Home Sale Price 1995* (Web address: http://icg.harvard.edu/~maps/maatlas.htm).

Cities and towns are developing detailed digital cartographic databases that include buildings, streets and alleys, utility lines, and even tree inventories. All of these layers may be used to create a map, or specific layers may be extracted. Demographers, geographers, librarians, planners, and citizens now have the capability to create maps on demand. Users are now able to decide specifically what they want or do not want to see on their map and create a map defined for their specific applications.

The Massachusetts Electronic Atlas is a Web-based (http://icg.harvard.edu/~maps/maatlas.html) electronic atlas with over 250 datalayers for Massachusetts's 351 cities and towns. It allows users from remote locations to access data, choose individual layers, zoom to specific geographies, create maps, and verify metadata authority fields (figure 11).

Internet mapping and GIS have the potential to radically change the way that people use geospatial information and, in the process, provide exciting new means to access, retrieve, and use data and maps. The impact of GIS technology will be fully realized as the unknown internet universe discovers and makes use of this unique form of information.

NOTES

1. Resolves. Massachusetts State Archives MSS. June 26, 1794.

2. Resolves. Massachusetts State Archives MSS. 5th June 1795.

3. Resolve. Massachusetts State Archives MSS. February 12, 1830.

4. *How Tis Done,* Chicago: Fidelity Publishing Co, 1879, p. 37.

5. Ibid., p.77.

6. Michael P. Conzen, "Landownership maps and county atlases," Agricultural History 58 (1984): 188–122.

7. *How Tis Done,* p. 49.

8. *Hardly a Man Is Now Alive: The Autobiography of Dan Beard* (New York: Doubleday, 1939), p 225.

9. Ibid., p. 229.

10. Ibid., p.266.

11. David Weaver, "The Remarkable Recent Evolution of Cartographic Production Methods," Boston Map Society, October 21, 1997.

6

The New England Plates

The title page from *La Geografia* reads: "The Geography of Claudio Ptolemeo of Alexandria with additional comments and facts by Sebastian Munster . . . and updated by Gastaldi . . . and translated into vernacular Italian by Pietro Andrea Mattioli . . . with additional information on modern names, cities, provinces, castles. [Printed] in Venice by Gio Baptista Pedrezano, 1548."

In this woodcut from *La Geografia di Claudio Ptolemeo Alessandrino* of 1548, Ptolemy holds a quadrant as an armillary sphere rests on a rock nearby.

PTOLEMY: THE ANCIENTS SPEAK

Throughout history, humans have employed intuition, observation, deductive reasoning, religious dogma, scientific investigation, and imagination to give form and comforting order to the unknown. The early Greeks applied nearly all these approaches, along with some astronomy inherited from the Egyptians, to arrive at an understanding of the earth that would not be significantly expanded in the West until the Renaissance.

Pythagoras intuited the earth's spherical shape in the sixth century B.C., and Aristotle and others later supported his finding. In the third century B.C., Eratosthenes calculated the earth's size by measuring the angle of the sun's rays at different points on the same meridian—a brilliant leap of deduction that placed him approximately two millennia ahead of his contemporaries.

In the second century A.D., Claudius Ptolemy, a leading scholar at the great research library at Alexandria, added his contribution. He was an astronomer, geographer, and cartographer—in short, a cosmographer, interested in the nature of the earth and its place in the universe. But it was his volume *Geographia,* containing an innovative world map, that resurfaced in late fifteenth century Europe with profound consequences.

In the text of *Geographia* and its world map, Ptolemy urged cartographers toward a scientific method. He attempted to construct a map projection that would show some of the earth's curvature on a two-dimensional sheet. He introduced the idea of using an accurate scale of distance in the creation of maps and divided the degrees of latitude and longitude into minutes and seconds for greater accuracy.

Ptolemy's maps were not accurate, but they were superior to any world map produced for the next twelve hundred years under the Christian supression of classical knowledge. With only the crudest measurements of longitude available, and for a limited number of locations, Ptolemy relied heavily on the accounts of travelers to construct his maps, noting their tendency to exaggerate the distances they traveled. Perhaps these exaggerations account for Ptolemy's elongated Asia and Mediterranean Sea, the latter shortened by Mercator in the sixteenth century—though still not sufficiently.

Despite his advanced thinking, however, Ptolemy could not accept the impressive size of the earth offered by Eratosthenes, one of his predecessors at the library at Alexandria who lived from about 276 to 196 B.C. Like most of his contemporaries, Ptolemy preferred a smaller size—one that indicated a less overwhelming area of unknown geography. Ptolemy's guess was 28 percent smaller than the earth's actual size. Nor could Ptolemy believe that the earth rotated around the sun, as his contemporary, Aritarchus of Samos, had divined.

Ptolemy's innovations and mistakes had significant consequences in fifteenth-century Europe when a monk, Jacopo Angelo, finally translated them from Greek into Latin. The translation roughly coincided with the invention of the printing press, making a large distribution possible. And Ptolemy's small earth with a long Asia wrapped around it set imaginations on fire.

Ptolemy's world map carried great authority. With a projection sophisticated for its time, its attempt at an accurate scale, and its ingenious plotting of the known world, it shone in comparison with contemporary maps produced in the early Renaissance. As printed woodcuts of his map and copies of his *Geographia* began to circulate in 1480, it influenced European geographers and cartographers, as well as navigators such as Christopher Columbus.

Ptolemy influenced scholars of fifteenth-century Europe because he speculated on the relative size of the earth, the continents and oceans, and because he set innovative and exacting standards for cartography. The relatively small earth he portrayed made a circumnavigation of the globe seem more attainable and helped—along with improvements in the design of ships, navigational equipment, and geographical knowledge—to launch the Age of Exploration and, eventually, the modern age of scientific investigation.

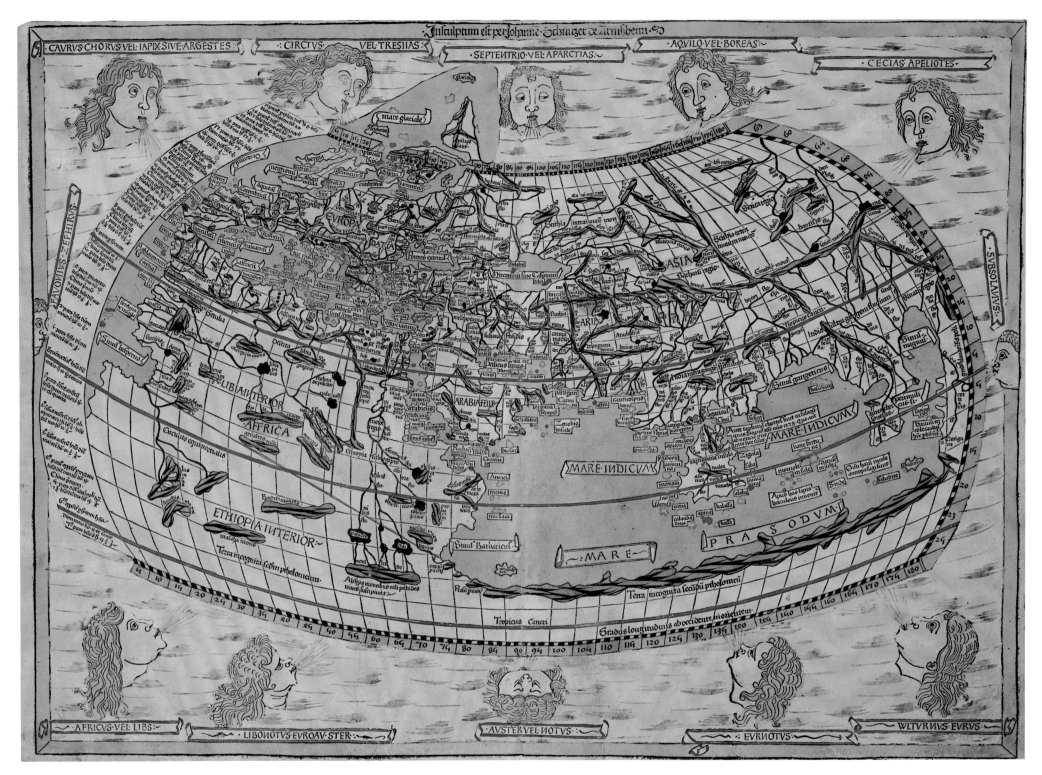

Plate 1
Claudius Ptolemy (ca. 90–168 A.D.)
{World}
From *Colophon: Opus Donni Nicolai Germani Secundum Ptolomeum . . .* (Ulm, 1486)
Woodcut. 40 x 55 cm.

Although Ptolemy influenced his contemporaries and later Arab geographers, his work was virtually unknown in the West until one of his later manuscript copies was brought to Europe and translated into Latin by Jacopo Angelo in 1406. His work was immediately accepted by Renaissance scholars as a great achievement of Greek science and his atlas, known as *Geographia,* was published and republished throughout Europe for nearly 250 years, eventually incorporating the early discoveries of the New World explorers.

The world map is on a modified conical projection and reveals the known world of Ptolemy's time, which had not yet been expanded by western European exploration. Columbus and his contemporaries relied on Ptolemy's work and set sail with little understanding of the vast oceans they must cover or knowledge of the American continent between Europe and Asia.

This copy, known as the Ulm edition, is characterized by its bold Germanic style and gothic lettering. It is the first edition of the *Geographia* printed north of the Alps, the first woodcut version of this map, and the first to be signed; the inscription reads: "Engraved by Johann, woodcutter from Armszheim."

The classical world's western boundary is shown by Thule, just north of Scotland, and this edition attempts to show Scandinavia in the extension on the northern boundary of the map. The Ulm Ptolemy is usually found in original coloring with the sea dark blue in one state and brown in another state. The brown color, reproduced here, is considered by scholars to have followed the first by several years.

COLUMBUS AND THE POWER OF POSITIVE THINKING

When Columbus approached the monarchs of Spain to request funding for a westward voyage to the Orient, Queen Isabella appointed a special commission to review his proposal. Although Columbus's research was thorough, his interpretations and source selections were biased by hope, allowing the commission, after six years of deliberation, to dismiss his estimate of the westward distance to Asia as overly optimistic, and his project as misguided.

Columbus's calculations were incorrect, but their audacity in charting the unknown is impressive, as was so much early cosmography. Like all European geographers and cartographers of this period, Columbus was heavily influenced by Ptolemy's *Geographia,* published in Latin for the first time in 1480, approximately twelve centuries after Ptolemy wrote it. But Ptolemy's measure of the earth was unrealistically small.

Believing in a small earth, Columbus also followed the theory of a contemporary Florentine physician that the intervening sea between Spain and Japan was narrower—certainly not two oceans as vast as the Atlantic and Pacific. Furthermore, Columbus had interpreted the century-old writings of Marco Polo in a way that allowed him to lengthen Ptolemy's Asia, bringing its easternmost coast closer to Europe. Finally, he found reason to reduce the accepted nautical length of a degree of longitude, effectively shrinking the Atlantic Ocean.

But, ultimately, Columbus's personality carried more weight than his calculations. He believed that God had granted him the destiny of a great westward voyage. He projected the confidence and knowledge gained in his experience sailing with the Portuguese in explorations of the North African coast, and, significantly, he was sophisticated enough to appeal to the Crown's commercial interests in gaining better access to Asian wealth. After being dismissed by the commission and packing his bags for France, Columbus was overtaken by a messenger from Queen Isabella, granting the sponsorship he had requested.

Columbus's flawed calculations nearly pinpointed the West Indies to which he eventually sailed. The great captain himself could not imagine the earth he so bravely explored; he claimed for a few years to have landed in the Orient, as he had promised he would do. While he held on to his claim of having found a new route to Asia, he lost the honor of having the New World named after him. When mapmaker Martin Waldseemuller published a map in 1507 showing smatterings of the new continents, he named them after Amerigo Vespucci, whose 1499 voyage to South America provided much of the new information displayed on his map.

Columbus's landing in the Indies as portrayed in the 1631 German book *Newe Welt und americanische Historien,* which reports that he received a gracious welcome and gifts of gold in exchange for his offerings of "shirts, caps, knives, mirrors and the like."

Hartman Schedel, *{World}* (Nuremberg, 1493). This map appeared in the second edition of the *Nuremberg Chronicle,* and was thus rather widely disseminated, just as news of Christopher Columbus's voyage was beginning to spread. Derived from Ptolemy, if fanciful and lacking detail, this was the last noteworthy world map to be produced without any indication of the New World.

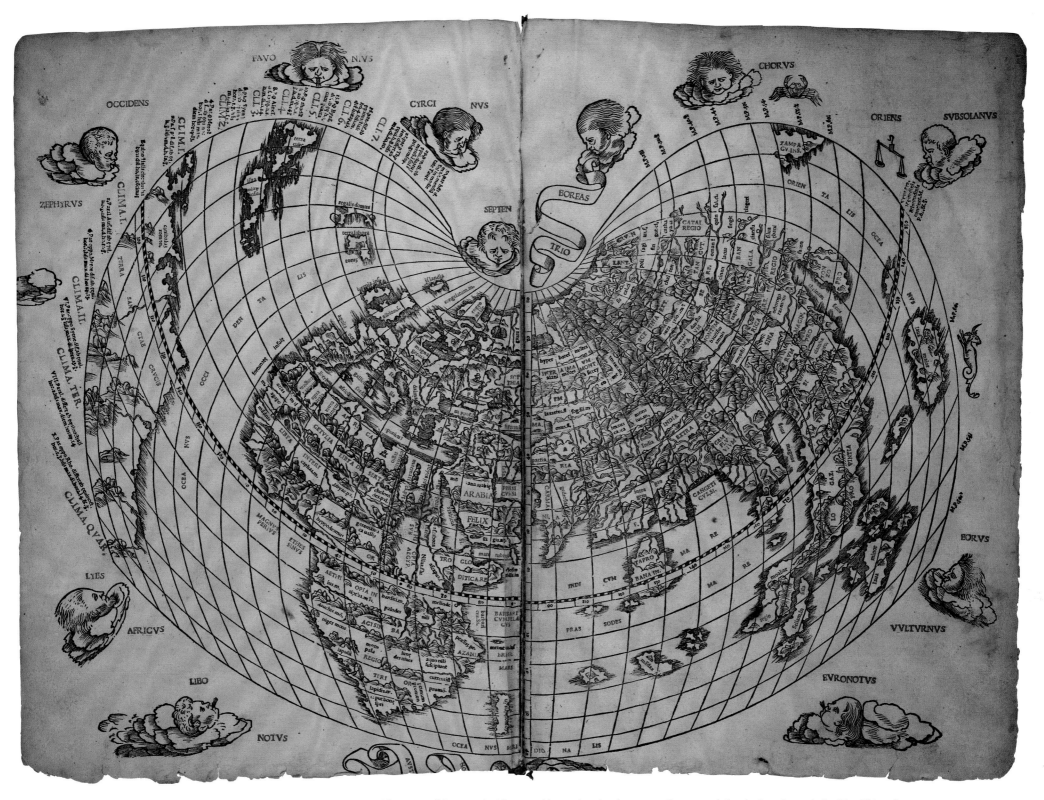

Plate 2
Bernardus Sylvanus
{World}
From *Claudii Ptholemaci Alexandrini liber geographiae . . .*
(Venice, 1511)
Woodcut. 57 x 42 cm.

This is one of the most significant world maps in printed map history and represents the earliest period of European discovery of the New World. It is the first map to be printed in two colors. The red capital letters combined with the decorative windheads and the unusual cordiform, or heart-shaped, projection make this among the most distinctive world maps.

The map is based on the Ptolemaic engraving style, emphasizing mountains and rivers, which leaves little space for geographical place names. The map is geographically interesting for the few place names it does show in Europe and South America and for identifying features such as Cuba, Hispaniola, and *terra laboratorus*—a probable reference to Newfoundland or the North American coast, although quite inaccurately shown just west of Ireland. Also of interest is the open eastern coastline of Asia and a western open coastline of a land labeled *regalis domus* just west of *terra laboratorus*.

While the map was not reprinted and is therefore rare, the cordiform projection was accepted and used by other cartographers such as Apianus (ca. 1520) and Vavassore (ca. 1540).

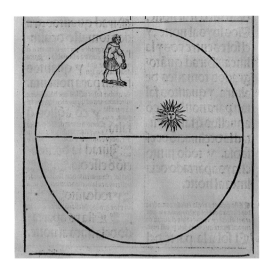

The woodcut shown here appears in the 1545 *Arte de Navagar* and illustrates the use of a mariner's astrolabe. A circle graduated in 360 degrees with two sighting vanes 180 degrees apart, the mariner's astrolabe was used to determine latitude by measuring the altitude of the sun at midday. This instrument (purely an altitude-measuring device) differs from the planispheric astrolabe (a time-finding and astronomical instrument) and was widely used by Portuguese and Spanish navigators in the late sixteenth century.

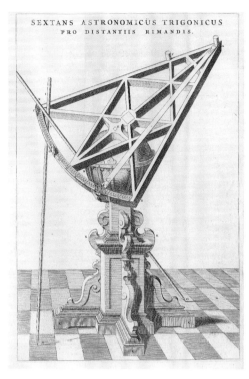

The astronomical sextant, shown here from a 1662 Blaeu atlas, was used on land to precisely measure star positions for producing celestial charts. Improvements in the mapping of the heavens became of crucial importance to navigation. The astronomical sextant is unrelated to the nautical sextant except that the frame of both instruments occupies 1/6 of a circle.

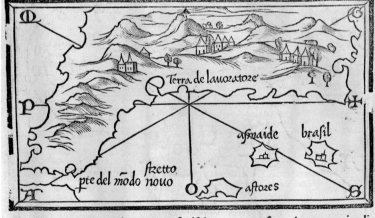

Benedetto Bordone, *{North America}* (Venice, 1528). Appearing in the same publication, *Isolario,* as the world map at right, this map is believed to be the first to show New England. If the large island landmass labeled "Terra de lavoratore" is a depiction of North America, then its northeast corner would be New England.

EARLY MAPS: WHERE ON EARTH ARE WE?

Mapmaking depended for over two millennia on three kinds of measurements of the earth: distance; latitude and longitude to pinpoint location; and slope, or topography. People have measured distance with rods or knotted cords for thousands of years. The surveyors of ancient Egypt, for example, had to reestablish property lines every year after the flooding of the Nile, for which they needed an instrument for measuring distances and one for establishing right angles, which they called a *groma*. And the Romans were sufficiently deft at measuring slope to construct their great roads and aqueducts, though their tools are lost to us.

The cartographers, geographers, sailors, and travelers of the ancient world needed to know where on the earth they were in relation to other places. Eventually the cartographer needed to know the exact latitude and longitude of different places in order to plot them on his grid of latitude and longitude and then connect the dots to make a map.

Instruments for measuring latitude were arrived at early, certainly by classical times. Like the modern sextant, they located a person's position north or south by measuring the height above the horizon of the North Star and, later, the noonday sun.

The great explorers of the fifteenth and sixteenth century could easily ascertain their latitude aboard ship, perhaps with an astrolabe. With clocks that could only tell them the hour, however, longitude was an educated guess: every minute that the solar time of two places differed represented a distance of sixteen miles in longitude.

To chart the new coasts and islands they observed in their travels, the intrepid explorers could rely on an instrument introduced in the twelfth century: the magnetic compass. As he passed along the coast, the captain recorded his impressions of the land mass and along which direction it seemed to run. These accounts and maps were then circulated among mapmakers in Europe, with some accounts, such as Magellan's, for example, likely to remain closely guarded for political reasons. The captain's inability to plot true points of longitude, and the difficulty of determining distance as he sailed or observed the coast, provided the creative variations in the shape of the new world on maps made before the eighteenth century. The compass itself, operating slightly differently throughout the world, also contributed to slight inaccuracies.

Measurement of longitude remained crude until the eighteenth century. In 1697, when the clocks ultimately needed for measuring longitude were still primitive, a Frenchman named Cassini tied the measurement of longitude to the observation of the eclipses of two of Jupiter's moons. After Cassini published his tables of these events, people could tell how far east or west of Cassini's telescope they were by the number of minutes at which an eclipse differed in time from those observed by Cassini. This onerous technique, however, was nearly impossible to apply at sea.

The English Parliament, responding to complaints that the difficulty of measuring longitude was jeopardizing British navigation, exploration, and trade, offered a prize of £20,000 in 1714 to anyone who could "discover the Longitude." A self-taught country clockmaker, John Harrison, finally claimed the prize in 1773 after devoting his life to developing and testing a marine chronometer that could withstand the shocks of sea voyages. By about 1750 accurate measurements of longitude contributed to a more modern and consistent image of the Americas.

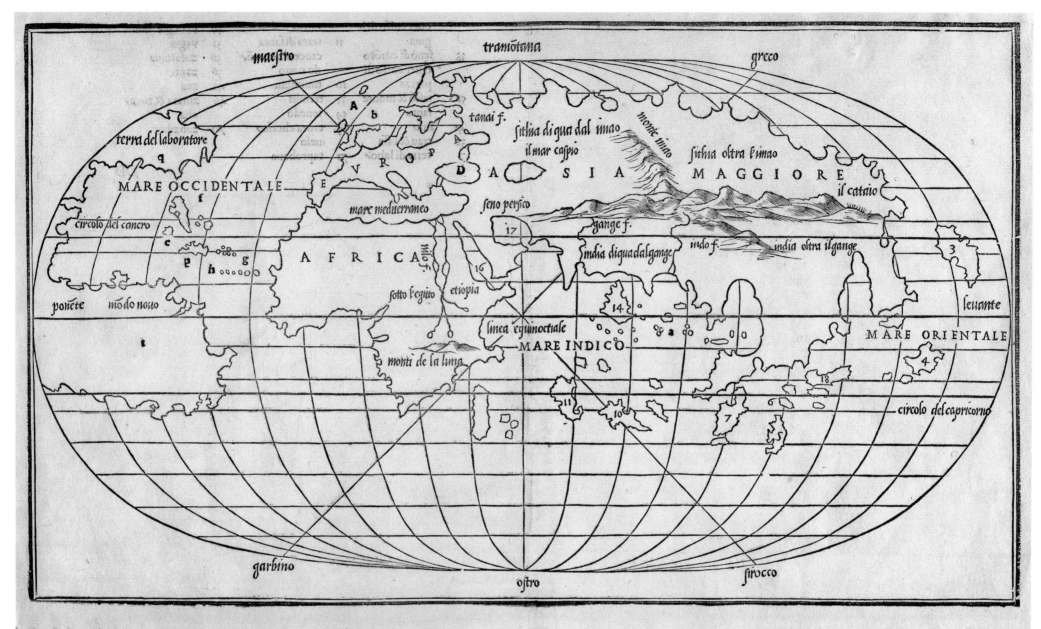

Queste linee che fono per il longo di questo vniuerfale da gli fapienti furono appellate li‑
nee parallele,& quelle che tengono forma curua in modo di arco,fono nominate meridia‑

ni,& il clima tiene da leuante fino in ponente,fi come fanno la linea, de lo equinottio,&
quella del tropico del cancro,& del capricorno.

Plate 3
Benedetto Bordone (1460–1531)
{World}
From *Libro . . . de tutte l'Isole del mondo* (Venice, 1528)
Woodcut. 21 x 38 cm.

Bordone's world map is one of the earliest using an oval projection following Roselli's ca. 1508 map, which pioneered this projection. While similar to Roselli's map, Bordone made several changes including the separation of Asia from America, although the (unknown) shape of the western edge of America would be left for others to delineate. He does retain the truncated South America form thereby creating an enclosure for the Caribbean Sea. The North American landmass, *terra del laboratore,* is by comparison to the Sylvanus map much more appropriately scaled and more accurately located.

Bordone published his atlas, or *Isolario,* and it was based on the first printed *isolario* by Bartolommeo dalli Sonetti, published in Venice in ca. 1485. Bordone expanded his atlas to include sixty-four maps. This world map is an outline, or index map, with numerals or script on each of the islands suggesting the detailed maps that are to follow. The *isolario* was popular in the fifteenth and sixteenth centuries and is related to the *portulano,* or pilot book; its objective was to display islands at a larger scale than the regional maps found in most atlases.

"Discovery of the Sea of Magellan" from the German book *Newe Welt und americanische Historien,* published in 1631. Magellan, presumably on his ship *Victoria,* which looms large on Munster's map of 1540, is shown consulting an armillary sphere, an ancient astronomical instrument composed of rings that depict the relative postions of the celestial equator and other zones of the celestial sphere.

FERDINAND MAGELLAN

Ferdinand Magellan (ca. 1480–1520) is not as well known in America as Columbus, and yet, in many ways, his accomplishment was even greater. He did not find the New World, but he found the way around it, through the strait that would eventually bear his name between the Island of Tierra del Fuego and mainland South America. While Columbus had sailed for only thirty-five days to find the New World, Magellan sailed westward from Seville for fifteen months, crossed the vast, uncharted Pacific, and discovered islands such as the Marianas and Philippines that no European had ever seen.

Although he died in the Philippines before completing his return to Europe, he is credited with circumnavigating the globe. He plotted and commanded an all-but-impossible voyage while keeping a loyal crew through it all. And he had sailed to the Philippines from Portugal years before on a course charted for exploring the Spice Islands. The crew that survived him actually traveled for twenty-one more months before reaching Spain again in September 1522 and completing the circumnavigation near the third anniversary of their departure.

Magellan's proposal for a westward voyage, like that of Columbus, was turned down by a Portuguese monarch and, again like Columbus, he turned to Spain. Unlike Columbus, however, he was considered a traitor by the Portuguese for at least two centuries after his death. He had been born in a noble Portuguese family. Orphaned at the age of ten or twelve, he began serving as a page in the Royal Court. After the passing of Dom João II, whose queen Magellan had served and who had rejected Columbus's bid, Magellan served Dom Manuel I, who disliked him and sent him on his first voyage at age twenty-five—to India. For a decade, Magellan remained a soldier and seafarer in the Portuguese effort to wrest dominion of African and eastern trade routes from the Arabs, and establish a series of outposts.

Because of his membership in the Portuguese court, Magellan's betrayal was taken personally by the Portuguese. Perhaps he had even shared with the Spanish his theory, developed with a scholar in celestial navigation, that the Line of Demarcation that had separated the Spanish and Portuguese territorial claims since 1494 could be drawn clear around the earth, where it would show, on the Pacific, or eastern, hemisphere, that the rich Spice Islands belonged to the Spanish. King Manuel, however, had not only declined his proposal to find the strait at the bottom of South America and a new route to the Spice Islands—perhaps he felt he had funded enough explorers—but had shown his contempt for Magellan by keeping his pay lower than that of other officers.

Magellan apparently had no family or heirs to preserve his papers—which were confiscated and lost—or his reputation, which probably suffered first from a Spanish effort to keep the Strait of Magellan a secret, and then from two centuries of posthumous attacks by his Portuguese countrymen. And perhaps his name is not as celebrated as Columbus's because his conquest was not a conquest of land, but of the sea and the globe and the mists of ignorance that enshrouded them.

NOVAE INSVLAE, XVII·NOVA TABVLA·

Plate 4

Sebastian Munster (1488–1552)

Novae Insulae, XVII Nova Tabula

From *Geographia universalis vetus et nova . . . Claudii Ptolemaei* (Basel, 1540)

Woodcut. 26 x 24 cm.

This is the earliest printed map to clearly show America as a separate landmass and was one of the most widely disseminated maps of the New World before the creation of the modern atlas. Munster produced sixty-one double-page maps for use in his editions of Ptolemy's *Geographia* and in his own *Cosmographia*. The maps are all woodcuts and while it is not known who carved them, it is believed that Hans Holbein created the borders on the verso of the maps.

The northeast section of America is named *Francisca* and is separated from the continent by the false sea of Verrazano. Both features are related to Giovanni da Verrazano's 1522–1524 voyage along the American coast when the waters of the Chesapeake Bay were thought to be the Indian Ocean. This concept was exaggerated even further with the reports of Cartier's voyages of 1534–1535 up the St. Lawrence River and into the Great Lakes when he was searching in vain for the mythical northwest passage. This map is the earliest to name the Pacific, *Mare pacificum,* and prominently shows Magellan's ship *Victoria.* Shown

directly above *Victoria* and much closer to the American landmass than to Asia is Zipangu (modern-day Japan), indicating that explorers and cartographers were still unclear about the scale of the Pacific Ocean.

Munster was a professor of Hebrew at Basel University and a well-known Hebraist, mathematician, and geographer. This new edition of Ptolemy's *Geographia* added a number of new maps to the modern section, including a modern map of the world. This "modern" map was printed at a time when the curiosity of the public was changing conservative academic views and standards concerning the extent of the known world.

Giovanni Battista Ramusio, *La Nuova Francia* (Venice, 1556). Ramusio's map shows yet another variation on The Land of Norumbega: "TERRA DENVRVMBEGA." It was based on the voyages of Giovanni da Verrazano for the French in 1524, and reflects his reports of the natives of that land: their habitat, clothing, hunting, and fishing practices—and the early mixing of natives with European explorers and fishermen.

THE LAND OF NORUMBEGA

The North American coast that first appeared on European maps was filled with new and changing place names designating mysterious and barely known places. After Verrazano's important voyage of 1524, tracing the North American coast from Florida to southern Canada, the name *Norumbega,* in various mutations, began to appear on maps of the New World. Some mapmakers, such as Giacomo Gastaldi in his 1548 map of *Tierra Nueva,* gave it a German twist and came up with a variation on Nuremberg.

The name Norumbega designated the area now known as northern New England. It comes from the Abenaki language spoken by native tribes of northern Massachusetts and southern Maine. To these tribes, *norumbega* meant "the quiet place between two rapids" or "where the river widens."

Throughout the second half of the sixteenth century, Norumbega appeared repeatedly on the maps of prominent mapmakers such as Gastaldi (at right), Abraham Ortelius, Oronce Fine, and Cornelis van Wytfliet (see plate 6). Meanwhile, Sir Francis Drake gave the name of New England (or Nova Albion) to the California coast during his 1577 voyage around the world. This may be taken as part of his long campaign to assert English interests over those of the Spanish, whose ships he regularly looted as a privateer for Her Majesty.

Norumbega, unexplored and unknown, was shrouded in myth. Verrazzano suggested that most of the New World was an isthmus dividing the Atlantic and Pacific Oceans. And the belief that Norumbega hosted a wealthy capital city inspired at least one voyage of exploration. English-sponsored explorers pressed for decades into the northern bays and riverways of Norumbega in their search for a northwest passage to Cathay.

While Norumbega beckoned, her coast became the site of increasing numbers of French and English trading expeditions seeking furs, probably some fishing trips, and certainly numerous voyages of exploration—whose captains often abducted natives to exhibit at home or sell as slaves, setting the tenor of relations between the two races.

Finally, in 1614, John Smith laid the matter to rest. He visited the northeast coast of the future United States and christened the area not Norumbega but New England. His subsequently published map (plate 7) and promotional pamphlets replaced many native place names with English ones and interpreted the region's resources in terms of their usefulness to the English economy.

And the settlement he urged did indeed begin within a decade after he heralded the advantages of the place. The name Norumbega eventually designated only a small area of Maine near Penobscot Bay, shrinking with the Indian lands, as the greater part of Norumbega was transformed into a landscape of British colonies more aptly described as New England.

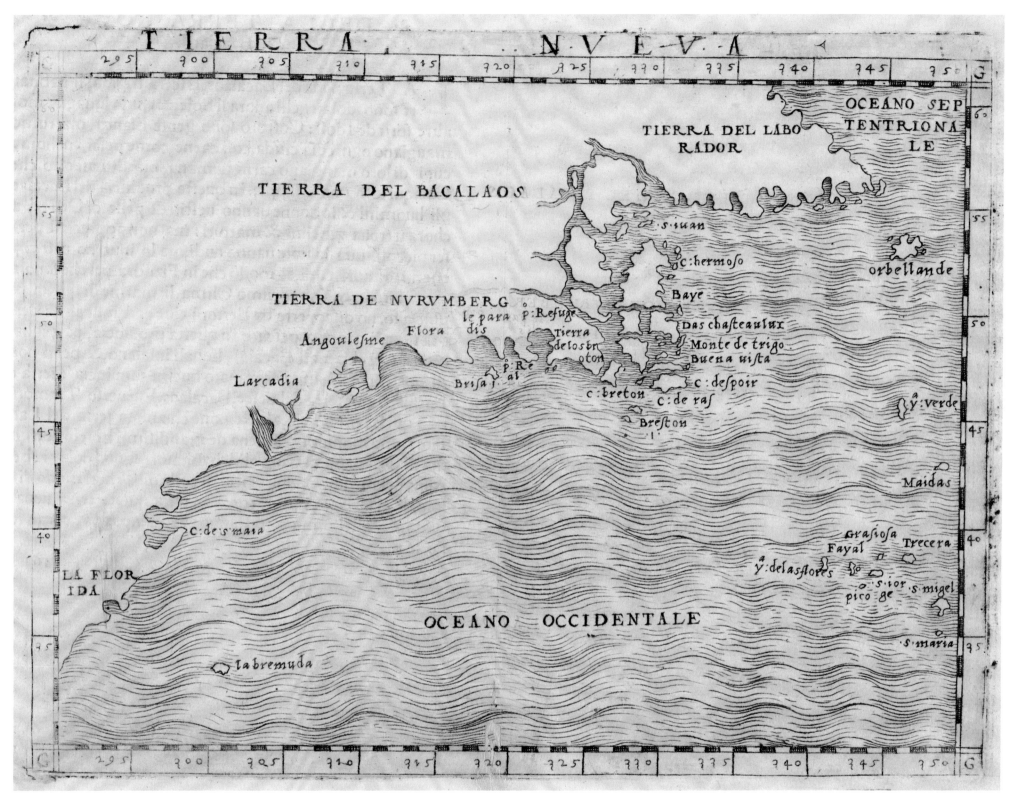

Plate 5
Giacomo Gastaldi (ca. 1500–ca. 1565)

Tierra Nueva

From *La Geografia di Claudio Ptolemeo Alessandrino . . .*
(Venice, 1548)
Engraving. 13 x 18 cm.

Gastaldi is one of the most important cartographers of the sixteenth century and the most significant Italian map-maker of his time. This is the earliest printed map to focus on the eastern seaboard of North America. While seem-ingly crude, a close review reveals the map to be quite advanced for the cartography of this period.

Its major features of the coastline are well rendered. South of *Tierra del Laborador* is a region of broken rivers and islands which is an early attempt to portray the St. Lawrence area and gulf. That portion of modern-day Canada is given the sixteenth-century name *Tierra del Bacalaos*. South of this name is the undulating coast called *Tierra de Nurumberg,* a variant on the Indian word *Norumbega.* This area is further defined by noting that the two bays in the area of *Larcadia* are the Chesapeake and the Delaware, while that of *Angoulesme* was Verrazano's name for New York harbor.

Off the coast of *La Florida* lies the island of Bermuda, its first appearance on a printed map. (This was also the earli-est map to use the place name Larcadia in Canada.)

This regional map attempted to reveal the discover-ies of the Verrazano and Cartier voyages while maintaining the Ptolemaic format of cartography. It appears in the first edition of Ptolemy's *Geographia* to contain regional maps of the Americas, and it is the first printed in a small format. It also reintroduced copperplate printing to map reproduc-tion, as it was the first important atlas to use this technique in the sixteenth century.

Jodocus Hondius, a prominent Dutch mapmaker of the sixteenth and early seventeenth centuries, and founder of a mapmaking dynasty, was a fan of Gerard Mercator's. After Mercator's death, and after Edward Wright established mathematical principles for Mercator's projection, Hondius was one of the first to adopt it. Also after Mercator's death, Hondius bought up Mercator's map plates to create the Mercator-Hondius atlas. The cartouche above, showing the two mapmakers seated together, comes from the 1635 reprint of that atlas.

GERARD MERCATOR

Gerard Mercator (1512–1594), creator of the first modern map projection, was born in Flanders. He attended university in Belgium and emerged a master of astronomy, geometry, geography, instrument making, and Latin.

The Low Countries, which then consisted of Holland, Belgium, and Flanders, emerged as the center of European mapmaking during Mercator's lifetime. The Dutch, in particular, excelled at the art of copperplate engraving, which, at that time, replaced woodcutting as the preferred form of map reproduction. Mercator lived not only in an exciting locus of the mapmaking world but in an exciting time when new voyages of exploration were constantly returning to supplement the available information on distant lands and seas. The captains of these voyages, in turn, relied on the latest and best maps and charts, such as those produced by Mercator.

Mercator began, however, with a domestic commission, surveying for three years to produce a map of Flanders. The accuracy of the map, replacing more artistic and fanciful versions, brought him wide acclaim.

Two globes by Mercator survive, along with two world maps, a large-scale map of Europe on six sheets, and a few smaller maps, plus his chronology of world history that attempted to sort out the confusion of dates that had occurred during the Middle Ages. Mercator labored lovingly to create the most faithful Renaissance rendition of Ptolemy's world map, and the most faithful compilation of Ptolemy's *Geographia,* free of interpretation by Renaissance scholars. His Ptolemaic map was reprinted for 150 years.

The earlier of his two world maps, printed in 1538 when Mercator was twenty-six, is known for being the first to christen both newly discovered continents with the name "America." In this map, Mercator also presented the theory (not widely accepted at the time) that an ocean separated the American and Asian

continents; he suggested the possibility of a northwest passage to Asia above North America. (Unfortunately, Mercator's support of the theory of a Northwest Passage to Cathay [China] may have contributed to a few icy and futile voyages, such as Martin Frobisher's exploration of part of Canada's east coast.) About thirty years later, in 1569, Mercator completed his six-sheet world map using the Mercator projection, for which his name survives to this day.

Mercator's novel projection worked by straightening out the curved meridians of the globe. As the distance between the straightened meridians artificially spread—instead of diminishing—toward the poles, he increased the distance between the parallels of latitude correlatively.

Mercator accomplished this innovation for the use of seamen, to allow them to plot a straight course that would not require many adjustments during a voyage. Scholars have pointed out that his world map was not really the best vehicle for demonstrating the new projection. The larger the area covered (and the further from the equator), the greater the distortion. Mercator's projection applies best to sea charts and to small areas near the equator.

In 1599, thirty years after Mercator's revolutionary world map appeared, English scholar Edward Wright worked out the mathematical formula for the Mercator projection. It was several more decades before navigators came to appreciate and rely on the convenience Mercator had created for them.

Working at the forefront of cartographic innovation, Mercator counted among his friends the mapmaker, map editor, and publisher Abraham Ortelius, who lived in Antwerp and with whom Mercator corresponded concerning maps and voyages of exploration. After Mercator's death, his son Rumold continued the family trade of mapmaking and carried his father's atlas project to publication in 1595, the first to use the term *atlas.* Rumold's reputation, however, never quite matched his father's. Indeed, few cartographers' have.

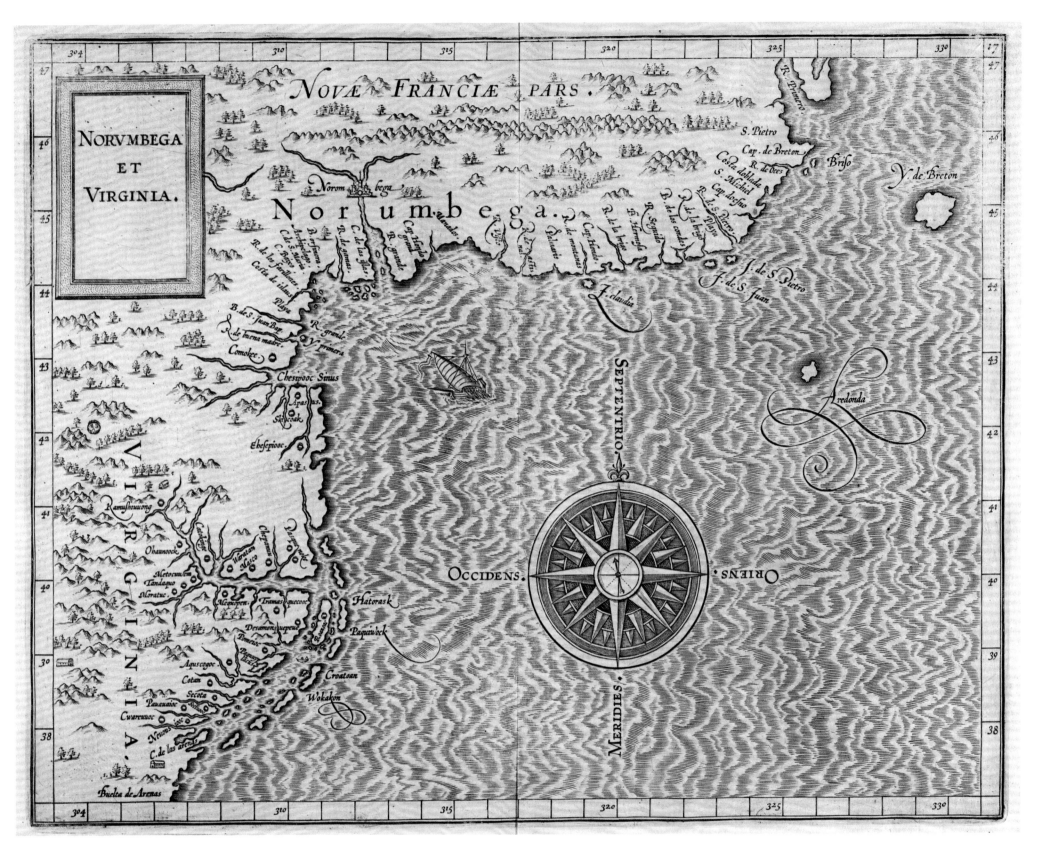

Plate 6

Cornelis van Wytfliet (d. 1597)

Norvmbega et Virginia

From *Descriptionis Ptolemaicae augmentum . . .* (Louvain, 1597)

Woodcut. 23 x 30 cm. (1607, State 2)

Wytfliet published the first atlas devoted solely to America. Despite the reference in the title to Ptolemy the atlas contains eighteen regional maps, a world map based on Rumold Mercator's map of 1587, and an accompanying text devoted to the discovery, natural history, and geography of the New World.

The map shows the east coast of America from the Carolina Outer Banks north into Canada and a distorted and oversized New England, named *Norumbega*. One of the major inaccuracies is the placement of the Middle Atlantic coast 4 to 6 degrees too far to the north. This results in the Chesapeake Bay, *Chesipooc Sinus,* lying at the same latitude as southern Maine. The map does name Virginia just after Sir Walter Raleigh's failure to settle a colony at Roanoke.

Wytfliet, a Flemish geographer, relied on John White's map of Virginia, published in 1590, for his topography and place names.

John Smith's portrait graced all of the various issues of his map of New England. The later portrait (shown above right) miraculously shows Smith's hair and beard gaining in luxuriance.

"... THE COUNTRIE OF THE MASSACHUSETTS, WHICH IS THE PARADISE OF ALL THOSE PARTS"

John Smith (1579–1631) left his father's farm in England to spend his early youth fighting and adventuring on the continent as a mercenary. He reported his feats of daring there in his *True Travells,* relatively little of which is now considered to be true. He was still a young man in his mid-twenties when fresh intelligence of the New World and its amazing resources began to lap at England's shores with the bow waves of returning European ships—and at the imaginations of a few of her citizens.

In 1606, Smith threw in his lot—as an adventurer rather than a colonist—with a company of about 150 sailing to Jamestown. Although John Smith is associated more with Virginia than New England, he spent only two-and-a-half years there, a time characterized by disease, famine, and hostile relations with the Indians.

During this desperate time, Smith's popularity waned more than once to the point that he was nearly hanged, and it waxed long enough to see him briefly serve as the colony's president. His return to England saved him from further threats of harm.

By 1614, the time of Smith's first exploratory journey for the Northern Virginia Company along the New England coast, eight European expeditions had passed along the same course. But Smith, a born adventurer, seems to have been the first to fall in love with the land. He spent the rest of his life promoting it.

When pirates captured Smith's ship at the start of a second voyage to New England in 1615, he spent his captivity writing *A Description of New England,* accompanied in its second printing by his map. In the exploration and promotion of New England, Smith seems to have found a higher purpose for the talents that served what historians portray as a basically narcissistic personality. Through his pamphlets describing New England and offering advice to prospective colonists, he sought to capture the public imagination and to serve as a heroic expert and visionary. And he did offer shrewd insights, such as his suggestion that the English fishing industry could be bolstered by a fishing station on the New England coast, along with some optimistic exaggeration, such as his claim that New England had the climate of Devon. Apparently he did not visit during the winter.

Smith was thwarted, however, in his desire to sell his services as an adventurer and guide to the colonists. Sir Ferdinando Gorges helped appoint him admiral of New England and hired him to accompany settlers to Maine in 1615, but Smith's first ship was dismasted and his second captured by pirates. The Plymouth Puritans assured him they had a more reasonably priced scout in Miles Standish. The frustrated admiral stayed home and wrote pamphlets.

The map that accompanied Smith's *Description of New England* eschewed the native place names and installed new English terms approved or chosen by the crown. Smith is credited with naming New England and making the first printed reference to the "Countrie of the Massachusetts [Indians]." But, fortunately for Smith's place in American legend, Prince Charles rejected Smith's suggestion for Cape Tragabigzanda (a reference to the romantic adventures of his youth) and substituted his own mother's name, calling it "Cape Anna." The maps do testify, however, to Smith's vanity. His portrait, along with heroic verses glorifying him, appear on each map, with his hair and beard growing slightly more luxuriant in the later issues.

Plate 7
Captain John Smith (1579–1631)
New England, The most remarqueable parts thus named by the high and mighty Prince Charles, Prince of great Britaine
From *The General historie of Virginia, New England and the summer isles . . .* (London, 1624)
Engraving. 30 x 35 cm. State 4

This is the foundation map of New England cartography, the first printed map devoted exclusively to the coast of New England, and the first to use the name *New England.*

Supported by several merchants in London, Smith's first voyage along the New England coast led to his second major cartographic achievement, the first being his 1612 map of Virginia.

The map was prepared in 1615, published in 1616, and modified and republished at least nine times. New England, Smith's Isles (Isle of Shoals), and Poynt Suttliff (Brant Rock) are the only names on the map proposed by Smith himself while *Plimouth, Cape Anna,* and the *River Charles* are names that correspond to their present locations. Colonial place-naming was often capricious: the Scottish name *Aborden* in place of the Indian name

Penobscot, and *Leth* in place of *Sagadahock,* are two of several names demanded by the fifteen-year-old Prince Charles of Scotland. As a testimony to the influence of Smith's map and book, the Pilgrims retained the map's name for their eventual landing site at Plymouth.

This State 4 of the map was printed several years before the founding of Boston in 1630. The name Boston, however, already appears. Brought to America by nonconformists from a town by the same name in Lincolnshire, it is here found on the map far to the north in what is currently the area near York, Maine.

The first leaf of King Charles's 1629 grant, *Charter of the Governor and Company of Massachusetts Bay in New England.*

THE COUNCIL FOR NEW ENGLAND

Although Queen Elizabeth sponsored many voyages of exploration, it fell to King James I to parcel out the new lands under English dominion so they might start to produce income. In 1606, King James awarded the vast territory of Virginia to a group of London merchants who eventually called themselves the Virginia Company. In 1620 he awarded the northerly territory of New England to a group of Plymouth merchants who would call themselves the Council for New England, and whose names appear on Sir William Alexander's map (at right). Both grants ran from sea to sea save for lands claimed by other "Christian states" or other grant recipients.

Alexander, a Scot and close ally of the Scottish King James, received the bulk of Canada's Atlantic Provinces: Newfoundland, New Brunswick, and Nova Scotia (which Alexander named), plus the Gaspé Peninsula and the title first viscount of Canada. His map names both a Province of Alexandria in Nova Scotia and a town of Alexandria in Newfoundland, but his efforts at colonization—focused on Nova Scotia—failed in the brutal climate.

The next most influential member of the Council for New England, who also received, with two others, most of northern New England, was Sir Ferdinando

Gorges. Eventually, most of Maine fell under his aegis. Sir Ferdinando's early ventures at colonizing also failed in savage winters, but Sir Ferdinando was genuinely fascinated by the New World and did not give up. In 1605, he had procured from the explorer George Weymouth three kidnapped New England Indians. The Indians lived at the Gorges home in Somersetshire, where Sir Ferdinando had them tutored in English so that he could learn from them about the New World. Two of the Indians accompanied one of his first colonial expeditions. In 1615, Gorges also hired John Smith to accompany another group of settlers as scout, but bad luck prevented Smith from reaching New England.

The name Gorges also appears on the lower Massachusetts portion of Alexander's map, indicating a grant to Robert Gorges (apparently along with others) of "All that part of the Maine Land in New England known as Massachusetts." Robert, the youngest Gorges, was eventually named lieutenant governor of New England. According to early records, as the council members sorted out the grant, Robert's parcel lay between the Charles River and Cape Cod, slightly overlapping the grant by which, in 1629, King Charles gave part of the New England Council's lands in Massachusetts to the Massachusetts Bay Colony—lands for which they had already received a somewhat shaky patent from the Council for New England.

Scholars disagree as to exactly how the Puritan colony of Massachusetts Bay obtained its patent from the Council for New England. Ferdinando Gorges was governor of the council at that time. One scholar suggests that he was out of the country when the Puritan-leaning Earl of Warwick, whose name appears on Alexander's map near the Massachusetts Bay, put the patent through. Another quotes the patent as granting the land so long as the arrangement is not "prejudicial to my son, Robert." Records in the Massachusetts Archives suggest that Robert Gorges had died around this time and that his property passed to his brother, John, who sold the huge tract to Sir William Brereton in January of 1628. In any case, the Massachusetts Bay Company felt insecure enough to apply to the king—through some influential London merchants—for a royal grant to the land. Their generous tract ran from three miles south of the Charles River to three miles north of the Merrimack.

The council members on Alexander's map were considered Lord Proprietors of the New World—that is, feudal lords with the right to collect rents, duties, and percentages. Their enterprises, which they directed from Great Britain, generally failed, although Gorges's colony in southern Maine eventually became the town of York. And their political fortunes were reversed in the English Civil War of 1641, which deposed the king and his royalist favorites.

Meanwhile, the Massachusetts Bay Company had shrewdly taken its royal charter and its governing board along to the New World, in case the king should decide to confiscate its charter as he had that of the London Company in 1624. A modest Puritan exodus from England swelled the Bay Colony's numbers. In the penance of New England winters, they thrived. Their charter gave them the right to self-government and to deed land through their General Court. When the king sent for the Massachusetts Bay charter in 1634, in order to install Sir Ferdinando Gorges and his business partner, Captain Mason, as governors of New England, John Winthrop readied the militia and had a beacon erected atop Beacon Hill to alert the colony to the arrival of British ships. The crown would not successfully reclaim Massachusetts until 1686, and then only to lose it, along with every other American interest, a century later.

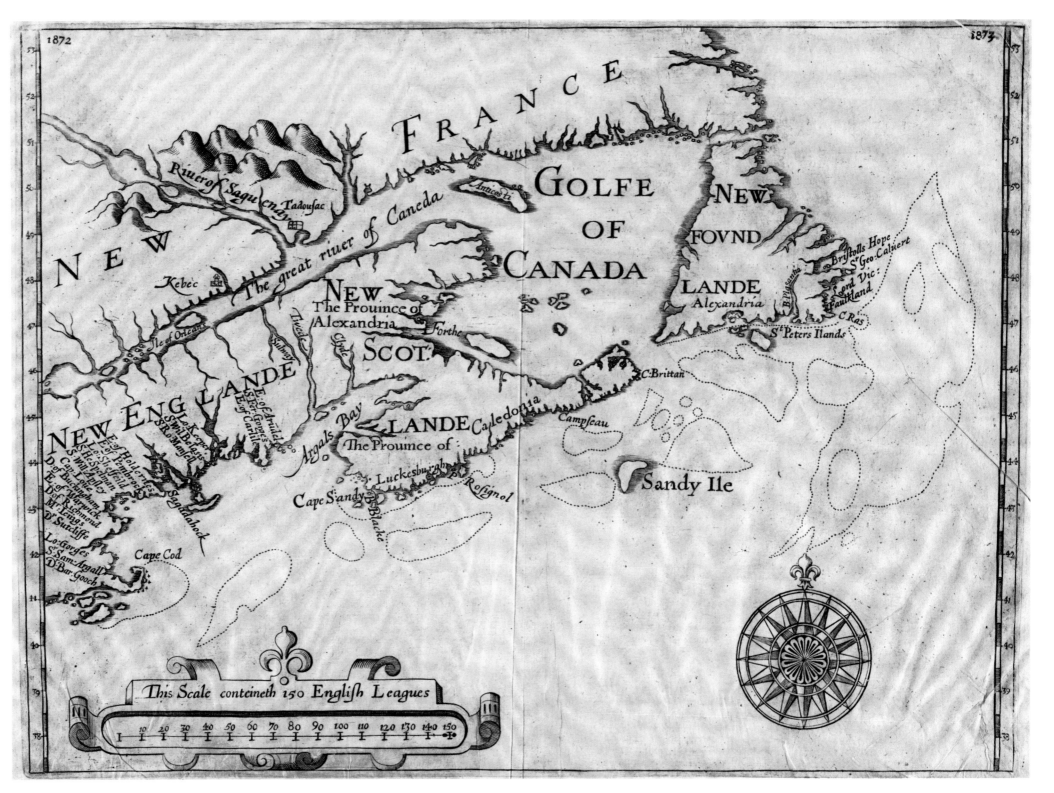

The map labels include:

1872 · 1873

FRANCE

GOLFE OF CANADA

NEW FOVND LANDE Alexandria

NEW ENGLANDE

NEW The Prouince of Alexandria

SCOT.

LANDE The Prouince of Caledonia

Riuer of Saguenay · Tadousac

The great riuer of Caneda

Kebec

Ile of Orleans

Forthe

Argals Bay

Cape Sandy

Luckesburgah

Rosignol

C: Brittan

Campseau

Sandy Ile

Bristolls Hope · St Geo: Caluert · Lord Vic: · Faultland · C: Ras · B: Plasantia · St Peters Ilands

Cape Cod

This Scale conteineth 150 English Leagues

10 20 30 40 50 60 70 80 90 100 110 120 130 140 150

Plate 8
Sir William Alexander, Earl of Stirling
{New England}
From *An Encouragement to Colonies* (London, 1624)
Engraving. 25 × 35 cm.

This map of the New England coast north to Newfoundland was one of the first to follow John Smith's 1616 map. Alexander's *Encouragement to Colonies* was published to promote his attempt to colonize Nova Scotia, or New Scotlande, but it was ultimately futile.

The map reveals the early scope of the proposed colony granted by James I and Charles I to the Council for New England. Originally, the intent was to colonize the English colonies with large English manors or estates that would be independently governed by English lords, who were the elite members of the council. This map shows the twenty patentees, reduced from an original forty, given land in a 1623 meeting of the council. The council was given control of the Americas between 40 and 48 degrees north latitude. Although Alexander shows the 40th parallel running through Buzzard's Bay, it actually falls closer to modern Philadelphia.

Alexander was the first viscount of Canada and received grants from Charles I for the area east of the St. Croix River and the Acadian peninsula. With the failure of the early estates and the competition from the newly formed Massachusetts Bay Colony, the plans for a feudal New England began to disintegrate.

The map reflects Alexander's Scottish interests and many of the place-names can be traced back to Scotland. It also shows the French colonies of *Kebec* and *Tadousac* and is one of the earliest maps to show Prince Edward Island.

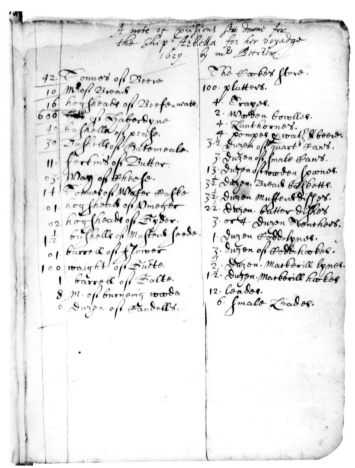

(*top*) While the exact date and artist are unknown, this portrait of John Winthrop was most likely rendered around 1630 and is attributed to the School of Van Dyck.

(*bottom*) This provisions list from 1629 is for Winthrop's ship, the *Arbella,* which actually set sail at the end of April 1630 at the head of a fleet of eleven ships. The *Arbella* was named after the wife of Sir Isaac Johnson, the largest stockholder in the Massachusetts Bay Company. Both Sir Isaac and Lady Arbella traveled with Winthrop, though neither he nor his wife would live out the year. Nor would about a fifth of the group of a thousand emigrees.

THE LOVE LETTERS OF JOHN WINTHROP

John Winthrop lived in tumultuous times. With a Catholic queen influencing King Charles, England became increasingly inhospitable toward those deprecatingly called Puritans—including the Winthrop family. Though born to a gentleman's life and respected as an attorney, John Winthrop was barred from court in 1629 as a known Puritan. Shortly thereafter, a group of the Governors and Company of the Massachusetts Bay drafted him as governor, to lead the conveyance of the company's charter and its entire government, with about a thousand emigrants, to the coast of Massachusetts.

Winthrop was no fan of democracy. He mistrusted the ability of commoners to govern themselves and is remembered as the paternalistic persecutor of Anne Hutchinson. But he is also known as a founder and generous, gifted, if magisterial political leader of the colony, famous for the words, "For wee must Consider that wee shall be as a City upon a hill. The eies of all people are upon Us."

Winthrop's personal letters to his wife Margaret reveal more intimately the love of God and strong domestic affection that fortified Winthrop throughout the travails of leading a colony through an arduous voyage; settling under the most dire conditions in a strange land; and thrashing out new models of government while being brought to face his own imperfections and the many flaws of his fellows.

While Winthrop spent months in London arranging the pilgrims' voyage, Margaret stayed behind at Groton to sell the family's manor home and give birth to their last child. She waited while the governor led his flock of almost a thousand to the winnowing hardships of colonial life. A year after his departure from London—and after the first winter badly reduced the immigrants' numbers—Governor Winthrop wrote to his wife from Boston as she prepared for her own voyage. Though he had lost one of his older sons at the trip's end and Margaret was to lose their new baby en route, Winthrop's letter contemplates divine mercy. "MY DEARE WIFE . . . blessed be his holy and glorious name that he hath so far magnified his mercy towards us, that when so many have been layd in their graves since we parted, yet he hath pleased to preserve us unto this hope of a joyful meetinge, that we may see the faces of each other againe, the faces of our children & sweet babes."

Plate 9
William Wood (ca. 1580–1639)
The South part of New-England, as it is Planted this yeare, 1639
From *New England Prospect* (London, [1634] 1639)
Woodcut. 18 x 30 cm. State 3

Only John Smith's 1616 map (see plate 7) and Alexander's 1624 map (see plate 8) preceded this careful depiction of New England. Wood's was the first printed map by a New England resident and the first to name the town of Boston located properly. Unaltered, it was reissued in 1635 and 1639 with new dates and reset titles.

Wood arrived in Massachusetts with his father in 1629 at the age of twenty-three and helped found the town of Lynn. He returned to England in 1633 to publish his *Prospect,* and the various editions of this work and map were influential in encouraging settlement of southern New England.

As the title page of the *Prospect* suggests, this map was intended to "both enrich the knowledge of the mind-travelling Reader, or benefit the future Voyager." The prospective colonist could find no better map and it would not be improved upon until John Foster's map in 1677 (see plate 12). It influenced even John Smith whose 1635 map includes a three-line inscription referring to Wood's map as the source for new information and shows new towns depicted on Wood's map: *Watertowne, Newtown* (Cambridge), *Medford, Charlestowne, Saugus* and *Dorchestr.*

Wood's outline of New England is somewhat crude compared to Smith's map but displays far greater accuracy for coastal Massachusetts. Over thirty English and Indian villages are named for the first time on a printed map. The delineation of the coast is far superior to that of inland areas and closely resembles a manuscript map of the region associated with John Winthrop. It is significant that both maps clearly delineate Cape Ann, Marblehead, Nahant, Deer Island, Charlestown, the Mystic and Charles Rivers, and the Boston peninsula.

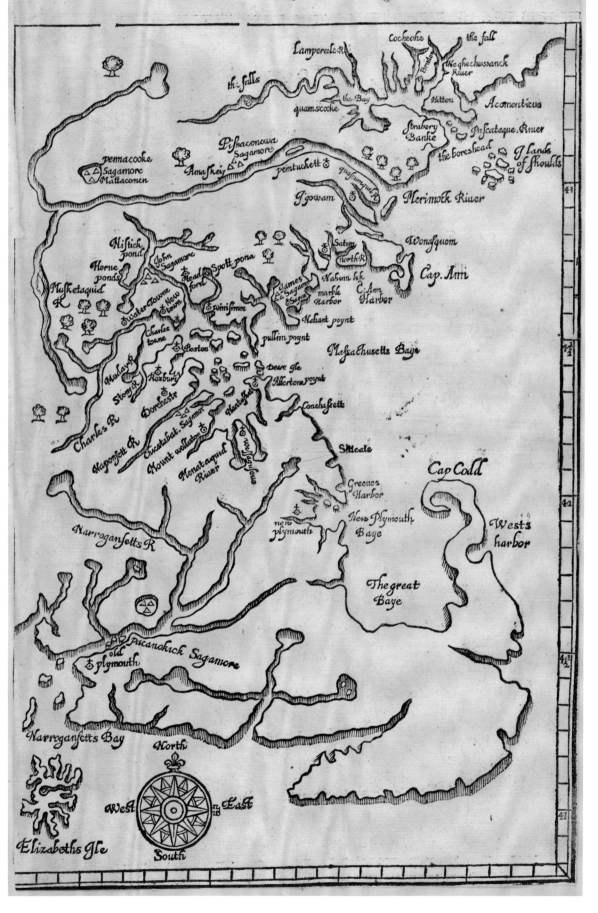

(left) The title page of Blaeu's 1635 atlas, in which Jan Jansson's map (at right) appeared.

(right) Jan Vermeer's ca. 1669 painting, *The Geographer,* painted during the period of Holland's mapmaking primacy, is one of several Vermeers that show maps and, in this case, also a globe.

THE GOLDEN AGE OF CARTOGRAPHY: DUTCH MAPMAKERS OF THE SIXTEENTH AND SEVENTEENTH CENTURIES

We know the sixteenth and seventeenth centuries in Europe as the time of the late Renaissance and early baroque periods. It was the age of exploration and colonization and yet ninety percent of the population worked at home on the farm. It was the Age of Reason and yet the Protestant Reformation and Catholic retribution led to the widespread torture and murders of the Spanish Inquisition. It was a period when enormous wealth poured into the major European powers and yet, perhaps because of that, it was a time of political instability and intense rivalry when the English Revolution occurred and most European nations were at war with at least one of their neighbors. It was a period when knowledge advanced against ignorance and yet the Black Death still mocked the value of human life.

The Low Countries were the birthplace of Gerard Mercator (1512–1594), the greatest geographer and cartographer since Ptolemy, at about the time that copperplate engraving delivered a long supremacy in mapmaking to the Dutch, who were already known as skilled engravers. By the seventeenth century, the

golden age of Dutch mapmaking was already decades old, and the death of Mercator, his son, and his colleague Ortelius had left Dutch cartography in the hands of mapmakers who specialized in publishing and collecting maps and who refined the engraving and painting of maps to an art form that made Dutch maps prized throughout Europe, particularly in France and England. Mapmaking flourished along with other arts and cultural hallmarks in Holland; this was also the age of Rembrandt as well as Vermeer, who depicted maps in the background of several of his paintings.

Mapmakers of this period had a ready market, for as exploration, overseas trade, and colonization increased, so did the demand for maps. Having emerged from a period of Spanish rule in 1568, the Dutch gradually became a colonial and financial power (through trade, banking, and insurance for traders). But first, in the sixteenth century, the Dutch became experts in the navigation of European waters by distributing the wealth of the Indies as it poured into Spain and Portugal. As coastal traders throughout Europe, the Dutch became so well acquainted with European waters that they were able to produce the first sea atlas or *Waggoner,* so called because of its author, Lucas Janssz Waghenaer. The *Waggoner* and its many imitations quickly became a necessity for the European navigator.

Although in the seventeenth century the Dutch remained somewhat at the mercy of the aggressive Spanish armada, the Dutch East Indies Company, established in 1602, controlled ports in West Africa, South Africa, the Middle East, much of the Indian coast, and throughout Sumatra, Java, and other parts of the East Indies. The Dutch West Indies Company, established in 1626 as trade shifted to the Atlantic and Caribbean, controlled ports in the mid-Atlantic portion of America's eastern seaboard, and in Northern Brazil.

The private enterprise of trading groups fostered both a great deal of cartographic activity and a great deal of secrecy concerning it, in order to maintain an economic and military advantage over rival and hostile nations. The Dutch East India Company possessed a "Secret Atlas," compiled by the best mapmakers of the nation and showing the best route around Africa and on to India and the Far East among endless islands and archipelagos.

During this era, the members of the great families of Dutch mapmaking competed, collaborated, and plagiarized, and they often intermarried. In the Hondius, Jansson, and Visscher families, as in Mercator's, the work of mapmaking was proudly handed down from father to son or son-in-law, as in the case of Jan Jansson, author of the map at right, who married Elizabeth Hondius, whose father purchased Mercator's plates after his death and issued the Hondius-Mercator atlas. These publishers and map artists lived at a time when the atlas had become popular, and money was to be made from assembling good collections of maps or charts of different regions. Dutch mapmakers of this period also produced the large world maps that represent the artistic pinnacle of mapmaking—often in double-hemisphere style—with their ornate borders and illustrations, including sensitively wrought figures representing explorers, their patrons, natives of new lands, or characters from other historical eras or mythology.

Competition with France and England continued to weaken Dutch economic primacy, and the War of Spanish Succession (1701–1714) ended it. By that time the maps of European mapmakers revealed a world nearly recognizable as our own, lacking only an understanding of the two poles, the interior of North America, and Australia and New Zealand.

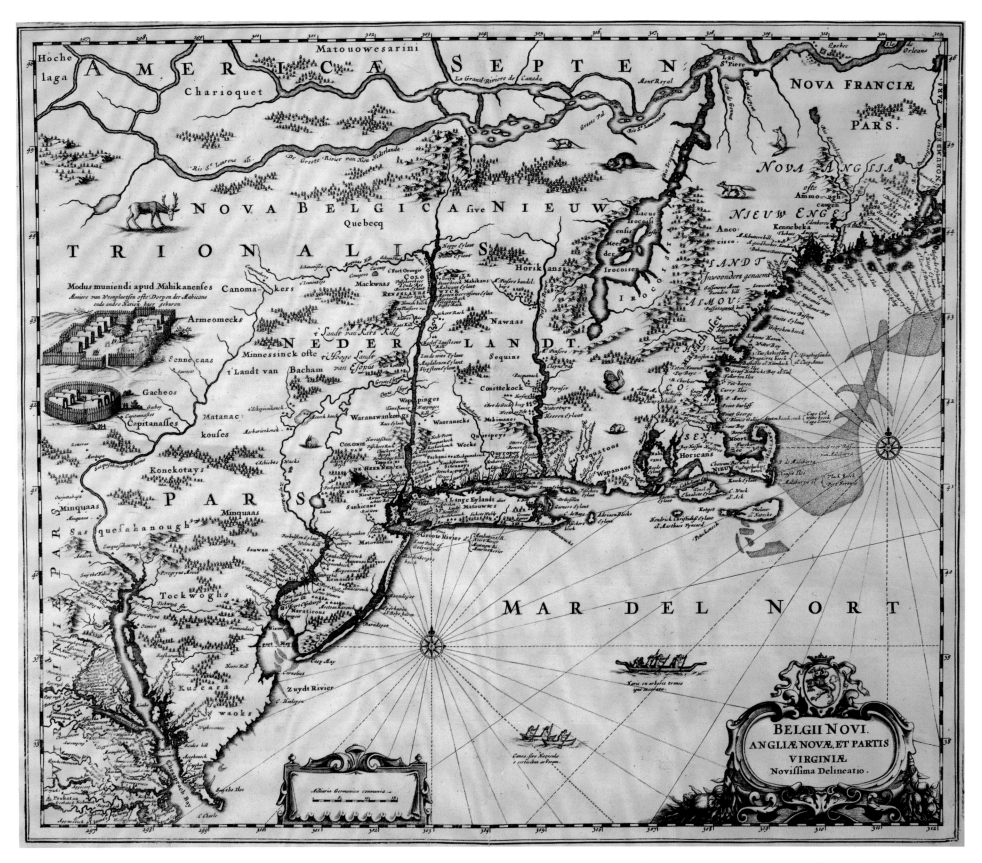

Plate 10

Jan Jansson (1588–1664)

Belgii Novi, Angliae Novae, et Partis Virginiae
Novissima Delineatio

Holland, 1651

Engraving. 45 x 53 cm.

This is arguably the most important map of northeast America produced during the latter half of the seventeenth century. No fewer than twenty-seven maps published in Holland, England, and Germany copied it almost exactly, and it formed the beginning of the famous Jansson-Visscher series. No other map of its time had such popularity or influence and few provided as much detail.

The New England portion of the map shows the most correct Dutch delineation to date. Boston, however, is shown on the north side of the Charles River and named *Briston*.

Massachusetts is named and the islands of Boston Harbor are shown as *Mattahunts Iles*. Several English placenames are found, such as Falmouth, Snowdon Hill, and Southampton.

A leading figure in the history of cartography, Jansson was born at Arnhem, the son of a publisher and mapmaker. He became a partner with his brother-in-law Henricus Hondius and, along with the mapmaking firm of Blaeu, would maintain Dutch mapmaking supremacy in the seventeenth century.

89

"Indians curing their sick" is an illustration from the 1631 German *Newe Welt und ameri-canische Historien.* In the worst European-borne epidemics to afflict native Americans, the sick outnumbered their caretakers, or the new contagions left no caretakers.

EARLY BIOLOGICAL WARFARE

While the earliest contacts between the peoples of the Old and New Worlds led in rare instances to friendship or interracial marriage, these initial contacts more often issued sparks of betrayal, murder, kidnapping, and enslavement. Most early European expeditions along the coasts of the Americas included the ritual kidnapping of Indians for exhibition or enslavement, which generally led to a less friendly reception for subsequent European parties of exploration.

Microbes, however, took a greater toll on the native population than human nature during this early period. Although Europe, Asia, and Africa shared much of the same germ pool, the isolation of the New World created a vulnerable host population in which Old World germs could suddenly and violently expand. Since no natives possessed immunity, there were hardly any healthy adults to care for the sick when epidemics of chicken pox, smallpox, or measles broke out.

The rampant spread of contagious diseases among the defenseless New World hosts resulted in a population loss that prepared the way for colonization. Many colonists found cleared land waiting for them. The Plymouth Colony established itself on the site of an agricultural village of the Patuxet tribe. Champlain had mapped the village in detail during his 1605 voyage. However, in 1617, a virulent epidemic raging through the native communities of New England carried off the entire population of the Patuxet hamlet. The epidemic also left the new English arrivals at Plymouth a friend and guide, Squanto, who returned from England, where he had been taken by force, to find no kin or community left to him in his native Patuxet-Plymouth village. He attached himself to the colony as a valuable adviser and interpreter.

Some Britons saw the advantage of biological warfare. There was at least one recorded instance during the later French and Indian War where officers caused a tribal outbreak of smallpox by seeing that the enemy received infected infirmary blankets.

Although the Indians, for their part, may have offered the colonists syphilis and some strains of flu in return, they apparently offered nothing quite as lethal as the contagious diseases of the Old World. As they faced continuing displacement and sociocultural disruption, the Indians remained vulnerable to disease, which furthered the downward spiral of demoralization and social disintegration in progress among native cultures. Estimates of the final loss of native population in the Americas range as high as ninety percent.

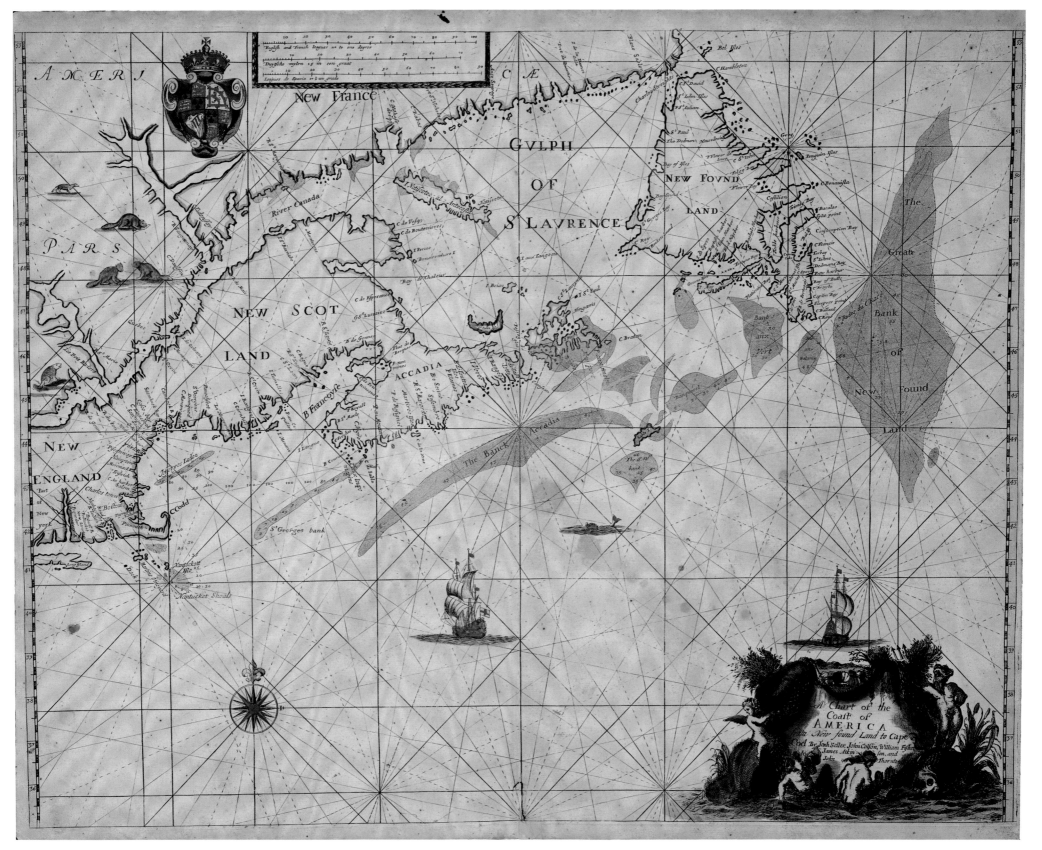

Plate 11
John Seller (fl. 1664–1680, d.1697)
*A Chart of the Coast of America from New Found
Land to Cape Cod*
From *Atlas Maritimus* (London: John Darby, 1675)
Engraving. 43 x 55 cm.

This chart is from the first edition of Seller's *Atlas Maritimus*, which is the earliest marine atlas published in England and the earliest English chart of New England waters. The chart shows islands, soundings, the lucrative fishing banks, and the towns of Boston and Charlestown.

John Seller began his business in London in 1658 as an instrument maker and teacher. His interest in chart and map publishing led him to create the concept for *The English Pilot*, a sea atlas of the world in four volumes (see plate 13 vignette). His plan called for the volumes to be divided between Northern Navigation (Europe), Southern Navigation (Europe), Oriental Navigation, and Western Navigation. Although he never completed this project, he did publish *The First Book* (1671), *The Second Book* (1672), and the *Atlas Maritimus* (1675), as well as other atlases and maps. His successors published the additional volumes and several editions throughout the eighteenth century (see plate 13). Seller's *English Pilot* succeeded in breaking the then Dutch monopoly on the publication of marine atlases.

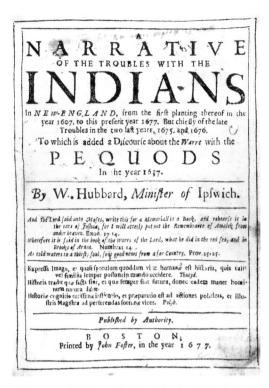

Title page of William Hubbard's book, *A Narrative of the Troubles with the Indians in New-England,* printed by mapmaker John Foster in 1677 and featuring Foster's map of New England, at right.

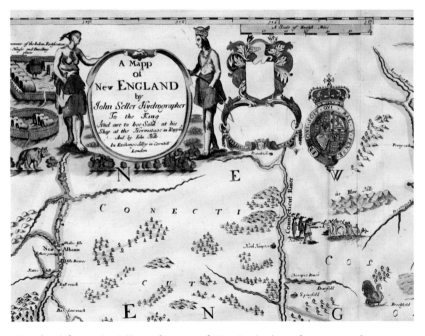

This detail from John Seller's 1675 map of New England (see frontispiece of chapter 3), also found in Hubbard's *Narrative,* shows a tiny perspective (at right of center) of the villagers of Hadley, led by William Goffe, repelling an Indian attack on the town of Hadley.

THE SINS OF THE FATHER: MASSASOIT, PHILLIP, AND KING PHILLIP'S WAR

The Wompanoag leader, Massasoit, and his son, King Phillip, were, respectively, the greatest friend and the greatest enemy of white settlers in seventeenth-century New England. Their differing attitudes toward the white man may be ascribed mainly to the growing intrusiveness of the English presence in Massachusetts during the fifty years that elapsed between Massasoit's early leadership and his son's—approximately from 1620 to 1670. Massasoit had initially dealt only with the colony at Plymouth. By 1662, forty thousand English colonists inhabited New England. They outnumbered native Americans about two to one.

In 1621, Massasoit signed a treaty with Governor William Bradford of the fledgling colony at Plymouth that basically ensured the colony's survival. The treaty made the colonists and the Wompanoag tribe military allies, swearing them to mutual protection in case of attack.

Massasoit further nurtured the colony at Plymouth by permitting two native guides to assist the colony. Squanto was a lone survivor of the native tribe at Plymouth that had been eradicated by disease. Hobamock was a member of Massasoit's council. Each of them provided valuable knowledge of the settlers' new environment, guiding the settlers' efforts in hunting, fishing, planting, and trading for furs, and serving as scouts and translators.

While Massasoit's special relationship with the colonists brought him political power among native tribes—he became the leader of a federation of local tribes—many of Massasoit's councilors, and many leaders of neighboring tribes, argued against his generosity toward the white settlers of Plymouth. But for forty years, Massasoit protected the settlers. And they, understanding their good luck, protected him.

By the time of Massasoit's death in 1662, the colonial encroachment on native land—and disruption of native culture—had expanded irrevocably. While Massasoit had futilely asked Governor Bradford to include in the Plymouth Treaty an injunction prohibiting the settlers from their incessant efforts to convert the Indians, by Phillip's time, it had become a capital crime for Indians to deny Christianity. Both of Massasoit's older sons felt distrustful of the white colonists who had betrayed their father in the treaty's finer points, and perhaps felt a need to avenge the way in which Englishmen had taken advantage of their father's honest nature. After Phillip's elder brother died—and Indians believed that whites had poisoned him—Phillip assumed leadership and laid the groundwork, through patient negotiation with potential allies, for King Phillip's War. The Nipmucks and Narragansett and other nations joined Phillip. Christian Indians and Mohegan mercenaries allied with the English.

The period between 1674 and 1676 was a time of terror for smaller colonial towns in the New England interior, and particularly in Massachusetts. Until the first brave was killed, King Phillip's warriors only harassed the settlers by acts such as killing livestock, but once the first Indian fell, fighting escalated and massacres ensued for both sides. Twelve English villages were destroyed, as were many Indian villages. Ultimately, the Indians fell in greater numbers.

By the war's end, approximately three thousand Indian men, women, and children had been slaughtered including, finally, Phillip himself. Many hundreds more, including Phillip's wife and son, were shipped to the Caribbean and other destinations as slaves. English casualties numbered about six hundred, though the colonists paid heavily in homes and cattle.

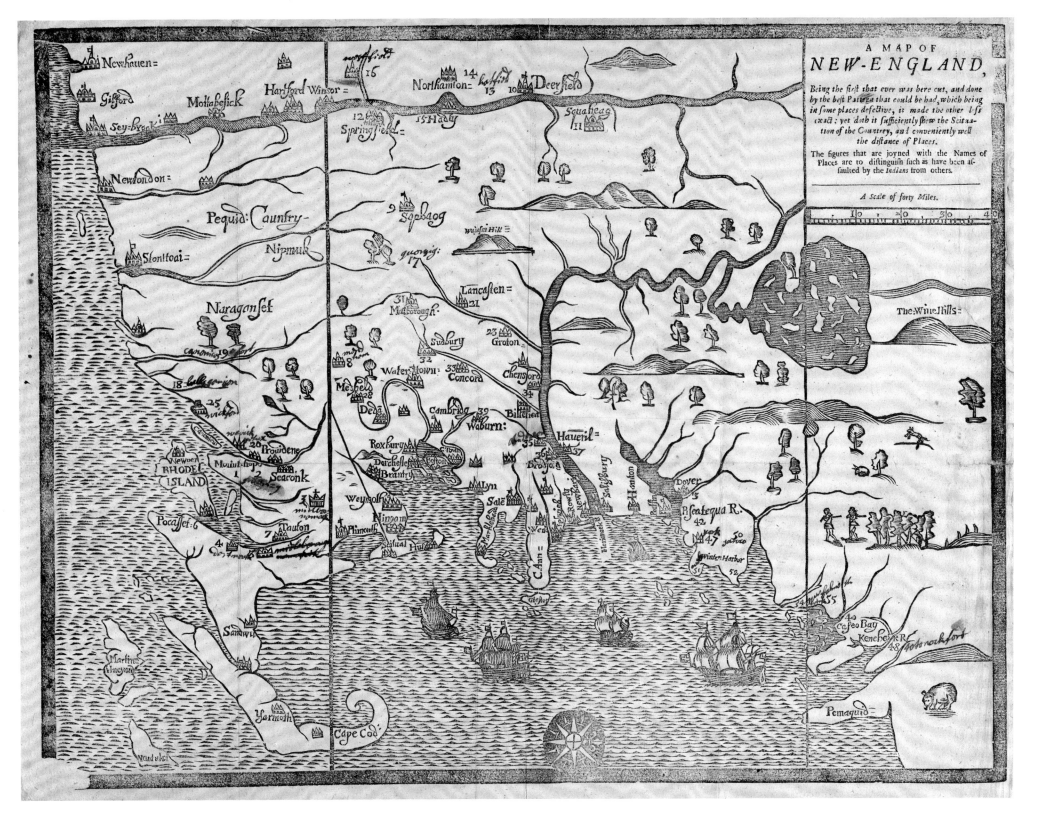

Plate 12
John Foster (1648–1681)
A Map of New-England
From *A Narrative of the Troubles with the Indians in New England* (London: William Hubbard, 1677)
Woodcut. 30 x 38 cm.

Originally printed in Boston, Foster's is the first map drawn, cut, and printed in America. His book was printed in London that same year and another issue of the map appeared with several style and spelling changes. The major difference is the naming of the White Mountains:

The London edition has become known as the "Wine Hills" version, as opposed to the rarer "White Hills" version published in Boston. Another difference is the addition of a town symbol between *Seaconk* and *Plimouth*.

The immediate occasion for publication of the map was the Indian massacres that took place throughout New England in 1675. The uprising was led by King Phillip, whose own village of Mount Hope is shown near Narragansett Bay.

The map is a significant improvement over earlier Dutch maps and shows, for the first time, the true geographical relationship between the Connecticut and

Merrimack Rivers and Lake Winnipesaukee. Similarly, the extent of English settlement can be derived from the more than fifty towns and villages named and numbered.

The two parallel vertical lines mark the boundaries claimed by the Massachusetts Bay Colony and originally surveyed by William Reed in 1665. The northerly line is based on the company's 1628 charter, which granted lands located south of an imaginary line three miles north of the Merrimack River. When it became clear that the Merrimack turned sharply to the north inland, surveyors for the colony claimed lands far to the north as shown, irritating the heirs of the Gorges grants, who also claimed these areas in New Hampshire and Maine.

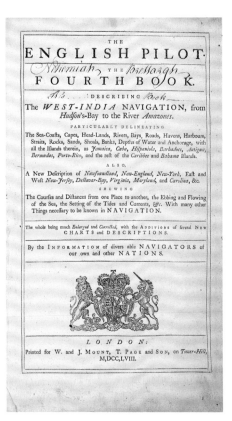

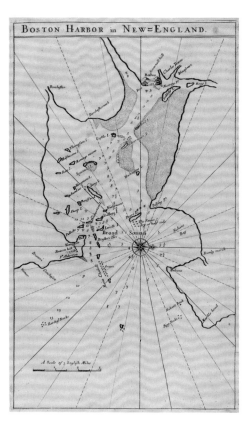

BOSTON HARBOR in NEW=ENGLAND.

(left) Title page from *The English Pilot, Fourth Book* (1730), in which the Thornton map (at right) appeared. *The Pilot* focused on navigation to North America and the Caribbean, and on the Atlantic coast.

(right) John Seller, *Boston Harbor in New-England* (London, 1689). The first edition of *The English Pilot, Fourth Book,* in 1689, but few subsequent editions, carried this plan of the Boston Harbor, believed to be the first published map of the harbor.

EQUIPPING THE ENGLISH PILOT

What was mapmaking like outside the cartographic capital of the Low Countries during the seventeenth century? In England, John Speed and others were bringing the mapping of the mother country up to date, but for most of the century, a mariner still might have a chart drawn for him as needed for a voyage or purchase a Dutch chart. But the English were eager to emulate the Spanish and Portuguese successes in exploration, conquest, and colonization, and to broaden their dominion. It seems a natural outgrowth of that spirit that John Seller, a compass-maker and writer of books on navigation, should have wished to break the Dutch monopoly on maps and to create an atlas of charts uniquely useful to the English navigator.

"Practical Navigation . . . ," wrote John Seller in his 1669 guide by that name (or *Praxis Nautica*), "consists of two general Parts, First, that which may be called the *Domestick* or more common Navigation (I mean Coasting or sailing along the shore). . . . Secondly, That which may more properly bear the name and principally deserves to be entitled the Art of Navigation, . . . that Part which guides the Ship in her Course through the Immense Ocean, to any part of the Known World. . . ."

John Seller's abiding regard for the art of navigation made him the right candidate to produce the work that he promised at the end of *Praxis Nautica*: "a Sea Waggoner for the whole World," by which he meant a sea atlas *of* the whole world for the British Empire. In 1671, 1672, and 1675, he published through a London printer the first three volumes of *The English Pilot*, an institution-in-the-making that was to outlive its founder by a century.

Seller's concept of the *Pilot*, and his ambitions to establish his country nearer the forefront of chart making, slightly exceeded his grasp. In order to make the first two volumes of *The English Pilot*, Seller procured Dutch maps and reengraved them with English names. He hadn't much choice given the state of English chart making. Critics rightly but embarrassingly objected that Seller's maps of British home waters were inaccurate.

Partly as a result, in 1681, the Admiralty commissioned Captain Greenvile Collins to make the first original survey of the British coasts. When, in 1693, a new *Coasting Pilot* was finally published, the improved charts still lacked latitude and longitude and, for international waters, the *Pilot* still relied on Dutch maps and charts. By this time, however, Seller had lost control of his brainchild to four collaborators who formed a gifted team with the necessary capital resources for Seller's ambitious project. Two of them, John Thornton, cartographer and engraver, and William Fisher, printer and bookseller, completed the fourth volume of Seller's *Pilot* and published it in 1689. Fisher had acquired the rights from Seller, perhaps because the latter lacked capital.

While Seller's fortunes declined, the *Pilot* thrived. It ultimately included five volumes or books. Book 1 covered southern navigation; Book 2 covered northern navigation; Book 3 covered Asia; Book 4 dealt with the New World; and Book 5 described the African coast and the passage there. *The English Pilot* was published periodically until 1800. Book 4, for example, was published at one- to five-year intervals, with editions produced annually during times such as the French and Indian War. Fisher's son-in-law, Richard Mount, joined the combine and remained an owner after Fisher's death. Over the ensuing decades, Mount's son, Fisher, and grandson, John, both helped to carry the enterprise forward, though its zenith of accuracy occurred under the Thornton-Fisher team.

Book 4 of *The English Pilot* contained the first published chart of Boston Harbor and its approach, with numerous islands and shoals, including detailed instructions for avoiding the Nantucket shoals, and progressing past Gay Head on Martha's Vineyard. The text includes instructions for navigating most of the New England coast under headings such as "Directions to sail into Plymouth" and "General Directions for him that shall fall in with the Coast of New England, coming from the East-ward." Though a few latitudes are mentioned in this first edition, longitudes are not, but the refinement of longitude, like the New World, was soon to open new horizons in the fields of geography and cartography.

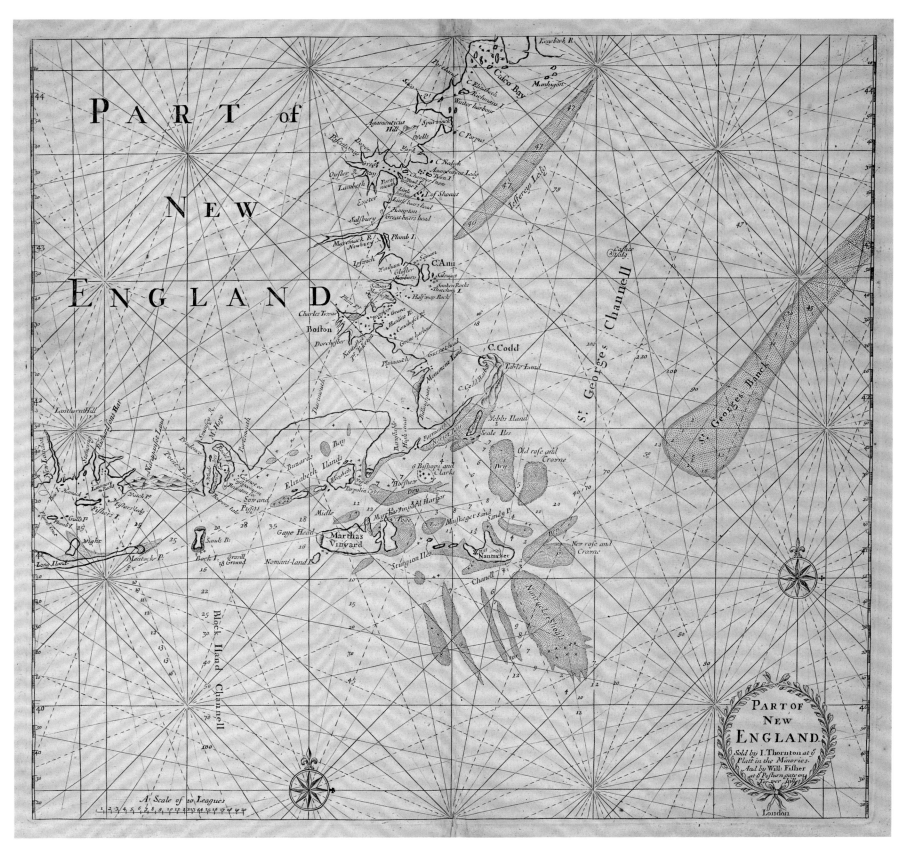

Plate 13
John Thornton
Part of New England, Sold by I. Thornton at ye Platt in the Minories
From *The English Pilot, Fourth Book* (London, 1689)
Engraving. 48 x 44 cm.

This detailed sailing chart reveals the shoals, banks, bays, capes, islands, and towns from Casco Bay in Maine to Rhode Island.

John Thornton was the leading English hydrographer at the end of the seventeenth century. His efforts rescued the failing *English Pilot* initiated by John Seller and established *The English Pilot, Fourth Book,* as the standard navigational guide for American waters for nearly a century. This map was the first chart to be accurate enough for navigational use. Its large scale and increased detail,

including soundings, were significant improvements over John Seller's chart of 1675 (see plate 11). Thornton's chart would guide merchants and immigrants alike to Boston during the active settlement period at the end of the seventeenth century.

This chart was published in the first and second editions of *The English Pilot, Fourth Book,* in 1689 and 1698. It was replaced by a *Large Draught of New England, New York and Long Island* in most copies of the 1706 third edition.

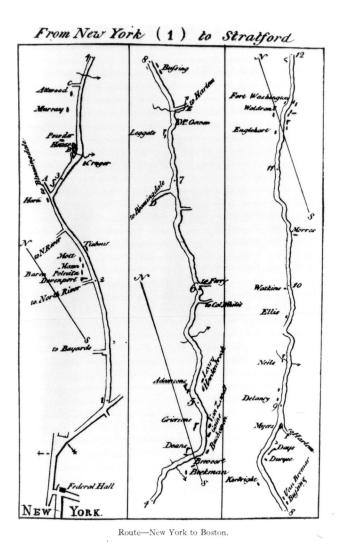

From New York (1) to Stratford

Route—New York to Boston.

This segment of an early map of the Post Road between New York and Boston shows the route from New York City to Fort Washington.

THE BOSTON POST ROAD

The nation's first roads followed native paths. The early governors of Massachusetts settlements such as Salem, Boston, and Plymouth were occasionally obliged to hike over these paths to one another, wading or being carried through large streams and small rivers.

Increasing foot traffic and the use of horses gradually widened these paths. Eventually, some combination of constant wear and deliberate attempts at improvement made these roads passable by carts, carriages, and other vehicles. In 1639, localities were charged with building and maintaining roads in their jurisdictions and later with operating ferries. That same year, the Boston-Plymouth

path was improved. But the Old Connecticut Path, which brought the earliest settlers from Boston to the rich Connecticut River Valley, and along which the Boston–New York post would travel as far west as Springfield, was not much improved until after 1700.

The inauguration of a postal route—agreed to by the governors of New York, Connecticut (John Winthrop's son), and Massachusetts for sharing news of important events—was a milestone in colonial progress. The first post rider set out from the fort on Manhattan Island in January of 1673 on his two-week journey to Boston. He carried official correspondence for Hartford and Boston and bags of letters designated for the towns he would pass through.

In winter, the post rider might reach only as far as the ferry from Manhattan to the mainland by the end of his first day, but during the long days and fair weather of summer, he was expected to ride thirty to fifty miles a day, and to find along the way fresh horses provided by cooperating governments. His progress might be hampered by the company of another traveler for whom he was expected to act as a guide, and who, meanwhile, often suffered from trying to keep up with the post rider. His route took him northeast through Stamford, New Haven, Hartford, and then into Springfield, Massachusetts. From there he turned eastward to ride to Worcester, and on to Boston. After a couple of days' rest, he started back to New York. This first rider made several one-month round trips before, in 1674, a Dutch fleet besieged New York and King Phillip's War curtailed travel in New England.

The post resumed again in 1685 with proper postal officials appointed in New York and Boston. Because the letters for a town might simply be left at the tavern where the post rider stopped, the legislation to refine this system was as abundant and as ineffectual as legislation ordering towns to improve the roads. In Boston, legislation in 1639 and again in 1677 attempted to prevent the miscarriage of letters by appointing a de facto postmaster, who received all letters.

In 1691 the British crown took control of the matter by issuing a royal patent to a postmaster for the colonies. The first colonial postmaster extended service from Portsmouth, New Hampshire, to Baltimore. By the Revolution, it extended south all the way to Charleston, South Carolina.

In 1753, Benjamin Franklin and his co-postmaster, Colonel William Hunter, took command of the colonial postal service and finally created an effective organization and rate system. By this time, the Boston Post Road was known as a highway. Featuring bridges and a decent width, it could carry a wagon or smaller vehicle. By attaching an ingenious measuring device to his wagon wheel, Franklin was able to measure off the Boston Post Road in one-mile lengths. Some of the stone mileage markers remain today.

In 1772, just before the disruptions of the Revolution, the first regular stage coach schedule was established between New York and Boston. Passengers made the journey in about six days by traveling nineteen hours a day, snatching their brief share of sleep in often-primitive accommodations. During the ride, passengers might be asked to help push the coach through mud. Overcoming such hardships, these early travelers along the old post road brought with them the future, although in barely discernable increments, and their path is now memorialized by superhighways that follow the routes of the first post riders.

75 | Degrees west from London | 70

PART OF

P. of North AMERICA

Fort la Mothe

Champlain Lake

NEW ENGLAND

NEW YORK

P. of the IRO: Onnoyoute QUOIS

NEW ENGLAND, NEW YORK, NEW JERSEY and PENSILVANIA.

By H. Moll Geographer. 1729.

5 10 20 30   60
English Miles

PENSILVANIA

NEW JERSEY

WEST JERSEY

EAST JERSEY

Hudsons R.

Delaware R.

Sasquahanough R.

The Greatest Fall
The Present Sasquahana an Indian Fort

Bucks C.
Philadelphia Co.
New Pennes
Town berry
Burlington
Philadelphia
Darby C.
Chester C.
Chichester
Brandy R.
Newcastle
Salem

Baltimore T.

PART of MARYLAND

Chesapeak B.

C. May Cou.
Woodland

Dellawar Bay
Kinlopen

C. May

Great Egg Harbour
Little Egg Harbour
Joe Sandy Land
Barnagat Bay
Manasquam R.
Shark R.
Shrewsbury
Sandy Point
Monmouth Cou.
Middletown
Raven R.
York Town

New York
Elizabeth Town
Perth
Amboy
Blewhill
Essex C.
Bergen Cou.

NEW YORK

Albanie

Massachusetts Col.

Deerfield
N. Hampton
Hadley
Springfield
Westfield
Squab
Enfield
Wethersfield
Middletown
cot Col.
Norwich
Hadham

CONNECTICUT

New London

LONG ISL.

Montang Pt.
East Hampton
South Hampton
Shelter I.

Saco R.
Sugar Loaf hill

NEW ENGLAND

Piscata
way
Kennebec R.
Penico ok
Winter H.

Dover
Baon I.
Shoales I.
Piscataway
Portsmouth
Hampton
Salsbury
Newbery
Rowly
Ipswich
C. Ann
Glocester
Manchester
Marble Head
Lyn

Boston Town & Harbour
Weymouth
Conihasset Rocks
Scituate
Marsfield

C. Codd

Plimouth Col.

Warwick
Wickford
Newport
Rhode I.
Block I.

Eastham
Monimoy
Yarmouth
stable
Old Rose and Crown

Nantucket I.
New Rose and Crown Sand
Nantucket Shoales

Mount Desert
Mount Desert Rock

Jeffery's Bank

Seale I.

St. Georges Bank

Sugar Loaf hill
Hechias
Lit. Manan I.
G. Manan I.
Wolves
Pt. Little Pro
FUNDY BAY
Long I.
G. Passage
Annapolis Royal
SCOTLAND
Sturgion Isles
P. Mouton
C. Sable
F. Sable

WESTERN OCEAN

WEST

An Account of ye Post of ye Continent of Nth. America as they are Regulated by ye Postmasters Genl. of ye Post House.

The Western Post setts out from Philadelphia every Fryday leaving Letters at Burlington and Pert Amboy and arrives at New York on Sunday night; the distance between Philadelphia and New York being 106 Miles. The Post goes out Eastward every Monday morning from New York, and arrives at Seabrook Thursday noon; being 150 Miles, where the Post from Boston setts out at the same time; the New York Post returning with the Eastern Letters, and the Boston Post with the Western, Bags are dropt at New London, Stommington, Rhode Island, and Bristol. The Post from Boston to Piscataway being 70 Miles leaves Letters at Ipswich, Salem, Marblehead and Newberry. There are offices keept at Burlington, Perth Amboy in New Jersey, New London and Stommington in Connecticott, at Rhode Island, Bristol, Ipswich, Salem, Marblehead and Newberry. and the 3 Great Offices are at Boston, New York & Philadelphia.

Plate 14
Herman Moll (d. 1737)
New England, New York, New Jersey and Pensilvania
From *Atlas Minor* (London, 1729)
Engraving. 21 x 28 cm.

This popular map of New England shows the Post Road from Boston to Philadelphia. The road, still referred to today in New England as the Boston Post Road, was included in Moll's *Atlas Minor* (1729). The text in the lower right is entitled: "An Account of ye Post of ye Contintent of Nth. America as they are Regulated by ye Postmasters Genl. of ye Post House" and describes the route east from Philadelphia and west from Boston. This exact account was also used on Moll's 1715 "Beaver" map of North America, known for its large inset view of beavers making dams.

Moll was a geographer and map publisher of Dutch origin who moved to England in 1678. He published one of the most respected general maps of British America in his 1715 *The World Described* in which he took up his adopted country's boundary disputes in America and used his maps to alert the English of French encroachments.

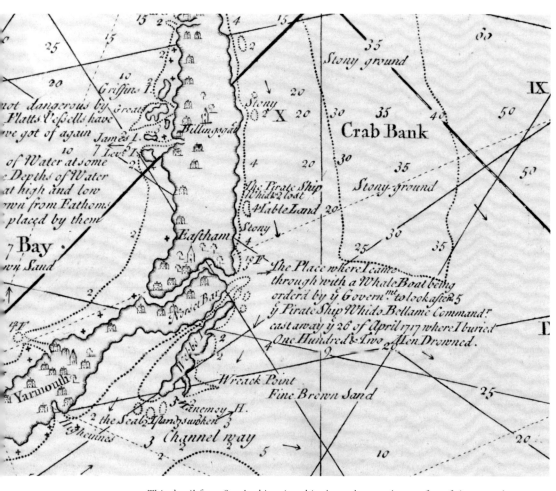

This detail from Southack's painstakingly made map shows a few of the notes documenting his travails as a government guardian of the *Whydah* wreck. It reads, "The Place where I came through with a Whale Boat Being ordered by ye governmt to look after ye Pirate ship Whido Bellame Command! Cast away ye 26 of April 1717 where I buried One Hundred & Two Men Drowned."

CYPRIAN SOUTHACK AND THE *WHYDAH*

The story of the *Whydah* begins and ends with treasure-hunting. And between the two treasure hunts comes the prosaic figure of Cyprian Southack, painstaking bureaucrat and mapmaker, whose chart of Cape Cod served as the liaison between the pirate captain Sam Bellamy, who perished with the *Whydah* in 1717 off the coast near Eastham, and a twentieth-century adventurer who discovered the wrecked pirate ship.

In 1717, "Black" Sam Bellamy was guiding the *Whydah* up the New England coast to Cape Cod where he had left his sweetheart the year before to seek the sunken gold of a Spanish Treasure Fleet that had perished off the coast of Florida. A handsome young seaman from the west coast of England with a poor man's hatred of the status quo, Bellamy was returning instead as the captain of a large slave ship that he had captured, outfitted with twenty-eight guns, and filled with stolen treasure. Two more recently captured ships, manned by Bellamy's crew, accompanied the *Whydah*.

Approaching Cape Cod, the pirates found themselves sailing into treacherous shallows in stormy weather and high seas, which finally drove two boats onto the shoals. On the outermost shore of the Cape, mountainous waves splintered the grounded *Whydah* to pieces, battering the bodies of the drowned pirates in and around the wreckage and finally tearing them away from it.

Cyprian Southack arrived almost two weeks later from Boston, as the royal governor's representative, to reclaim and hold for the owners whatever valuables could be salvaged. Southack entered the outer reaches of Cape Cod as an unwelcome and helpless intruder. On Cape Cod, where pilfering wrecks was a regional pastime, news of the *Whydah*'s fate had spread so quickly that it caused a traffic jam of wagons on the sparsely populated part of the Cape near Eastham. The sly locals, with bits of treasure stowed in closets and barns, gave Southack no help as he searched almost fruitlessly for pieces of the wreck and the treasure he presumed it contained. The weather, too, conspired against Southack as he awaited an opportunity to dispatch divers to the wreck. After trudging over the sand and arranging the burial of 102 pirate bodies that had washed ashore during his days of searching, Southack returned practically empty-handed to Boston.

The only real fruit of Southack's labors was his later-published chart of New England, including Cape Cod, with its autobiographical detail of his futile search for the *Whydah.* In the 1980s, treasure-hunter Barry Clifford saw a copy of Southack's map with its faithful sense of detail and marking of the location of the *Whydah* wreck. Indeed, Clifford explored the area indicated on the map and, pinpointing the wreck with remote sensing equipment, ultimately found the ship's hold, salvaging the ship's bell and an array of smaller artifacts.

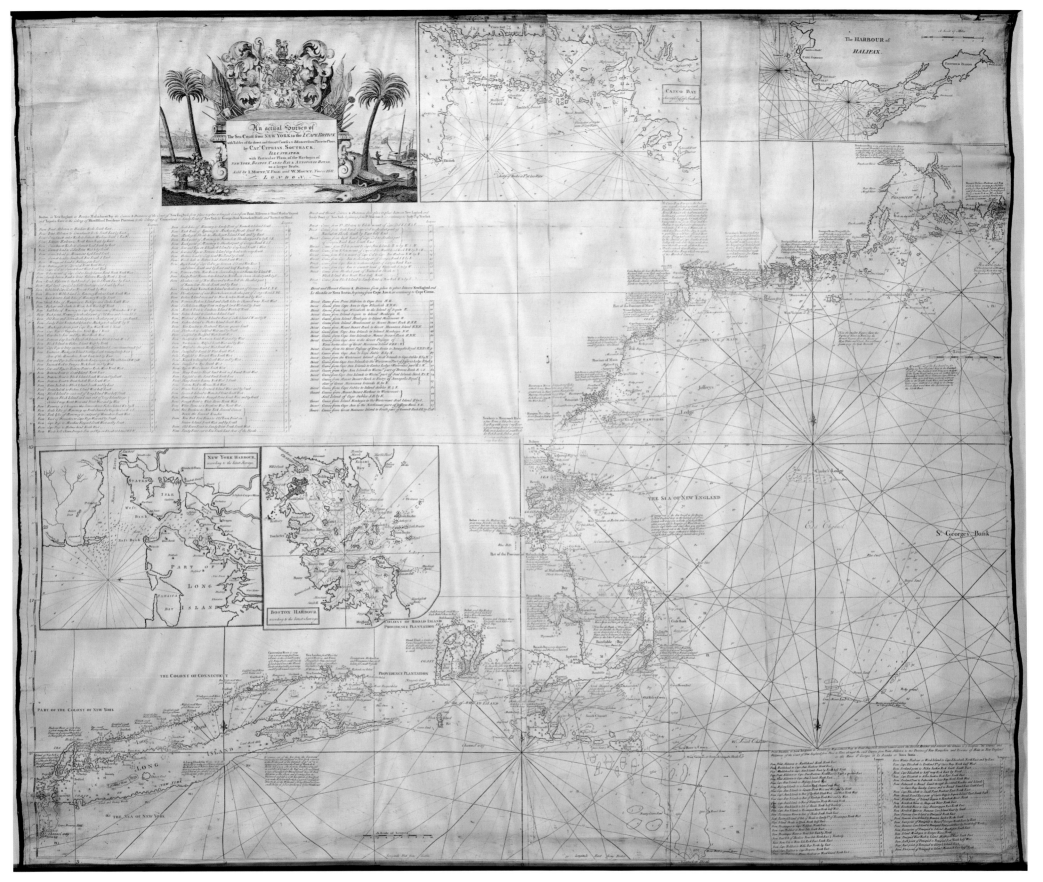

Plate 15
Cyprian Southack (1662–1745)
An actual Survey of The Sea Coast from New York to the I. Cape Briton
(London, 1734)
Engraving. 127 x 108 cm.

This unusual wall map of New England, in six sheets, includes the four western sheets from Southack's landmark chart of the coast from New York to Cape Breton.

Southack lived in Boston after 1685 and is recognized as America's earliest chart maker. His extensive experience as a navigator and privateer in American waters enabled him to produce several charts of the New England coast, including an eight-sheet chart of the New England and Nova Scotia coast, finished in ca. 1734. It is the earliest chart of any part of North America produced by an American. The chart was engraved in London where it was published in several editions and sheet formats. In the issue reproduced here, the western or New England section of the chart is mounted as a wall map and Southack's chart of Boston Harbor has been added to the map as an inset.

99

Edwin Willard Deming painted *Braddock's Defeat* in 1903, one hundred and fifty years after its occurrence in the French and Indian War. When Braddock arrived in the colonies with an imperious manner and many British troops at his command, only to march them off to a catastrophic defeat, the British and Americans were stunned, the French pleasantly surprised.

ONE SEVEN-YEAR WAR LEADS TO ANOTHER

Any modern resident of Massachusetts or Rhode Island might take pleasure in imagining the picturesque villages of Jefferys's map showing some of the oldest and most thickly settled portions of the New England coast. The eastern towns of modern Massachusetts are nearly all in place. Their names bring to mind the tidy common ringed by dignified clapboard houses, many of which were already old in the era of Jefferys's map, and vestiges of which can still be found in these towns.

The bucolic scenes that the map brings to mind, however, belie the turmoil of colonial life. Still somewhat primitive by European standards, the colonist's daily life was also fraught with political intrigue and frequent threats of war. Only five years after the end of King George's War with France (1744–1748), twenty-one-year-old Major George Washington was on his way through the wilderness to confront the French with an ultimatum from Governor Dinwiddie of Virginia concerning control of the Ohio Valley. England and France would formally declare war in 1755 (the year when the first edition of the Jefferys map was published), after skirmishes in the American interior had already broken out.

Though France and England fought the Seven Years War, or French and Indian War, over their rights to expansion in the American interior, the war was actually triggered by competition among the American colonies to expand westward, particularly into the Ohio Valley where the French were hastily putting up fortifications.

In this period of American history, the colonies were very much rivals for new territories. Massachusetts and Connecticut, with their sea-to-sea charters, were being blocked on their western borders by New York, with whom Massachusetts carried on a lengthy boundary dispute. In seeking and receiving a land grant to expand into Ohio territory, Virginia settlers (whose original, vast charter also ran sea-to-sea) were seen to be infringing on the rights of Pennsylvanians.

Yet during the seven-year period that the colonies hosted the British army—and especially after the war when colonists found themselves saddled with an occupying army—many colonials found they had something in common: a profound vexation with British rule. The well-financed British army and navy brought with them to the colonies the social caste system that was gradually being shed in America. For example, their forms of recruitment were closer to impressment. The navy, by far the worst offender, rounded up 800 sleeping men from New York City one morning between midnight and 6 A.M. In the army, disciplinary infractions among the army's enlisted men might bring 300 lashes with a cat o' nine tails.

Americans found that they ranked rather low in the British system. During the war's first two years, all American officers, regardless of rank, were required to report to British captains. The British requests for money, men, supplies, equipment, and especially quarters, were peremptory (as might have been expected from an army fighting on the colonists' behalf) and did not show a great regard for the processes of the colonial assemblies. While British troops were required by law to be quartered in public houses, a shortage of available space in the colonies led to quartering in homes and usurpation of property.

Nonetheless, as the British-American military collaboration was smoothed out in the war's later years, Massachusetts and other colonies raised armies of thousands. The little towns on Jefferys's map, with their pastoral commons, sent men by ship to take Nova Scotia and on foot to fight on the frontier at Ticonderoga and Crown Point. Massachusetts's governor William Shirley (see figure 8 in chapter 4) was briefly head of all American and British forces in the colonies and had lost his son in the first large-scale battle. Governor Pownall, his successor, later tried to explain to Parliament the colonists' apprehension concerning the standing army that Britain had left behind.

The Seven Years War and the British army left behind in its aftermath fomented the tensions that produced, after fifteen years, the American Revolution. Colonists resented both British attitudes and the residual army that occupied their frontiers, towns, and cities. They further resented King George's efforts to tax them in order to support these unwelcome irritations.

Plate 16
Thomas Jefferys (ca. 1710–1771)
A Map of the most Inhabited part of New England
From *The American Atlas . . .* (London: Robert Sayer and John Bennet, 1774)
Engraving. 2 sheets each 53 × 98 cm. Third edition

Jefferys was a prolific English engraver, geographer, and publisher of several important maps of America. The north half of the map includes new townships in New Hampshire and Vermont, and the inset plan of Fort Frederick in the 1755 first edition has been replaced with *A Plan of the Town of Boston,* a note relating to the boundary between New Hampshire and New York, and a changed imprint to reflect the new 1774 date.

Jefferys's business declared bankruptcy in 1768; Robert Sayer acquired most of his stock and published many of Jefferys's maps in *The American Atlas.*

Jefferys's map is derived from Boston physician William Douglass's *This Plan of the British Dominions of New England in North America,* published posthumously by his heirs in 1753 (see figure 2 in chapter 4). Douglass's map was the most detailed map of New England for its time. Its rarity, and the existence of Jefferys's more famous map, robbed Douglass of the recognition that he deserved.

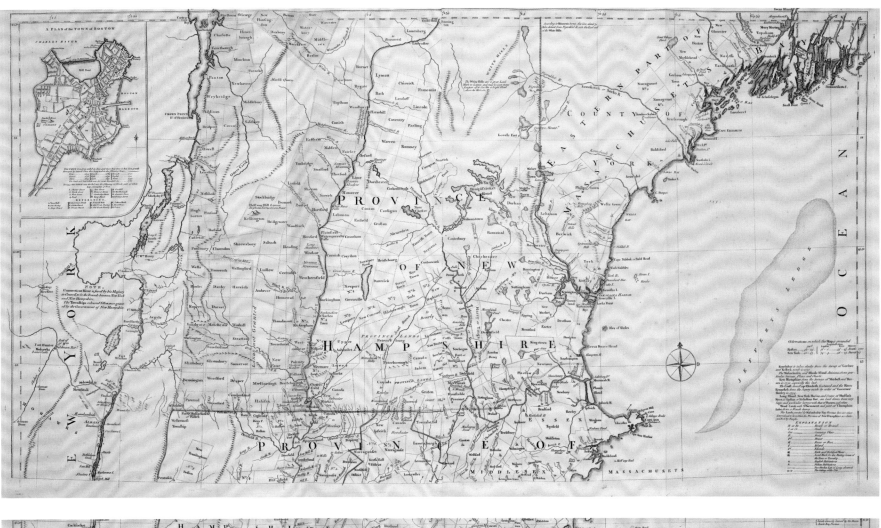

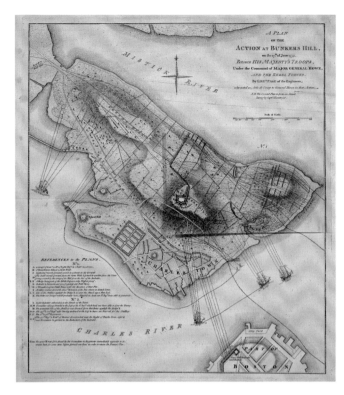

Thomas Page, *A Plan of the Action at Bunkers Hill, on the 17th of June 1775, Between His Majesty's Troops, Under the Command of Major General Howe, and the Rebel Forces* (London, 1775). This is the most detailed, informative, and commonly used delineation of the Battle of Breed's (here called "Bunkers") Hill. The overlay shows the initial attack that was repulsed, while the same area of the map beneath the overlay (lower illustration) shows the later progress by the British troops up the hill to just outside of Warren's redoubt. The mapmaker, Lieutenant Page, identifies himself as aide-de-camp to General Howe during the engagement.

MAPS AND THE REVOLUTION

Maps played two critical parts in the American Revolution. They were equipment without which the officers planning battles could not proceed (as in the example of the map at right, which served British officers). In addition, the plans sketched of various key battles in the war described the war's progress to the public.

A plan might be published within a month of the battle it represented, providing the equivalent of a modern news report. These battle maps were often made by the well-trained British engineers observing the battles. They appeared mainly in England, where a large public waited in suspense for months-old news of the war.

The plan illustrated at left was published in London with General Burgoyne's narrative of the Battle of Bunker Hill, in which Charlestown burned. The map shows troop and ship positions, gives the names of key ships and commanding officers, and shows the direction of troop movements, notably the Americans' retreat.

General Burgoyne's fluent description evokes images of today's battle-side television coverage, but encoded with the slight bravura of the eighteenth-century British general. His letter to his nephew, Lord Stanley, from which the text is taken, reports:

> And now ensued one of the greatest scenes of war that can be conceived: if we look to the height, Howe's corps ascending the hill in the face of entrenchments, and in a very disadvantageous ground, was much engaged; and to the left the enemy pouring in fresh troops by the thousands, over the land; and in the arm of the sea our ships and floating batteries cannonading them: strait before us a large and noble town in one great blaze; the church steeples, being of timber, were great pyramids of fire above the rest . . . the roar of cannon, mortars, and musquetry; the crush of churches, ships upon the stocks, and whole streets falling together in ruin, to fill the ear; . . . and the reflection that perhaps a defeat was a final loss to the British empire in America, to fill the mind; made the whole a picture and a complication of horror and importance beyond any thing that ever came to my lot to be witness to.

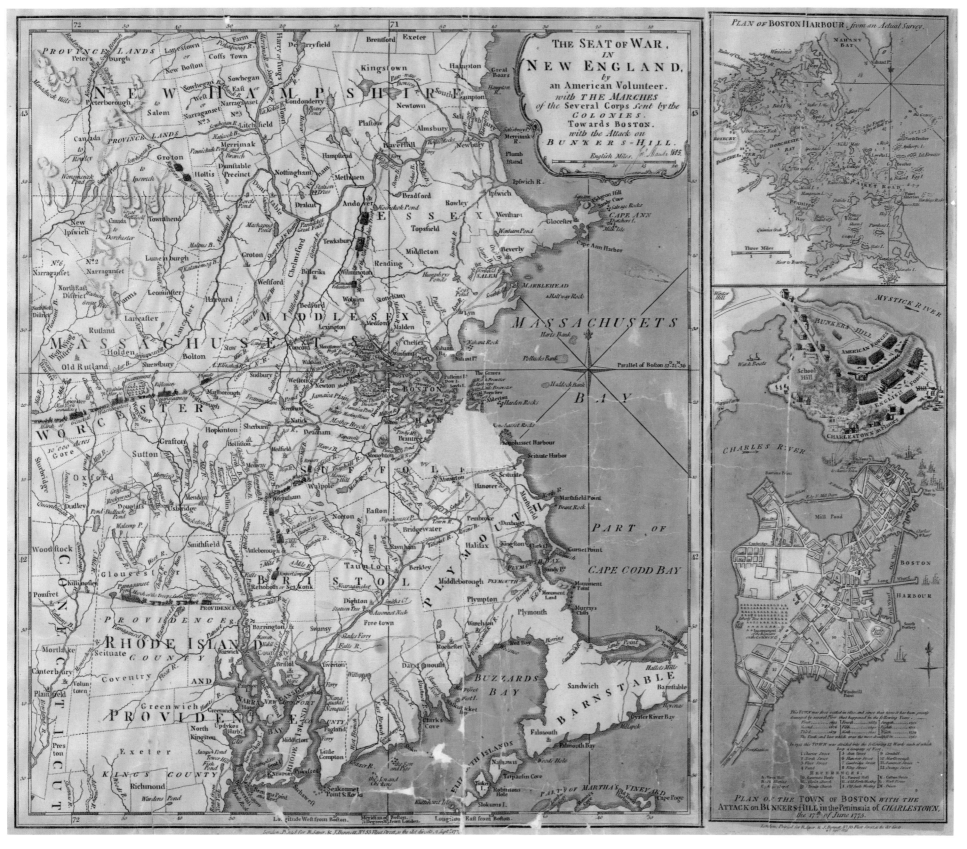

Plate 17
Robert Sayer (1725–1794) and John Bennet (d. 1787)
The Seat of War in New England, by an American Volunteer with the Marches of the Several Corps sent by the Colonies towards Boston, with the Attack on Bunkers-Hill
(London: R. Sayer & J. Bennet, 1775)
Engraving. 46 × 54 cm.

This map shows troops marching to Boston from Connecticut, New Hampshire, and Rhode Island. Two insets provide greater detail on Boston. The first is a general chart of Boston Harbor while the second shows the dramatic attack on Breed's Hill (mistakenly called Bunkers Hill on the plans in the vignette at left) in Charlestown and the town of Charlestown in flames.

Robert Sayer began his career as a map publisher with Philip Overton in 1745 and worked on his own after Overton's death in 1751. His acquisition of Thomas Jefferys's assets in 1768, and eventual partnership with John Bennet in 1770, created a famous map publishing firm.

This firm is well known for their Jefferys publications including the *General Atlas* (1773), *American Atlas* (1774) (see plate 16), *North American Pilot* (1775–1776), *West India Atlas* (1775), and *American Military Pocket Atlas* (1776). This latter title was known as the "Holster Atlas," as it was often carried by British officers in their holsters; it included in a portable format six larger folding maps that the British army believed provided essential topographic information.

Boston Light on Little Brewster Island, the first lighthouse in the New World, as it appears today. Although the structure has been modified over the years, the tower itself was last rebuilt in 1783 after the British destroyed it during the Revolution.

BOSTON LIGHT

Many islands crowd Boston Bay—called Massachusetts Bay in colonial times—and guard the entrance to Boston's inner harbor. The islands are a navigational hazard at night or in bad weather, but by day their familiar shapes herald the harbor to incoming vessels and serve as landmarks to guide the sailor.

As early Boston's maritime commercial interests boomed, and her bay and harbor filled with sails, the idea of a lighthouse at the entrance to the bay gained ground with merchants, shippers, and captains. In 1713, a prosperous merchant, John George, Jr., petitioned the legislature to consider building a lighthouse "for the direction of ships and vessels in the nighttime." The legislature appointed a committee, and the committee ventured into the harbor with several prominent shipmasters, visited and surveyed a number of islands, and recommended that the lighthouse be erected on "the Southernmost Part of the Great Brewster"—actually Little Brewster Island, connected by a sandbar to the larger one. Their recommendation became an act of the legislature. The result was the construction of a lighthouse in 1716 on Little Brewster Island, previously called Beacon Island.

Mr. George died not long after making his proposal, and his wealthy, attractive widow soon became the last and most beloved wife of the Reverend Doctor Cotton Mather. But his initiative in suggesting a lighthouse resulted in the construction of the first modern-style lighthouse in the New World. And, although a few ancient prototypes of the lighthouse existed, only the French and English had each built a stone light tower in the previous century: the Eddystone Light House in the English Channel and the Corduan at the mouth of France's Gironde River.

Since oil lamps were replacing candles at about this time, historians assume that the first light in the old stone tower was probably an oil lamp—fueled first by fish oil, and later whale oil and kerosene. In 1719, a cannon was added to the island's equipment to warn ships in fog.

The rise of lighthouses in eighteenth-century Massachusetts gave rise to the role of "keeper," yet another addition to Massachusetts's culture of the sea. The early light keepers, who needed an assistant or two to manage the light, lived on the island, usually with family, or a servant or helper. The early keepers seem to have hired themselves out as harbor pilots and occasionally had a farm or real estate interest on neighboring islands. They kept ice and snow off the glass under the hazardous conditions of winter storms and they rescued the survivors of shipwrecks.

The first keeper was himself drowned two years after the completion of Boston Light. George Worthylake, his wife, and daughter died off Noddle's Island, when a sudden squall took their sailboat. Thirteen-year-old Benjamin Franklin made a best-selling ballad out of "The Lighthouse Tragedy."

A few small fires damaged the lantern in its first century. During the Revolution, colonial troops dismantled the light to prevent its helping the British; in 1776, the retreating British stopped to detonate it. It was rebuilt in 1783.

Shipping interests grew stronger and notions of a protective government did, too. Six other lighthouses were built on points and islands outlying Massachusetts harbors, and buoys were arranged as channel markers at Newburyport and Boston. A post-Revolution national government took responsibility for the lighthouses in 1790 and 1791, and built still more.

No other coastal state had more than one lighthouse at the time the U.S. government took charge of them. Several had none. Today, there are over a thousand along the American coast. Boston Light is now a national landmark in the Harbor Islands National Park Area, and is cared for by the U.S. Coast Guard.

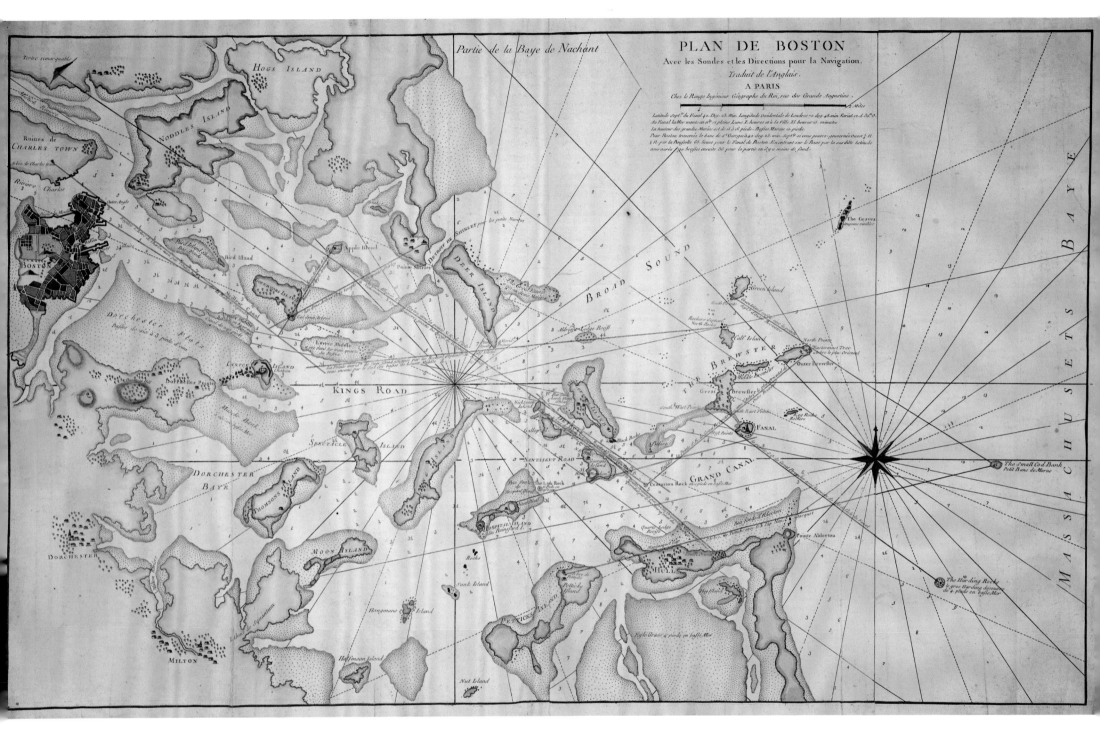

Plate 18
George Louis Le Rouge (fl. 1740–1780)
Plan de Boston
(Paris: Ingenieur Geographe du Roi, 1778)
Engraving. 51 x 84 cm.

This map shows Boston Harbor in fine detail with its islands, shoals, fortifications, and Boston peninsula. This is the French edition of Sayer & Bennet's *Chart of the Harbour of Boston* published in 1777 and included in the *North American Pilot*.

Le Rouge's *Atlas Ameriquain Septentrional* (1778) was considered the best collection of French maps for North America during the Revolutionary War. It contains French versions of maps originally published by William Faden and Thomas Jefferys including the large map of North America by John Mitchell.

Le Rouge's *Neptune Americo-Septentrionale* (1778) became the official reference of the French Navy for North America and included twenty-five detailed hydrographic charts showing soundings, shoals, and significant topographic features.

This portrait of Des Barres by artist J. Gambardella (ca. 1925), was copied after an earlier painting by Des Barres himself.

JOSEPH FREDERICK WALLET DES BARRES

Joseph Frederick Wallet Des Barres (1721–1824) created the *Atlantic Neptune*, a collection of the handsomest, most detailed, and most accurate charts of American coastal waters ever undertaken at that time. Unfortunately, they were used against American forces during the Revolution.

Des Barres arrived at this assignment from the British Admiralty by a circuitous route. Born of French Huguenot parents who had emigrated to Switzerland, he grew up and attended university in Basel, where he studied with highly regarded mathematicians and faced some continuing persecution. He may have fled to England after killing an antagonist in a duel. There, in 1753, at age thirty-two, he entered the Royal Military College. He graduated just in time to be appointed a Lieutenant in the Royal American Regiment, shipping out for the French and Indian War under General Howe.

Des Barres faced action at Schenectady, Lake George, Ticonderoga, and the shelling-siege of Quebec. His first surveying assignment seems to have been to prepare plans of the battle site at Quebec and of the city itself, and a survey of the harbor. Shortly thereafter he was sent to survey Halifax, Nova Scotia and prepare plans for its dockyards and fortifications. In 1763, with his work increasingly recognized, though never rewarded to his satisfaction with promotions or salary, Des Barres was assigned to survey the entire coast of Nova Scotia.

Now Des Barres's talents and energy began to shine. He had the benefit of working with the increasingly refined cartographic instruments of the mid-eighteenth century. And, although he was constantly frustrated by misunderstandings with the British military bureaucracy, he had the benefit of working within a large organization, which allowed him to assemble a good size staff and, when the opportunity to produce the *Atlantic Neptune* came along later, to use the work of others in the organization who had charted southerly American waters.

Des Barres spent ten years surveying the Nova Scotia coast from spring to fall. Winters, he headed home to Castle Frederick in Falmouth, where he kept a teenage mistress who bore him six children during his long absences from his English wife and his other eleven children. During the long New England winters, Des Barres and his staff drafted their surveys into charts.

Des Barres finished the charts of Nova Scotia in 1773, which made him just the candidate sought by the Admiralty in 1774 to produce charts of the American coast for British naval ships as the first skirmishes of the Revolution broke out. Des Barres collected charts and published them in five volumes, by region, as the *Atlantic Neptune,* in 1777, 1780, 1781, and 1784. (Some scholars mention other editions.) The charts were highly praised and were superior to American charts, surpassing even the knowledge of American navigators. Collectors now prize them.

With the end of the Revolution came the demise of the English Board of Trade that had governed many American affairs. Des Barres found he could not get paid for his work on the *Atlantic Neptune,* but he was promoted to major and sent as lieutenant governor to Cape Breton. He selected a deep, sheltered harbor for the site of his new capital and drew up plans. Quarreling with his fellow officers led Des Barres to be recalled after only two years. In England he pursued a long campaign to recover his good name; this echoed his earlier campaigns to receive payment and presaged later campaigns to rectify the state of his American and Canadian landholdings, most of which were mortgaged, and which, at one time, amounted to 80,000 acres.

If these suits show a querulous nature they must also be taken as an indication of the energy that allowed Des Barres to pursue his difficult assignments diligently, and allowed him to live to the ripe old age of 103. From age eighty-three to ninety-two he served as governor of Prince Edward Island and was, reportedly, still spry at the age of 100.

Plate 19

Joseph F. W. Des Barres and George Callender

{Boston Harbor}

From *Charts of the coast and harbors of New England . . . By J. F. W. Des Barres* (London, 1781)

Engraving. 72 × 52 cm. Second edition

In 1764 the British, recognizing that the existing charts of the North American coast were inadequate, began a new survey of the coast using the most advanced hydrographic instruments available. The northern part of the survey, under the direction of Samuel Holland, began at the Bay of Fundy and worked southward. One of the surveyors was Joseph F. W. Des Barres, the compiler, editor, engraver, and publisher of the charts that are known collectively as the *Atlantic Neptune*. No two sets of the *Atlantic Neptune* are identical. Each volume was composed of charts selected for

a particular purpose or mission. Many volumes also contain views of harbors, drawn to help navigators recognize important landmarks. The *Atlantic Neptune* is considered one of the finest examples of eighteenth-century printing, and much of the credit is due to Des Barres. The chart reproduced here was based on surveys of Boston Harbor made in 1769 by George Callender. The Des Barres chart was the basis of many maps of Boston issued during the Revolution (see plate 18, for example).

Samuel McIntire figurehead (ca. 1800).

MARITIME MASSACHUSETTS IN 1790

By 1790, the year of Matthew Clark's chart at right, the destruction and sacrifice of the Revolution and the difficult years of reconstruction finally lay behind. Massachusetts had begun to recover the maritime prosperity that had fueled her growth since colonial times. The atlas from which Clark's chart comes, the first marine atlas published in America, served the cod fisherman and whalers who were recovering their trade from wartime decimation as well as the mercantile adventurers who, in the face of limitations on trade with the British West Indies, were forced to configure new trade routes.

After experimental voyages to China by New York, Boston, and Salem ships during the early to mid-1880s, the Massachusetts China Trade took off. In 1890, three Salem ships returned to port from the grueling route of up to 41,000 miles or eighteen months passage, and one to Boston. Their cargoes of teas and silks held great promise, and a trade developed with Russia as well. The new level of accuracy and detail that Clark's map represented helped many a captain navigate safely through home waters with new swiftness and confidence.

Though Philadelphia and New York had long outstripped Boston in size, the maritime supremacy of Massachusetts remained secure for a few more decades. With shipping proceeding from Boston, Salem (which in 1790 was the sixth largest city in America), and Newburyport, fishing from Gloucester and other ports, and whaling from New Bedford and Nantucket, maritime Massachusetts now entered a period of prosperity that grew steadily until Jefferson's Embargo of 1807 and the War of 1812.

Not only did maritime Massachusetts fuel the entire Massachusetts economy, it also ran the Commonwealth, as historian Samuel Eliot Morison describes it, "by the simple device of apportioning the state senate according to taxable wealth." Thus, during this time, the struggling farmers of the interior, and the poorer citizens of Boston itself, fared badly, for merchants supported inequitable tax measures. By 1790, however, reviving maritime wealth began to ease life somewhat for the farmers as mercantile goods became abundant once more and farm products regained some of their value.

After the War of 1812 the superior access to western markets of ports such as New York and Philadelphia began to create a shift in the Massachusetts economy. Ships needed to return to the best points of distribution for their cargo and while Boston survived for a while in this hierarchy—until the arrival of railroads in the 1830s—the smaller coastal towns such as Salem and Newburyport lost business and population more quickly.

Massachusetts's economy shifted from maritime commerce to industry. In the old ports at Salem, Newburyport, and Nantucket one still finds the grand houses of eighteenth- and nineteenth-century sea captains and merchants; Gloucester still hosts a fishing industry. But these are remnants of a bygone prosperity.

Plate 20
Matthew Clark (1714–1798)
Chart of the Coast of America
From *Charts of the coast of America from Cape Breton to the
entrance of the Gulf of Mexico* (Boston, 1790)
Engraving. Chart sizes vary

Clark advertised his charts in the July 5, 1790, *Boston
Gazette* as having just been published. Clark was then sev-
enty-six years old. This example represents the New
England section from the first marine atlas published in
America. This section is shown in three sheets (sheets five,
six, and seven) of the eighteen charts that were offered for
separate sale or as an untitled volume. These charts resemble their British counterparts but have added local information including soundings, shoals, channels, currents,
and towns and harbors.

Of particular interest is the inset map of the
approach to Boston, since it is the first chart of the harbor
surveyed and printed in America. The charts were designed
for Boston merchants, as well as for ship navigation, and
include the earliest accurate survey of the Nantucket Shoals.

Although the charts are generally uniform in design,
they vary in scale. They are usually found joined in pairs so
that adjacent shorelines could be studied and their identification aided by the shoreline profiles that were included.

Clark's charts also introduce Osgood Carleton, a
well-known Boston surveyor, publisher, and mathematician. The Boston Marine Society, an organization of New
England shipmasters, recommended him as the person to
sign the plate and proof sheets of each chart on behalf of
the society. He was to sign all of the charts that would be
sold separately and at least one of the bound volumes. In
spite of these approvals, Clark's charts were generally
thought to reveal limited planning and hasty execution.
They did serve local mariners for some time, however, and
added additional information not available on the Des
Barres charts.

The ca. 1830 watercolor of J. and T. H. Perkins Co. ships *Levant* and *Milo* was copied after an oil painting by an unknown Chinese artist.

A ledger sheet made by Ephraim Bumstead a few months after his arrival in Canton, China shows the expenses of J. and T. H. Perkins Co., mainly related to the freighting of the ship *Rose,* bound for Nantucket. Note the large payments to Houqua, Canton's most powerful merchant and an important influence on, and ally of, John Perkins Cushing.

JOHN PERKINS CUSHING AND THE BRAHMIN OPIUM FORTUNES

In 1803, while his ship lay berthed at Providence before the five-month voyage to China, sixteen-year-old John Perkins Cushing wrote blithely to his grandmother, "On my account you may rest perfectly easy for I have every thing to make me happy. A beautiful ship[,] an excellent captain and good officers. . . . Uncle Tom H. P. has not said anything to me about my adventure altho I suppose he has put it under the care of Mr. Bumstead until we arrive at Canton."

Uncle Tom was Boston's Thomas Handasyd Perkins—shortly to become the most powerful shipping magnate of early nineteenth-century America—who had raised his nephew, orphaned at age ten. On his "adventure" in China, Cushing was to serve as assistant to Ephraim Bumstead, agent for the Perkins shipping firm, whose trade with China had become its mainstay. In April 1805, Perkins learned that Bumstead had died after only a year in China, leaving his barely eighteen-year-old nephew as the firm's sole representative in Canton.

Shortly after this shocking news came the first Perkins shipment of China teas, purchased and loaded under Cushing's supervision. Around his twentieth birthday, Cushing emerged from Canton for a six-week visit to Boston as a full partner in Perkins & Company.

After another dozen years in Canton, Cushing had translated a gentlemanly nature into a reputation for honesty, intelligence, and generosity. He had formed a close friendship with Houqua, the wealthiest and most powerful of the Hong merchants, renowned for qualities similar to Cushing's. He had also sniffed out the opium market in China at his uncle's request, and helped to lay the groundwork for the lucrative American opium trade that followed. No foreigner in Canton enjoyed more prominence or success and, through Cushing's good work, Perkins & Company came to monopolize at least half of the American trade with China.

Since opium smuggling was illegal in China, Cushing cleverly concealed his opium trading through an alliance with the Boston firm of Bryant & Sturgis, whose operatives smuggled in the opium that paid for Cushing's purchases. Their joint interests were called The Boston Concern. Even after his retirement, Cushing continued to enhance his princely fortune through investments in opium ventures, apparently with no moral qualms accruing to his "honest" nature. Opium operations brought no shame to well-to-do Americans and the hazard of smuggling at Chinese ports was no worse than other inconveniences or risks associated with long voyages and shifting market conditions. At the same time, the particularly magnanimous brand of charity for which Cushing and some of his relatives were known may have forestalled any twinges of conscience.

Finally, at forty-three, in 1831, Cushing returned for good and retired, marrying Mary Louise Gardiner, daughter of the rector at Trinity Church, the next year. Soon thereafter they moved with their first child to a grand new estate in Watertown, which Cushing named Bellmont—which later became the name of the town that was apportioned off from Watertown in the area of the estate.

For the rest of his life, having lived so much of it as an orphan and expatriate, Cushing stayed close to Watertown. His diligently recorded diary begins on the day of the move to Watertown, and bears most attentively on his lavish gardens and green houses, gardeners' work, horticultural purchases, and each day's weather. Among the plant shipments Cushing received from around the world were some from his old friend, Houqua, whose luxurious garden may have first ignited Cushing's interest in horticulture. One can imagine Cushing inspecting his first shipment of Chinese peonies and traveling—through the easier routes of memory—to the exotic scenes of his youth.

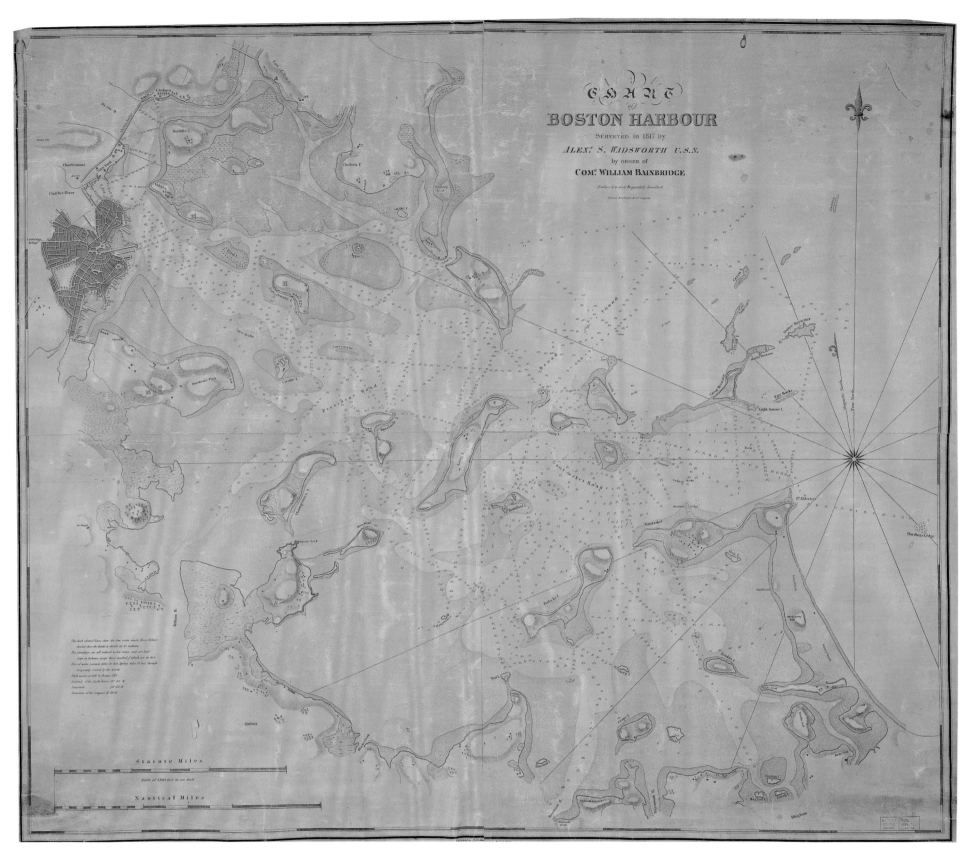

Plate 21
Alexander S. Wadsworth
Chart of Boston Harbor
(Philadelphia: John Melish, 1819)
Engraving. 90 x 105 cm.

In 1817 Alexander Wadsworth of the U.S. Navy surveyed the first official naval chart of Boston Harbor. The chart was prepared by order of and is inscribed to Commodore William Bainbridge, the recent commandant of the Charlestown Navy Yard and, in 1817, a member of the board of commissioners who ran the navy.

Wadsworth indicated not only the shoreline of all the landforms in the harbor but also their high points, surrounding tidal flats, marshes, and fortifications. In addi-

tion, he recorded many soundings in the shipping channels and between the islands, making this chart an important source of information about the condition of the harbor at that time. Although Wadsworth's rendition of the Boston peninsula and South Bay is somewhat schematic, one can easily see the outlet of South Bay, which became the Fort Point Channel. Also clearly depicted is the topography of Noddles Island, which would soon be developed as East Boston.

This wood engraving of Ferdinand Hassler, who commanded the first federally mandated survey of the American coast, appeared in *Harper's New Monthly Magazine* (March 1879).

THE UNITED STATES COAST SURVEY

After the American Revolution, and after Joseph F. W. Des Barres achieved a level of accuracy and detail for coastal charts of America to which others could only aspire, American shippers, ship captains, and navigators began to demand better charts of the coast. Initially, private publishers met this demand. This meant that areas such as Boston, a large port with a long merchant marine history, supported an active map and chart trade, and New York did as well. The ancient Boston Marine Society, representing the interests of shipmasters, hired Osgood Carleton, a highly respected teacher of mathematics and astronomy with hydrographic experience, to certify the accuracy of new charts of Massachusetts waters (see plate 20). The southern coast, however, was relatively neglected and, in the 1790s, Congress responded to public demand by passing occasional legislation initiating specific regional surveys.

Finally, in 1807, on the recommendation of the American Philosophical Society of Philadelphia, whose members included President Thomas Jefferson, Congress authorized a "Survey of the Coast." As it progressed over the next few decades, the survey gradually evolved into an agency of the U.S. government. Its supervisor was a new favorite of the Philosophical Society, Ferdinand Rudolph Hassler (1770–1843), a mathematician recently immigrated from Switzerland to whom meticulousness was second nature.

After delays in the bureaucratic process and the disruptions caused by the War of 1812, Hassler returned after four years in Europe, where he had supervised the crafting of the necessary instruments, and assembled a reference collection. It was 1815, and he spent the next year scouting possible locations for the creation of the base line for the survey with members of his new military staff.

The army and navy had done a limited number of coastal charts and maps addressed to specific undertakings, such as the building of coastal fortifications or the evaluation of a site being considered for a naval station. Some of their charts had been circulated by private publishers. Hassler was able to draw on the talents of some of the accomplished officers and to train younger, less experienced ones. Unfortunately, it appears that one naval officer was so zealous in his belief that the military should be in charge of the Coast Survey that he managed to delay the entire enterprise fourteen years by getting Congress to enact his view as legislation.

Work on the survey seems to have stopped or slowed until the act was repealed in 1832 and Hassler took over again at the age of sixty-two. The coast now ranged not just from Maine to Georgia but on to Florida, which the United States had purchased back from Spain in 1819, and around it to the Gulf of Mexico. Over the next few decades, the American coast would expand to include the Gulf states of Alabama, Louisiana, and, finally Texas, which the United States won from Mexico in 1848, along with New Mexico and California—the Pacific Coast.

Hassler lived just long enough to see the first fruits of his labors realized. By 1843, when he died, his operation had an extensive surveying department, a computing center, and engraving and printing facilities. His engravers were at work on a six-sheet chart of New York Harbor showing a new deep water channel that one of his surveyors had discovered.

The Coast Survey continued to produce impressive harbor charts (see figure 8 in chapter 5), although it was slowed by the loss of personnel to military duty during the Mexican War and the Civil War. Its esprit de corps fell a casualty to the Civil War, and it never entirely recovered. With a growing nation and rapidly progressing technologies, however, the bureaucracy itself was forced to change, and a series of new agencies would fall heir to the original Coast Survey office.

Plate 22
U.S. Coast Survey
Plan of the Inner Harbor of Boston
(1847)
Engraving. 2 sheets 56 × 91 cm. and 65 × 91 cm.

The U.S. Coast Survey was established in 1807 by President Jefferson. Under the direction of Ferdinand Rudolph Hassler, its first director, the first coastal surveys were produced in 1818 and then, owing to bureaucratic haggling, suspended until 1832. After Hassler's death in 1843, Alexander Dallas Bache, a scientist and great-grandson of Benjamin Franklin, was appointed superintendent of the Coast Survey. More charts were published during Bache's administration, one of them the first officially commissioned chart of Boston Harbor, which was surveyed in 1847 at the request of a state commission investigating possible development of the South Boston Flats.

The survey was made under the direction of Lt. Charles H. Davis of the navy. The state commission, which contributed to the cost of the survey, had asked that it determine the original shoreline of South Boston. This shoreline is marked with a dotted line as is the line 1650 feet seaward from it that delineated the limit of privately owned flats. The chart also shows accurately the amount of the Boston Wharf Company wharf that had actually been filled, in contrast to other schematic representations (see plate 36). And although the chart's purpose was to survey the South Boston Flats, the topography of the eastern end of South Boston and of Castle and Governor's Islands is rendered with the careful detail that characterized Coast Survey charts.

The 1847 U.S. Coast Survey chart had a large influence on Boston mapping, for the chart's original and 1847 shorelines of South Boston were reproduced on many subsequent maps.

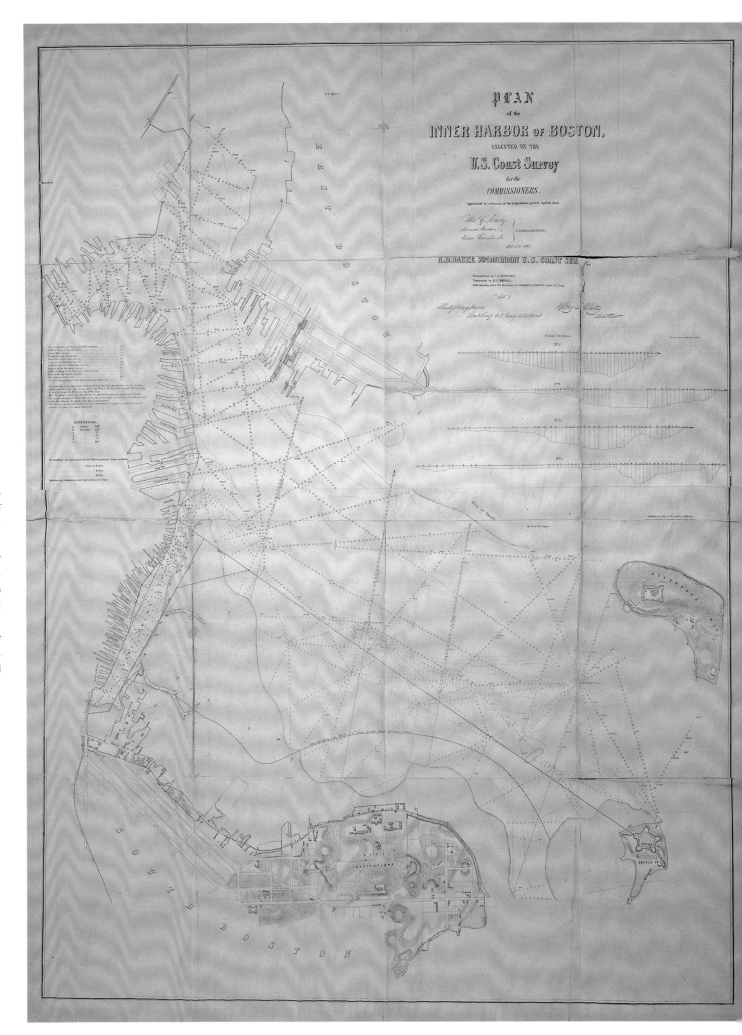

NASA high-altitude infrared photograph of the Boston metropolitan area (1980). The blue color indicates the area of urbanization: buildings, streets, parking lots, and other paved areas. Foliage and earth reflects infrared radiation and therefore the red indicates the open and natural areas of the region. Compare this maplike photograph to the 1893 Charles Eliot plan covering approximately the same area (figure 16 in chapter 8). The success of Eliot's vision to encircle turn-of-the-century Boston with a ring of open space is apparent by comparing the red in the NASA photograph with Eliot's plan for acquiring "public reservations."

MAPS AND THE U.S. GOVERNMENT

From Ptolemy to Mercator and well into the eighteenth century, the task of making a map could be accomplished by one individual, although actual surveying required the employment of assistants. As the accuracy of maps increased in

response to both demand and technical innovations, however, mapmaking became a government business, made up of multiple specialized disciplines. Currently, mapmaking in the United States lies in the hands of several government agencies, each employing cadres of scientists whose specialties range from quasars to marine sciences.

Since Ferdinand Rudolph Hassler's work supervising the Coast Survey, in which he established in New Jersey the first base point for a survey of the east coast, over a million geodetic survey points have been designated by descendent organizations of the Coast Survey. Meanwhile, mapmakers and earth-measurers have gone on to refine other aspects of their science. Measurements of distance on the earth can now be made with the help of quasars. The word *quasar* is short for QUASi-stellAR radio source—that is, celestial bodies four to ten billion light years distant that emit powerful radio energy. The radio waves of quasars strike different parts of the earth's surface at different times as the earth rotates, just as the sun's rays do.

Manmade satellites orbiting the earth are also programmed to assist those trying to pinpoint exact locations. Cellular phones and other consumer technologies are now available that can take advantage of this Global Positioning System, as the government calls it.

The complex mutations of government agencies keeping abreast of the latest advances in geodesy (the measurement of the earth) and geology (the study of the physical composition of the earth) began after the Civil War. First, in 1871, a congressional act expanded the Coast Survey's responsibilities to include the interior of the growing United States. The Coast Survey had already produced some interior maps for Union forces during the Civil War.

In 1878 the Coast Survey gave way to the United States Coast and Geodetic Survey and in 1879 a Geological Survey was established by Congress under the Department of the Interior. While still in its infancy, the United States Geological Survey prepared the map of Boston at right. The agency now employs geologists, geographers, cartographers, hydrologists, and biologists. Its various bureaus supervise all kinds of mining, oil, and water power concerns.

Before its functions were absorbed by a new office in the National Oceanic and Atmospheric Administration (NOAA) in 1970, the Coast and Geodetic Survey had prepared nearly one thousand nautical charts of U.S. waters and ten thousand aeronautic charts of U.S. air space. In both world wars, about half the Coast and Geodetic Survey staff was commissioned in the armed services where they played key roles in the planning of battles, troop movements, fleet movements, and intelligence operations in all theaters of the wars.

The NOAA now includes the National Weather Service; the National Marine Fisheries Service; the Office of Oceanic and Atmospheric Research; the National Environmental Satellite, Data and Information Service; the National Ocean Service; and the National Geodetic Survey. It is the scientists of the National Geodetic Survey who are charged with using quasars and satellites to study the motion of the earth's crust, gravity, polar motion, tides, and orbit.

Yet, even as the increasing sophistication of our study of the earth and its place in the universe brings us vast distances from the work of Ptolemy and Mercator, modern science leaves us facing a vast ocean of space. As we regard this new frontier, we can surmise the feelings of early cartographers who faced an earth too expansive for their tools and a blank and impenetrable ocean guarding its secrets.

Plate 23
U.S. Geological Survey
Massachusetts, Boston quadrangle
(Washington, surveyed in 1898–1900)
Lithograph. 45 × 33 cm.

The U.S. Geological Survey was created on March 3, 1879, and was an outgrowth of the early surveys of the West. President Hayes signed the bill and discontinued the three remaining western surveys. The earlier surveys had supplied extensive geographical information about the western United States but had become rivalries for appropriations and geographical limits. It was decided that a single permanent bureau would be more beneficial for the investigation of the nation's geology and mineral resources.

Clarence King was appointed as its first director and, after discussing the survey's role with Congress, he realized that a scientific classification of the nation's lands was required and that topographic mapping should be an integral part of this effort. The survey's annual budget included annual allocations for surveying and mapping as well as for updating, revisions, and new surveys.

It did not take long for the federal surveys to reach Massachusetts; surveys began in 1884 in the Dedham, Haverhill, Holyoke, Housatonic, Newburyport, Northampton, and Sheffield regions. The next year surveys began in the Boston area, resulting in the first topographic map of Boston (see figure 10 in chapter 5).

Topographic maps are a unique blend of physical geography and man-made human cultural features. Thus, we see an excellent delineation of the coastline, the course of rivers, locations of ponds and reservoirs, and the land's physical geography shown by brown contour lines. This information is supplemented with cultural information such as towns, roads and railroads, cemeteries, bridges, and place names. These maps provide a wealth of information and this particular map presents an accurate delineation of Boston and its surrounding region at the turn of the century. Comparing similar maps over a period of time reveals the growth of Boston and the eventual growth of its suburban core.

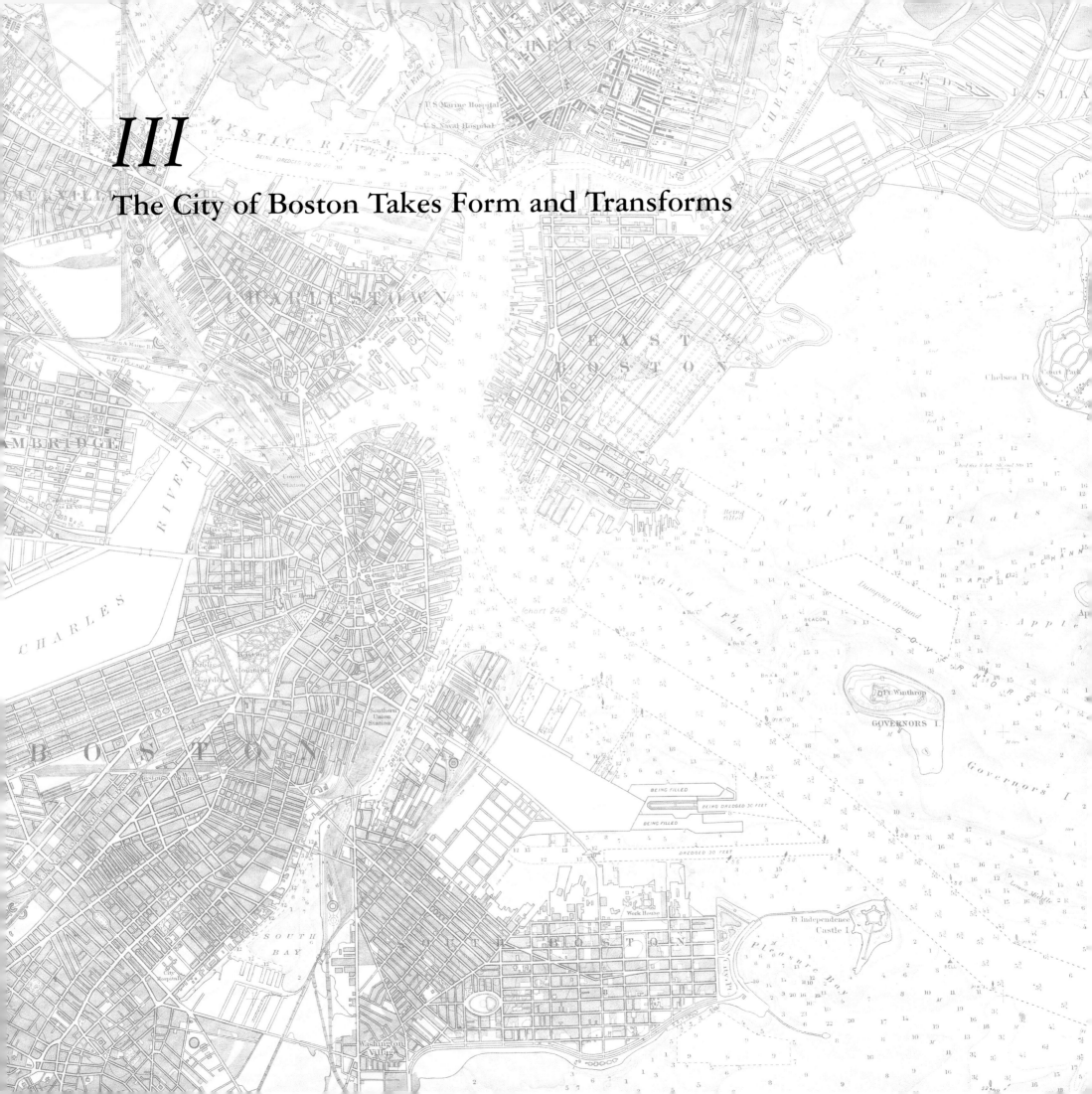

III
The City of Boston Takes Form and Transforms

N

0   1/2 Mile

Frontispiece Composite map of land-making projects. This map graphically shows the growth of Boston's land area and change in its shoreline from 1630, when Boston was established, to the present. This enormous transformation in size and shape resulted from filling in the tidal flats that once surrounded the city, a development discussed in the following chapter. The map itself is a composite of the computerized historical maps that are shown separately and described in chapter 2.

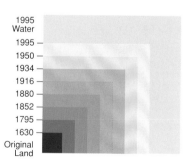

1995
Water

1995 —
1950 —
1934 —
1916 —
1880 —
1852 —
1795 —
1630 —
Original
Land

19th Century excavation

1995 shoreline with no historic changes shown

MapWorks•99

7

Gaining Ground: Boston's Topographical Development in Maps

Nancy S. Seasholes

Walt Whitman once compared maps of Boston to a sheet of writing paper that had been crumpled up, thrown down, and stamped flat.[1] He was referring to the maze of streets that the maps depict, but one can also trace other developments on these maps—the growth of different sections of the city, for example, or the proliferation of wharves along the waterfront. Certainly, however, one of the most dramatic changes illustrated by the maps is the enormous transformation of the city in both size and shape. Part of the increase in area is, of course, due to the annexation of adjacent but once-separate towns such as Roxbury, Dorchester, and Charlestown. Much of the expansion and altered configuration on the waterfront side of the city, however, has resulted from the addition of thousands of acres of land made by filling in areas once covered by water, a process known as *land making.* Land has been made in Boston for many reasons—commercial developments, new residential areas, transportation routes and facilities, and parks—and the progress of this land making can be traced on successive maps of the city.[2]

Boston was established in 1630 on a small peninsula roughly the shape of a three-lobed leaf, the lobes being hilly promontories separated by deeply indented coves and the stem a narrow neck connecting the peninsula to the mainland, a landform that still existed in the late eighteenth century (see plate 28). During the seventeenth and eighteenth centuries some land was added to this constricted peninsula to accommodate the growing town. Most of this land was created by a process known as *wharfing out*—extending wharves out from the shore and eventually filling the slips, or docks, between them. Wharfing out was facilitated by Massachusetts's unique riparian law, which gives shoreline property owners rights to the adjacent tidal flats down to the low tide line or 1650 feet from the line of high tide, whichever is closest to shore (in other states private property ends at the high tide mark), a law passed in the 1640s to encourage the building of wharves. Archaeologists have found that land was also made along the shore of one cove in the early eighteenth century by laying down a gridwork of timbers and then dumping fill on top of them.[3] And some land was created in the eighteenth century when several enclosed docks, which had been excavated in the seventeenth century to provide shelter for the small ships of that era, were filled in both because

they could not accommodate larger eighteenth-century ships and because, since their enclosure prevented them from being adequately flushed out by the tide, they had become odoriferous receptacles for sewage and filth. A comparison of the 1722 Bonner and 1743 Price maps (see plates 24 and 26) shows, for example, that Faneuil Hall is built on land made by filling in part of the Town Dock (see also plate 26 vignette), which once extended inland as far as the eponymous Dock Square. For the most part, however, the land of the original Boston peninsula sufficed for the town for almost two hundred years.

In the 1790s, however, Boston began to grow rapidly. The economy, which had been depressed since the 1740s, revived with the inauguration of the China trade, and the population, which had also been static since the 1740s, almost doubled between 1790 and 1810. But with most of the original peninsula already occupied, the town clearly needed more land and the question was where this land was to be obtained. Expanding to a site on the mainland was not even considered at the time—commerce was focused around the wharves on the harbor side of the original peninsula and surrounding areas either did not have developed harbors or were part of other towns (see plates 29 and 30). So the solution adopted by Bostonians at the turn of the nineteenth century was to *make* more land by filling in the large expanses of tidal flats—areas covered with water at high tide but exposed mud flats at low—and marshes—low-lying land usually above the high tide line but interlaced with tidal creeks—that surrounded the peninsula.

Where Bostonians acquired the concept of large-scale land making is not clear. Some have assumed that, because the areas filled were so vast, the method used to make land must have been based on the Dutch model of diking, pumping, and draining to reclaim land from the sea.[4] But contemporary accounts make it clear that land in Boston was not created by a process of reclamation. Instead, the technique used to make land was related to the technique used to construct wharves—a structure, usually a stone seawall, was built around the perimeter of an area to be filled and then fill was dumped into the area enclosed until the level of the fill was above the level of high tide. Whatever the origin of the idea and method, however, it is clear that at the beginning of the nineteenth century Bostonians embarked on massive land-making projects.

Some of the first projects made land for residential use. In 1803–1805 the westernmost peak of Beacon Hill (known as Mount Whoredom, as Page acknowledges on his 1777 map [see plate 28], thanks to the red light district on its north slope, but renamed Mount Vernon as more suitable for a residential area), was cut down as a speculative venture to develop house lots on the hill. The dirt was dumped on the flats in the Charles River at the foot of the hill, creating the land where Charles Street now runs, as one can see when comparing this area on the 1796 Carleton and 1814 Hales maps (see plates 31 and 32). Between 1804 and 1806 new land was created on the east side of the Neck as part of a deal made when South Boston was annexed in 1804. The speculators intending to develop South Boston planned to connect it to the main part of Boston with a bridge from the north side of South Cove, the large cove on the east side of the Neck that can be seen on the Frentzel and Pelham maps (see plates 27 and 29). But the owners of wharves in the cove, realizing such a bridge would impede access to their wharves, convinced the speculators to build the bridge much further south on the Neck—on the line of present East Berkeley Street—by offering to build a new street to the bridge. The tidal flats between this new street, originally called Front Street but later renamed Harrison Avenue, and the shore were then filled as part of the project, as can be seen in a comparison of this area on the 1796 Carleton and 1814 Hales maps (see plates 31 and 32). And between 1807 and 1828 the Mill Pond, a large cove that had been dammed off in the mid-seventeenth century to power some tide mills but had become polluted and filthy and thus, at a time when it was thought diseases were caused by bad odors, considered a health hazard, was filled to make house lots for working-class residents. The Mill Pond before it was filled is shown on the 1796 Carleton map (see plate 31) and when the project was in process on the 1814 Hales map (see plate 32). The area created by filling the Mill Pond is now known as the Bulfinch Triangle, for the street plan was drawn up by architect Charles Bulfinch who, as one of the town's selectmen, was on the committee appointed to devise such a plan (figure 1). The Mill Pond was filled with gravel obtained by cutting down the central peak of Beacon Hill, now the site of the rear wing of the State House (figure 2).

Other early land-making projects created land for commercial use. Between 1803 and 1807 India Wharf, a "modern" deepwater stone wharf with handsome brick buildings designed by Bulfinch, was built where Harbor Towers is now located. As part of the project, two new streets—Broad and India—were laid out and filled across the old zigzagging wooden wharves between State Street and the new India Wharf, creating two broad thoroughfares along the waterfront, as can be seen in a comparison of the 1796 Carleton and 1814 Hales maps (see plates 31 and 32).

At least one of the early land-making projects spawned a later one. In order to replace the public grist mill that had been discontinued when the Mill Pond was filled, the entire Back Bay of the Charles River was

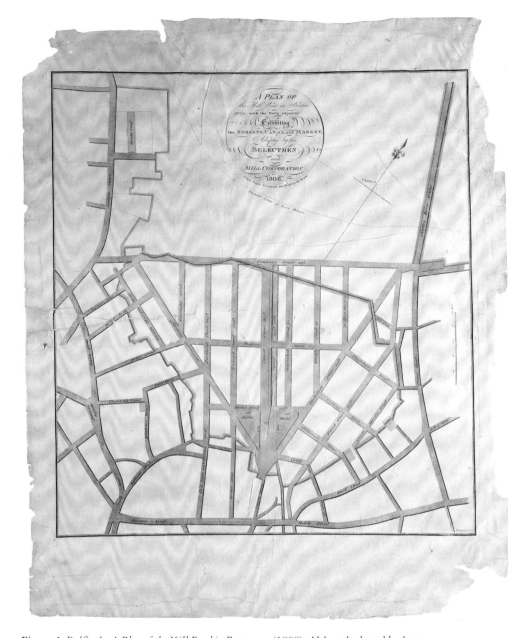

Figure 1 Bulfinch, *A Plan of the Mill Pond in Boston . . .* (1808). Although altered by later developments, some of the street plan that Bulfinch devised for the Mill Pond in 1808 is still intact, particularly the left-hand side, the two prominent diagonals—now Merrimac and North Washington Streets—and Causeway Street across the base of the triangle. The canal down the middle has been replaced by the tracks of the Green and Orange Lines and the Central Artery now slices across the right-hand side of the triangle.

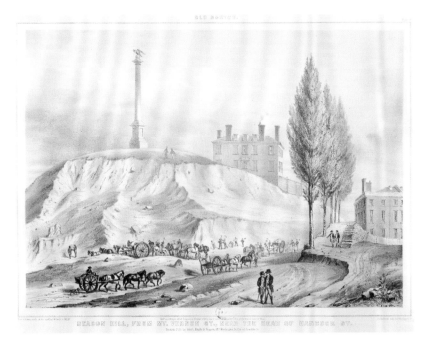

Figure 2 Drawing by J. R. Smith of cutting down Beacon Hill, seen from Mt. Vernon Street (1811). Drawn at the scene in 1811, this view gives some idea of the height of the original crest of Beacon Hill, now the location of the rear wing of the State House, which was estimated to have been sixty feet higher than at present. The view also shows the methods used in early land-making projects—dirt and gravel were dug by hand with picks and shovels and carried in horse-drawn tip carts. The house in the center was on Bowdoin Street and soon had to be taken down, its foundation undermined by cutting down the hill behind it.

dammed off in 1818–1821 to power other tide mills. The new Mill Dam extended on the line of present Beacon Street all the way from the foot of the Common to Sewall's Point in Brookline, now Kenmore Square. A cross dam (on the line of present Hemenway Street) was constructed on Gravelly Point, a marshy promontory in the vicinity of today's Massachusetts Avenue, dividing the Back Bay into two basins, as shown on Hales's 1830 map of Boston (see plate 34). At high tide, water entered the full basin through gates in the main dam, flowed through sluiceways in the cross dam, powering mills there, and then ran into the receiving basin where, at low tide, it drained out through gates in the main dam back into the river. A toll road (now Beacon Street) on top of the Mill Dam provided another link between the Boston peninsula and the mainland in addition to four bridges that had been built since the late eighteenth century, all shown on the 1826 Annin and Smith map (see plate 33).

In 1822 Boston adopted a city form of government, the former town meeting system no longer practical for the more than 40,000 inhabitants and 7000 voters. As a fitting project for the new city, Josiah Quincy, the second mayor, decided to replace the old crowded central market near

Faneuil Hall with a new one (see plate 33 vignette). The docks and wharves east of Faneuil Hall were filled in and a long central market building, now called Quincy Market, flanked by two blocks of stores, the North and South Market buildings, were built on the made land (see figure 4 in chapter 8), resulting in what Quincy called a "noble improvement" (figure 3; see also figure 8 in chapter 1).[5] After the new marketplace opened in 1826, two new streets—Commercial and Fulton—were extended to the North End in 1827–1830 by filling the intervening flats and wharves, somewhat as India and Broad streets had been created south of the market area earlier in the century. The Faneuil Hall Market project, as it was then called, and the projected Commercial and Fulton Streets are shown on the 1826 Annin and Smith map (see plate 33), and the two new streets are shown completed on the 1835 Smith map (see plate 35).

More residential land also continued to be made for Boston's burgeoning population. After the Mill Dam was completed in 1821, owners of property along the shore of Back Bay south of the Common began to

Figure 3 Lithograph by John Andrews of Faneuil Hall Market from the east (1827). When the Faneuil Hall Market project was completed in 1826, Commercial Street ran next to the water in front of the new buildings, as can be seen on the 1826 Annin and Smith map (see plate 33). In Andrews's view, one can see the new central market building, now called Quincy Market, with Faneuil Hall behind it and the North and South Market buildings on either side. The vantage point from which Andrews drew the view has long since been filled in and is now the location of Marketplace Center.

fill in their flats, aided by a city-built dike that cut off the water of the receiving basin. Filling of this area south of the present Public Garden was completed in the mid-1830s, creating what was once called the Church Street District and is now the Bay Village and Park Square areas, the area on the shore between the railroad tracks on the 1835 Smith map (see plate 35). To encourage residential development of what were known as the Neck Lands, now the section of the South End south of East Berkeley (formerly Dover) Street, in 1829 the city decided to improve access to them by building two new streets—Front Street (now Harrison Avenue) on the southeast side of the Neck and Tremont Street on the northwest. Front Street was filled and constructed between 1831 and 1836. To build Tremont Street, the city constructed a dike in the receiving basin that joined the dike on the west side of the Church Street District and by 1836 had filled the intervening flats. The filling that created these two new streets, as well as that of the flats between present East Berkeley Street and the Church Street District, which were filled by their private owners, can be seen in a comparison of the 1826 Annin and Smith and 1835 Smith maps (see plates 33 and 35). And although not for residential use, most of the land now the Public Garden was created in the 1830s when a dike was extended from the one on the west side of the Church Street District to the Mill Dam and the enclosed flats filled (see plate 36 vignette), a development that can be traced by comparing the 1835 and 1846 Smith maps (see plate 35 and figure 4).

The introduction of railroads in the 1830s not only revolutionized transportation but also created a need for yet more land in Boston. The first three railroads to enter the city were all completed in 1835 and all had depots on made land. In addition, two of them, the Boston & Providence and Boston & Worcester, crossed the receiving basin in Back Bay on embankments that had been built up above the water (figure 5). The Boston and Providence depot was on made land about where the Park Plaza Hotel is today. The Boston and Lowell depots were on land that had been created for that purpose by filling flats north of Causeway Street, shown on the 1835 Smith map (see plate 35)—the area where the O'Neill Federal and Registry of Motor Vehicles buildings are now located.

The depots for the Boston & Worcester Railroad were on newly made land in South Cove. A more direct bridge to South Boston had finally been built in 1827–1828 approximately where the Dorchester Avenue Bridge is today, virtually cutting off the wharves in South Cove just as the owners of these wharves had once predicted and as the 1830 Hales map shows (see plate 34). The wharf owners had then decided it would be more profitable to fill the cove than to keep it open for shipping and in the early 1830s offered to pay one of the new railroads to locate its terminals there. The Boston & Worcester accepted. Filling began in 1833 and by 1839 the part of South Cove north of what is now the Massachusetts Turnpike had been filled in, as shown on the 1835 Smith map (see plate 35). The rest of South Cove, between what are now the turnpike and East Berkeley Street, was filled in the 1840s, creating land on which housing for railroad workers was soon erected. Part of the South Cove project also involved constructing wharves along the Fort Point Channel, which was the outlet of South Bay—the large tidal bay that lay between the Neck and South Boston. This additional filling in South Cove can be seen in a comparison of that area on the 1835 and 1846 Smith maps (see plate 35 and figure 4).

Land was also added in the 1830s to parts of Boston beyond the original peninsula. In South Boston, which had begun to develop rapidly after the opening of the new bridge in 1828, Cyrus Alger, the owner of an iron foundry, filled a large triangle on the west side of the South Boston peninsula, shown on the 1835 Smith map (see plate 35), in order to create more land for his iron works and in the process formed the east side of the Fort Point Channel opposite the South Cove wharves on the west. And the Boston Wharf Company began to construct an enormous wharf north of the seawall that ran along First Street on the north side of South Boston, as can be seen in a comparison of the 1835 and 1846 Smith maps (see plate 35 and figure 4). The development of East Boston also began in the 1830s. In 1833, an heir of Noddles Island in Boston's harbor, which is shown on the 1830 Hales map (see plate 34) and was a virtually uninhabited series of hills and marshes on which livestock were raised, formed the East Boston Company to develop the island as a new residential and industrial section of the city. By the 1840s the waterfront facing the harbor was lined with wharves of various maritime industries, as indicated in an inset on the 1846 Smith map (figure 4).

Although not yet part of Boston, land was also added to Charlestown, the town on the peninsula just across the Charles River from Boston and clearly visible on the Frentzel and Pelham maps (see plates 27 and 29). Settled by a group of Massachusetts Bay colonists in 1629, a year before Boston, Charlestown's development had been quite similar to the larger town's. In the seventeenth and eighteenth centuries wharves had been built along the Charlestown harborfront, an enclosed Town Dock had been developed, and the head of the bay between Charlestown and what is now Somerville had been dammed to power tide mills, developments shown on the Pelham map (see plate 29). In the first half of the nineteenth century, land was made in Charlestown for railroads, just as it was in Boston, since Charlestown's location ensured that most railroads entering Boston from the north would cross Charlestown. In the 1840s the Fitchburg Railroad filled about fifteen acres on Charlestown's southwestern waterfront and the Boston & Maine created an island in the river for an engine house and other service structures (figure 6). One reason for making land in Charlestown was unique to that city, however. In 1800 the federal government had purchased a thirty-five-acre tract on Charlestown's southeast waterfront for a navy yard—a shipyard for repairing or constructing U.S. Navy ships. Over the years land was added to the

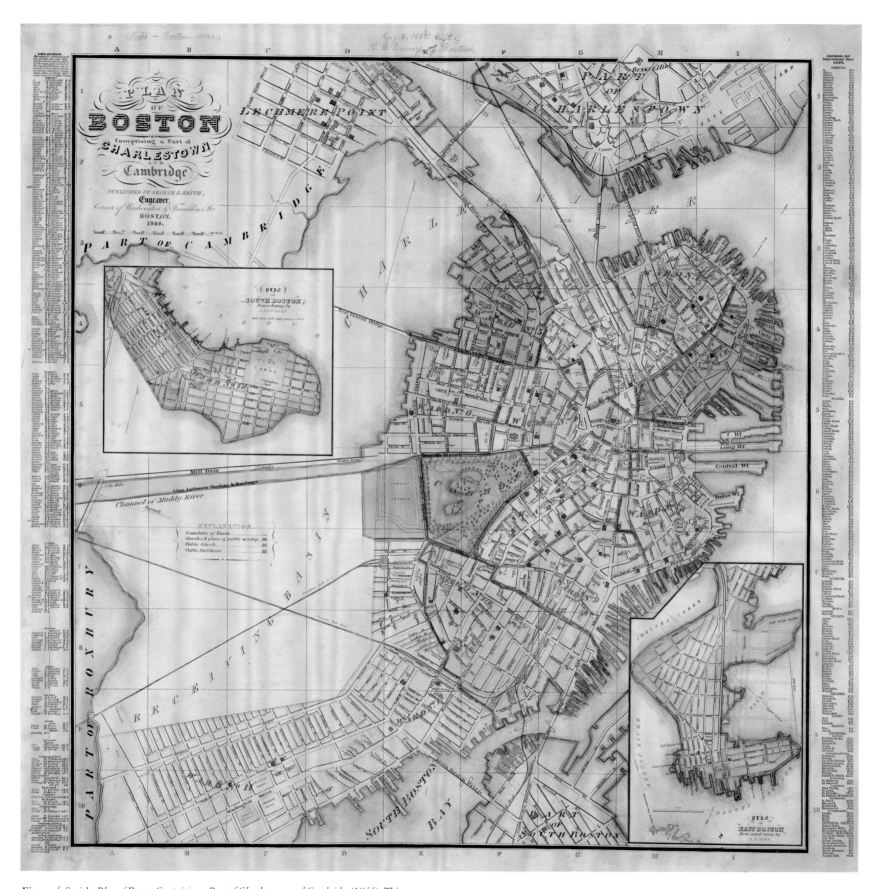

Figure 4 Smith, *Plan of Boston Comprising a Part of Charlestown and Cambridge* (1846). This map is an update of the 1835 Smith map (see plate 35) which was, in turn, an update of the 1826 Annin and Smith map (see plate 33). The 1846 Smith map is more accurate than the 1848 Dearborn (see plate 36) and is thus a better reference for tracing the land making of that era.

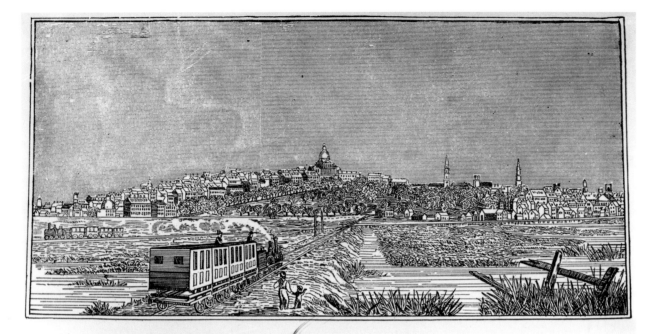

WORCESTER AND PROVIDENCE RAILROAD CROSSING.

navy yard by wharfing out, enclosing and later filling timber docks (areas on the waterfront in which shipbuilding timber was stored in salt water), and creating land for the huge shiphouses in which wooden sailing ships were constructed, eventually more than doubling the size of the original navy yard (figure 6).

By the mid-1840s, Irish immigrants, fleeing the potato famine in Ireland, were pouring into Boston. Between 1840 and 1850 the city's population grew from 93,383 to 136,881—an increase of 46.6 percent—and by 1850 almost 26 percent of Boston's residents were Irish-born. The city's response was to encourage well-to-do Yankees (euphemistically called the "business classes"), who were valued both as voters and as taxpayers, to remain in the city rather than move to the suburbs. So in the 1840s the city began to develop the South End, the one still relatively unoccupied section, as a desirable residential area by laying out a series of squares and parks, planting trees, and grading streets.

As part of the development of the South End, the flats along South Bay were filled, a project undertaken so that the sewers, which at the time simply discharged raw sewage at the nearest shoreline, could be extended to deep water rather than drain onto the flats, the city could profit from the sale of the made land for house lots, and new wharves could be constructed on South Bay. The South Bay Lands project, as it came to be called, involved filling all the flats and marshes in the bay south of present Malden Street, an area shown on Chesbrough's 1852 reconstruction of the original shoreline and areas of made land (see plate 37). To carry out the project, the city contracted in 1848 with a William Evans, who built

a railroad spur across South Bay from the Old Colony Railroad in South Boston, shown on both the 1852 Chesbrough and 1852 Slatter and Callan maps (see plates 37 and 38), in order to bring gravel fill from Quincy—a precursor of the method used to fill Back Bay a decade later.

Back Bay was another land-making project designed to attract wealthy residents. The Mill Dam project had not been a success—the dam had not only failed to provide adequate power for the tide mills but it also prevented sewage, which drained into the receiving basin from surrounding areas, from being carried off by the tide. The railroad embankments built across the basin in the 1830s further impeded the flow of water (figure 5), and by 1849, in the words of a city report, Back Bay had become "a great cesspool . . . [with] a greenish scum, many yards wide, stretch[ing] along the shore of the basin . . . whilst the surface of the water . . . bubbl[es] like a cauldron with the noxious gases that are exploding from the corrupting mass below."[6] The solution, almost all agreed, was to extend the sewers out beyond the Mill Dam and to fill the area enclosed by the dam.

In 1854, the Boston Water Power Company, which operated the mills, and the state—the two major owners of the flats in Back Bay—divided the receiving basin, the state getting the area now between Beacon and Boylston Streets from Arlington to a line between Exeter and Fairfield and the Boston Water Power Company all the rest. The Boston Water Power Company began filling its flats in 1855 and the state its area in 1858 (figure 7). The state contracted with two railroad builders, who arranged to have gravel brought nine miles from suburban Needham on

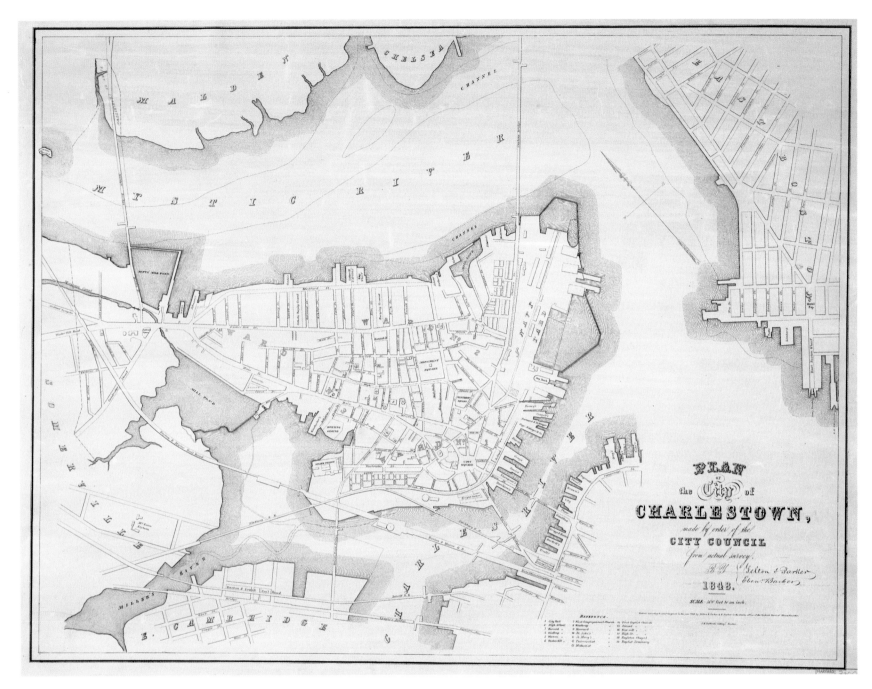

Figure 6 Felton and Parker, *Plan of the City of Charlestown* . . . (1848). In 1848 Charlestown followed Boston's earlier lead and adopted a city form of government. One of the first acts of the new City Council was to order a plan made of the new municipality; surveyors Felton and Parker and Ebenezer Barker were hired for the project. The resulting map gives a good picture of Charlestown after two centuries of development.

Figure 7 Photograph of Back Bay from the State House (1858). In this view one can see the Mill Dam, now Beacon Street, stretching across Back Bay toward the Brookline hills in the distance. In the middle distance is the cross dam, on the line of what is now Hemenway Street, which met the main dam at a point now on Beacon Street between Hereford Street and Massachusetts Avenue. The two white buildings are the flour mills that were powered by the dam. Moving closer to Boston, one can see the unfilled flats belonging to the state, the trees on the line of what became Arlington Street, the rather barren Public Garden crossed by a few paths, and then, on the nearer side of a row of larger trees, the Common. The dome of the State House was a favorite vantage point for early panoramic photographs such as this one.

an existing railroad and then built a special track to Back Bay—much as
gravel had been brought by rail to fill South Bay a decade earlier. In
Needham the gravel was dug by steam shovels (figure 8), a train of thirty-five cars was loaded in ten minutes, and, with three trains each making
twenty-five trips a day, fifty-three of the state's one hundred acres were
filled by 1864 (see the 1860s photograph in plate 39 vignette). The rate
of filling then slowed, but the state's part of Back Bay was nonetheless
completed by 1876. The Boston Water Power Company arranged to have
its flats in the receiving basin filled by the same contractor but, with a
much larger area to be filled, the company's section was not finished until
the 1880s. The successive stages of filling Back Bay can be seen in a series
of reconstructed plans (figure 9).

While Back Bay was being filled, land was also being made elsewhere in Boston. By the 1850s the old docks on the central waterfront
were too narrow for the large new steamships then being built, so parts of
these docks were filled in and new buildings constructed on the made land
(figure 10), as can be seen in a comparison of this area on the 1852 Slatter
and Callan and 1862 City Engineer's maps (see plates 38 and 40). Then,
in the late 1860s and early 1870s Atlantic Avenue was constructed right
across these docks and wharves, drastically truncating them and slicing
the wharf buildings in two in order to lay a railroad track—a vivid
demonstration of the decreasing importance of the central waterfront and
the rising ascendancy of railroads over ships.

The Atlantic Avenue project arose, ironically, out of concern about
the decline of Boston's commerce, especially in relation to New York.
Shipping freight through Boston was impeded by lack of a rail connection
between the depots in South Cove (near present South Station) and those
in the Mill Pond/Causeway Street area (near present North Station). To
provide such a connection, it was originally proposed that tracks be laid
on streets that went around the central waterfront, but some began to
advocate shortening the route by building a new street across the wharves,
as shown on the 1870 City Surveyor's map (see plate 41). The final impetus for the Atlantic Avenue project was the need for a site on which to dispose the dirt from nearby Fort Hill, which was being cut down at the time
(figure 11; see also plate 41 vignette). Construction of Atlantic Avenue
across the wharves and docks began in 1869 (figure 12), filling of the
then-landlocked docks on the shoreward side of the street began in 1870,
smashing through the wharf buildings apparently occurred soon thereafter (figure 13), and in 1872 the new street was ready to have railroad
tracks laid on it (see figure 4 in chapter 1).

Meanwhile, concern that Boston was losing shipping to New York
City was manifesting itself in other ways. Although the real problem was
that New England had no large bulk export product and so, as a port,
Boston was always dependent on imports, in the mid-nineteenth century
the loss of shipping was usually attributed to problems of Boston Harbor.

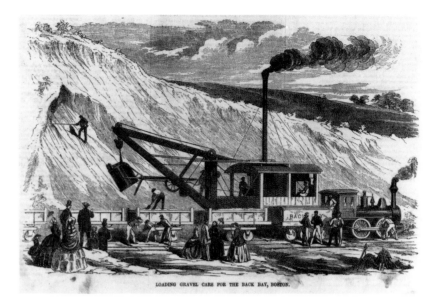

LOADING GRAVEL CARS FOR THE BACK BAY, BOSTON.

Figure 8 Engraving of a gravel train in Needham (1858). This engraving, which was
published in *Ballou's Pictorial* in October 1858, shows a gravel train being loaded in
Needham by one of the new "steam excavators" (shovels). When a train arrived in
Needham from Back Bay, it was divided into two sections. Each section was then attached
to a locomotive and pulled past one of the steam shovels, which filled an entire car with
just two shovelfuls. The presence of ladies in the drawing suggests that it was made on a
day of a VIP or public visit to the site.

Figure 9 Reconstructed plans of Back Bay by Fuller and Whitney (1851, 1861, 1871, 1881). In 1881 the firm of Fuller and Whitney, the surveyors for the Back Bay project, drafted a series of reconstructed plans of Back Bay showing the various stages of its filling.

The 1851 plan shows Back Bay just before the major land-making project began. The new land west of Tremont Street had recently been filled by the Boston Water Power Company.

The 1861 plan shows the state's flats filled beyond Clarendon Street and the Boston Water Power Company's flats being filled south of Boylston Street. A tongue of newly made land extending south from the intersection of the railroad tracks had probably been filled in order to lay a track for the gravel trains.

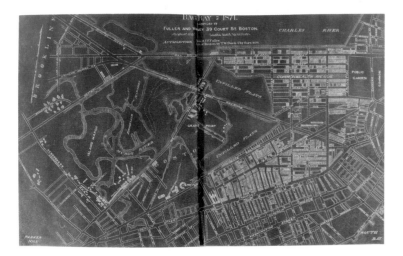

By 1871 the state's flats, which extended to a line between Exeter and Fairfield Streets, had been filled, but the Boston Water Power Company still had large unfilled areas.

By 1881 all the flats east of the original Gravelly Point had been filled and the marshes west of the point were being filled to create the Back Bay Fens.

Figure 10 Photo of the west end of the State Street Block (1998). In 1856 the head of the dock between Long and Central Wharves was filled and in 1857–1858 the State Street Block was erected on the newly made land, as can be seen in a comparison of the 1852 Slatter and Callan and 1862 City Engineer's maps (see plates 38 and 40). The western end of this handsome granite building remains as it was designed by architect Gridley J. Fox Bryant, but the eastern end was chopped off when the Central Artery was constructed in the 1950s.

Figure 11 Photograph of cutting down Fort Hill (ca. 1870). Fort Hill was cut down by a number of contractors, one of whom, John Souther, had operated the steam shovels in Needham that dug the gravel to fill Back Bay (figure 8). Souther also used steam shovels on Fort Hill, one of which is visible in the middle distance in this photograph. The shovel loaded dirt into small cars, which ran by gravity on movable tracks down to the docks. Dirt was also carried in horse-drawn tip carts, similar to those used earlier in the century on Beacon Hill (figure 2; see also plate 41 vignette).

Contemporaries focused on two main aspects of the harbor: its reduction in size as the result of extending wharves and filling tidal flats and its deterioration in quality thanks to shoaling of the shipping channels and erosion of the harbor islands. Reduction in size caused by encroachments into the harbor had been regulated since the 1830s when lines were set limiting how far wharves and fill could extend. Shoaling of the shipping channels was also thought to be related to fill for, at a time when the accepted theory was that the channels were kept open by the force, or *scour*, of the ebb tide, filling obviously reduced the amount of available water and thus, presumably, the scour. With no clear answers, however, in the late 1850s the city finally prevailed on the federal government to appoint a commission of experts to study Boston Harbor and make recommendations to prevent its further deterioration.

The U.S. Commissioners on Boston Harbor worked from 1860 to 1866, submitting ten reports on various topics. The commissioners increasingly focused on the South Boston Flats, the vast expanse of grass-covered mud flats that extended almost a mile north from the South

Figure 12   Detail from 1870 bird's-eye view, showing construction of Atlantic Avenue. In this detail from F. Fuchs, *View of Boston, July 4th, 1870* (see frontispiece to chapter 1), one can see Atlantic Avenue being constructed across the dock between T Wharf on the right and Commercial Wharf on the left. In order to build the new street, a seawall was constructed on its seaward side and then the shoreward side was filled. Dirt brought down from Fort Hill was piled in high mounds until ready to be used.

Figure 13 Photograph of India Wharf Building (ca. 1870). This photograph was taken from Central Wharf, looking at the India Wharf Building across the dock that separated the two wharves (see plate 41). The apparently inexplicable fence across the water at the left of the photograph is actually on Atlantic Avenue, which had already been constructed across this dock. (One can see a boat moored in the open part of the dock on the seaward side of Atlantic Avenue.) This photograph was probably taken to record the India Wharf Building just before the center section was demolished in order to permit the completion of Atlantic Avenue.

Boston shore where the Boston Wharf Company was building its huge wharf shown on the 1852 Chesbrough and 1852 Slatter and Callan maps (see plates 37 and 38). Whether this wharf decreased or increased the scour in the Fort Point Channel had been an issue in the 1850s. The U.S. Commissioners eventually concluded that it aided the scour and, to improve the scour in both the Fort Point and main shipping channels, recommended that a seawall be built around the South Boston Flats. After some urging by Boston business interests, the commissioners also agreed that the flats enclosed by the wall could be filled (see figure 33 in chapter 8). And so the South Boston, or Commonwealth, Flats project, which eventually became one of the largest land-making projects ever conducted in the city, began not as a commercial development but as a harbor improvement.

Getting the project started was not easy, however. The state's commissioners envisioned the made land as a locus of shipping and railroad terminals, but had a hard time convincing railroads to acquire and fill sections of the flats. The project did not officially begin until 1873 and most of the land made by 1878, the mile-long lobster-claw shaped area with what is now Fan Pier at the tip that is shown on the 1880 Boston Map Company map (see plate 43), was filled by the state and the Boston Wharf Company. Despite the difficulty of attracting railroads or other buyers for the new land on the South Boston Flats, the commissioners kept plunging ahead with the project—as soon as one area was filled they contracted to fill the next. By the 1890s hundreds of acres had been filled on the South Boston Flats, as shown on the 1896 Coast and Geodetic Survey chart (see plate 44), most of them virtually unoccupied except for the Boston Wharf Company and the New York, New Haven, & Hartford Railroad properties near the Fort Point Channel.

The development of railroad and shipping terminals was also the reason for most of the land made in Charlestown in the late nineteenth century. In the late 1870s and early 1880s the bay between Charlestown and Somerville was filled in and soon a vast Boston & Maine Railroad freight yard was laid out on the new land. In the 1880s and 1890s the Hoosac Dock and Elevator Company and then the Fitchburg Railroad extended and widened the wharves southwest of the Navy Yard to handle grain and other products shipped from the west through the Hoosac Tunnel in the Berkshires. And in the late 1880s and early 1890s, the Boston & Maine Railroad completed the long-projected Mystic Wharf on the north side of Charlestown, creating about 86.5 acres that soon became one of the major shipping terminals in the harbor. All these developments are shown on the 1896 Coast and Geodetic Survey chart (see plate 44).

While land was being made for shipping terminals, land was also created during other improvements to the city's infrastructure. In the late 1870s and early 1880s, for example, Boston finally modernized its antiquated sewage system. The old sewer system was blamed for the city's high death rate in the 1870s, for, at a time when it was still believed that diseases were caused by foul odors and filth, the sewers were certainly a source of both. Raw sewage was discharged at seventy outlets ringing the city where, instead of being flushed away by high tide, it was often brought back in by the incoming tide and lay exposed on the flats at low tide. In 1876 a special sewer commission recommended that new sewers be built to carry sewage from the existing lines to pumping stations. There the raw sewage would be raised high enough to flow by gravity through outfall sewers to sites located far from habitation, where, still untreated, it would be discharged into the ocean at ebb tide. It was decided to locate the first pumping station and beginning of the outfall sewer in the recently annexed Dorchester section of the city at the Calf Pasture (now Columbia Point)—a marshy promontory on which, as its name implied, Dorchester residents had once pastured calves. Construction of the pumping station, a large dark granite building that still looms between the JFK Library and the UMass/Boston campus, began in 1879. As part of the project, the end of the Calf Pasture was filled and squared off to make a wharf, and a long pier was built over the sewer that ran from the pumping station to a shaft that descended 160 feet to the outfall tunnel, made land that is shown on the 1880 Boston Map Company map (see plate 43). (The tunnel was bored a mile and a third through bedrock under the harbor to Squantum Neck and from there a causeway carried the outfall sewer to the point of discharge on Moon Island.) The Main Drainage system, as it came to be called, went into operation in 1884.

At the time when the Main Drainage system was being proposed and constructed, Boston's park system was also being inaugurated. Bostonians had been agitating for public parks since the late 1860s, a city park commission proposed a system of ten parks in 1876 (see map in plate 43 vignette), but only one, what is now the Back Bay Fens, was approved in 1877—and not because it would provide a recreational area but because it would solve a sewage problem. The full basin of Back Bay had become very polluted by the sewage draining into it from Stony Brook and the Muddy River. The city's plan was to build new sewers to carry these two streams directly into the Charles River and to turn the full basin into a holding area for storm overflows from Stony Brook. The plan was modified somewhat by Frederick Law Olmsted, the famous landscape architect, who was hired in 1878 to work on the Back Bay Park and became the designer of the Boston park system (see plate 43 vignette). Olmsted's plan for Back Bay (see figure 6 in chapter 1) called for a great deal of dredging (figure 14), filling, and construction of bridges, and the park was not completed until the 1890s. (The design of the Back Bay Fens soon became obsolete, however, when the Charles River Dam was built in the first decade of the twentieth century, turning the waterway in the park from salt to fresh and removing the need for a holding basin, and the park was then altered [see figure 6 in chapter 1 and figure 23 in chapter 8].)

Figure 14 Photograph of dredge in Back Bay (1882). In order to convert the Back Bay Fens into a holding basin for storm overflows from Stony Brook, the waterway through the park was dredged to the level of low tide. (The dredged material was deposited on the sides to shape the waterway in accordance with Olmsted's plan.) The dredge pictured here was typical of those used in many late nineteenth-century land-making projects. The row of mansard-roofed houses and other buildings in the background were on present Hemenway Street.

Meanwhile, in 1881 the city had approved six more of the ten parks originally proposed (see map in plate 43 vignette). In some sections of the city, the proposed parks were on the waterfront, either because those were the only areas still available or because, in the days before air-conditioning, waterfront locations were valued for their cooling breezes. All these waterfront parks needed to be filled. In the West End, a narrow strip along the Charles River was filled and developed in the mid-1880s to create a park called Charlesbank for residents of the densely packed tenements in that neighborhood (figure 15), land making that is shown on the 1896 Coast and Geodetic Survey chart (see plate 44). In South Boston, Marine Park was created in the 1880s and early 1890s by filling the east end of the peninsula and building one bridge to enclose part of Pleasure Bay and another to connect the park with Castle Island (figure 16), a development that can be seen in a comparison of this area on the 1880 Boston Map Company map and the 1896 Coast and Geodetic Survey chart (see plates 43 and 44). In East Boston, Wood Island Park, now buried beneath the fill of the airport, was made in the 1890s when the marsh between the two hills on the Wood Island promontory was filled and the area landscaped (figure 17), a project that again is shown on the 1896 Coast and Geodetic Survey chart (see plate 44). And as part of a "second wave" of parks, begun in the 1890s to provide playgrounds and recreational areas in parts of the city omitted from the original plan, new parks were created by filling areas on the Mystic River in Charlestown, on the harbor in the North End, and on Savin Hill Bay in Dorchester.

Land was also made for some of the parkways constructed to link the original parks, an idea included in the original park proposals and adopted by Olmsted, creating what is now called the "emerald necklace" (see map in plate 43 vignette). Riverway and Jamaicaway, linking the Back Bay Fens and Jamaica Pond, were built in the early 1890s by filling in the Brookline side of the Muddy River. The Strandway, now Day Boulevard in South Boston and originally part of the link between Franklin and Marine Parks, was constructed during the late 1890s and early 1900s by filling in the entire southern shore of South Boston, as can be seen in a comparison of the 1896 and 1916 Coast and Geodetic Survey charts (see plate 44 and figure 18). And although not part of the mainland parkway system, Neptune Road, now part of the airport, was filled in the mid-1880s to create a parkway, shown on the 1896 Coast and Geodetic Survey chart (see plate 44), that connected Wood Island Park with the rest of East Boston.

The Charles River Basin was also transformed into a park when the first Charles River Dam was constructed in the first decade of the twentieth century, although, as in the case of the Back Bay Fens, the immediate impetus for the project was sanitary rather than recreational. In the late nineteenth century the Charles River was still a tidal estuary and at low tide the flats, onto which raw sewage had been discharged for years, were

Figure 15 Photograph of Charlesbank (ca. 1900). Olmsted's design for Charlesbank included a promenade along the river screened from the city by a landscaped embankment. None of his original design survives, all of it having been destroyed in the various modifications of the park in the 1930s and 1950s, and Charlesbank today is a rather barren field on the river across from Massachusetts General Hospital.

Figure 16 Photograph of Marine Park (ca. 1892). Marine Park was very popular with South Boston residents, who came to enjoy the sea breezes and promenade along the pier that enclosed the south side of Pleasure Bay.

Figure 17 Photograph of Wood Island Park (ca. 1907). Wood Island Park is now buried beneath airport fill in the area behind present Terminal E. This photograph was taken on the steps leading down from the station of the Revere Beach and Lynn Railroad, which runs along the left side of the photograph and is now also obliterated by the airport, looking at the men's gymnastic ground and boys' playground. The harbor can be seen in the right background and Orient Heights in the left.

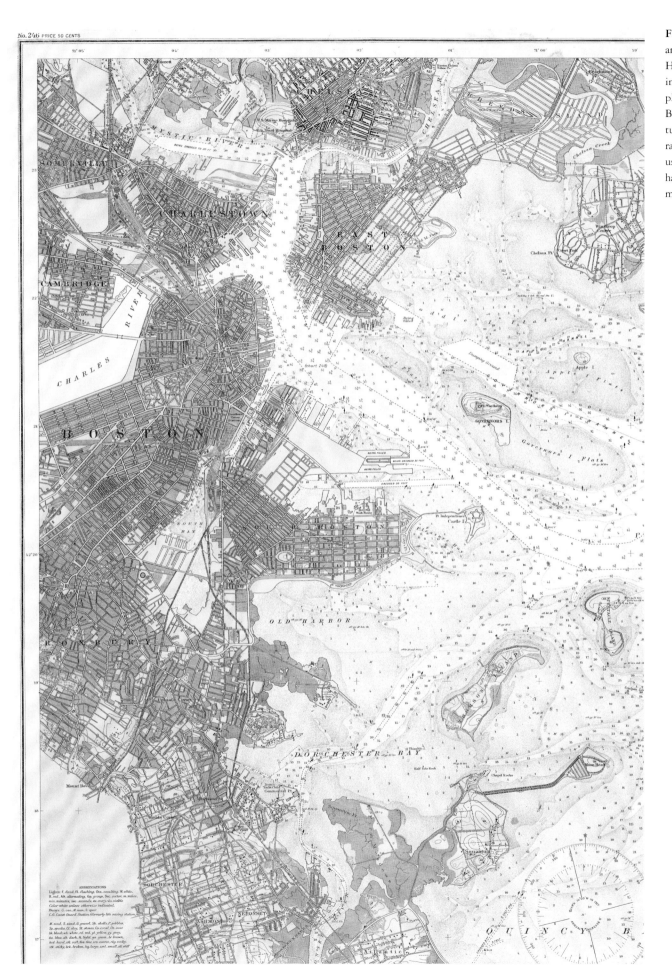

Figure 18 Detail from 1916 U.S. Coast and Geodetic Survey chart of Boston Harbor. This chart is an update of those in a series first published in 1896 (see plate 44). The most accurate maps of Boston at the turn of the twentieth century were not really maps at all but rather coastal charts prepared for naval use, so in several instances these charts have been used to illustrate the land making during this period.

both unsightly and malodorous. In 1894 a special board recommended that the problem be solved by building a dam to maintain the river at a constant level, keeping the flats always covered with water. The dam would also transform the river basin from salt water to fresh and the shores would be landscaped, creating a "water park" similar to the Alster Basin in Hamburg, Germany, a plan that Bostonians had been advocating since the 1850s (see figure 20 in chapter 8). The 1894 dam proposal was defeated, however, but was revived in 1901 and finally approved in 1903. The first Charles River Dam was constructed between 1905 and 1910 on the site of Craigie's, or the Canal, Bridge between Boston's West End and East Cambridge, making the land where the Museum of Science now stands (figure 19). As part of the project, a narrow "esplanade" was created on the Boston side of the river (figure 20) by filling a strip between the Longfellow Bridge and Charlesgate, as one can see in a comparison of the 1896 and 1916 Coast and Geodetic Survey charts (see plate 44 and figure 18).

Figure 19 Photograph of Charles River Dam (ca. 1913). The first Charles River Dam included a seven-acre park on the up-river side, an area that remained open until the Museum of Science was constructed on it in 1951. In this photograph taken soon after the dam was completed, one can see the also recently completed viaduct, which still exists, that carried the elevated tracks across to Lechmere.

Figure 20 Photograph of the Esplanade (ca. 1916). Taken from a building on Embankment Road looking west, the photograph shows the narrow "esplanade" that had recently been created along the river—the area where Storrow Drive now runs. The photograph can be dated by the presence on the Cambridge side of the river of the main building at MIT, which was completed in 1916.

Figure 21 Photograph of Fenway area (1909). This photograph, taken by Baldwin Coolidge on October 12, 1909, looking east across the Fens from the end of Jersey Street, shows apartment buildings along what is now Hemenway Street and, behind them, the dome of the recently completed Christian Science Mother Church.

While land was being created for parks, land was also made in the late nineteenth century to create more space for Boston's rapidly expanding populace. Construction of the Back Bay Fens in the 1880s and 1890s encouraged the filling of the surrounding marshes, creating solid land in what are now the Fenway and Longwood areas on which apartment buildings were soon erected (figure 21). In the same period, the neighboring flats along the river were filled, creating the Bay State Road area. In East Boston, which had not grown very much since a financial panic in 1857 had dealt a deathblow to its wooden shipbuilding industry, the population began to increase rapidly in the mid-1880s thanks to a large influx of Jewish immigrants from eastern Europe. The resultant need for more housing is probably why, in the 1890s, the East Boston Company finally began to fill the flats inside a seawall it had built in 1850 across what was called the Basin—the large expanse of flats between Jeffries Point and Wood Island that is shown on the 1896 Coast and Geodetic Survey chart (see plate 44). The company continued to fill the Basin for the next several decades, creating some of the land that is shown on the 1916 Coast and

Geodetic Survey chart (figure 18) and is now under the entrance and exit roads of the airport. Breed's Island, surmounted by the steep Orient Heights, was originally separate from the rest of East Boston and developed by a different venture, the Boston Land Company. In the 1880s this company laid out house lots on Orient Heights and in the early 1890s created more land for house lots by filling low-lying areas at the foot of the heights, as shown on the 1896 Coast and Geodetic Survey chart (see plate 44).

The major land making in Boston at the turn of the twentieth century, however, was done for commercial projects. At the end of the nineteenth century, concerns arose about Boston's port facilities. As with the agitation about the harbor in the mid-nineteenth century, these concerns again reflected the realization that Boston's importance as a port had declined relative to New York and major European ports. This time, however, the problem was identified as a lack of publicly owned modern docks and wharves served by railroads. In 1897 a state board appointed to investigate the "wants of the port of Boston for an improved system of docks and wharves and terminal facilities" recommended that the state acquire part of the Noddles Island Flats, east of the Basin in East Boston and shown on the 1896 Coast and Geodetic Survey chart (see plate 44), for a major port development and build a "model" dock with "every modern appliance" on the South Boston Flats.[7] The state commissioners quickly took fifty-seven acres of the Noddles Island Flats by eminent domain, landing them in a ten-year lawsuit with the East Boston Company, and rushed to construct the new pier on the South Boston Flats. Soon called Commonwealth Pier (now the World Trade Center), the pier, built between 1897 and 1901 (figure 22; see also figure 32 in chapter 8), was the largest one on the East Coast at the time and can be seen in a comparison of the 1896 and 1916 Coast and Geodetic Survey charts (see plate 44 and figure 18).

The concern about port facilities was soon caught up by the City Beautiful movement, which swept the nation in the first decade of the twentieth century and, at least in Boston, focused not only on beautifying the city but also on improving its infrastructure. Two commissions were appointed to recommend public improvements for metropolitan Boston. One improvement that resulted in more land was Fish Pier (see figures 32 and 34 in chapter 8), built next to Commonwealth Pier on the South Boston Flats in 1910–1913 and shown on the 1916 Coast and Geodetic Survey chart (figure 18), for use by the Boston fishing fleet, which had hitherto been based at T Wharf in the city proper. Another was the construction of the largest dry dock in the world at the east end of the most recently filled section of the South Boston Flats, also shown on the 1916 Coast and Geodetic Survey chart (figure 18). Filling the area surrounding the dry dock started in 1914, work on the dock itself in 1915, and, after many delays, the project was finally completed in 1919. In 1915 filling of the Noddles Island Flats finally began, initiating the port development in East Boston that had been contemplated for so many years (figure 23). About the same time filling also began, with material dredged in the harbor but formerly dumped at sea, of a channel north of Governors Island off East Boston. Work on filling the Noddles Island Flats and the Governors Island dumping ground, both indicated on the 1916 Coast and Geodetic Survey chart (figure 18), for a port development continued throughout the rest of the teens and into the early 1920s, but then the project took an unexpected turn.

At the end of World War I, airplane enthusiasts began to agitate for construction of a landing field in Boston that would serve the needs of the incipient air mail service, commercial and military aviation, and recreational fliers. After a long search for an airport location, the area being filled on the East Boston Flats for a port development was finally selected in 1921. The site's advantages, some of which still obtain, were cited as its proximity to the city, distance from densely populated areas, suitability for sea as well as land planes, and, last but certainly proven not least, room for expansion. It was originally thought that the airport would not replace the port development but simply occupy the site until the port project was

COMMONWEALTH PIER NO. 5, DEC. 28, 1912. UNDER CONSTRUCTION.

Figure 22 Photograph of Commonwealth Pier (1912). In spite of the rush to construct Commonwealth Pier, the pier then lay unfinished—and unused—for the next decade. Finally, in 1912 a new board assumed responsibility for the development of harbor facilities and moved quickly to have passenger and freight structures built on the pier. The board also sought shipping business but, with the bad luck that seemed to plague the development of Commonwealth Pier, leased half of it to a German line whose sailings were then curtailed when World War I began in 1914.

under way. Grading and surfacing the area already filled began in 1922 and the first plane landed on June 4, 1923, the year the airport officially opened. Filling the East Boston Flats continued throughout the 1920s, and by 1930 several hundred acres had been created between Jeffries Point and Wood Island in an L-shaped configuration, shown on a 1930 aerial photograph and the 1934 Coast and Geodetic Survey chart (figure 24 and see also plate 47), that had been determined by the location of the central anchorage basin in the still-planned port development (figure 23).

At the same time the airport was being created, the South Boston Flats project was finally being completed. In 1918 the U.S. Government had bought a strip of made land next to the dry dock for an army supply base from which to ship war matériel to Europe. This land was on the north side of the Reserved Channel, the waterway that had been left open to provide access to the wharves on the original north shore of South Boston. As part of the 1918 agreement, the federal government deepened the Reserved Channel, dumping the dredged material onto the flats between Marine Park and Castle Island. When dredging of the Reserved Channel was finished, the state continued filling this area, finally joining Castle Island to the mainland in the late 1920s, as can be seen on the 1934 Coast and Geodetic Survey chart (see plate 47), and, more than fifty years after it had begun, completing the South Boston Flats project.

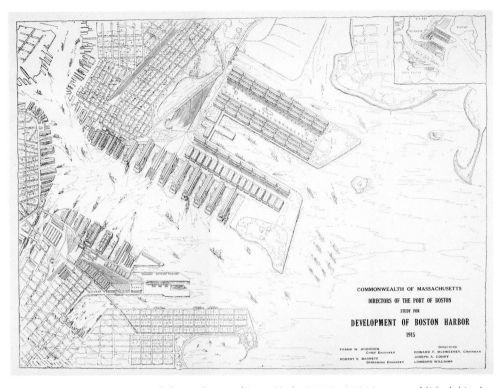

Figure 23 *Study for Development of Boston Harbor* (1915). A 1915 report published this plan showing the extensive complex of shipping and rail terminals planned for the East Boston Flats, the area now occupied by the airport, as well as for the South Boston Flats.

Figure 24 Aerial photograph of Boston (1930). In this early aerial photograph, one can see the made land of the airport extending out toward Governors Island from the Jeffries Point section of East Boston, much as it appears on the 1934 Coast and Geodetic Survey chart of the harbor (see plate 46). One can also see Wood Island Park next to the airport and, north of East Boston, Charlestown with the lobster-claw- like Mystic Wharf, then Boston itself before the second phase of the esplanade was filled along the river, and finally, at the lower left, Fan, Commonwealth, and Fish Piers in South Boston.

While all this filling was occurring in the harbor, land was also being made along the shore of Dorchester for what was originally called Old Colony Parkway and is now Morrissey Boulevard. First proposed in 1906 and then advocated by the City Beautiful movement and the commissions on metropolitan improvements (see plate 45 vignette), Old Colony Parkway (so named because the route first proposed paralleled that of the Old Colony Railroad, now the MBTA Red Line) was intended as a major automobile route between Boston and the South Shore (see plate 45 vignette). The original proposal was for a highway on the west side of Savin Hill, but was changed in 1914 to the present one on the east side of Savin Hill—a route that would obviously require considerable filling across Savin Hill Bay as well as across the marshes of the Calf Pasture and the cove between the Calf Pasture and Savin Hill, as the 1916 Coast and Geodetic Survey chart indicates (figure 18). Filling the Calf Pasture and the cove began in 1918 and continued into the mid-1920s, but filling the section across the mouth of Savin Hill Bay did not start until 1925. Two arms of land were created for the parkway—one extending south from Savin Hill on which Malibu Beach is now located and the other north from Commercial Point—and, when the drawbridge connecting these filled areas was completed in 1928, the entire Old Colony Parkway, which is shown on the 1934 Coast and Geodetic Survey chart (see plate 47), was finally opened to traffic.

Other filling in the 1920s created land for railroads. One locus of this land making was South Bay. After the completion of the South Bay Lands project in 1861 (see above), wharves had been built on the northwest side of the bay, Swett (now Southampton) Street constructed on a causeway across the bay in the 1870s, and some land created in the 1860s on the South Boston side for railroads and iron works, as shown on the 1880 Boston Map Company map (see plate 43). Although the bay was polluted by sewage that continued to drain into it even after the Main Drainage system was constructed, proposals to fill it were always defeated by arguments about the importance of the wharves on the west side, which handled bulk goods like lumber and coal. Some filling was nevertheless permitted in the early 1900s to provide new wharves to replace those on the Fort Point Channel that had been displaced by the construction of South Station in 1897–1898. These new wharves in South Bay were created in 1902–1904 by filling a large area north of what is now Southampton Street. This created land now just south of the huge incinerator with the three prominent stacks (until recently visible from the Southeast Expressway), land making that can be seen in a comparison of this area on the 1896 and 1916 Coast and Geodetic charts (see plate 44 and figure 18). By the teens, however, attitudes about filling South Bay had changed—storm overflows from nearby sewers had turned the bay into a stinking "nuisance" (a term once used to describe an obnoxious smell or appearance)—and in 1920 when the New York, New Haven, & Hartford Railroad requested permission to fill its part of the bay in order to make land for railroad yards, the state commissioners readily agreed. Filling continued throughout the 1920s, and by 1930 almost all of South Bay had been filled except for the channel and turning basin that served the remaining wharves, as can be seen on the 1934 Coast and Geodetic Survey chart (see plate 47).

The Boston & Maine Railroad also created a large amount of land in the late 1920s. When the railroad built North Station in 1928, it received permission to fill a large area of flats behind the station so that passengers in the rear cars of trains could disembark on solid ground instead of on trestles. The project, which also involved filling sizable areas on the Cambridge and Charlestown side of the river, began in 1927 and continued for several years, creating the land, shown on the 1934 Coast and Geodetic Survey chart (see plate 47), where the Spaulding Rehabilitation Hospital is now located.

By the late 1920s it was clear that the Charles River Basin, created in the first decade of the century when the Charles River Dam was built (see above), had not become the water park originally envisioned. Wind-whipped waves bouncing off the bordering seawalls created a chop that

Figure 25 Photograph of the Esplanade (1935). This photograph was taken from the same vantage point as the ca. 1916 photograph of the esplanade, and makes an interesting comparison with that view (figure 20). The early 1930s filling doubled the width of the Esplanade and added the lagoon between Exeter and Fairfield Streets that is now right next to Storrow Drive. Back Street, which runs next to a seawall built in the 1860s when Back Bay was being filled, has been conveniently labeled on this photograph from the Metropolitan District Commission archives.

Figure 26 This aerial photograph was taken in October 1952 by the U.S. Department of Agriculture, which in the 1930s had begun photographing all counties in the country in order to record their land use. The photograph is actually a mosaic of aerial photographs taken at a scale of 1:20,000 (the index numbers can be seen on each of the individual photos). Comparing these 1952 photographs with the 1934 Coast and Geodetic chart (see plate 47) reveals changes that had occurred in Boston in the interim. Most noticeable is the tremendous amount of new land at the airport, created between 1943 and 1947 by pumping dredged material over tidal flats and around the former Governors and Apple Islands. Other parts of East Boston had been filled as well—most of the basins on either side of Wood Island Park and what is now Constitution Beach. In South Boston, the U.S. Navy had done considerable filling during World War II, creating another dry dock, piers, and a quadrilateral quay on the harbor front; extending land at the end of the Reserved Channel; and extending the made land north of Castle Island. Columbia Point, formerly the Calf Pasture, had been greatly enlarged after years of being used as a trash dump and its northern shore had been squared off for the Columbia Point housing project. The size and shape of Spectacle Island had also been transformed by trash fill as well as by erosion. And in Boston Proper, new land had been added to Charlesbank park and new islands created along the Charles River to compensate for the land taken by the construction of Storrow Drive.

made the basin too dangerous for small boats and rowing shells and, in addition, the Esplanade was too narrow for boathouses. In 1929 a special commission recommended that the Esplanade be widened and extended to the Cottage Farm (now Boston University) Bridge with a shore that sloped down to the water instead of ending at a seawall, that new recreational areas be provided, and that a highway be built on the embankment. Not surprisingly, the last proposal raised a storm of protest. The recreational improvements were to be financed by a gift of $1,000,000 from Mrs. James J. Storrow, but when she joined one of the groups opposing the highway, the commissioners dropped the road from the plan in order to retain her gift. Most of the filling was done in 1932 and the project, completed in 1935, not only doubled the width of what was named the Storrow Memorial Embankment but also created several familiar landmarks—the "Make Way for Ducklings" islands near present Community Boating, which were intended as a haven for small boats, a music shell, and the existing lagoon between Exeter and Fairfield Streets (figure 25; cf. figure 20).

In the period between World War II and the late 1980s even more land was added to Boston. Perhaps most dramatic was the transformation of the airport. Renamed in 1943 for General Edward Lawrence Logan, a South Boston native who had served in World War I, the small landing field of the 1930s was transformed into a modern airport between 1943 and 1947 by filling in hundreds of acres, covering the former Governors and Apple Islands, completely surrounding Wood Island Park, and extending the airport close to the shores of Winthrop and the former Breed's Island, as can be seen in a 1952 aerial photograph (figure 26). Another period of expansion began in the late 1960s—Wood Island Park, Neptune Road, and the Basin were swallowed up and the Bird Island Flats filled, as shown in a 1999 aerial photograph of the city (see plate 50).

Dramatic changes also occurred at the Calf Pasture. In the 1880s a gas company had filled in and squared off the end of the Calf Pasture south of the Main Drainage pumping station, as shown on the 1896 Coast and Geodetic Survey chart (see plate 44), and for many years this company and the sewage works were the only occupants of this marshy promontory (figure 27). In the 1920s, however, the Calf Pasture began to be used as a dump; by the end of World War II its size had been increased by many acres and its shape transformed (see plates 47 and 48). This large expanse of made land was cheap and attracted some new occupants. In 1948 Boston College High School purchased a seventy-acre site on Old Colony Parkway as the location for a new school to replace the one in the South End that it had outgrown. The first building was constructed in 1949–1950 on the existing fill, and the school created some additional land in the 1950s by filling in the area between Morrissey Boulevard and the Calf Pasture, as can be seen on a composite map of Boston's land making (frontispiece). In 1950 the Boston Housing Authority selected a site

Figure 27 Aerial photograph of Calf Pasture Point (1923). Taken in 1923 from the south, this aerial photograph shows Calf Pasture Point as it appeared for many years (see the 1896, 1916, and 1934 U.S. Coast and Geodetic Survey charts in plates 44 and 47 and figure 18) with the Bay State, later Boston Consolidated, Gas Company tanks on the south side and Main Drainage sewage works on the north. The building at the end of the long pier covered the shaft that descended 160 feet to the tunnel leading to Squantum Neck; this building is now on the right-hand side of the perimeter road, just before the entrance to the Massachusetts State Archives.

on the north side of the Calf Pasture as the location for an enormous public housing project. Most of the site was already filled with trash, but the housing authority squared off its edges with additional fill and, in 1951–1954, constructed what was called the Columbia Point Housing Development (frontispiece and figure 26). (This ill-conceived project of high-rise apartment buildings, whose name changed that of the Calf Pasture to Columbia Point, eventually failed and was replaced in the 1980s with the present Harbor Point development.) In 1968 the University of Massachusetts decided, after four years of wrangling about a site, to locate its new Boston campus at the end of Columbia Point, south of the long pier that had been built in the 1880s over the Main Drainage outfall sewer (figure 27). Most of the area was already filled with a thirty-foot depth of trash (figure 28) and the university only had to do a little

Figure 28 Aerial photograph of Columbia Point (ca. 1970). This aerial photograph shows Columbia Point from the east. The site chosen for the Boston campus of the University of Massachusetts is at the left foreground, filled with about a thirty-foot depth of trash and south of the long pier that once extended from the pumping station to the building over the shaft to the outfall tunnel (figure 27). In the background, the Columbia Point housing project can be seen on the right-hand side and Boston College High School on the left.

Figure 29 Aerial photograph of Columbia Point (ca. 1978). This aerial photograph makes an interesting comparison with one taken of the same area about 1970 (figure 28). During the decade, the University of Massachusetts had been constructed, its shoreline squared off with a little filling, the lagoon at the northeast tip formed by the L-shaped dike filled in, and construction of the Kennedy Library begun on that site.

additional filling to straighten the shoreline. Construction began in 1970 and the new campus opened for classes in 1974. UMass/Boston, as it is familiarly called, was joined by another high-profile neighbor when the John F. Kennedy Library, also after a controversial search for a site, finally decided in 1977 to locate the library at Columbia Point. The site, at the northeast end of the point, had been an open lagoon formed by an L-shaped dike built in the 1950s (figure 27). Most of this lagoon had been filled in 1970 with material excavated while UMass was being constructed and the rest was filled during the construction of the library (figure 29), which opened in 1979.

More land was also made along the Charles River. The highway that had been omitted when the Esplanade was widened in the 1930s (see above) was finally approved in 1949 as one solution for Boston's postwar

"traffic mess." Ironically named Storrow Drive in spite of Mrs. Storrow's opposition in 1929, this highway was constructed in the early 1950s on the part of the Esplanade that had been filled in 1906–1909 and, to compensate for the land taken, more land was created by filling new islands and lagoons along the river (figure 30) and by widening Charlesbank park, as can be seen in a comparison of the area on the 1934 Coast and Geodetic Survey chart and a 1952 aerial photograph (see plate 47 and figure 26). Then, in the 1970s, a new Charles River Dam was constructed to replace the one built in the first decade of the century (see above). A hurricane in August 1955 had raised the level of the Charles River Basin to a height that caused severe flooding, especially in areas of made land, and vividly demonstrated that the first dam was inadequate. After many studies, the site selected for the new dam was that of the old Warren Bridge

Figure 30 Photograph of Storrow Drive under construction (January 26, 1951). Taken from about the same vantage point as the ca. 1916 and 1935 photographs of the Esplanade (figures 20 and 25), this photograph of the construction of Storrow Drive makes an interesting comparison. In the foreground is the tunnel for inbound traffic, which had been added to the project in order to preserve seating at the Hatch Shell. To the right a billboard bravely proclaims the "New Embankment Highway" and behind it dredges work filling new islands to compensate for the land taken for the drive.

between Boston and Charlestown, the westernmost of the two bridges to Charlestown visible on the 1934 Coast and Geodetic Survey chart (see plate 47). Construction of the new dam began in 1974 and continued throughout most of the 1970s, creating some new land, most of it on the Charlestown side of the river, as can be seen in a 1999 aerial photograph (see plate 50).

Other areas filled since World War II include South Bay. The turning basin and docks at the south end, visible on the 1934 Coast and Geodetic Survey chart and in a 1952 aerial photograph (see plate 47 and figure 26), were filled in the 1950s when the Southeast Expressway was built. But, incredible as it may now seem, the open channel along the northwest side was not completely filled in until the late 1960s when, after decades of complaints about its pollution, it was finally covered over and the outflow carried underground into the Fort Point Channel, as shown in a 1999 aerial photograph (see plate 50).

More land was even made on the South Boston Flats. In 1920 the U.S. Navy had purchased the huge dry dock built by the state in South Boston during the preceding decade (see above), and the site became an annex of the Charlestown Navy Yard. In 1940–1943 the navy filled an area north of the dry dock and constructed four new piers and another dry dock between this new land and Fish Pier as well as filling a large area at the end of the Reserved Channel and adding more land north of Castle Island, all shown in a 1952 aerial photograph (figure 26). The four piers were filled in during the 1980s to make land that became the New England terminal for imported Subaru cars, a site shown on a 1999 aerial photograph of the area (see plate 50) that was soon known as Subaru Pier. This newly made land was soon taken over by the project constructing a new tunnel across Boston Harbor and putting the Central Artery underground—the "Big Dig"—and became a dump site for excavated dirt before it was transported to its final resting place on Spectacle Island in the harbor (see figure 35 in chapter 8).

The filling of Subaru Pier in the 1980s is the most recent land-making project on the Boston mainland. Not surprisingly, the pace of land making has now slowed—most of the tidal flats that once surrounded the city are now filled in and an extensive permitting process is required to fill more. But when one compares a modern image of Boston with a map made before much filling was done (compare plates 27 and 50; see also frontispiece), one can clearly see how dramatically the city has been transformed by the land making of the last two hundred years.

NOTES

1. Walt Whitman, *Specimen Days* (1882; reprint, Boston: David R. Godine, 1971), 108.

2. The account of Boston's land making presented in this chapter is based on Nancy S. Seasholes, *Gaining Ground: Landmaking in Boston, 1630s–1980s,* forthcoming.

3. Nancy S. Seasholes, "Filling Boston's Mill Pond," *Historical Archaeology* 32, no. 3 (1998): 124–127.

4. See, for example, Michael P. Conzen and George K. Lewis, *Boston: A Geographical Portrait* (Cambridge, Mass.: Ballinger Publishing Co., 1976), 9.

5. Josiah Quincy, *A Municipal History of the Town and City of Boston, during Two Centuries from September 17, 1630, to September 17, 1830* (Boston: Charles C. Little and James Brown, 1852), 202.

6. Boston, City of, *Documents of the City of Boston for the Year 1849,* no. 36 (Boston: City Printers, 1850), 3, 4.

7. *Report of the State Board on Docks and Terminal Facilities, January 1897* (Boston: State Printers, 1897), 5, 83, 85.

Frontispiece Central Boston (1996). Long Wharf is just to the right of center with the State Street (formerly King Street) axis extending into the city and terminating at the Old State House, barely visible amid its contemporary skyscraper neighbors. To the right of this axis lie Faneuil Hall and the Quincy Markets with the new City Hall and Government Center area immediately behind. The aerial covers much of the area of the Shawmut Peninsula, dramatically enlarged over the course of its settlement.

Experiencing Boston: Encounters with the Places on the Maps

Alex Krieger

Cotton and Increase Mather, Harriet Beecher Stowe, Henry David Thoreau, John Singleton Copley, Oliver Wendell Holmes, Louisa May Alcott, Alexander Graham Bell, and generations of Adamses, Cabots, Lowells, and Kennedys—a roll-call of notable Bostonians is, indeed, impressive.[1] But come to Boston, and places, too, engulf you—many urbane, endearing, enduring, and evolving places. For in addition to their social, political, and artistic achievements the citizens of Boston, more so than the citizens of many American cities, have understood the value of place-making.

The setting itself made this inevitable. Hilly, oddly shaped, ringed by tidal flats, and with only a narrow (and sometimes impassable) neck to the mainland, the original Shawmut Peninsula was unlikely to produce a straightforward town plan. The early maps portray the fragile circumstances well (see plate 18). The young settlement clings to the small peninsula amid a complex geography of shoals, marshes, and islands. The determination to make a home on this less-than-hospitable terrain made place-making an early priority. It also required imagination, organization, and enterprise.

To transfer cargo from sea to land across unnavigable flats required the building of docks, wharves, piers, and canals. To take advantage of the tides for commerce, mill dams and seawalls were needed. Improving access to the rest of the region necessitated the construction of long bridges, toll roads and, later, railroad trestles. Making the hills more suitable for homes and farms meant leveling the steepest slopes, and to accommodate a growing population, additional land had to be found or made. Fortuitously, the leveling of the hills generated fill material that, if properly disposed into the coves, would create land. Land reclamation schemes ultimately quadrupled the acreage of the original peninsula.[2] (See the growth diagrams in chapter 2.)

The collagelike fabric of today's Boston is the result of this nearly continuous manipulation of the city's geography. Each major venture left a physical presence, in the form of a specific neighborhood, a distinct pattern of streets, or a sequence of open spaces. The pattern of the fingerlike piers pointing out to sea, the tight-knit Federal fabric of Beacon Hill, the geometric street network of the Bulfinch Triangle, and the grid of the Back Bay are all examples. To this the twentieth century has been adding its own characteristic realms: a downtown of skyscrapers ringed by suburbs and interconnected by the umbilical cords of highways and transit lines. Many cities experience eras of rapid growth between periods of stability or even recession. In Boston this dynamic is portrayed in accentuated fashion; each growth period producing major alterations to the landmass itself.

Many analogies are used to describe the complex organisms that are modern cities. The notion of a palimpsest seems particularly suited to Boston.[3] Most everywhere in Boston there are layers to decipher. One can seek the evidence of earlier presences, the traces of old maps.

THE AVENUE(S) LEADING FROM THE SEA

Examine a map of the Shawmut Peninsula from Bonner's time on (see plate 24) and you observe a fingerlike pattern of streets leading to and extending over the water as wharves. The one that reached furthest out to sea yet anchored itself most profoundly to the peninsula was Long Wharf, begun under the direction of Captain Oliver Noyes in 1711. Long Wharf was the virtual extension of the town's principal commercial street, King Street, far into the harbor. Paul Revere's famous 1770 engraving portrays its mercantile thrust well (figure 1; see also figure 1 in chapter 1). A third of a mile long, and seemingly straining under the weight of the goods it was holding, Long Wharf was the arrow pointing back to the Old World.

At the town end of Long Wharf, King Street intersected with the road that connected the peninsula to the mainland, today's Washington, then Cornhill, Street (figure 1). If this were a Roman town the intersection of King and Cornhill (today, State and Washington) would be where the Cardo and Decumonus met; the center of things. The main public market flourished there, and along the market's edges the first meeting house, the governor's house, and by 1657 a "Town House" for governing the burgeoning settlement appeared.

Two years after Long Wharf was begun, following a fire (a frequent urban event), a new masonry Town House was built, whose exterior walls survive in today's Old State House.[4] From the porch on the second floor

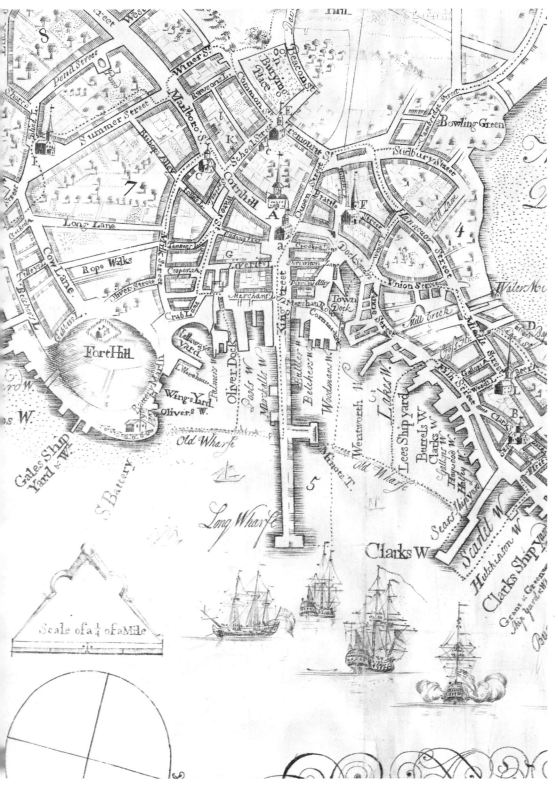

Figure 1 The Long Wharf / King Street axis as delineated in the 1728 William Burgis map of Boston (see plate 25).

the colonial governor could look straight down King Street to a commanding view of Long Wharf and the harbor, as Queen Elizabeth did when she helped Bostonians celebrate the Bicentennial in 1976 (figure 2). Two hundred years earlier the same porch witnessed the first Boston reading of the Declaration of Independence, after a fourteen-day trip from Philadelphia. It had been fifteen years since, in 1761, the Town House hosted an eight-hour speech by James Otis, Jr., denouncing the Writs of Assistance, which many historians identify as one of the first steps toward independence from British rule.

After the War of Independence King Street became, more appropriately, State Street. Likewise, General Washington lent his name to the cross street at which this Great Street (its original name) terminates. You can still stand at the end of Long Wharf and, peering under the soon-to-be-demolished Central Artery, see its terminus at the Old State House, today surrounded—but not diminished—by a ring of skyscrapers (figure 3). These modern monoliths house some of Boston's leading financial institutions and herald the city's Financial District. This, too, seems predestined as the Old State House, and even its wooden predecessors, contained a "merchants' exchange," the colonial forerunner of today's stock exchange.

As one hopes of a two-and-a-half-century-old structure, the Old State House seems to rest securely on its site, even though directly beneath it cross two subway lines. Today thousands of daily commuters emerge from underneath this venerable Old State House, it having added subway entrance to the many functions it has performed over the years. Moving across one of the busiest intersections in the downtown, the more observant commuters take note that they are crossing the site of the 1770 Boston Massacre (see plate 27 vignette).

Such resonances over time are many. A hundred yards or so to the north of the Long Wharf/State Street axis lay the original Town Dock, at the head of which Faneuil Hall was built in 1742, rebuilt after a fire in 1761, and doubled to its present size by Charles Bulfinch in 1805.[5] Upon taking the mayor's office in 1823, Josiah Quincy made it a high priority to modernize the area of the Town Dock. The markets that today bear the mayor's name opened in 1826, being rather unsentimentally constructed right on top of the older dock, and in a sense constituting Boston's earliest waterfront urban renewal (figure 4; see also plate 33 vignette). In their present, more festive guise the Quincy Markets form a key midpoint along the tourist route connecting the State House atop Beacon Hill, the twentieth-century Government Center, and the harbor.

These adjacent corridors—along State Street and through the Quincy Markets constitute Boston's mythic Walk-to-the-Sea (figure 5 and frontispiece). Just about any story about Boston can begin along them. Around this double axis the city has evolved, prospered, and occasionally waned over more than three centuries. Few American cities can boast of an equally rich palimpsest.

Figure 2 View from the Old State House looking down State Street to Long Wharf with the elevated Central Artery (soon to come down) obstructing the view of Boston Harbor.

Figure 3 The Old State House at the head of State Street nestled amid its tall contemporary neighbors.

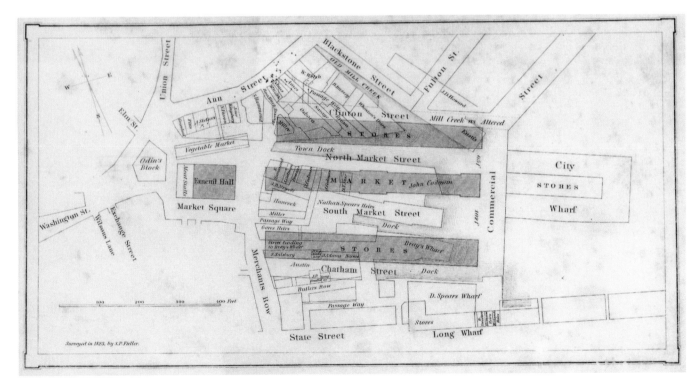

Figure 4 A reproduction of an 1823 engraving, after a survey by S. P. Fuller, found in Josiah Quincy's *A Municipal History of the Town and City of Boston,* published in 1852. It shows how the then new Quincy Markets were built over the Town Dock (see plate 33 vignette and figure 8 in chapter 1).

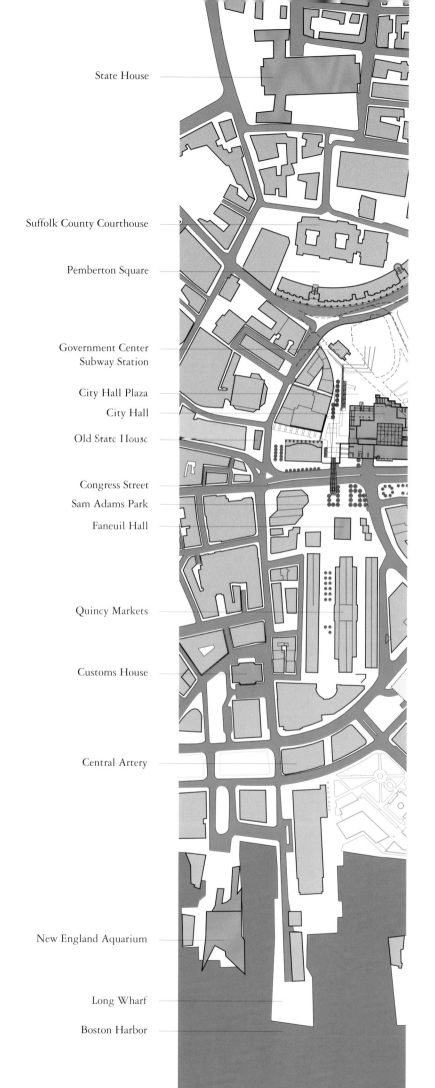

State House

Suffolk County Courthouse

Pemberton Square

Government Center
Subway Station

City Hall Plaza
City Hall

Old State House

Congress Street
Sam Adams Park
Faneuil Hall

Quincy Markets

Customs House

Central Artery

New England Aquarium

Long Wharf

Boston Harbor

Figure 5 Plan illustrating the "Walk-to-the-Sea" from the state capitol atop Beacon Hill through City Hall Plaza and the Quincy Markets to Long Wharf and the harbor.

THE WATER'S EDGE

Both King Street and the Quincy Markets terminated at the water. The use of the waterfront, access to it, and its design have been fundamental concerns since the founding of the city. Like the tide itself, however, the immediacy of the water's edge has ebbed and flowed in the consciousness of Bostonians. During the seventeenth, eighteenth, and nineteenth centuries piers and wharves formed what Walter Muir Whitehill called the avenues to Boston from the parts of the world that really mattered.[6] Well beyond the turn of the twentieth century, ambitious schemes for the enlargement of port facilities held the attention of municipal authorities and promoted new landfill projects. Today, a continuous and publicly accessible corridor of open space is a planning priority—indeed, a matter of law for all development near the water. Even the airport, which, like the railroad a half-century earlier, supplanted many port functions, somehow, inevitably, wound up on the harbor's edge. By air one still comes to Boston via the harbor.

But precisely because the harbor was the setting for so many of the city's enterprises, awareness of the water's edge diminished over the years. Although the city was founded on a virtual island, encountering water today often requires a search. Come to Dock Square, site of the original Town Dock, and you will not be within sight of the harbor. The Back Bay no longer refers to the great cove of the Charles River estuary but to a fine neighborhood. A recently opened shopping center called South Bay Plaza is located on but recalls only in name the area of a once-vast cove separating the Shawmut and South Boston peninsulas. After so much land making, the sense of living on a seacoast is sustained more often by memories and symbols, or a shift in wind direction bringing the smell of the sea, than by actual contact with water.

In fact, throughout most of the first half of the twentieth century this most intensively used part of the city—the edge between land and sea—was emptying. A much-diminished port, obsolete maritime infrastructure, pollution, and decay resulted in a sort of ever-receding land-side tide. The not-so-busy wharves began to store a different kind of commodity: parked cars for the downtown (figure 6). The waterfronts of many industrial-era cities experienced a similar fate, and many have yet to recover.

Few at mid-century would have predicted that within a generation the bustle at the waterfront would return, not in the form of warehouses, customhouses, longshoremen, or clipper ships, but courtesy of homes, cultural institutions, tourists, and pleasure craft. The waterfront is a center of action again, only in redefined use and desires. A long-standing expa-

Figure 6 Aerial view (ca. 1964) showing how by mid-century many of the historic wharves had lost their mercantile functions to become parking lots. Long Wharf, with some of its historic structures intact, lies to the bottom. Compare to the frontispiece showing the present uses and character of the same wharves.

Figure 7 View of Rowes Wharf, an acclaimed office, hotel, retail, and residential project (developed and built in the mid-1980s by the Beacon Companies, founded by Norman B. Leventhal). It occupies several of those mid-twentieth-century parking lots at the top left portion of figure 6.

triate returning to Boston would surely be shocked that Rowes, Burroughs, Lewis, and Mercantile Wharves are now all elegant residential addresses, not places of industry; that life in the Charlestown Navy Yard is directed by homeowners' associations instead of naval protocol; that forty-seven miles of shoreline are being steadily converted to a continuous public promenade called Harborpark; or that some of the most valuable real estate is down along the wharves, not at a safe distance up the slopes from the harbor (figure 7).[7]

HIGH GROUND

Near the ocean, high ground is always important, a relief from unpredictable tides, muddy shoals, and stale air. Boston's higher grounds were occupied as early as it was feasible, though the steepest areas required leveling to make them suitable for settlement.

The small Shawmut Peninsula itself had five peaks: three clustered to form Trimount, today's Beacon Hill; Copps Hill in what became the North End; and Fort Hill overlooking the harbor to the south but today beneath the Financial District. From the harbor today Boston does not appear to be particularly hilly, not nearly as dramatic as the earliest engravings suggest (figure 8). The skyscrapers far exceed the height of the original terrain, forming a kind of artificial mountain that seems to emerge directly out of the harbor (figure 9). Abstractly, these products of commerce and business acumen recall the topography of the original peninsula.

It is from the Charles River and Cambridge that the original profile remains discernible. The Trimount, having lost nearly sixty feet and two of its peaks, is still perceptible, forming one of the most beloved contemporary views of the city. A dense mass of red-brick houses is crowned by the gilded dome of the State House. But the grand profile of the capitol is no longer viewed against the sky, as it was a century ago. Instead it stands as an animated actor against a more sober backdrop of skyscrapers (figure 10; see also plate 32 vignette).

Other peaks were also cut down. No longer a hill, and with no remains of a fort, Fort Hill no longer exists (see figure 11 in chapter 7 and plate 41 vignette). In the mid-nineteenth century a commercial development leveled the hill, the fort having been replaced with a circular square at the beginning of the century. In turn, this development succumbed at mid-twentieth century to make way for an elevated highway.[8] In the spirit of a palimpsest, however, traces persist—the area became the site of the city's second tallest skyscraper, called International Place. And once the highway is placed underground, as is currently proceeding, a new Fort Hill Square is planned near the original site (figure 11; see also plate 41 vignette).

Figure 8 A detail of a 1774 Paul Revere engraving indicating—in an exaggerated form—the hilly topography of the original Shawmut Peninsula.

Figure 9 View northward toward downtown from Columbia Point ca. 1988 with South Boston in the mid-ground. The twentieth-century silhouette abstractly amplifies the original hilly profile of the Shawmut Peninsula.

The hilly terrain was not limited to the Shawmut Peninsula. A listing of neighborhoods turns up much further topography: Dorchester Heights, Savin Hill, Meeting House Hill, Mission Hill, and Bunker Hill among them. Indeed, in a crescent-shaped figure surrounding the Shawmut Peninsula a series of hills eventually became outer neighborhoods, each generally marked by a meeting house, monument, or institution near the hill's crown.

A good example is the First Church of Roxbury in John Eliot Square with its majestic view of downtown (figure 12). The town of Roxbury, or Rocksbrough, named for the many protruding rock ledges that characterized this uplands area, was founded in 1630, the same year as Boston. The community immediately centered on a small hill, which the present church and square occupy. The meetinghouse dates to 1804 but is, in fact, the fifth church built on the same site; the first is believed to have been constructed in 1632.[9] The physical characteristics and demographics of the area surrounding Eliot Square have changed many times, but the iconic quality of a neighborhood surrounding a white clapboard New England meetinghouse and its pastoral common persists.

In Charlestown there is Breed's Hill, which everyone confuses with Bunker Hill, since the monument commemorating that Revolutionary War battle sits atop it. There was no mistake in siting the monument. The famous "Battle of Bunker Hill" actually took place on Breed's Hill. Place-labeling confusion aside, the composition of hilltop open space, a tall landmark, and surrounding neighborhood here, too, remains. Atop Dorchester Heights in South Boston is a beautiful oval-shaped square with a monument to General Washington at its center; though crowding it to the east is South Boston High, made infamous during the city's 1970s struggle over school integration (figure 13). South Boston was once a peninsula as autonomous as Shawmut, and perhaps because of this the residents of "Southie" have maintained a strong sense of independence, ever resistant to changes imposed by outsiders. Back on the Shawmut Peninsula is Copps Hill, named after a person but occasionally appearing on maps as Corpse Hill. It still commands some of the best views of the inner harbor while, indeed, serving as the burial ground, and major open space, for the North End.

A much broader arc of topography includes the Blue Hills, Stony Brook Reservation, the Middlesex Fells; higher ground still, which toward the end of the nineteenth century began to be acquired by a group of enlightened citizens determined to preserve these natural wilderness areas. Not unlike Rome's fabled ring of seven hills, Boston's high ground provides open air and fine places to dwell, along with a sense of regional containment.

Figure 10 View of Beacon Hill crowned by the gilded dome of the 1798 State House set amid the background of twentieth-century Boston.

Figure 11 A proposal for a new Fort Hill Square to be built near the original site as part of the depression of the Central Artery project.

The hills helped produce one of Boston's exemplary qualities—the existence of many desirable residential areas in proximity to the downtown. One first thinks of Beacon Hill, a truly urbane neighborhood occupying the highest remaining ground on the Shawmut Peninsula (figure 10).[10] Originally part of the three-peaked Trimount (from which Tremont Street got its name) and too steep to settle, it was flattened and became the most fashionable residential address during the early years of the nineteenth century, a status it retains to this day. Attesting to its desirability, a haughty resident once remarked: "Why should I travel when I'm already there?" (see plate 32 vignette)[11]. Earlier, sailors and others were glad to pause there, too, when the hill's western slope, quite prominently labeled on early maps, was known as Mount Whoredom (see plate 28).

But Beacon Hill is not the only place to live downtown, nor were the hills the only places deemed suitable for settlement. Two of Boston's most urbane downtown neighborhoods, the South End and the Back Bay, were created on fill and thus on flat land. From the observatory atop the John Hancock Tower (which houses an interesting exhibit on the growth of Boston) one can survey the contrasting patterns of these adjacent neighborhoods.

The Back Bay was platted for affluent home seekers who could no longer easily find suitable property on crowded Beacon Hill (see plate 39 vignette). With a central spine, Commonwealth Avenue—worthy of a Haussmann—the aspiring mansions of the Back Bay proudly lined their broad, straight, and tree-lined boulevards. To contemporaneous Bostonians the Back Bay was impressive less for its grand architecture, which borrowed equally from French and English styles, than for its rational, modern layout (with sewers, for example) in the manner of Napoleon II's Paris.[12] In the South End, settled a bit earlier and by a more working-class population, the more modestly scaled rowhouses form a checkerboard pattern of traditional perimeter blocks and small green squares. Around these shared open spaces, such as Union Park and Chester Square, the more common local association with English, rather than French influences, is evident. In the South End there are many more vestiges of Georgian London than of Napoleon's Paris (figures 14a and 14b).

Such distinctions, with their often equally sharp boundaries, are characteristic of Boston neighborhoods. Sometimes the architectural differences are the most pronounced. Other times it is topography, or the era of building, or the particular platting of streets and blocks. Often the physical differences are reinforced by ethnic or socioeconomic ones: "Irish" South Boston, for example, or the "Italian" North End, along with "Brahmin" Beacon Hill or "black" Roxbury. Of course such labels can promote troublesome, not just unifying, sentiments about neighborhood

Figure 12 A characteristic neighborhood ensemble; an important local institution, the First Church of Roxbury, commanding a public square, John Eliot Square in Roxbury, overlooking downtown.

identity. Boston remains a city of strongly defined neighborhoods. Mostly it benefits from this. Sometimes it suffers from an attendant tribalism.[13] In Boston the dialectical relationship between neighborhood lines and the wariness of one neighborhood toward an adjoining one seems part of the physical fabric itself.

Figure 13 Another "high ground": Dorchester Heights on Telegraph Hill in South Boston. The tower commemorates General Washington's campaign to seize this strategic hilltop and thus force the British to abandon Boston Harbor. To the right is South Boston High.

Figure 14a Union Park in the South End, one of the dozen-or-so squares reminiscent of Georgian London.

Figure 14b A portion of the South End with its characteristic townhouse block pattern.

The Common came first, and although it is America's oldest public green, it was for generations used (quite pragmatically) for grazing, military training, public punishments, burials, assemblies, festivals, play fields, and garden plots. Its transformation into a park paralleled the emergence of adjacent Beacon Hill as a fashionable place to live. And as the mid-nineteenth-century drive to fill the Back Bay advanced, a thirty-year debate to determine the use of the ropewalks at the swampy, western edge of the Common resolved itself in favor of an enlargement to the Common.

Between 1824 when, at considerable cost, the city bought back the land it had given away for free in 1794, and 1859 when the Back Bay Act definitively secured the land for public purposes, local entrepreneurs—and at times the city council itself—looked for opportunities to subdivide the land into house lots. It almost came to pass. The advocates for a public garden prevailed and set in motion a campaign that would produce one of the most extensive urban open space systems in America (see plate 43 vignette).

Various plans to construct a municipal park system preceded Frederick Law Olmsted's arrival in Boston in 1878. Some were even more ambitious then Olmsted's own plans for (what others would later call) an "emerald necklace" (figure 15).[14] By the time of his engagement, the Boston Park Commissioners had produced a diagrammatic map that determined the park system's future alignment (see plate 43 vignette). Indeed, Olmsted came to Boston because he believed that its park advocates would provide him with the best opportunity to expand upon the limited achievement (in his own terms) of New York's Central Park. Though expansive, Central Park was but a single park. Olmsted's goal was to permeate the increasingly harsh, dense, and expanding industrial city with the healing effects of nature provided in proximity to the daily activities of city dwellers. Combining Olmsted's vision with their own beliefs in the importance of open space, Bostonians pursued park planning as a fundamental concern of city planning: a means to direct city expansion and population density, influence the local economy, improve health and sanitation, and, of course, beautify the city.

By the late 1880s as the emerald necklace was taking root, a campaign for a much more comprehensive regional network of open space began to gather support. Charles Eliot, Olmsted's most able disciple, and Sylvester Baxter, a journalist and editor, initiated this less-often appreci-

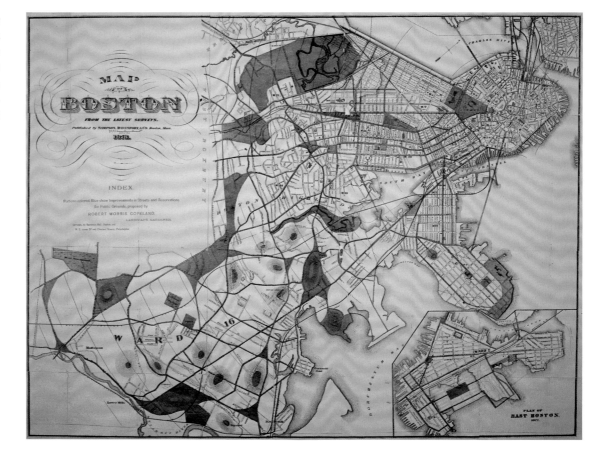

Figure 15 Robert Morris Copeland, *Map of Boston from the Latest Surveys* (1872). One of several proposals for a system of parks for the city that preceded Frederick Law Olmsted's arrival in Boston. The plan appeared in a 1872 pamphlet entitled *The Most Beautiful City in America: Essay and Plan for the Improvement of the City of Boston,* written by Robert Morris Copeland, a landscape gardener and tireless advocate for civic improvements.

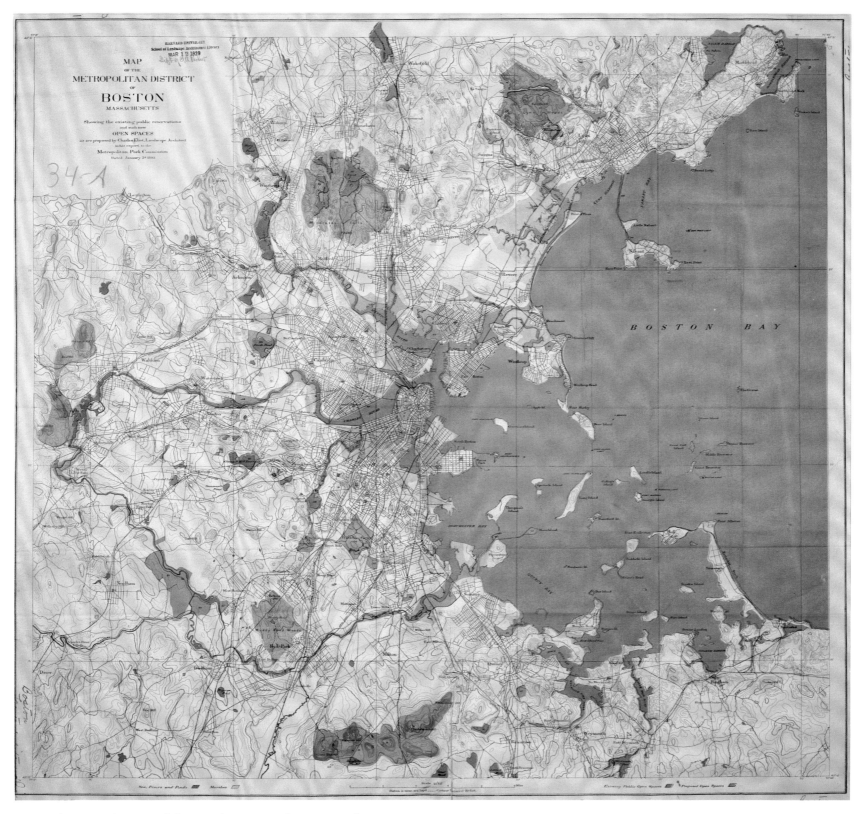

Figure 16 Charles Eliot, *Map of the Metropolitan District of Boston, Massachusetts* (1893). This plan, compiled by one of the founders of the Trustees of Reservations and a disciple of Frederick Law Olmsted, sought to expand Olmsted's ideas for a metropolitan-scaled open space system. The plan formed the basis for the Metropolitan District Commission, which was established in the same year. Compare Eliot's dream to the reality achieved a century later in the NASA high-altitude photograph on p. 114.

ated but even more audacious plan to encircle Boston with a second "green" ring. By the turn of the century an impressive 15,000 acres of what they termed "public reservations" had been assembled, including thirty miles of river frontage, ten miles of ocean shoreline, and twenty-two miles of right-of-way for parkways.

Along with preserving the New England landscape, Eliot and Baxter called for more cooperation between Boston and its thirty-eight neighboring communities. Problems of sewerage, road building, and even social services, they argued, required metropolitan alliances. They envisioned their visible ring of natural reservations as an emblem of a new political ring. Their efforts resulted in the formation of what is now the Metropolitan District Commission and a still-evolving hope for regional governance.[15] Comparing Eliot's 1893 metropolitan open space plan, which shows both necklaces (figure 16) to a contemporary high-altitude aerial photograph of the region (see plate 23 vignette) reveals the success of their vision.

That legacy continues. Recent examples of urban revitalization incorporating open space are many. A vast parking lot at the harbor's edge, land once used for maritime purposes, was transformed into Christopher Columbus Park during the 1970s. An unsightly, dilapidated garage was replaced by an underground garage and a street-level park at Post Office Square in the 1980s[16] (figure 17). In the 1990s, the overhead Central Artery is being placed underground with a system of civic and open spaces planned for its surface. This massive undertaking became conceivable after the successful conversion of the Southwest Corridor (a seven-mile-long stretch of demolitions for a highway that was never built) into a series of parks and boulevards, a new subway line, and neighborhood institutions during the 1980s and 1990s. And the transformation of the old Eastern Railroad corridor in East Boston into a three-mile linear park is underway. The park will connect the inner harbor to Belle Isle Salt Marsh, one of the last sizable vestiges of the original salt marsh geography.

With such examples Bostonians have, again and again, successfully reenacted the battle over the use of the obsolete ropewalks at the base of the original Common.

Figure 17a and b Before and after views of Post Office Square. For many years a thoroughly unmemorable parking garage, the site was redeveloped by a group called the Friends of Post Office Square, who with the city's assistance purchased the garage, replaced it with a seven-level underground garage, and built a public park above. In honor of the founder of the Friends of Post Office Square, the park was rededicated by the mayor of Boston in 1997 as the Norman B. Leventhal Park at Post Office Square.

It was Captain John Smith, seeking the favor of the fifteen-year-old future King Charles I, who sought out the young prince's advice about place names for his 1616 map of New England. Somehow the references to the "Massachuets" River in Smith's written account of his journey were replaced by the clear label of "The River Charles" on his canonical first map of the region (figure 18; see also plate 7). The solicitous renaming of the river took far less effort than the task of preserving its banks as a great public park. One of the longest campaigns on behalf of public place-making involved this other Boston waterfront.

The potential of a grand basin between Boston and Cambridge captivated the imaginations of generations of Bostonians and produced a succession of schemes from the 1840s until the 1930s, when the Charles River Esplanade began to assume its current character. Robert Gourlay's 1844 metropolitan-scaled crescent (figure 19), published well before the start of the filling of the Back Bay, was followed by Charles Davenport's romanticized evocation of Hamburg's Alster Basin in 1875 (figure 20) and by several plans by Olmsted to connect the river to his emerald necklace. Nearly a dozen separate proposals for islands in the middle of the river, evoking the qualities of the Seine, the Tiber, and the Thames, explored the virtues of intimate scale and density of activity along the river (figure 21).[17] Marvelous projections of esplanades, terraces, and pleasure drives argued for reserving both banks for public purposes long before waterfronts were recognized as bucolic civic amenities.

Figure 18 *(top)* Detail from the John Smith map (see plate 7).

Figure 19 *(bottom)* Robert Gourlay, *General Plan for enlarging and improving the City of Boston* (1844). Perhaps the most visionary plan ever produced for Boston, anticipating many things including the need to redesign the banks of the Charles River Basin into a grand residential esplanade. Gourlay's home town of Edinburgh and his knowledge of London and Bath influenced his plan. His intent was to prepare Boston to accommodate a million people, which he (correctly) predicted would occur within a century. A decade before Boston had even seen a horse car, he recommended a network of suburban commuter railroad lines that would extend underground as they entered the city. Not steam, but compressed air, distributed from a central station like electricity today, would power his moving machines. His Beacon Street railway predicted the Green Line alignment quite well, and his tunnel between the State House and the South Ferry clairvoyantly anticipated both the Blue Line and the Callahan Tunnel to East Boston.

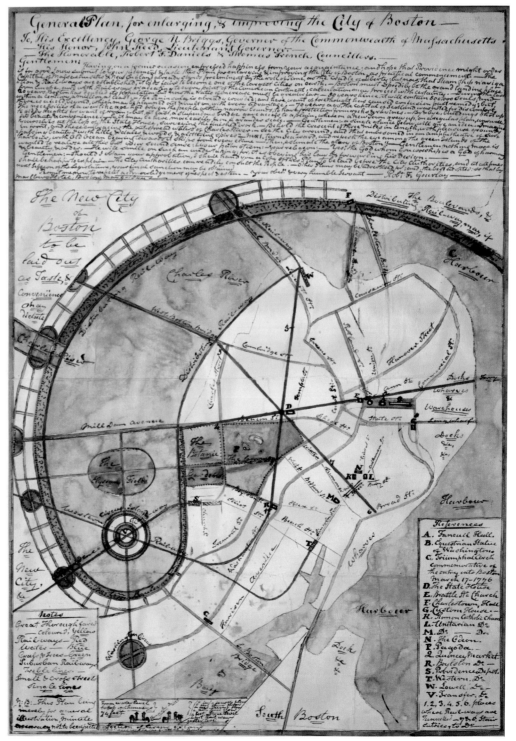

NEW BOSTON AND CHARLES RIVER BASIN.

Figure 20 *New Boston and Charles River Basin* as proposed by Charles Davenport and drawn by Albert Coolidge in 1875. Another of the many proposals—this one evoking Hamburg's Alster Basin—that continued the campaign begun by Robert Gourlay (figure 19) to capture the banks of the Charles River for civic and recreational purposes.

Figure 21 One of more than a dozen proposals over a twenty-year period to create an island in the middle of the Charles River Basin. This version was drawn in 1907 by Ralph Adams Cram, one of Boston's most illustrious architects of the period, for a report on municipal improvements. A rationale common to most of the island projects was to minimize the width of the basin, reducing the spans of the various bridges being proposed to connect Cambridge and Boston. But the real impact of these was to further the long campaign that eventually led to the construction of the Charles River Esplanade.

Some of these evocations were drawn in protest against a quite different possibility. During the nineteenth century, industrial activities, not parks, were thought to be the most sensible uses for waterfronts. Since the Back Bay of the Charles River was criss-crossed with railroad trestles, one idea for filling in the bay involved relocating the tracks to the river's edge (figure 22). The rationale was simple. The Beacon Street mill dam was already a heavily used road and workaday environment. Enlarging it to include the railroads would unencumber the middle for residential block development. That is where the real estate value was assumed to be, not along the muddy, tidal river's edge. Indeed, Commonwealth Avenue and several preceding versions of centrally located oval-shaped lakes were intended to create a more hospitable, marketable setting around which to build homes.

In the end, financial and bureaucratic obstacles, not the visionary rendering of riverfront parks, prevented the moving of the tracks. (These were finally removed in the 1950s, when the Prudential Insurance

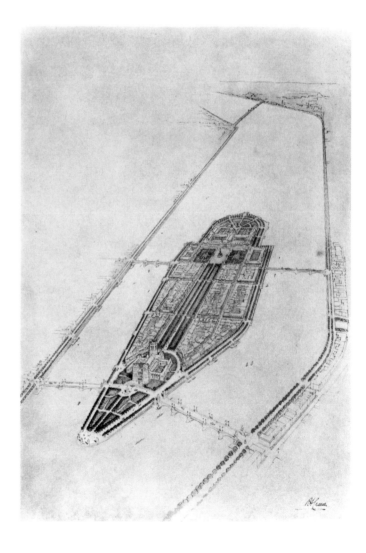

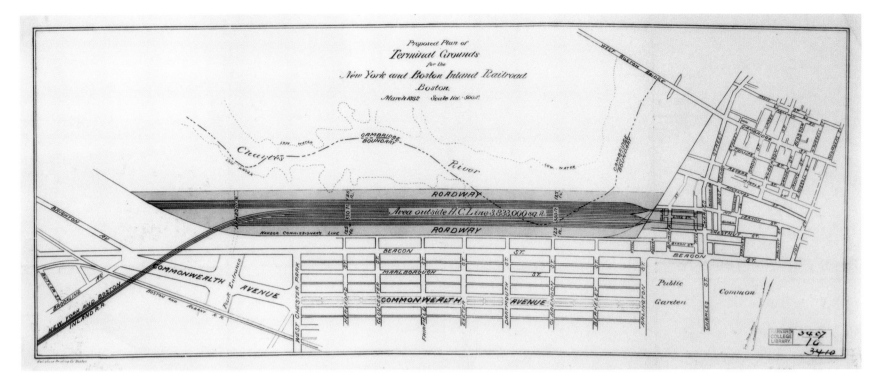

Figure 22 *Proposed Plan of Terminal Grounds for the New York and Boston Inland Railroad*
(1882). A fate common to many American urban waterfronts, shorelines devoted to railroad yards, temporarily loomed as a possibility for the Charles River. Fortunately, visions
of a different possibility such as those of Gourlay (figure 19), Davenport (figure 20), Cram
(figure 21), and others eventually prevailed.

Company of America built its headquarters on the largely abandoned rail
yards splitting the Back Bay and the South End.) Having avoided a riverfront incursion by the railroad, the eventual creation of the recreational
basin was, nonetheless, propelled by a transportation imperative. The controversial decision in the late 1940s to construct a high-volume road along
the Back Bay embankment to relieve downtown traffic provided the final
impetus to finish the Esplanade. As Nancy S. Seasholes describes in her
essay, the construction of Storrow Drive, along with the earlier damming
of the river to control tides, galvanized the effort to implement the (by-
then) ninety-year-old plan to preserve the river's edge for everyone's enjoyment.

No plans to build pleasure islands in the Charles River were ever
realized. But, today, the eighteen miles of continuous public access along
both the Cambridge and Boston edges of the Charles River Basin (popular
training ground for aspiring Boston Marathoners) constitute one of the
treasures of the metropolitan area. And perhaps these riverfronts are one of
the reasons the Charles carries the local moniker of the "People's River."[18]

SPOKES AND CIRCUMFERENTIALS FOR THE HUB

For a long time, connecting the peninsula to outlying areas was the main
concern of regional mobility. Contemporary street maps still reveal several intertwined spider's webs in which the dominant lines are those radiating outward. The "spokes of the Hub," Bostonians call these, and among
them are virtually every major artery of pre-twentieth century Boston:
Washington Street (the original neck), Tremont Street, Columbus
Avenue, Huntington Avenue, Commonwealth Avenue, Cambridge Street,
Hanover Street, Dorchester Avenue. That so many are called avenues is
noteworthy. Each has, over time brought life to the center of the city, and
provided a route for outward expansion.

Commonwealth Avenue is the most famous of these and the most
beautiful, best portraying American civic ambitions at the turn of the
nineteenth century (see plate 39 vignette). But if "Comm. Ave." is the
most cosmopolitan, Huntington Avenue is the most revealing. It is a virtual X ray through one hundred years of American urbanization (figure

Wanderers), and even the headquarters of the Society for the Prevention of Cruelty to Animals. These institutions sought greener, healthier, more generous grounds, away from the congestion and tumult of the industrial city, just as families seeking homes in the suburbs would later do.

Move out along Huntington Avenue and some of Boston's other radiating spokes, and you will see the traditionally nucleated civic elements of the city give way to the linear corridors of contemporary suburbia. A recent campaign extolling the virtues of Boston, however, has recognized this unusual collection of cultural resources. The phrase "Avenue of the Arts" has been added to each Huntington Avenue street sign. The hope accompanying this sign (harbored in many cities) is that after a century of retreating from cities, appreciation for cultural institutions and the districts they form will lead to a new appreciation for cities overall.

Of course, cities that develop along radial lines eventually cry out for connecting rings. Many Bostonians can describe those moments of frustrated awareness when it becomes apparent that to get from point A to point B requires traversing two sides of a triangle. The public transportation system has a similar flaw; getting from Copley Square to Harvard Square on the subway requires first going to Park Street, some 105 degrees to the east of where the proverbial crow would fly. The transportation imperative of the twentieth century, therefore, has been to connect the spokes with a stronger pattern of circumferentials.

Another look at a contemporary map reveals the efforts to achieve these circumferentials. The park system, with its connecting boulevards, was the first attempt to intersect the radiating road network and ring the city. In the mid-twentieth century circumferential highways like Route 128 did so as well. And at the end of the century there is talk of a circumferential transit corridor—an Urban Ring—that would reduce the "two-sides-of-the-triangle" problem as well as increase the sense of proximity to the neighborhoods encircling Boston's traditional urban core.[19]

PLACES RENEWED

For nearly a half-century, between World War I and the late 1950s, Boston hibernated, losing its old industrial and mercantile economic base and a good third of its population. People came to regard it as a town without a future, described more than once as a "hopeless backwater." Even a newly elected mayor, Collins in 1960, spoke about a "malaise of the spirit" and how ashamed people were about the state of their city.[20] The shame, along with eventually unacceptable economic stagnation, instigated what many first considered a hopeless effort at large-scale redevelopment. Propelled by practical-minded visionaries and generous federal urban renewal subsidy programs, a near-desperate period of demolition and reconstruction ensued. At the height of the era of urban renewal one quarter of the city was designated an urban renewal area.

23). Beginning at Copley Square, one of Boston's cherished urban nodes, Huntington Avenue eventually becomes Route 9, infamous collector of sprawl far in the western suburbs. Between the malls of Route 9 and the Back Bay lies a remarkable transition through time, changing land uses, and evolving visions of urbanity.

We generally think of suburbanization as a movement of homeowners, not cultural institutions. From the late nineteenth century onward, however, various institutions sought new sites along Huntington Avenue, especially where the avenue paralleled Olmsted's park system. Among these were museums (including the Museum of Fine Arts), performance halls (as Symphony Hall, Jordan Hall, the Boston Opera House [now demolished], and the present home of the Huntington Theater Company), schools (including Northeastern University, Wentworth Institute of Technology, and the Massachusetts College of Art), hospitals (eventually consolidating into the Longwood Medical Area), orphanages (such as the Home for Little

The 1950 *General Plan for Boston* set the tone. Labeling, for example, the West End as "an obsolete neighborhood," it depicted "a new plan" for this apparently tired and run-down district immediately to the north of Beacon Hill (figure 24).[21] The "new" was meant literally. Modernization was not to come from preserving, adapting, or fixing up, but through complete reconstruction along new block patterns and architectural forms. For the moment, at least, Boston's old architecture and historic neighborhoods were only impediments to progress, reminders of work left to be done.

The *General Plan* may have been, in part, inspired by the audacity of planners like Martin Wagner, a young disciple of Walter Gropius. In 1947 he published the ultimate reconstruction plan; the entire peninsula cleared in favor of a continuous megastructure following the alignment of a superhighway (figure 25).[22] Selected survivals of the old city—the historic monuments—would remain as pavilions in a vast park that covered the Shawmut Peninsula. A 1964 photo of downtown shows how perilously close to Wagner's vision Boston came, its heart virtually demolished, its planners confident that only a step this radical would produce economic and social revival (figure 26).

Those skeptical of such heavy-handed ways to renewal looked at Wagner's question-mark-shaped new city and asked, whither Boston? But in response to such skeptics a Karl Marx phrase (without attribution) was frequently used: "You can't make an omelet without cracking some eggs."

The old West End was selected to be one of the first eggs. The modern omelet of Charles River Park left few palimpsest-like reminders of the past, but may have (inadvertently) accelerated the formation of neighborhood activists, preservation groups, and advocacy planners who eventually organized to save the Back Bay and much of the South End from comparable renewal efforts. But a famous sign along Storrow Drive at Charles River Park—which reads "If you lived here, you'd be home now"—is a reminder of the noble, if naive, hope of the times. New environments such as Charles River Park, *built in the middle of the city,* would stem the flow of middle-class citizens decamping Boston for the suburbs.

Among the most impressive achievements of the initial decade of renewal was the conversion of another sixty acres of decrepit and congested downtown—the local haunt of sailors on leave—into a modern-day acropolis for government. Seedy Scollay Square was self-consciously renamed Government Center and was intended to symbolize the reemergence of the "Cradle of Liberty" as a vital modern city (figures 27a and 27b). At the heart of this Government Center was a monumental ten-acre plaza and an even more monumental new city hall. The subject of an international design competition held in 1962, both plaza and city hall received instant and prolonged international acclaim. That particular strand of mid-century modern architecture called the "New Brutalism" was believed to properly represent a newly confident Boston emerging from its lengthy decline.

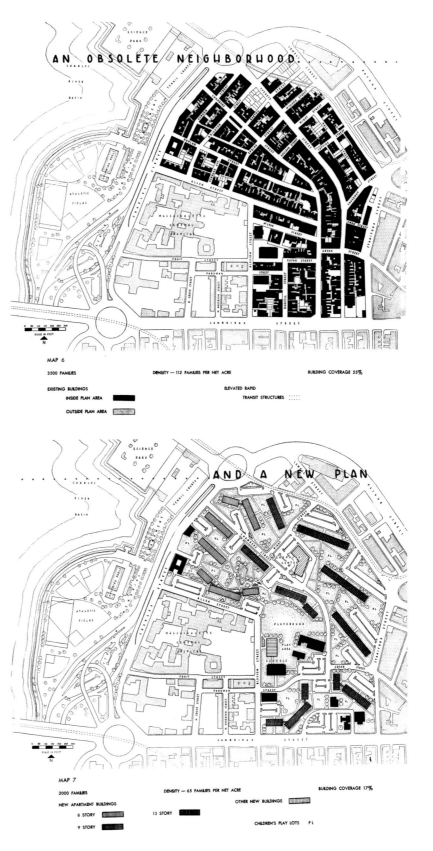

Figure 24 *The General Plan for Boston,* published by the City Planning Department in 1950, contained this rather harrowing analysis of how to achieve renewal. What was eventually done was quite similar. Today's planners would be inclined to reverse the titles of the two drawings.

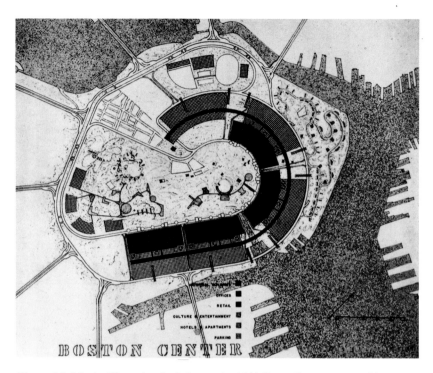

Figure 25 Martin Wagner's submission to the 1944 *Boston Contest,* a competition sponsored by several major institutions to seek the best planning ideas for renewing Boston. Wagner's "renewal" would have come at the expense of first demolishing most of the city, something that the federally sponsored urban renewal programs of the 1950s and 1960s came close to achieving (figure 26).

As the century closes Government Center is in the process of being renewed again, and for many not a moment too soon.[23] While taking pride in the achievements of renewal and reinvestment, most Bostonians never grew to love their new city hall or the austere plaza in which it aloofly sat. The subsequent rejection of the radical means of urban renewal and the increased interest in traditional urban patterns, history, local activism, and public input to planning led to a different assessment of the symbolism of Government Center. As the downtown renewed itself relying on a mixture of commercial, cultural, and residential investment, Government Center's great size, indifference to history, and functional isolation came to represent, for many, the shortcomings of mid-century, top-down planning.

Having been "renewed" beyond recognition in the 1960s, the present replanning aims to reveal bits of the old Scollay Square palimpsest. Among the ideas is to restore Hanover Street, which, like twenty-one other streets, was vacated to make room for Government Center. Another is to reduce the segregation of uses by adding new uses to the space, including a hotel to form a new edge for the plaza. (During its turn-of-the-century heyday Scollay Square boasted three hotels.) A third goal is to reduce the starkness of the plaza through a richer design of the landscape. However this particular effort at renewing urban renewal will conclude, it has served as a reminder that renewal should be an ongoing rather than an epochal process.

Figure 26 By 1964 it might have seemed to some as if Martin Wagner's plan was being implemented. The view shows the extent of the demolition in Scollay Square in preparation for the future Government Center area. The federal office project, today's John F. Kennedy General Services Administration complex, is seen under construction.

Figures 27a and b Photographs of the Scollay Square area looking toward Fanueil Hall taken in 1911 and 1985 from approximately the same vantage point. Few buildings of the earlier era remain. One notable survivor is the Sears Crescent, seen beneath and to the left of the Lipton's Teas sign in the 1911 photo. Faneuil Hall and the Old State House also, thankfully, survive.

Figure 28 A 1930s view of downtown, then and since 1915 dominated by the singular, campanile-like Customs House Tower. Compare this view to the present Boston skyline depicted in the frontispiece. In the foreground one can see a portion of the radiating rail spurs from which Fan Pier got its name.

Modernizing Boston has also meant building higher. In 1915 the city's century-old Customs House received an addition. It was twenty-six stories high and was constructed right on top of the dome of the original Greek Revival building. Modern-day preservationists would surely not have the courage, and yet the new Custom House became one of Boston's most beloved landmarks. For many years the Custom House Tower dom-

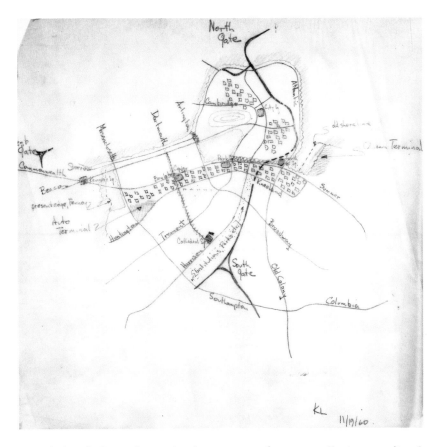

Figure 29 *(top)* The earliest graphic representation of the "Tall Spine," an idea for channeling the expansion of the downtown into a dense band of development over an old rail corridor and the Massachusetts Turnpike, which border the Back Bay. It was sketched by Kevin Lynch during a 1961 meeting of a Boston Society of Architects committee formulating an urban design plan for central Boston.

Figure 30 *(bottom)* The "Tall Spine" nearly forty years in the making as it appears from atop the Blue Hills to the south of the city.

inated the skyline, almost in the manner of a campanile in a medieval town (figure 28). Few tall buildings were built in Boston during its decades of economic stagnation. Indeed, until the deluge of development in the 1970s and 1980s, a skyscraper under construction was a welcome sign of progress. No more.

As this is being written tall buildings are perceived as unwelcome intruders. They are blamed for overwhelming the traditional scale and character of the downtown. They are accused of causing congestion, robbing sunlight from the street, being symptomatic only of periodically inflated real-estate markets. Few recall that at mid-century a theory emerged for locating tall buildings in and around the central core.

In 1961 Kevin Lynch, a noted urban planner and MIT professor, conceptualized a "tall spine" for Boston.[24] Lynch foresaw the need to channel contemporary-scaled development away from fragile historic districts. He projected the expansion of the downtown into a dense linear band between the historic neighborhoods of the Back Bay and the South End, filling a corridor of largely abandoned rail yards and paralleling the then recently constructed Massachusetts Turnpike (figure 29). Being more optimistic about tall buildings then Boston's current planners, and mindful that they are as characteristic of the twentieth-century American city as the Back Bay or Beacon Hill were of the nineteenth-century city, Lynch hoped to marshal them into a coherent pattern.

The logic of Lynch's doodle has unofficially guided the physical transformation of the commercial core. After four decades of building, the spine is visible and evokes an unanticipated historical association. From points in the harbor as well as from the high ground at the periphery of the city, Boston's tall silhouette seems to spiral outward from the Shawmut Peninsula to form a line marching southwest-ward. As one recalls the original configuration of the Shawmut Peninsula, with its narrow neck to the mainland, this figure seems to be reemerging out of glass, steel, and concrete. Nonsense, you say; but climb atop the Great Blue Hill and take a look! (figure 30).

Figure 31 A 1996 aerial view of several of the inner islands with the city in the background. Many unused and some harshly misused over time, the thirty-three islands in Boston Harbor nonetheless constitute one of the great open space treasures of the metropolitan area. The islands are listed on the National Register of Historic Places as an archaeological district and are administered as a national park area by a partnership of federal, state and local agencies under the jurisdiction of the secretary of the interior.

THE ARCHIPELAGO

From atop the Blue Hills, or the upper floors of Boston's skyscrapers, one glimpses another realm—of islands (figures 31 and 35; see also plate 18 vignette). Today's metropolitan region of nearly four million people bears little resemblance to the fragile settlement that first took hold on the isolated Shawmut Peninsula. How can we evoke what the early settlers encountered? Some of the thirty-three islands, many uninhabited and barely used, that grace Boston Harbor may provide an inkling.

Under a management plan being developed by the National Park Service, this archipelago is in search of a modern destiny. Native Americans (of course) and the early colonists used the islands well; for farming, fishing, cattle grazing, lumbering, some quarrying, and hunting (deer were known to swim out to Deer Island to avoid wolves), and periodically as summer resorts. Gradually, especially from the mid-nineteenth century on,

the range of uses diminished. The islands became repositories for unwanted things such as waste or invalids. They proved useful for the internment of the sick, the orphaned, and those who broke the law. They provided homes for unsavory industries such as the rendering of horse carcasses. Some disappeared in the path of landfill projects; Bird, Apple, and Governor's are now simply part of the East Boston and Logan Airport landmass. And the most consistent use on many was military defense.[25]

Many of the islands have experienced several lives. It is hard today to imagine Sheep Island as a popular grazing area because erosion has reduced its size from twenty-five to less than two acres since colonial times. One can surmise how Hangman Island got its name and be glad that the practice has ceased. On Thompson Island a trading post was established in 1626, four years before the founding of Boston. It contains one of the best-preserved tidal ponds and salt marshes on the islands; a great asset for the Outward-Bound program for Boston schoolchildren housed on the island. The island's nurturing of children dates back to 1883, when the Boston Asylum of Indigent Boys moved there. The small Rainsford Island somehow managed to host both a quarantine hospital and a summer resort for over a hundred years, accommodating tourists between epidemics.

During World War II nine of the islands were fortified. One of these, Georges Island, is still dominated by the formidable Fort Warren. Begun in 1833, it served as an important military encampment and a prisoner-of-war facility during the Civil War. It was modernized and outfitted for each subsequent naval threat including the Spanish-American War and both world wars. After its decommissioning in 1951, and a (fortunately) aborted plan to use it for storing hazardous waste, the responsibility for the island shifted to the Metropolitan District Commission, and its life as a recreational area began. Today it is among the few harbor islands used as a public park, with regular ferry service from Boston.

The island with the longest service record for defense, extending from the 1630s to World War II, is Castle Island. Yet no hostile shots were ever fired to or from it, nor is it today an island, having been connected by a bridge to the South Boston peninsula in the 1890s as part of Olmsted's design for Marine Park. Its Fort Independence, the eighth fort believed to have occupied the site, dates to the 1830s. Over the years a host of facilities were housed on the island including a mid-eighteenth-century hospital for smallpox isolation, a use common to several of the islands. While no longer an island, Castle Island is today the eastern terminus for the city's park system, becoming the bead that allows Olmsted's emerald necklace to touch the sea. There are few better settings from which to view—atop a rampart whose foundations date back to the first years of the city—both the inner urbanized harbor and the still scarcely populated islands of the outer harbor (see figure 11 in chapter 1).

Gazing due east from downtown one encounters a vast, unnaturally flat, and strangely unfilled expanse of land (figures 32 and 33). The Commonwealth Flats have never been full, having been created to accommodate a great future port and completed about the time that Boston's maritime functions began to wane. But this century-long emptiness is soon to end, for this is the direction of Boston's downtown expansion as the twentieth century closes. The question is less *when* than *what* will be built there, and in what increments of size?

Having large tracts of undeveloped land so close to the downtown leads, on the one hand, to proposals for those things that contemporary American cities covet but find it hard to make room for—convention centers, stadiums, courthouses, hotels, retail/entertainment complexes, and the like. On the other hand, the residents of nearby South Boston, for whom the present flats have represented a barrier to the harbor, see an opportunity for new neighborhoods taking advantage, at last, of the harbor setting. Finally, there are those who still give priority to industry, seeking to maintain Boston's long tradition of sustaining livelihood from the sea by arguing for a competitive modern port.

There may well be room for all of these futures, for the area of the Commonwealth Flats is as large as the original Shawmut Peninsula itself.

Figure 32 View of the Commonwealth Flats area looking west toward downtown (1998). A turn-of-the century land-making venture to create a modern port that, as luck would have it, would never fully be needed for its intended purpose. Underutilized for much of its life as Boston's maritime industries waned, the area has recently been rechristened the Seaport District and is currently the subject of substantial planning and redevelopment efforts. Indeed, the infilling has begun; one can see a new hotel in the foreground and the new Federal Courthouse on Fan Pier.

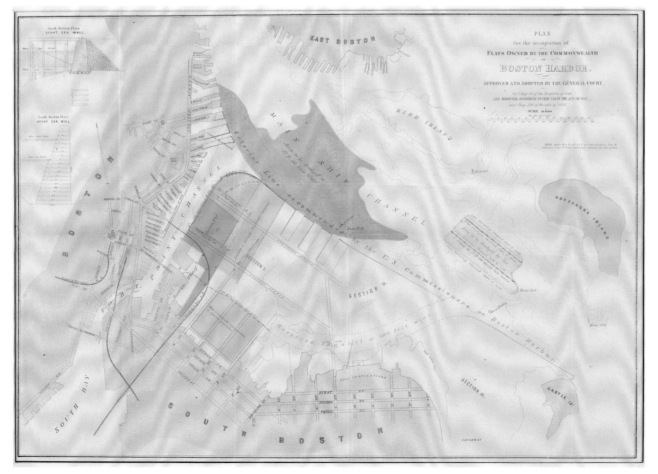

Figure 33 *Plan for the occupation of Flats Owned by the Commonwealth in Boston Harbor* (1870). The approximate area that would eventually be filled to create the Commonwealth Flats area of South Boston as shown in the *Fourth Annual Report of the Board of Harbor Commissioners*. The main purpose of the map was to show the southwesterly line of demarcation for the main shipping channel so that a masonry seawall might be built followed by the dredging of the channel to improve navigability. Compare with the contemporary view in figure 32.

But it is unlikely that it will take three centuries to fill up—hence, the worry. Contemporary Americans are rapacious users of land. As the twentieth century closes, and a new harbor tunnel to the airport opens, land speculators, planning consultants, anxious public servants, naysayers, and construction cranes abound. A new Boston could emerge here "overnight," minus the grace and intricacy that only time and history can produce. But is the specter of a Bostonian "edge city," like those along the beltways encircling Atlanta or Houston or Washington, D.C., the only fear, or is it the sense that something more basic is at risk?

Here, after all, are survivals of a working waterfront. A fishing fleet still anchors there, and several fish processors conduct their business. There are two dry docks, neither in use. There is a cruise ship terminal and a container port. There are unique maritime facilities such as the New England Fish Exchange—Fish Pier, for short (figure 34). Built in 1913, Fish Pier was once (and may still be) the world's largest pier devoted exclusively to the fishing industry. Two parallel warehouses 730 feet long project out into the harbor. At their harbor end a neoclassical headhouse is symmetrically placed. For many years it was the venue for daily fish auctions. What the Uffizi is to art in Florence, Fish Pier was to fishing in Boston. They even share a plan configuration. As office towers for financial institutions and convention center hotels are planned for the area—neither less essential to Boston's current economy than fish were a generation or two earlier—many are determined that Fish Pier, and something of the fish and fishermen, are allowed to persist into the next iteration of the flats.

DIGGING STILL

Looking out over this next Boston and the islands beyond reminds us that the moving of earth is still an important ingredient of the Boston palimpsest. As the very highway, the Central Artery, whose construction eradicated the remains of one hill (Fort Hill) is replaced by an underground highway, the excavations are producing a new hill, on an island no less. In a reversal of precedent, one harbor island is gaining height. A half-century's worth of the city's garbage, piled on Spectacle Island (one of the harbor's most abused) is being capped to create a new island park and promontory with the three million cubic yards of dirt dug up for the Central Artery and Third Harbor Tunnel projects (figure 35). In Boston, somehow, this does not seem so out of the ordinary.

Boston continues to shape and remake itself. Of all American cities one cannot say about Boston, as Gertrude Stein said of her native Oakland, that there is no there there. History-making and place-making have always thrived in parallel. And one looks in anticipation to how future maps of Boston will record the continuation of both enterprises.

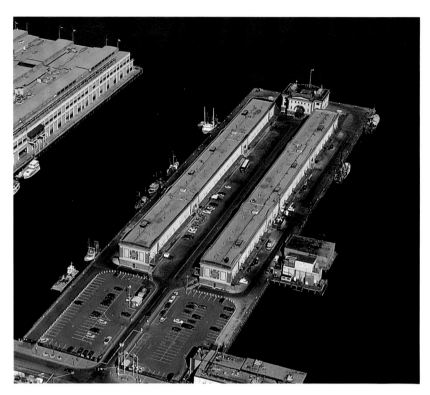

Figure 34 The New England Fish Exchange, or Fish Pier, completed in 1913. It remains the actual and certainly the symbolic home of the Boston fishing fleet.

Figure 35 Spectacle Island with Boston in the background, June 1996, as it is being transformed with excavated material from the Central Artery / Third Harbor Tunnel project. Evidence of Native American visits to the island date back to 500 A.D., but for the past century or more it has served the city as a dump. The polluted soil is being capped by the highway project to create a 105-acre public park.

NOTES

1. For some, such names—not the physical environment—are what comes to mind when Boston is mentioned. A generation ago Boston's official Bicentennial guide began with the following passage, a curious opening to a tourist's guide: "Say New York or Chicago or Los Angeles or San Francisco or even Philadelphia—and you think of place. But say Boston and you think, first, of people. Dozens of names start rolling like a drumbeat." See Cleveland Amory, "Boston in the 'Proper' Spirit," introduction to *Boston: The Official Bicentennial Guidebook* (New York: E. P. Dutton & Co., 1975).

2. In popular language the term *landfill* is used to describe the various topographical changes that have been made in Boston. This is, of course, technically inaccurate. As Nancy Seasholes describes in her essay, *land making* is the more appropriate term.

3. A *palimpsest* is a medieval writing surface, usually a parchment, from which earlier writing has been imperfectly erased to make room for a newer text. The scarcity of paper in the medieval world required its reuse, not unlike land in the city always under pressure to redevelop. Reading a palimpsest, like experiencing a city, reveals successive layers of content, the partial erasures—survivals of earlier texts or histories—remaining no less poignant than the uppermost one.

4. For a good overview of its history see James L. Bruce, *The Old State House* (Boston, 1965).

5. See the Peter Faneuil / Faneuil Hall vignette (plate 26 vignette).

6. Walter Muir Whitehill, *Boston: A Topographical History,* 2d ed. (Cambridge: Harvard University Press, 1968).

7. The idea for converting land at the water's edge for public purposes gained initial momentum with the *Downtown Waterfront Urban Renewal Area* plan published by the Boston Redevelopment Authority in 1964. Twenty years later a specific program to pursue a *continuous* public edge along the waterfront was approved by the city. See *HarborPark* (Boston: Boston Redevelopment Authority, 1984). The initial scope of a seven-mile stretch of the central waterfront from Charlestown to South Boston has since been expanded to encompass nearly forty-seven miles of shoreline including portions of the Mystic River, Chelsea, East Boston, and the perimeter of the airport, and stretching all the way to the Neponset River along Boston's southern border.

8. The combined Central Artery/Third Harbor Tunnel Project is currently, at around eleven billion dollars, the largest public works project in the United States. Its origins date back to the 1970s. Planning, design, and construction began in earnest in the late 1980s. Completion is scheduled for approximately 2004. Its history, of course, has not yet been written. See the Central Artery vignette (plate 50 vignette).

9. Among this old congregation's many illustrious pastors was John Eliot, who is remembered for his humane interest in the local Indians, very rare for a mid-seventeenth-century ministry. In a less famous, though parallel, event to Paul Revere's "midnight ride," William Dawes left the First Church to warn patriots in these parts about the approaching British troops.

10. See the Beacon Hill vignette (plate 32 vignette). See also Barbara W. Moore and Gail Weesner, *Beacon Hill: A Living Portrait* (Boston: Century Hill Press, 1992).

11. Quoted in Michael P. Conzen and George K. Lewis, *Boston: A Geographical Portrait* (Cambridge, Mass.: Ballinger, 1976).

12. For a history of the Back Bay see: Bainbridge Bunting, *Houses of the Back Bay: An Architectural History, 1840–1917* (Cambridge: Harvard University Press, 1967); Mona Domosh, *Invented Cities: The Creation of Landscape in Nineteenth Century New York and Boston,* especially chapter 4 (New Haven: Yale University Press, 1996); Lewis Mumford, ed., *Back Bay Boston: The City as Work of Art* (Boston: Museum of Fine Arts, 1969); Whitehill, *Boston.* See also Back Bay vignette (plate 39 vignette).

13. The literature on the city's neighborhoods, ethnic histories, and demographic changes is vast. The following provide a good starting point for additional reading: Herbert Gans, *The Urban Villagers: Group and Class in the Life of Italian Americans,* rev. ed. (New York: Free Press, 1982); Oscar Handlin, *Boston's Immigrants, 1790–1880* (New York: Atheneum, 1959); Brett Howard, *Boston, A Social History* (New York: Hawthorn Books, 1976); Mel King, *Chain of Change: Struggles for Black Community Development* (Boston: South End Press, 1981); Anthony J. Lukas, *Common Ground: A Turbulent Decade in the Lives of Three American Families* (New York: Knopf, 1985); Thomas O'Connor, *South Boston, My Home Town: The History of an Ethnic Neighborhood* (Boston: Quinlan Press, 1988); Stephan Thernstrom, *The Other Bostonians: Poverty and Progress in the American Metropolis, 1880–1970* (Cambridge: Harvard University Press, 1973); William Whyte, *Street Corner Society: the Social Structure of an Italian Slum* (Chicago: University of Chicago Press, 1943). In 1995 The Boston Landmarks Commission published a series of pamphlets on each of thirteen Boston neighborhoods under the general title of *Exploring Boston's Neighborhoods.*

14. For the best overview of Frederick Law Olmsted's work on the Boston Park System see Cynthia Zaitzevsky, *Frederick Law Olmsted and the Boston Park System* (Cambridge: Harvard University Press, 1982). See also the Frederick Law Olmsted vignette (plate 43 vignette).

15. *A History and Description of the Boston Metropolitan Park* (Boston: Commonwealth of Massachusetts, Metropolitan District Commission, 1900).

16. A good overview of how Post Office Square came to be redeveloped is found in the *Urban Land Institute Project Reference Files* 24, no. 3 (January–March 1994). See also Julia Collins, "There Was a Parking Lot . . . ," *Landscape Architecture,* September 1992.

17. *Report Made to the Boston Society of Architects by its Committee on Municipal Improvements* (Boston, 1907). See also Alex Krieger, *Past Futures: Two Centuries of Imagining Boston* (Cambridge: Harvard University Graduate School of Design, 1985).

18. Max Hall, *The Charles: The People's River* (Boston: David Godine, 1986).

19. While the idea of a circumferential transportation corridor for Boston dates back to the early part of the century (as plate 45 vignette describes) and is most clearly manifested today by Route 128 and Interstate 495, the present initiative seeks to achieve a similar circumferential corridor via public transportation by designing a new line that would connect many of the city's outlying neighborhoods and early suburbs. See George Thrush, *The New Urban Ring* (1994), a Northeastern University publication that followed a series of urban design charrettes held in 1992–1993 to discuss the merits of such a "ring."

20. Thomas H. O'Conner, *Building a New Boston: Politics and Urban Renewal 1950 to 1970* (Boston: Northeastern University Press, Boston, 1993).

21. For the most comprehensive account of the life in the West End leading up to urban renewal see Gans, *The Urban Villagers.* For excellent historical accounts of the period of Boston urban renewal see O'Connor, *Building a New Boston,* and Lawrence W. Kennedy, *Planning the City upon a Hill: Boston Since 1630* (Amherst: University of Massachusetts Press, 1992).

22. Martin Wagner, "Der Neubau Der City," *Baurundschau* (Germany), no. 17/18, September 1948. See also William R. Greeley, ed., *The Boston Contest: A Master Program in the Metropolitan Area* (Boston, 1944).

23. At the request of Mayor Thomas Menino, the Trust for City Hall Plaza, a non-profit organization funded by approximately three dozen major Boston corporations and institutions, was formed in 1995. The trust's mandate is to help the city of Boston develop a long range plan for the redesign, programming, and maintenance of City Hall Plaza.

24. Kevin Lynch's ideas about a "Tall Spine" were worked out in the context of the Committee on Civic Design of the Boston Society of Architects. This group met during 1960–1961 and produced a report. See Robert Sturgis, "The Architect's Plan for Boston," *Journal of the American Insitute of Architects* (January 1, 1962): 35–39. Eventually the idea was partially incorporated into *The 1965–1975 General Plan for Boston,* published by the Boston Redevelopment Authority in 1965.

25. Emily and David Kales, *All About the Boston Harbor Islands* (Hingham, Mass.: Hewitts Cove, 1983). One of the last associations of local Indians with the Harbor Islands was also related to defense. During King Phillip's War (1674–1676) the Massachusetts Bay Colony revoked the civil rights of all Indians and set up internment camps for them on the harbor islands.

9
The Boston Plates

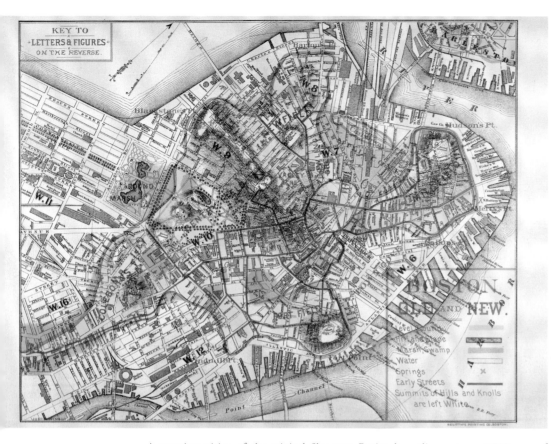

A superimposition of the original Shawmut Peninsula outline onto an 1880 map of Boston. The diagram, titled *Boston, Old and New* was prepared by Justin Winsor and used as the frontispiece for volume 1 of his *Memorial History of Boston, including Suffolk County, Massachusetts* published in 1882.

A superimposition of the 1795 shoreline onto a 1995 aerial photo.

THE BONNER MAP: THE FIRST PRINTED MAP OF BOSTON

On May 14, 1722, the *Boston News-Letter* ran an advertisement that read, in part: "MAP OF BOSTON.—A Curious Ingraven Map of the Town of Boston, with all the streets, Lanes, Alleys, Wharffs & Houses, the Like never done before, Drawn by Capt. John Bonner. . . ." The like certainly never had been done before, for the map in question is the first surviving printed map of Boston as well as the first town plan printed in what is now the United States.

Bonner was a navigator and a shipwright, and his maritime orientation is undoubtedly the reason he shows waterfront features in great detail but renders inland topographical features rather sketchily. He depicts the many wharves lining the shore, for example, but gives almost no indication of the three steep peaks of Beacon Hill.

To show settlement, Bonner used the convention of houses lining the streets. He depicts these houses and other buildings not in any normal perspective, however, but as if they had toppled over backward. Furthermore, the houses are schematic rather than representations of actual dwellings, so that the number of houses Bonner shows on a given street usually does not indicate the number that were actually there. His use of the house convention does, however, indicate the relative density of settlement in various areas. In the legend, Bonner provided a key to churches and public buildings and listed the dates of major fires and smallpox epidemics.

Bonner's map gives a good picture of Boston after a hundred years of development. The North End and the area around Town, or East, Cove were thickly settled. Wharves lined their shores, a graphic illustration of Boston's position as the leading port in the American colonies. Other indicators of the town's maritime economy were the number of shipyards on the waterfront and the ropewalks, which manufactured naval cordage, on Fort and Beacon Hills and in the West End. The Mill Pond, with its Mill Dam located approximately where Causeway Street is today, is clearly shown some eighty years prior to being filled in to form today's Bulfinch Triangle (see figure 1 in chapter 7). Long Wharf, built in 1711–1715, extended majestically almost a third of a mile out from shore across the tidal flats in the Town Cove to deep water, enabling ships to load and unload directly onto the wharf without the use of lighters. (The "Old Wharfe" that intersected Long Wharf along the outer limit of the flats was the remains of a barricade that had been built across the harbor in the 1670s during a war with the Dutch.) From Long Wharf, King (now State) Street ran straight up through the bustling town to the Town House, the site of today's Old State House. From this point, Cornhill, now Washington Street, extended south to the Neck, providing Boston's only land link with the mainland.

Bonner drew and published his map, but it was engraved and printed by Francis Dewing, who had come to Boston from London about 1716 and had published some of Cyprian Southack's charts (see the frontispiece to chapter 4). Although Dewing's name appears on an edition of Bonner's map published in 1725, Dewing's association with the map actually ended in 1722 when, suspected of counterfeiting, he fled to England.

Only one copy of the original state of the Bonner map is known to have survived (the one reproduced here). It was updated and reissued at least nine times during the eighteenth century and reprinted in facsimile form many times since, a testament to its popularity and importance.

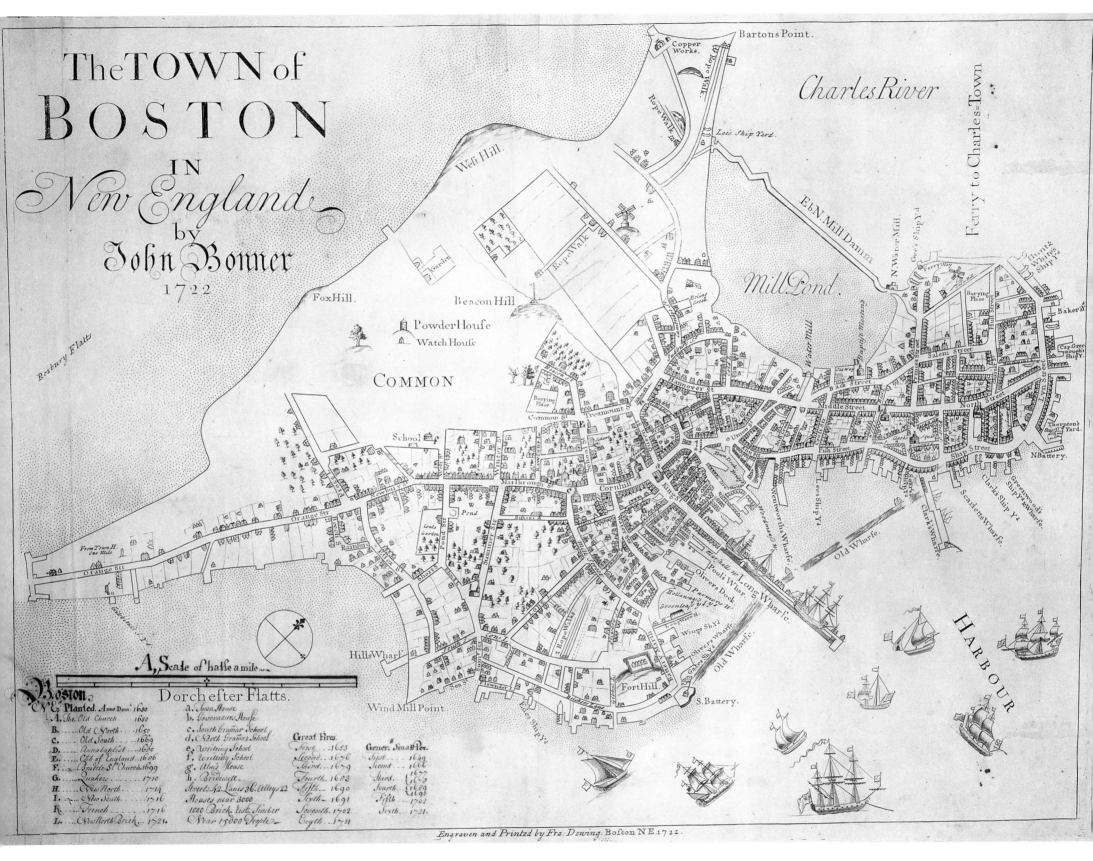

The TOWN of BOSTON IN New England by John Bonner 1722

Charles River

Bartons Point.

Copper Works.

Ferry to Charles=Town

Lei's Ship Yard.

Rope Walk

West Hill.

E b N. Mill Dam en

Mill Pond.

Garden

Rope Walk

Fox Hill.

Beacon Hill

PowderHouse

Watch House

COMMON

School

Orange Str

From Town H One Mile

Orange Str

A, Scale of halfe a mile

Dorchester Flatts.

Boston

E &c. Planted. Anno Dom: 1630
A. ... The Old Church ... 1630
B. ... Old North ... 1650
C. ... Old South ... 1669
D. ... Annabaptist ... 1690
E. ... Ch. of England. 1606
F. ... Brattle St. Church. 1699
G. ... Quakers ... 1710
H. ... New North ... 1714
I. ... New South ... 1716
K. ... French ... 1716
L. ... NewNorth Brick. 1721

a. ... Town House
b. ... Governours House
c. ... South Gramar School
d. ... North Gramar School
e. ... Writing School
f. ... Writing School
g. ... Alms House
h. ... Bridewell
Streets 42 Lanes 36 Alleys 22
Houses near 3000
1000 Brick. Rest Timber
Near 15000 People

Great Fires.
First ... 1653
Second ... 1676
Third ... 1679
Fourth ... 1683
Fifth ... 1690
Sixth ... 1691
Seventh. 1702
Eighth. 1711

Gener. Small Pox.
First ... 1649
Second ... 1666
Third ... 1677
Fourth ... 1689
Fifth ... 1702
Sixth ... 1721

Wind Mill Point

Hills Wharf

FortHill.

S. Battery.

HARBOUR

Engraven and Printed by Fra. Dewing. Boston NE. 1722.

Plate 24
John Bonner (1643–1726)
The Town of Boston in New England
(Boston, 1722)
Engraving. 43 × 59 cm.

Peter Pelham's 1728 portrait of the Reverend Dr. Cotton Mather was the first mezzotint produced in America (a method of engraving on copper or steel by burnishing away a uniformly roughened surface). Since the colonies lacked a capable portraitist, Pelham painted the portrait, too. It would be Pelham's stepson, however, John Singleton Copley, who would become the first great portrait painter in America. And Pelham's son, Henry, would become a mapmaker (see plate 29 and accompanying vignette) and engraver who helped immortalize the Boston Massacre with a hastily produced engraving (copied by Paul Revere) of the scene.

COTTON MATHER, AMERICAN GOTHIC

Cotton Mather (1663–1728) inherited the names of two of the most revered ministers in the Massachusetts Bay Colony. Grandfather John Cotton was the teacher at Boston's First Church. Grandfather Richard Mather, the minister at Boston's Second, or North, Church, was being eclipsed by his own son, Increase Mather, Cotton's father. This legacy proved both a burden and a blessing.

Cotton Mather's awareness of this legacy is reflected in his academic achievements—he entered Harvard College at eleven. It showed also in his overdeveloped respect for authority and in a preoccupation with his own potential to serve it. He created prayers and exercises for his older Harvard classmates, which got him beaten for his trouble. He was ordained young, and entered young into the political spotlight where, as a twenty-six-year-old minister among gray-haired colleagues, he took a role of leadership during the unrest that followed the arrival and expulsion of the first royal governor in Massachusetts.

Mather's eager deference to authority probably cost him his place in history. It led him to support the judges of the Salem witch trials, who were old family friends and mentors, many years his senior. While privately he urged the judges to be cautious with inconclusive evidence, he publicly supported them and his firm belief in demonic possession supported their conclusions. As the arrests, torture, and executions mounted, along with public outcry against the apparent cruelties, Mather's critics recognized some of his serious limitations.

Mather matured into a more humane man, worn down by changes in his political fortunes and the loss of ten of his fifteen children along with their two mothers. A few years before his death at sixty-five, he made his final and happiest marriage. He took refuge in performing good works, urging others to perform them also, and in liberalizing the strictures of the Puritan religion to permit tolerance of other forms of Protestantism.

Although Mather ministered diligently to a congregation of about 1,500, many of whose members loved him, and although he published 388 titles during his lifetime, mainly religious instructions and histories (including *Magnalia Christi Americana* for which he is usually remembered), and helped to found Yale University, he represented to succeeding generations the last gasp of Puritanism's dangerously repressive tenets.

Critics disagree as to whether Mather is more to be pitied than censured. He was Puritanism's most energetic scion at a time when religious zeal, and Puritan values, were waning in the colony. Mather witnessed political upheaval and increasing social permissiveness. He saw the English Crown revoke the Bay Colony's charter, claim Massachusetts as a royal vassal, and install a crown-appointed governor who made possible the erection of the first Anglican Church in Puritan Boston—the original King's Chapel.

Cotton Mather died in 1728, the year Burgis published his map of an increasingly proud and prosperous Boston—the Boston of the Long Wharf. By the middle of the next century, many of the great writers and intellectuals of Boston and Concord—Hawthorne, Melville, Harriet Beecher Stowe, and John Greenleaf Whittier—were slandering or ridiculing him. Their scorn, and his own weaknesses of character, helped to make him a symbol of the religious intolerance that was once a founding principle of the Bay Colony.

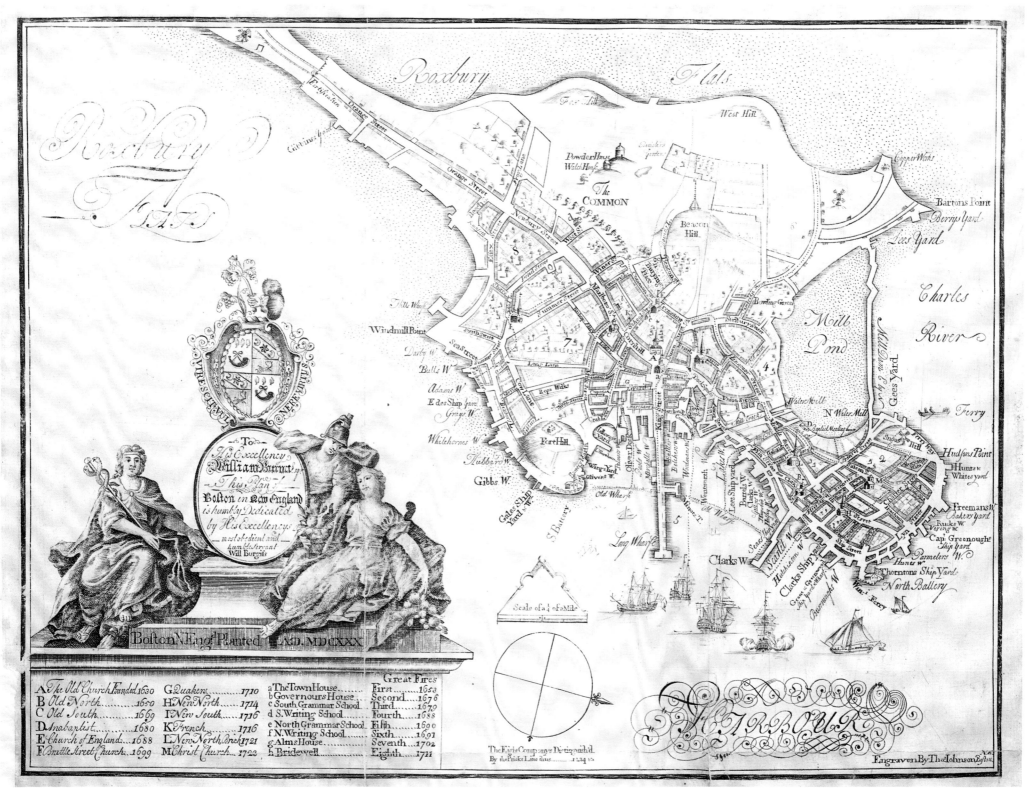

Plate 25

William Burgis (fl. 1716–1731)

To His Excellency William Burnet, Esqr. This Plan of Boston in New England is humbly Dedicated by His Excellency's most obedient and humble servant Will Burgis

(Boston, 1728)

Engraving. 26 × 37 cm.

Soon after the appearance of the Bonner map (see plate 24), in 1728 a second plan of Boston was drawn and published by William Burgis. Burgis had been trained in England and had come to Boston from New York in 1722. Although his map is more professionally executed than Bonner's and about half its size, Burgis clearly based his map on his predecessor's and copied much of the information, even using the same letters for the same churches and public buildings. There are differences between the two maps—Burgis aligned the Boston peninsula differently, used hatching to indicate built-up street fronts, and showed only public buildings in perspective. He also represented topographical features, such as the hills, more convincingly. But probably the most distinguishing feature of the Burgis map is its elaborate cartouche, testimo-ny to the skill of engraver Thomas Johnston (see chapter 4), with its dedication to William Burnet, the governor from 1728 to 1729. Burgis's map has been termed "one of the most attractive examples of urban cartography ever produced in America," yet it was published only once and was not a commercial success.

Burgis is also known for several skillfully drawn views, among them, the southeast view of Boston published by William Price in 1725 (see figure 7 in chapter 4) and one of Harvard College (see figure 2 in chapter 1).

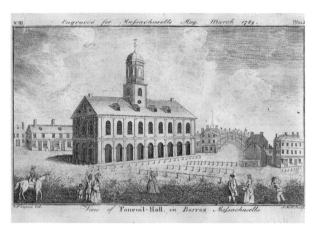

This engraving of Faneuil Hall must have been made sometime between 1784, when the adjoining part of Town Dock was filled in, and 1789, when the engraving was published in *Massachusetts Magazine.* The engraver has creatively moved the cupola from the front of the building to the center to create a more harmonious view. The railings on the newly made land enabled vendors at the town market to tie up their horses.

In 1805 the Charles Bulfinch addition to Faneuil Hall doubled its width and height, as can be seen in the contemporary photograph taken from the new City Hall.

ization of public meetings in Boston, which had heretofore occurred mainly in the churches, or "meeting houses," as the Puritans called them. Before long, the Sons of Liberty would be voicing their incendiary arguments for revolution there.

At the age of forty-three, after only six years of enjoying his legendary inheritance, Peter Faneuil died. The death of this civic-minded figure was truly a loss to Bostonians and lamented as such. It was now his younger brother Benjamin's turn to enjoy Uncle Andrew's legacy. Andrew had favored Benjamin initially, but had cut him out of his will when he learned that Benjamin planned to marry. Andrew had warned both his nephews that their marriages would be grounds for disinheritance. Benjamin, however, fell in love and defied his uncle's wishes. Although he intended his defiance to remain a secret, his uncle learned the truth and sent him packing. But after his brother Peter's death, Benjamin was able to enjoy his marriage and his uncle's fortune.

Bostonians rebuilt Faneuil Hall after a 1761 fire, expanded it with help from Charles Bulfinch in 1805, and renovated and fireproofed it in 1898. The modern renovation, done under the auspices of the Rouse Company in the 1970s, made Faneuil Hall and the Quincy Markets the first East Coast example of historic buildings converted into a "festival marketplace." The revival of Faneuil Hall helped bring life back to downtown Boston, and such marketplaces became a popular ingredient in the refurbishing of historic downtowns in many American cities.

This detail from the 1722 Bonner map shows the configuration of the Town Dock prior to the construction of Faneuil Hall.

PETER FANEUIL AND FANEUIL HALL

It was, in a sense, Andrew Faneuil's money that built Faneuil Hall, first shown on the Price map at right. But it was the public spirit of his nephew and heir, Peter Faneuil, that gave the money to the town of Boston in 1742. Andrew Faneuil had come to Boston as a French Huguenot refugee. By 1691 he was operating as a Boston merchant. In 1709 he built one of Boston's most impressive mansions on seven acres of land facing King's Chapel across Tremont Street. Andrew died in 1737, one of Boston's wealthiest and most prominent citizens.

Peter Faneuil, who had managed his uncle's business affairs for many years, inherited Andrew's tremendous wealth, and apparently reveled in it, although in a responsible way. He gave lavish parties and generously contributed to the welfare of his fellow Bostonians. Around 1740 he offered to build the town a central marketplace for produce and foodstuffs. Many townsfolk and farmers had long opposed markets of this kind. They expected a small number of licensed dealers to raise prices for consumers while lowering payments to farmers. But by a margin of only seven votes the townsfolk voted to accept Faneuil's offer and, in 1742, the handsome new marketplace was completed, with a capacious second story meeting room over the market. The new meeting hall permitted further secular-

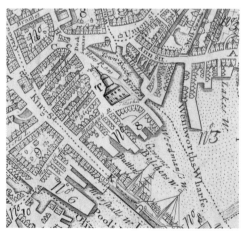

By the time of the 1743 Bonner-Price map, from which this detail was taken, Bostonians had filled in half of the Town Dock, making the land on which Faneuil Hall was built. The hall and new marketplace are shown beside the letter T.

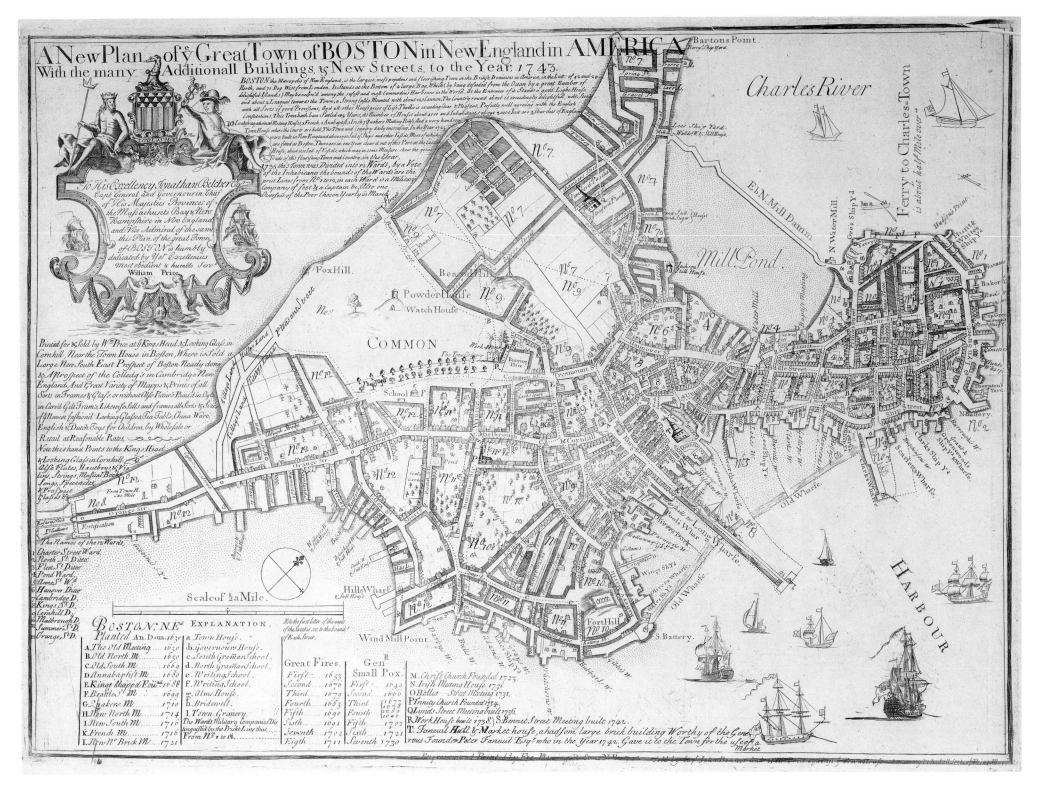

Plate 26

William Price

A New Plan of ye Great Town of Boston in New England in America with the many Additionall [sic] *Buildings & New Streets to the Year 1743*

(Boston, 1743)

Engraving. 42 x 60 cm.

Bonner died in 1726 at the age of eighty-three and the engraved plate of his map became the property of William Price, a cabinetmaker and merchant who sold maps, prints, and other goods in his shop on Cornhill Street. Price had

apparently published the 1725 edition of the Bonner map and, after acquiring the plate, issued updates engraved by Thomas Johnston in 1732 and 1733, and again in 1739, 1743, 1760, and 1769 (see chapter 4).

Price added a great deal of written material to Bonner's rather simple map (see plate 24)—a new title, historical information about Boston, a cartouche with a dedication to Governor Jonathan Belcher, an advertisement for the wares sold in Price's shop (indicated by a pointing hand on Cornhill), and, in the legend, new buildings and a list of wards. Price also abandoned Bonner's convention of indicating settlement with houses and instead adopted Burgis's method of using cross-hatching along street frontages.

A comparison of the 1743 Price with the 1722 Bonner shows many of the changes that had occurred in the intervening years. Most striking is the number of new streets laid out, particularly in the West End, on Beacon Hill, and in the Old South End—the area between Summer Street and the Neck where many wharves were also added. Many of those wharves had distilleries where rum was produced from West Indian molasses. The 1743 Price map also shows the newly built Faneuil Hall, completed a year earlier on land created when part of the Town Dock was filled in the late 1720s (see vignette at left).

179

This scene of the Boston Massacre, by William Champney, is notable for its rare and accurate portrayal of Crispus Attucks, the person being shot, as an African American.

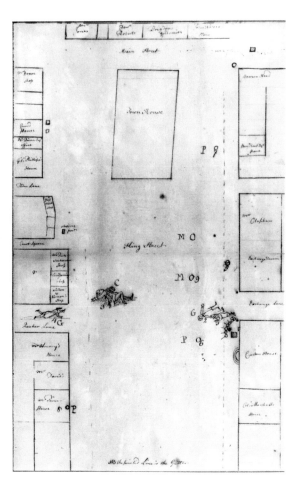

Paul Revere's plan of the site of the Boston Massacre, drawn for use in the courtroom.

THE BOSTON MASSACRE

In the firmament of American myth, the story of the Boston Massacre burns brightly. The version taught to school children was created by another bright star in the same firmament: Sam Adams, bold leader of the Sons of Liberty. In that version, a few unarmed Americans are martyred to the tyranny of Britain. What actually occurred, however, on that snowy March evening long ago when eight British soldiers confronted a mob of three or four hundred angry Bostonians is more complicated.

By 1770 British troops had been stationed in Boston for two years, and prescient minds on both sides predicted bloodshed. Hiller Zobel, author of a thoroughly researched 1970 account of the "massacre," quotes Lt. Col. Dalrymple, the commanding officer in Boston, writing late in 1769: "The crisis I have long expected comes on very fast, and the temper of the times is such that if something does not happen of the most disagreeable Kind, I shall with pleasure give up my foresight."

Radical mob violence had become commonplace in Boston. Resentment against taxes and punitive trade policies ran high. Mobs menaced loyalists, tarred and feathered suspected informers and harassed soldiers.

The regiments in Boston had no mandate except to support the civil officials who were royal appointees. But royal officials dared not call upon the military to enforce their will or even to maintain the peace for fear of igniting further violence. Soldiers found that civil laws prevented their taking any action against the individual citizens or mobs that threatened them. A soldier who roughly laid hands on a citizen could be hauled into court.

It was precisely this restriction that enabled a large snowball-throwing, club-wielding mob to taunt eight members of the 29th Regiment and their captain on the evening of March 5, 1770. Three or four hundred strong, and pressing close to the soldiers on three sides, the incensed townsmen screamed at the group of frightened soldiers, "Fire! Damn your bloods, Fire!" and "They dare not fire!" And a well-dressed gentlemen behind them seems to have urged them in earnest to fire on the out-of-control crowd in a voice that some mistook to be the captain's.

Finally, a few inhabitants began attacking the soldiers with sticks and clubs, and were repulsed by bayonets. One club struck a soldier's head, sending him to the ground. The enraged and wounded soldier was the first to fire into the crowd; his immediate neighbor followed, then a few more. Captain Preston, who had tried to call the mob off his eight soldiers and prevent further firing, was hustled off to jail with the others.

Although the deaths of five citizens became a propaganda opportunity for Samuel Adams, his cousin, John Adams, gave them an excellent defense in the trials that followed. A jury at least partly loyalist, and the general confusion at the scene, in which no two witnesses saw the same thing, contributed to Captain Preston's acquittal.

Except for the first and second soldier to fire, whose actions were clearly witnessed, the other soldiers were acquitted because their actions had been obscured in the melee. Ironically, Kilroy, the soldier who was knocked to the ground and then jumped up and fired, and the soldier beside him who fired second, who should have benefited most from arguments of self-defense, were convicted of manslaughter. A legal maneuver helped them avoid the death penalty and got them off with the slightly less barbaric punishment of thumb-branding or burning. All returned to England.

After a tense peace of two years, Britain placed all Massachusetts officials on British salary, and under British control. After the Boston Tea Party in 1773, Britain closed Boston Harbor, and thereby the city's livelihood, and assumed military control of the Massachusetts government. The first Continental Congress met in 1774 and a state of war rapidly ensued.

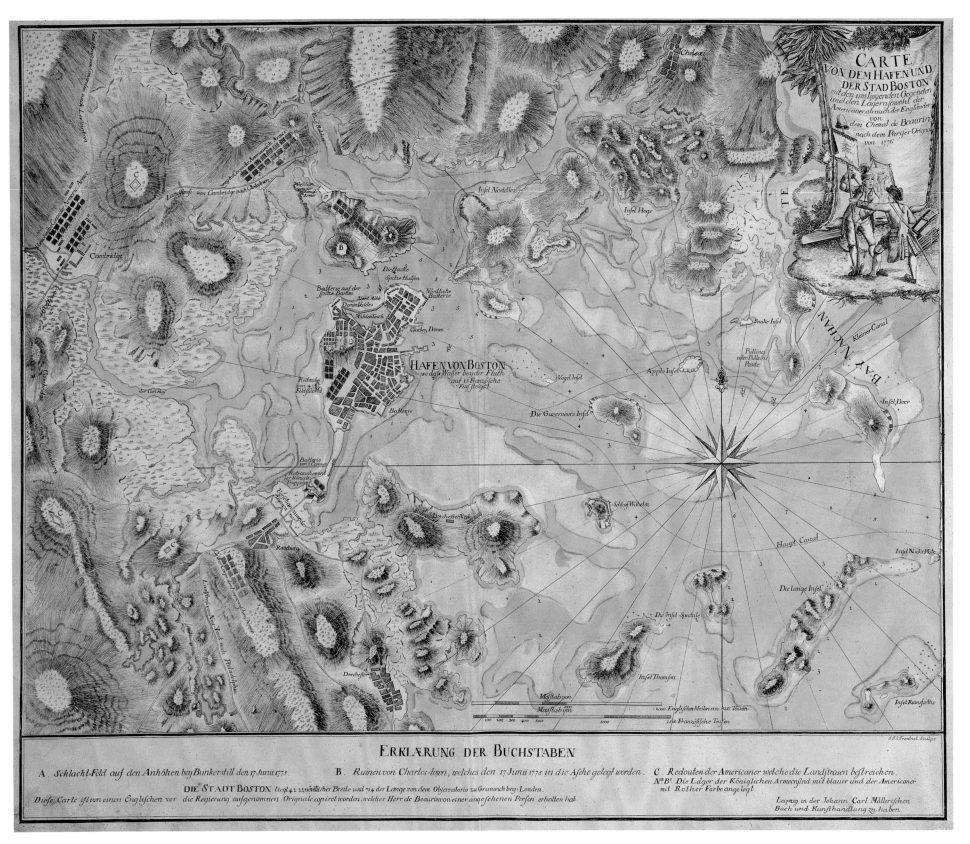

Plate 27

George Friedrich Jonas Frentzel (1754–1799)

Carte von dem Hafen und der Stad Boston

From *Geographische Belustigen zur Erklærung der neuesten Weltgeschichte. Stuck 1.* (Leipzig: J. C. Muller, 1776)

Engraving. 51 × 61 cm.

This unusual topographic map is engraved with elaborate hachures and is a direct copy of Beaurain's 1776 *Carte du Port et Havre de Boston.* The legend below the map reveals the number and caliber of artillery and the location of American and British troops in considerable detail. The town of Boston as well as roads, houses, farms, and other cultural features, are shown.

This is the only German map of Boston during the Revolutionary period. There is a reference to the battle of June 17, 1775, and the "Ruinen von Charles-town."

Frentzel was an engraver in Leipzig, Germany, and is best known for his twenty-sheet map of Saxony and Bohemia published in 1780.

181

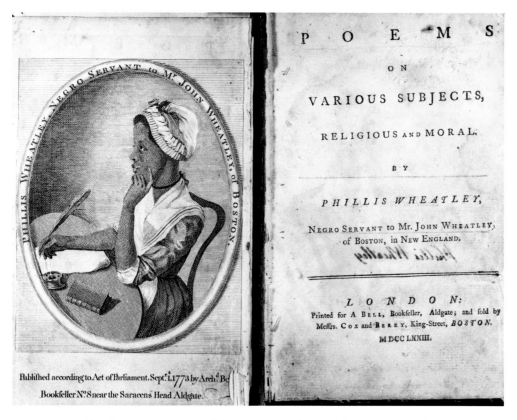

Frontispiece and title page of the 1773 *Poems on Various Subjects, Religious and Moral,*
by Phillis Wheatley.

THE GILDED CAGE OF PHILLIS WHEATLEY

The events and characters of prerevolutionary Boston had an unusual witness in
the person of a young slave girl named Phillis, living in the Wheatley home on
King Street by the Old State House. Phillis Wheatley arrived in the Wheatley
household in 1761 as a sickly seven-year-old weakened by the long passage on the
slave ship *Phillis*.

Once established in the Wheatley household, Phillis displayed an impressive gift for language and a strong religious devotion. Her mistress, Susannah
Wheatley, whose children were grown, cherished her in the role of child prodigy
rather than servant. But with her place as a black slave still closely circumscribed,
her role also included something of the exotic pet.

The Wheatleys encouraged her gifts, lavishing care and learning on her.
They also limited her contact with other slaves and blacks, whom they considered
beneath her. Yet when they attended the Old South Meeting House, Phillis was
required to sit in an African corner with other blacks.

As Phillis's poems became more accomplished in her early teens, Susannah
Wheatley promoted her little prodigy so effectively that Phillis found herself having tea with the most prominent Boston families including, awkwardly enough,
the Fitch family, owners of the *Phillis*.

As Phillis's poetic talents blossomed, the violent incidents of prerevolutionary Boston unfolded at her front door and provided the occasion for poems
that would be widely circulated and appreciated. Wheatley's poems commemorating the arrival of the British war ships in Boston Harbor, and the murder of an
eleven-year old boy by a Tory in heated discussion over taxation, afforded her an
opportunity to sympathize with the longing for liberty and the resentment of
tyranny and injustice that she could rarely express in regard to slavery. These popular subjects, showcased by her talent, gave her an excellent entree into the public imagination.

As Phillis's celebrity grew in America and England, Susannah Wheatley
helped her to publish a book of her poems in London, making her the second
woman and the first African American to publish in the colonies. The popularity of the book highlighted Phillis's uniqueness as a star slave, and the Wheatleys
decided to grant her freedom.

For a while, Phillis continued to enjoy the home, company, and patronage
of the Wheatleys. Within a space of about four years, however, the deaths of the
Wheatleys and the progress of the Revolution left Phillis alone in a shattered
Boston whose populace had little time or appetite for poetry.

With her golden cage gone, Phillis now tried her wings and found them
clipped. She married and the marriage began well, but her husband's employment
prospects dwindled. Within six years she was dead, ground down by poverty and
the physical demands of three pregnancies. All of her children died in infancy, the
last only hours after Phillis herself passed away in a grim rooming house. Her
funeral was unattended. Although she died in obscurity, her work was revived by
abolitionists in the next century as proof of the stature of black humanity.

Plate 28

Thomas Page (1746–1821)
*A Plan of the Town of Boston with the
Intrenchments &c. of His Majesty's Forces
in 1775 from the Observations of Lieut.
Page of His Majesty's Corps of Engineers;
and from the Plans of other Gentlemen*
(London, 1777)
Engraving. 49 x 43 cm.

Sometimes a historical event triggers a burst of
mapmaking. In 1775 and 1776, when Boston
was the theater of war, an enormous number of
maps of the town were produced. Many of
these maps traced the fortifications erected by
both the British and the colonists. A good
example is the map drawn by a Lieutenant
Page, a member of the royal engineers and an
aide to General Howe.

Page's map, which was drafted in 1775
but not published until 1777 by William
Faden in London, shows the British fortifications on the Neck and Fort Hill, just as its title
announces. But it also includes more detail
about the Boston peninsula than many of the
contemporary maps, probably because it is at a
larger scale. It is one of the first to label the
westernmost peak of the Trimountain (now
Beacon Hill) with its popular name—Mount
Whoredom. Among other details, Page shows
a T-shaped appendage in the middle of Long
Wharf—a remnant of the 1670s barricade and
the beginning of T Wharf (see plate 17
vignette for another example of Page's work).

A recently discovered imprint of this
map dated 1775 reveals a different engraving
and several other variants from this 1777
impression, which is more commonly known.

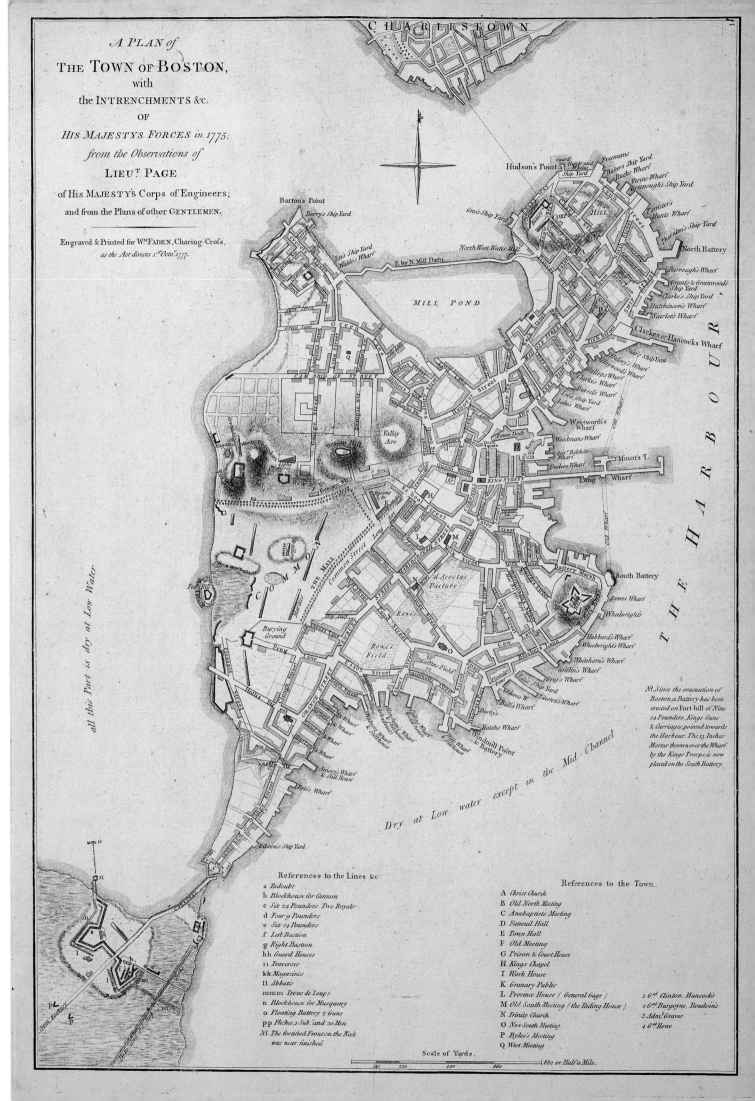

In 1752, when John Singleton Copley painted his younger half-brother, Henry Pelham, as the *Boy with a Squirrel,* Copley was himself a young man, painting a showpiece to send to England for critical review. Copley went on to a brilliant career, and his young subject grew into an accomplished engraver and mapmaker who, in 1777, authored the marvelous plan of Boston at right. This painting now hangs in Boston's Museum of Fine Arts, along with others of Copley's best.

JOHN SINGLETON COPLEY: THE ARTIST'S BOSTON

John Singleton Copley, the half-brother of engraver Henry Pelham, who made the accompanying map, can be called the father of American painting. Seventeen-thirty-eight, the year of Copley's birth, produced two great American painters. The other, Benjamin West, left to study abroad at an early age. Although West trained and influenced other American painters, his work followed contemporary fashion more closely and is arguably less original than Copley's.

The Boston of Copley's childhood, though briefly still the largest city in British North America before New York's ascension to that rank, was still transforming itself from a rough town, despite the large fortunes accruing to shipping magnates and merchants. Its little peninsula housed roughly 16,000 souls in a few thousand homes situated on streets that had acquired official names only a few decades before. On Boston's busy waterfront, Copley's widowed Irish mother ran her tobacco shop. This Boston had lately given birth to many of the doers and thinkers of the American Revolution, a few of whom became the subjects of famous Copley portraits.

Culturally, America was still a backwater. Cities grew and settlements expanded through commerce and land speculation. While government-related issues occupied many great American minds of this period, America had produced nothing in the area of fine arts, nor was there an audience for them. And although American architecture was progressing modestly, and the decorative arts had begun to flower in Boston and other seaports—through gifted silver smiths, cabinet makers, and engravers—America had no painters of note and no public institutions concerned with the arts, nor did it provide many opportunities for an American student to learn painting. Only portraiture, an art supported by the vanity or sentiments of the wealthy, sustained the first great artist to cultivate his talent on American soil.

Copley, although considered by historians a timid man, nonetheless possessed native genius and was strong enough to allow his sensibilities to guide him. While West and others urged Copley to move abroad before provincialism could stifle his gifts, Copley lingered in Boston, starved for a glimpse of real art and a public who might appreciate it, but completing one remarkable portrait after another despite his lack of schooling.

For almost a decade before the Revolution, Copley painted both radical Whigs and moneyed Tories. His eloquently simple portraits of a few prominent leaders of the mutinous Sons of Liberty—including Paul Revere at his artisan's table, Samuel Adams presenting radical petitions, and John Hancock at his desk—make up a remarkable gallery of American icons. Copley's best paintings show a searching realism, simplicity, and intensity that captured expression and personality deftly rather than fashionably.

Copley's rising reputation allowed him to marry into the class of his wealthy clients and purchase a home and land overlooking the Common, just down Beacon Street from the imposing Hancock mansion. Unfortunately, Copley's enhanced position and Tory in-laws required him to flee to London as the Revolution loomed—or so he believed. His arrival in London finally made it possible for him to paint in art's fashionable circles. Yet fashion seemed to have a diluting rather than an enriching effect on his work. His earlier work—closely intertwined with the American experience—is generally more powerful.

Plate 29
Henry Pelham
A Plan of Boston in New England with its Environs
(London, 1777)
Engraving. 98 x 70 cm.

Henry Pelham's large map of Boston, drawn in 1775 and 1776 and published in London in 1777, is another product of the Revolutionary era. The map, an aquatint engraved on two sheets by Francis Jukes, is considered one of the most beautiful maps of Boston ever produced. It was undoubtedly from John Singleton Copley, his half brother, that Pelham learned to draw and paint.

Pelham, a Loyalist, had access to British military maps and was allowed to visit the front lines in order to obtain information for his map; in the upper-left-hand corner he reproduced a copy of the pass issued to him on 28 August 1775 by John Urquhart, the town major, permitting him to map fortifications in Boston and Charlestown.

Pelham's finished map shows these fortifications and the lines of fire emanating from them. But it also shows the towns surrounding Boston—what are now East Boston, Charlestown, Cambridge, Brookline, Roxbury, and Dorchester—in glorious detail with all the roads and every house. Pelham evidently did not obtain this information about the adjacent countryside from the Des Barres chart (see plate 19), for the two differ in some details, such as the number and location of houses. Perhaps Pelham surveyed all this countryside himself. Whatever the origin of his information, however, his map remains an invaluable source of information about the late eighteenth-century Boston area—many of the roads are now modern streets and some of the houses still exist.

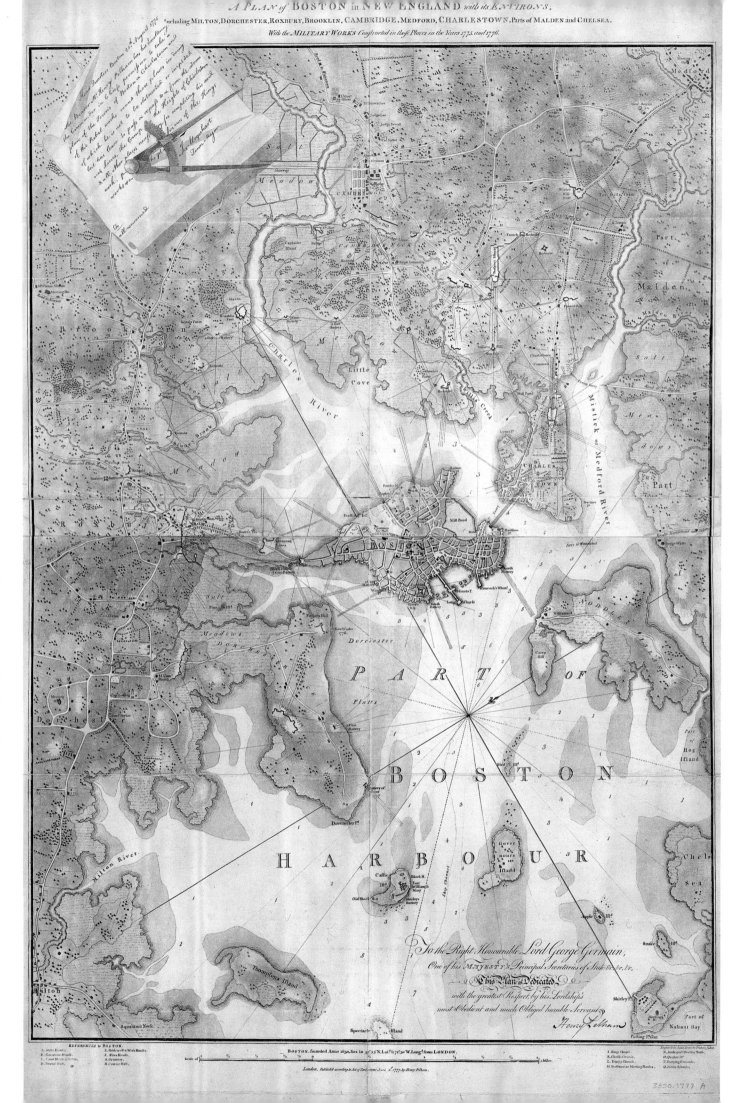

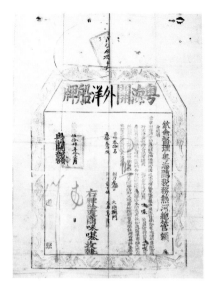

With this Chinese customs clearance, the Salem ship, *Astrea,* inaugurated the Massachusetts China Trade, returning to home port in 1790. At that time, and for several decades after, the Chinese required foreign ships to moor in a harbor about twelve miles downriver from Canton, China, the only port open to foreign goods.

An example of a silver teapot and stand from the Boston China Trade (ca. 1790–1800).

THE BOSTON CHINA TRADE

For a while in America, there was no wealth like that to be made in shipping. And among the shipping magnates of America's young Atlantic seaports, the Bostonians were an intrepid breed.

The China Trade, one example of this ingenuity, was an invention born of necessity around 1790, shortly before Carleton's map at right came out. In that year, Thomas Handasyd Perkins returned from China as supercargo on the Salem ship *Astrea*. Invigorated with new ideas about the China Trade, he immediately moved with his brother to Boston. Boston had room for new merchants after many had fled to England at the advent of the Revolution. Perkins knew that a Boston ship, the *Columbia,* also returning in 1790, had successfully offered Pacific Coast furs to the Chinese. He set out to emulate that success. While British ports around the world remained closed to American ships after the Revolution, the Perkinses and other merchants and shippers sought new territories for trade such as Russia and China. Those who succeeded in plying new trade routes and cultures—such as the Derbys of Salem, or the Perkinses and their gifted nephews, the Forbes brothers—achieved a wealth that tided them up to the pinnacle of Boston's nineteenth-century aristocracy.

Although Boston's trade with China peaked for only half a century, it brought a bustling prosperity to Boston that endured with some vicissitudes through Jefferson's Embargo of 1807, the War of 1812, and the Opium Wars between Britain and China (1839–1842). Not only the shippers and merchants thrived, but captains, shipbuilders, sail cutters, rope makers, coopers, and new schools of navigation.

A group of financial institutions evolved to help stabilize the risks of the China trade. The marine insurance companies insured ships laden with the investments of wealthy men. The commercial banks lent the capital that shippers needed when cash did not flow smoothly from one venture to the next.

Bostonians relied heavily on Pacific Coast furs, purchased for trifling sums from the native tribes there, to tempt the Chinese, who looked contemptuously on foreigners. Until the harvesting of Pacific sea otters ended, ships from Boston, and to a lesser extent Baltimore, New York, and Philadelphia, anchored off the Northwest Coast, loading as many as 14,000 furs in one hold before setting sail for the Far East.

After up to five months of sailing from their Atlantic ports, the ships arrived in China hoping to sell their loads of furs for six-figure profits at Canton the only Chinese port open to foreigners. They were allowed to anchor twelve miles downriver while Chinese boatmen ferried their goods to the various merchants' warehouses, or hongs, of Canton. The American ships then loaded up with Chinese teas, silks, porcelains, and finely wrought silver for an additional handsome profit back home.

After the sea otter's demise, Americans were forced to consider paying silver for their Chinese purchases, which, since North America had no silver, reduced their profit margins. But the Chinese opium habit had grown. It could now accommodate inferior grades of the drug such as those from Turkey. Before long, American shippers were stopping in Turkey on the way to China, and opium fueled the American China trade for about three decades. During this time, Boston dominated all other American seaports in the China Trade, and the Perkins firm, in alliance with others, dominated the Boston share of the market.

Finally, in 1839, China, having failed for decades in her efforts to control the smuggling of opium, confiscated a British opium ship. The British, defending with all the resources of their empire their right to smuggle drugs to the Chinese population, humiliated the Chinese in the three-year Opium War, forcing them to pay the costs of the war, cede Hong Kong, and open more ports to foreign trade.

At around this time, the Bostonians discovered the vast Chinese market for cottons from the new Massachusetts textile mills. Perkins and others gained an early monopoly on cotton mills in eastern Massachusetts, and cotton replaced opium as the staple trade commodity of Boston's China traders.

Through their vast wealth and generosity, T. H. Perkins, his nephew, John Perkins Cushing, and other shipping magnates fueled the growth of many of Boston's cultural and philanthropic institutions during the first half of the nineteenth century. The heyday of the Boston China Trade passed, however. New York, with more rail lines and greater access to interior markets, surpassed Boston in the shipping trade by mid-century. By the time of the Civil War, no maritime industry in Boston could bring in wealth comparable to that of the bygone China Trade.

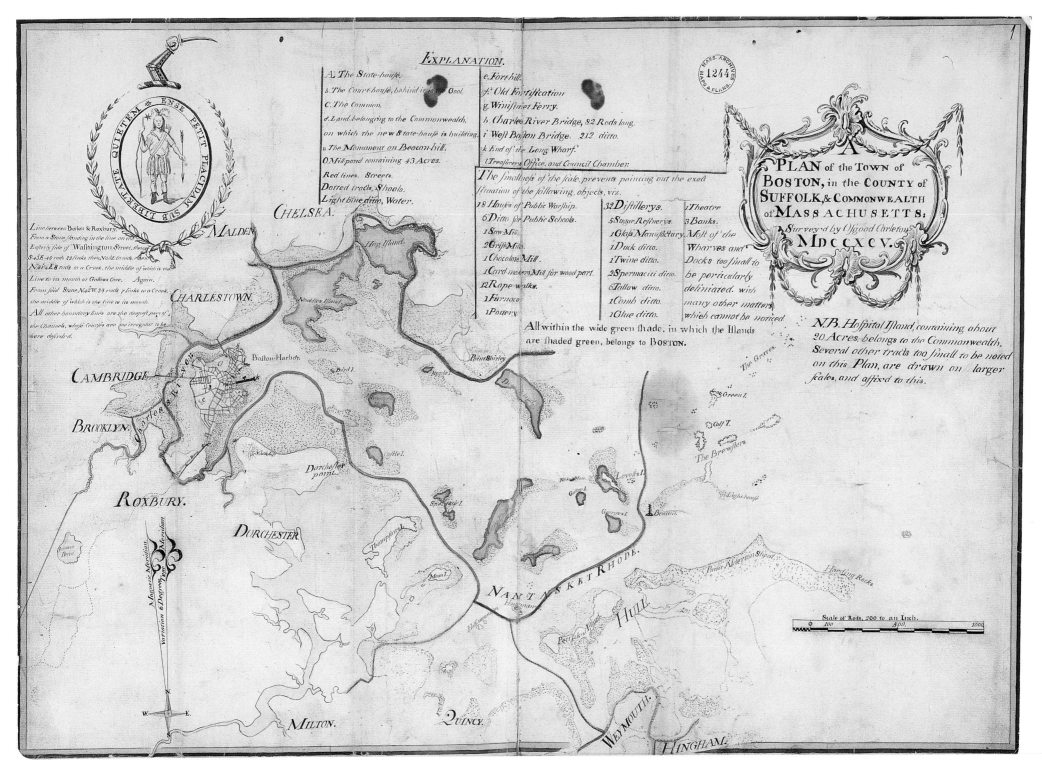

EXPLANATION.

A. The State-house.
b. The Court-house, behind it is the Goal.
C. The Common.
d. Land belonging to the Commonwealth, on which the new State-house is building.
n The Monument on Beacon-hill.
O Millpond containing 43 Acres.
Red lines, Streets.
Dotted trade, Shoals.
Light line ditto, Water.

e. Fort-hill.
f. Old Fortification
g. Winisimet Ferry.
h. Charles River Bridge, 82 Rods long.
i West Boston Bridge. 212 ditto.
k End of the Long Wharf.
l Treasurers Office, and Council Chamber.

The smallness of the scale prevents pointing out the exact situation of the following objects, viz.

18 Houses of Public Worship.
6 Ditto for Public Schools.
1 Saw-Mill.
2 Grist Mills.
1 Chocolate Mill.
1 Card makers Mill for wood part.
12 Rope-walks.
1 Furnace.
1 Pottery.

3 ½ Distillerys.
5 Sugar Refinerys.
1 Glass Manufactury.
1 Duck ditto.
1 Twine ditto.
2 Spermaciti ditto.
Tallow ditto.
1 Comb ditto.
1 Glue ditto.

1 Theatre
3 Banks.
Most of the Wharves and Docks too small to be perticularly deliniated. with many other matters which cannot be noticed

All within the wide green shade, in which the Islands are shaded green, belongs to BOSTON.

A PLAN of the TOWN of BOSTON, in the COUNTY of SUFFOLK, & COMMONWEALTH of MASSACHUSETTS. Survey'd by Osgood Carleton MDCCXCV.

N.B. Hospital Island, containing about 20 Acres, belongs to the Commonwealth. Several other tracts too small to be noted on this Plan, are drawn on larger scales, and affixed to this.

Scale of Rods, 200 to an Inch.

Plate 30
Osgood Carleton (1742–1816)
A Plan of the Town of Boston, in the County of Suffolk, & Commonwealth of Massachusetts
(Boston, 1795)
Manuscript. 37 x 22 cm.

Osgood Carleton was born in New Hampshire in 1742, served briefly before 1760 in the British army, where he learned surveying, fought on the American side at the Battle of Bunker Hill, and after the war opened a school in Boston where he taught mathematics, cartography, and navigation. In 1794, at his urging and that of the

Massachusetts Historical Society, the Massachusetts legislature directed every town in the state to have an accurate plan made at a scale of two hundred rods to the inch showing boundaries, rivers, bridges, county roads, churches, and court houses.

Carleton surveyed the plan of Boston himself. The prominent green line snaking through the map represents the boundary of Boston and the red lines the places where this boundary intersected those of adjoining towns ("Brooklyn" of course meaning Brookline). One can see that in 1795 only some of the harbor islands were considered a part of Boston, Noddles and Hog Islands—now East Boston—among them. Carleton showed the first two

bridges connecting Boston and the mainland—the Charles River Bridge, built in 1785–1786 to Charlestown on the site of the present Charlestown Bridge, and the West Boston Bridge, built in 1793 to Cambridge on the site of the present Longfellow Bridge. He used letters to locate other features, and, owing to the small scale of the map, he simply listed the number of churches, public schools, factories, theaters, and banks.

Carleton did compile a map of Massachusetts, but because the legislature did not approve it, he and John Norman, the engraver, published it themselves in 1798. A state-approved version, engraved by Joseph Callendar and Samuel Hill, was published in 1801 (see chapter 4).

(left) Engraving of John Adams by an anonymous artist, after Gilbert Stuart, ca. 1840s.

(right) Oil portrait of Abigail Adams by Mather Brown, 1785.

This unusually informal photograph of Henry Adams at his writing desk was taken by his wife Marian Hooper Adams at their Beverly Farms home in 1883.

THE ADAMS FAMILY

Every city has its dynasties. Boston's great families appear throughout the nation's history as well as its own. And of these families, none is as notable as the Adamses.

Samuel Adams (1722–1803), a founder of the radical Sons of Liberty that fomented so much revolutionary fervor in mid-eighteenth-century Boston, was probably the most incendiary firebrand in the movement to end British rule. He gave ringing speeches in Faneuil Hall, helped organize the protest against the Stamp Act in 1765, led the Boston Tea Party in 1773, and indoctrinated his more conservative younger cousin, John, in politics.

Sam, as well as John Adams (1735–1826), served in both sessions of the Continental Congress. There, John helped Thomas Jefferson draft the Declaration of Independence, beginning a lifelong friendship and rivalry. Adams's and Jefferson's opposing political views helped shape the national outlook on democracy. Adams, in the Puritan mold, mistrusted the common man and argued for "a government of laws, and not of men."

For Adams, a man's first obligation was to his community. Jefferson, on the other hand, was the great champion of personal liberty; in his view, individuals' rights were the guiding principle.

When Adams attained the presidency in 1797, after two terms as George Washington's vice president, Jefferson served as his vice president; Adams was ousted by Jefferson in the election of 1800. Their correspondence lasted until their deaths—both on the 4th of July, 1826. Adams's last words were of Jefferson—"Thomas Jefferson still surv— . . ." In fact, Jefferson did not survive Adams. His views on personal liberty, however, found more fertile ground in American culture than did Adams's views of community.

Abigail Adams (1765–1813), wife of President Adams, was a woman of restless intelligence and a clever pen who maintained a close involvement with her husband's work. Her letters have provided historians with a treasure trove of information. She argued issues of women's education (she was for it) and slavery (she was against it) with thoughtfulness and strength. Indeed, her pronouncements to her husband in surviving letters echo the Revolutionary slogans of her cousin-in-law, Sam Adams. In the spring of 1776, she wrote to her husband of her position on women's rights, "[We] will not hold ourselves bound by any laws in which we have no voice, or representation." The heady atmosphere of the Revolution was bringing into question other traditional assignments of power.

John and Abigail Adams had five children, including John Quincy Adams (1767–1848), sixth president of the United States. Young John Quincy Adams began his career in federal service with a stint as foreign minister to the Netherlands, Prussia, Russia, and Great Britain—much as his father had served as minister to France and England during and after the American Revolution. John Quincy Adams then served as a U.S. senator and finally secretary of state before becoming president in 1825.

Never a popular president, this Adams also served only one term, losing, in the first notoriously dirty American campaign, to Andrew Jackson. After a brief, bitter retirement in Quincy, Adams returned to Washington as a congressman, making for himself a more distinguished career. In his later years, he strongly supported his mother's unpopular cause of abolition.

Of John Quincy Adams's four children, only Charles Francis Adams (1807–1886) survived long enough to carry on the Adams tradition of public service—in Congress and as President Lincoln's minister to England during the Civil War (although he was actually the vice president's choice). Two of Charles's sons, Henry and Brooks, became scholars and writers. Henry Adams's (1838–1918) works include a nine-volume history of the Adams and Jefferson administrations, and the classic *Education of Henry Adams.* Brooks Adams (1848–1927) wrote *The Law of Civilization and Decay* (1895) and later *America's Economic Supremacy* (1900), in which he predicted the rise of America and Russia as superpowers.

John Adams's prophesy that he must "study politics and war so that my sons may study mathematics and philosophy . . . in order to give their children a right to study painting, poetry, music, architecture" was not entirely borne out by the evolution of the family interests. His descendants included a railroad chairman and expert, a secretary of the navy, and a chief executive of Raytheon, a defense contractor (see plate 48 vignette). Yet the Adamses continued, in one venue or another, to contribute to American policy debates for five generations, with their allegiances consistently focused on Boston, Washington, and the Old House at Quincy, now a national landmark, where so many of them found respite from the call of political and intellectual life.

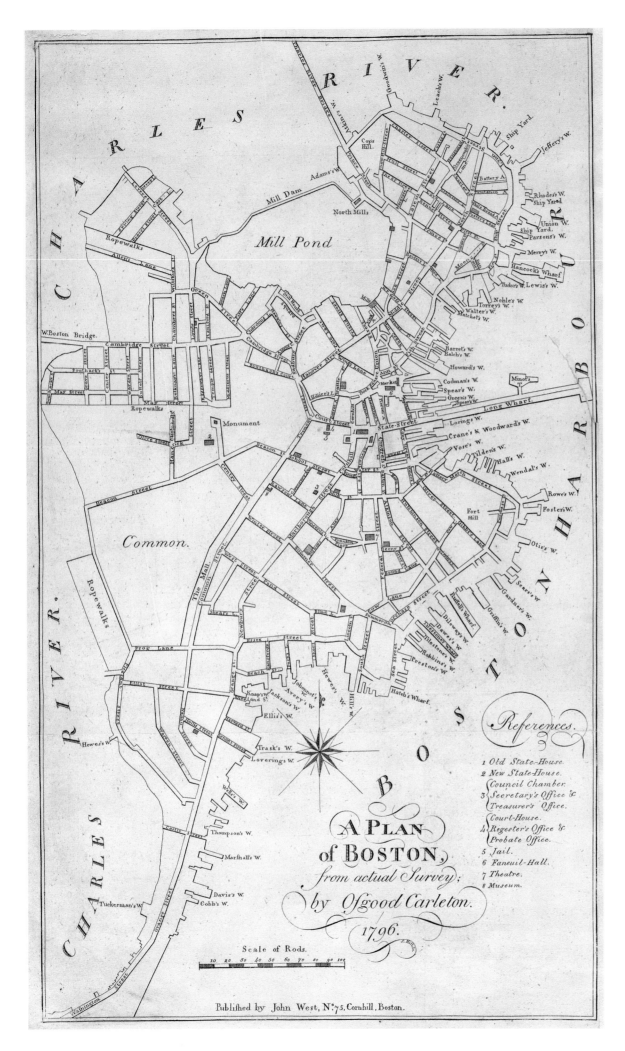

Plate 31
Osgood Carleton (1742–1816)
A Plan of Boston from actual Survey
(Boston, 1796)
Engraving. 21 x 36 cm.

In 1796, Carleton produced a larger-scale and more detailed map of the Boston peninsula than his 1795 map (see plate 30), which was published by John West in the *Boston Directory.* The directory, an alphabetical list of all the town's inhabitants with occupations and addresses, always included a map to serve as a guide to the streets cited in addresses.

Carleton's map is the first detailed map of the town since the Revolutionary era and shows some of the changes that had occurred in the interim: ropewalks had been relocated from Fort Hill to newly made land at the foot of the Common, South Battery had been replaced by Rowes Wharf, and the part of the Town Dock north of Faneuil Hall had been filled in. The first two bridges constructed to provide new connections between the Boston peninsula and the mainland, indicated on the 1795 plan, are more clearly shown here as the extensions of Cambridge Street and Prince Street.

In this detail of the Winsor map (see plate 24 vignette) (1880–1881) one can discern the ancient Trimountain summits, labeled B, C, and D.

This view of Beacon Hill reveals the densely knit red brick fabric of Beacon Hill.

BEACON HILL

To the earliest Massachusetts settlers, the Shawmut Peninsula was "Trimountain," a steep ridge with three summits. As the town of Boston grew on the Shawmut Peninsula, the steep slopes of the Trimountain were slow to be developed but still were integral to its history.

In 1634, Governor Winthrop had a beacon erected on the central summit, thereafter known as Beacon Hill, "to give notice to the country of any danger." The danger that worried Governor Winthrop was King Charles's intention to revoke the Bay Colony's charter and install a royal governor. The lookouts watched, therefore, for British ships.

Various slopes of the three hills took their names from their most prominent residents. The Reverend John Cotton lived on the eastern end-slope of the ridge, facing the harbor. This last hill was known as Cotton Hill in the neighborhood that John Cotton shared with Governors Vane and Endicott, but was called Pemberton Hill along Tremont Street where a few lavish estates, including that of Andrew Faneuil, were later sited.

The westernmost hill, bordering the Charles River, was called Mount Vernon by the Mount Vernon Proprietors who developed it at the end of the eighteenth century, but its earlier names reflect a colorful past. In the eighteenth century, its northern slope hosted a rougher riverfront community that gave rise, during the Revolution, to the name Mount Whoredom, a favorite destination of British soldiers bivouacked on the Common and elsewhere in Boston. On its southeast side were eighteen acres owned by the painter John Singleton Copley between 1769 and 1795, whose house faced Beacon Street. This slope was briefly known as Copley's Hill.

Just up Beacon Street from Copley, near the top of Beacon Hill where the State House now sits, was the estate of wealthy John Hancock, featuring a large, grand house. And there began the story of Boston's first great real estate development venture, and largest land moving project to that date.

The legislature had designated a committee to search out a site for a new State House. Serving on that committee was the future mayor, Harrison Gray Otis. Otis's committee settled on the late John Hancock's estate near the peak of Beacon Hill and, just weeks before the State House cornerstone was laid in Hancock's former pasture in July 1795, the Mount Vernon Proprietors, in whom Otis was a principal investor, purchased Copley's neighboring eighteen acres.

The Mount Vernon Proprietors included not only Otis, but Charles Bulfinch, the architect of the new State House. They bought up most of Mount Vernon with the idea of building a genteel residential neighborhood of stately houses in generous gardens. To accomplish this, the tops of Beacon Hill and Mount Vernon dug down and spread in the shallows of the Charles, where they created the new land for Charles Street.

Bulfinch lacked the financial resources to stay long in such rich company, but he designed the homes of some of the proprietors, including Otis. After earlier designing a house on Cambridge Street for him, which now houses the Society for the Preservation of New England Antiquities, Bulfinch designed a still extant home for Otis at what became number 85 on the new Mount Vernon Street. Not long after, Otis commissioned yet another house by Bulfinch at 45 Beacon Street to which he moved in 1808.

The War of 1812 slowed construction and sales on Beacon Hill, but building resumed afterward at a vigorous pace, with a combination of custom-built houses and large blocks of row-houses built on speculation. In 1826, the proprietors laid out the charming Louisburg Square roughly where the peak of Mount Vernon once stood, but the houses around it were not built until the 1830s and 1840s. Row houses crowded around Otis's Mount Vernon house and other early freestanding mansions.

By mid-century, although not all the Beacon Hill flat had been created, most of the streets we know looked much as we see them today. By this time, Boston was no longer a postrevolutionary town but an increasingly gracious and rapidly growing city. With sea-facing neighborhoods such as the old North End and Fort Hill given over to immigrants, Boston's leaders envisioned making more land—in the South End and Back Bay—to host more elegant residential neighborhoods for the middle and upper classes.

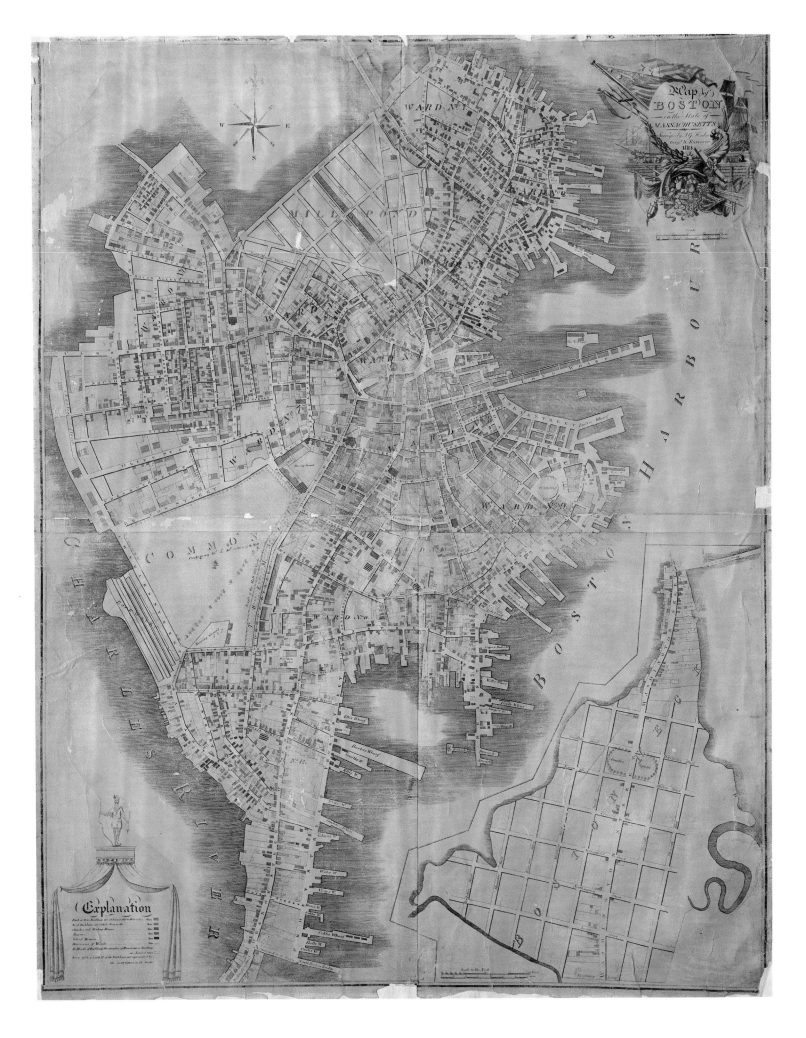

Plate 32

John G. Hales (1785–1832)

Map of Boston in the State of Massachusetts

(Boston, 1814)

Engraving. 72 x 92 cm.

Surveyed by John G. Hales and engraved by T. Wightman, Jr., this was not only the most accurate map of Boston yet produced but also the first to show all the buildings. Hales used different shadings to indicate the material from which a building was constructed (wood or brick/stone), often showing a row of similar buildings as one, as well as to indicate the churches, taverns, and schools. He also showed property lines, data that, when coupled with those about buildings, make his map an invaluable source of information about Federal-period Boston.

Hales was born in England in 1785 and is first listed in the Boston Directory in 1818. Later characterized as a "rapid, possibly hasty" worker, Hales produced other maps of Boston including an 1819 survey of Boston and its vicinity, and an 1823 map that was updated frequently and became the standard map of the city (see plates 33, 35, and 39 and figure 4 in chapter 7). In 1830, when the legislature ordered a map made of every town in the state, Hales did the surveys of many towns including Boston (see plate 34).

A comparison of the 1814 Hales and the 1796 Carleton maps shows the changing shoreline. Beginning on the east side of the Neck, Front Street (now Harrison Avenue) provided a new route between the town and the new bridge to South Boston, annexed in 1804; at the base of Fort Hill, India Wharf had been built and Broad and India Streets laid out over the former wharves; the Mill Pond, which appears to be filled in, was actually being filled at the time; in the West End, a new almshouse and Almshouse Wharf had been constructed; and, at the foot of Beacon Hill and the Common, Charles Street had been laid out on newly made land. A third bridge had also been built to connect Boston with the mainland. Just visible at the top of the map is the Lechmere, or Craigie's, Bridge, erected in 1809 between the West End and East Cambridge on the line of the first Charles River Dam, now the site of the Museum of Science.

In this 1824 portrait by Gilbert Stuart, Mayor Josiah Quincy sits in front of Quincy Market holding the architectural plans of his namesake.

mother, the future mayor suffered many trials typical of an eighteenth-century upbringing. From the age of three onward, on his mother's instructions, Quincy was taken from bed every morning by servants who dipped him in cold water. When he was six, his mother sent him to board in Andover, where he attended the new Phillips Academy that his maternal grandfather had founded. He wrote later of the severity of the discipline and pointlessness of the academic exercises he had endured: "I cannot imagine a more discouraging course of education than that to which I was subjected."

After several years during which, on the basis of his academic performance, no one held out much hope for his future, Josiah Quincy began to live up to the family name. He graduated Harvard with honors, and invited Governor Hancock to the celebration. His oratory skills attracted the same admiring attention his father's had. At first, after graduating, he lived quietly with his mother in Boston. In order to be near her, he signed on with a lawyer of no special accomplishment and turned down a choice apprenticeship.

Not long after his marriage, Quincy's family and political connections drew him out of "that domestic repose in which you seem to place too much of your delight," as his third cousin by marriage, President John Adams, teased him. Young Quincy was given the opportunity to run as the Federalist candidate for the state senate, and shortly thereafter for a seat in Congress, where he served as the House minority leader before leaving Washington in 1813 to return to Boston. In 1823, he began the first of six years as mayor of Boston.

Quincy's accomplishments as mayor helped shape the city. He modernized the old Town Dock and augmented Faneuil Hall with three additional elegant market buildings, which became known as the Quincy Markets (see figure 3 in chapter 7 and figure 4 in chapter 8). He bought the muddy ropewalk land at the base of the Common for development as a new public garden. He cleaned up the lawless West End of Boston and raised sanitation standards throughout the city, with the result that mortality rates in Boston declined. He strengthened the police force and fire department. He rode around the city at dawn each morning on horseback, unnerving some people as he surveyed conditions. After six years as mayor he had made the enemies he had expected to make as a vigilant administrator, and lost the next election gracefully.

For the next sixteen years, he served as president of Harvard College. Then, in his seventies, Josiah Quincy retired to study and write, serving occasionally on a board or committee. He continued in this manner until the age of ninety-two, outliving his wife and many good friends. He waited patiently for what he referred to as his "summons to join them," and a few months before his death, he wrote, "The light of the sun is withdrawing; but, blessed be Heaven, the light of the evening star reveals the hope of a coming immortality."

JOSIAH QUINCY, MASTER BUILDER

Josiah Quincy (1772–1864), Boston's "Great Mayor," could trace his lineage—a tenuous but distinguished line—back to Edmund Quincy, who arrived on the boat that bore Reverend John Cotton to Boston in 1633. A man of some rank, Edmund was promptly elected to the first General Court but died within a year, leaving a wife, son, daughter, and a large tract of land that became one of several Quincy ancestral estates and gave the town of Quincy its name.

Edmund Quincy's great-great-grandson, Josiah, also died young, as a minor hero of the Revolution in 1775, leaving behind his three-year old son, another Josiah, and a young widow. Despite, or perhaps because of, his devoted

Plate 33
William B. Annin and George G. Smith (fl. 1820–1833)
Plan of Boston Comprising a Part of Charlestown and Cambridgeport
(Boston, 1826)
Engraving. 54 x 53 cm.

In 1823 John G. Hales surveyed a map of Boston, which was updated and issued every few years. The 1826 version, updated by Stephen P. Fuller, was published by Smith,

Annin, and J. V. N. Throop. Annin and Smith were engravers, producing maps drawn on copper plates, but soon adopted the new process of lithography, a simpler and less expensive method where the map was transferred mechanically to a stone, from which it was printed.

This 1826 map shows many changes since Hales's 1814 map (see plate 32). Central Wharf had been added between India and Long wharves as a third deepwater wharf, and the old Town Dock filled in to make land for the Quincy Markets. Filling of the Mill Pond was virtual-

ly completed. The entire Back Bay of the Charles River had been cut off by a dam built in 1818–1821 on the line of present Beacon Street in order to power tide mills. The proposed street grid on the west side of the Neck, is an indication that the city was already contemplating filling in its part of what was called the receiving basin. Meanwhile, a trapezoidal area just north of the Mill Dam, now the Brimmer Street area of Beacon Hill, had already been filled by private developers.

PLAN
OF
BOSTON
Comprising a Part of
CHARLESTOWN
AND
Cambridgeport

Engraved & Published by ANNIN & SMITH & J.V.N.THROOP
From actual Survey,
With Corrections by S.P.FULLER, Surveyor. 1826.

SCALE

EXPLANATION

Boundaries of Wards
Churches & places of public worship
Public Schools
Public Buildings
Declivity of Hills

(left) An African-American girl stands in front of the African Meeting House at Smith Court on Beacon Hill in this photograph taken around 1832.

(right) A mezzotint portrait of William Lloyd Garrison by John Sartain, ca. 1835.

BOSTON IN 1830: THE QUIET REVOLUTION

The Boston of 1830 was still, in many ways, Bulfinch's Boston, and its historic maritime commerce still prosperous. Yet, the transformations that would ultimately yield a recognizably modern society were at hand. While Boston's land-mass had, in the early nineteenth century, expanded with modest but increasingly ambitious land-making projects, economic and social shifts were restructuring the society it housed.

Soon, immigration and industrialization would change the physical character of the city, its economy, and its social composition and dynamics. The Boston of 1830, already crowded with a burgeoning population of 60,000, was to double this number in roughly fifteen years, owing partly to an influx of immigrants, mainly Irish. Shortly thereafter, many of Boston's more prosperous citizens would leave the city to commute by horse-drawn streetcars from the suburbs. And cheap immigrant labor powered a growing number of factories in early industrial Massachusetts.

The Boston of the 1830s also experienced social changes more difficult to quantify. Emerson was about to resign as pastor of the Second Church of Boston to pursue his own Transcendentalist philosophy. A new state board of education was founded in 1837 with Horace Mann at its head. A growing number of social reformers filled Boston's lecture circuit and interjected new topics into public discourse. The rights of the disenfranchised became more widely considered, though much of polite society still found such topics foreign and even offensive. Blacks, Indians, women, children, the mentally ill, and the prison population all had champions who worked in or visited the Boston area.

William Lloyd Garrison (1805–1879), born in Newburyport, turned in a Newburyport slave trader in 1829, and shortly thereafter, in 1831, founded the New England Anti-Slavery Society in Boston, rapidly gaining a national reputation as an abolitionist leader. Between 1831 and 1865 Garrison published *The Liberator.* In its last issue it carried the new post-civil-war amendment to the Constitution outlawing slavery. Garrison was passionate in his unpopular work and his associate, Wendell Phillips, supported not only the abolitionist cause but the rights of Indians, women, and laborers.

Many of the early suffragists were also abolitionists such as Lucretia Mott (1793–1880) who was born on Nantucket and lectured in Boston, where she helped Garrison found the New England Anti-Slavery Society not far from State Street. She also helped to found a similar society in Philadelphia. Mott turned her concern to women's rights after officials of the World Anti-Slavery Convention in London (1840) refused to seat her as a delegate because of her sex. She convened the first conference on women's rights in Seneca Falls, New York, in 1848.

Lydia Maria Child (1802–1880), born in Medford, was an abolitionist and author. She wrote for children and, from 1826 to 1834, she edited the nation's first children's magazine, *Juvenile Miscellany.* We still remember Child's ballad "Over the River and through the Woods."

Samuel Gridley Howe (1801–1876) began teaching blind students in his father's Pleasant Street house in Boston and eventually founded the Perkins School for the Blind with generous assistance from Thomas Handasyd Perkins of China Trade fame. He spoke for abolition and prison reform, and in 1843 married Julia Ward Howe (1819–1910) of New York, later the author of the "Battle Hymn of the Republic." His suffragist wife worked not only for women's rights but for world peace.

Dorothea Dix (1802–1887) of Maine also brought her work to Boston. She championed the rights of the mentally ill. Her work led to legislation establishing state mental hospitals and ending the practice of incarcerating the mentally ill in prisons, the condition of which also drew her attention.

The social reformers working in Boston throughout the nineteenth century were parts of national movements converging on the ideals of a more equitable society, in which those in power felt obliged to speak for the less powerful. In Massachusetts, with its history of political activism, the energy of nineteenth-century social reformers may be seen as part of a continuing tradition. The ideals of those early reformers that pertained to the social responsibility of a humane government remain alive today in the form of the liberal political bent for which the Boston and Masssachusetts are known.

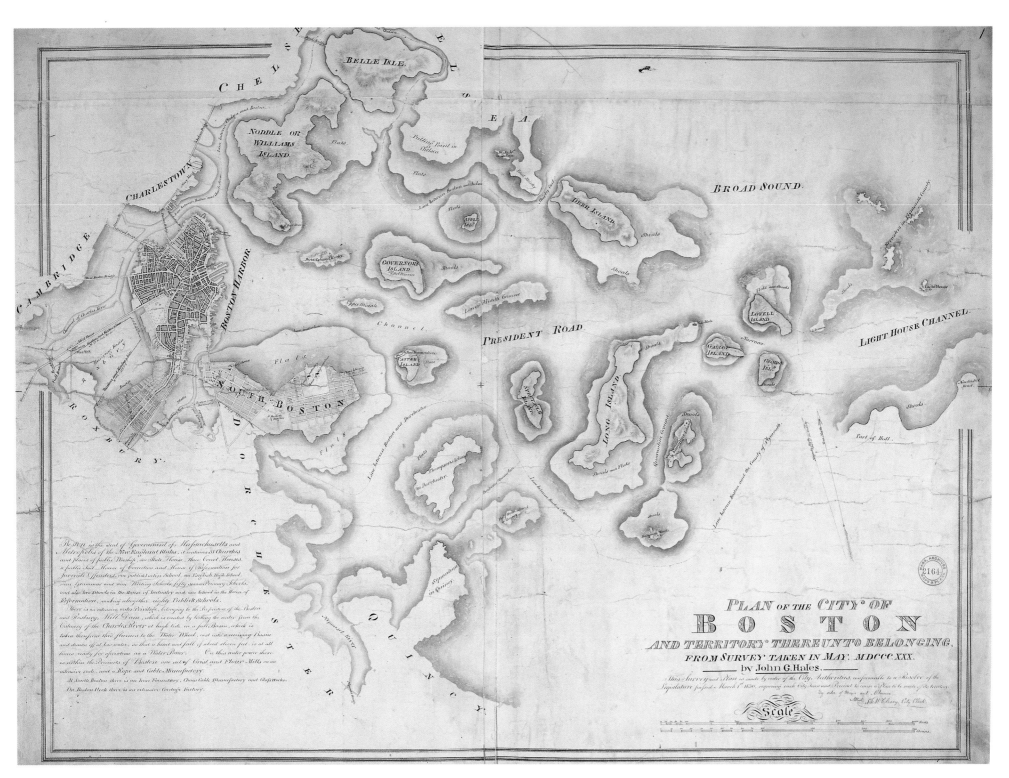

Plate 34
John G. Hales (1785–1832)
Plan of the City of Boston and territory thereunto belonging
(Boston, 1830)
Manuscript. 72 x 98 cm.

By 1830 the map of Massachusetts that Carleton had compiled from the 1794 surveys (see plate 30) needed updating. The legislature again directed each town to produce an accurate survey. This time the town plans were to be at the scale of 100, rather than 200, rods to an inch and to include, in addition to the items required in 1794, all roads, public buildings, topographical features, mills, mines, iron works, meadows, and woodlands. The legislature also recommended that towns be reimbursed for the expense of the survey if their plans were lithographed, and although the Boston plan remained in manuscript form, many town plans from the 1830 survey were published.

The map depicts Boston and all its harbor islands with their surrounding flats. Hales shows the many bridges that by 1830 connected the Boston peninsula with the mainland and met the state's requirement to include public buildings and industries by describing them in a written explanation. He gave particular attention to the Mill Dam project in Back Bay, where a dam, built in 1818–1821 on the line of later Beacon Street, was powering grist and flour mills as well as a rope and cable manufactory.

195

This engraving of Margaret Fuller, published by Johnson Fry and Company, was patterned after an original painting by Alonzo Chappel.

MARGARET FULLER AND THE TRANSCENDENTALISTS

Over the West Boston Bridge shown in Smith's 1835 map at right, Timothy Fuller clattered home on the stagecoach from his Boston law office to Cambridgeport. There, he heard his young daughter, Margaret (1810–1850), who was kept up late on his instructions, recite her *Virgil* and other Latin verses.

Despite her promising talents, Timothy Fuller saw no point in encouraging her gifts beyond a certain measure of domestic facility. After completing grammar school she begged to be sent to the new school where Ralph Waldo Emerson and his brother were teaching, but her father sent her instead for a final year of study at a girls' academy in the country. After that she helped at home and educated herself late at night and early in the morning. As a young woman, she became known as a provocative conversationalist, by turns erudite and irritating, whom a number of young scions of Harvard came to admire if not to court—to her disappointment.

When she finally managed an introduction to Emerson, she was twenty-five, and her father had died. She visited the Emersons at Concord and received a copy of Emerson's new book, *Nature,* a manifesto of Transcendental thought, which Boston had greeted with divided opinion. Emerson recruited Fuller along with his wife, Henry David Thoreau, Bronson Alcott, and other local intellectuals and literati to meet as the Transcendental Club.

Transcendentalism emphasized the existence of the soul, the unity of God, man, and nature, and reliance on the individual's experience, uninterpreted by doctrine or tradition. The Transcendentalists were, in a way, the natural inheritors of Anne Hutchinson's argument that a state of grace was a matter between God and the individual rather than a result of church learning or good works, and they heralded today's New Age variations on spirituality.

Ralph Waldo Emerson and Margaret Fuller were Transcendentalists by disposition and conviction. In their own early experiences of family and church, Emerson and Fuller each found much to transcend. Emerson, the brother, son, and grandson of ministers, grew up with cold, severe parents. Fuller, for her part, chafed under a dictatorial father and a society that offered her no reward for her gifts. They both relied heavily on their own observation of miraculous nature—for Fuller beginning as a child in her mother's garden—as a source of inspiration and faith.

By the time Fuller met the brilliant Emerson, she was attempting to support her own writing and study, her ailing mother, and her younger siblings. Emerson had arranged for her to teach in Bronson Alcott's school, but she was never paid for her services. When Emerson approached her about editing the *Dial,* a magazine he envisioned to convey the Transcendental message, she accepted, but found it a thankless task. Fuller contributed some of her own material to the *Dial* between 1840 and 1842, but she eventually transcended the Transcendentalists, along with her family, and her hometown. After she published her translation of Eckermann's *Conversations with Goethe,* she passed the *Dial* back to Emerson (who pursued it for less than a year before giving up on it), and began to travel within the Northeast, which seemed to free her muses.

As she was poised to publish her best-known work, *Woman in the Nineteenth Century,* Horace Greeley invited her to become literary editor of his *New York Tribune,* a post she took up at thirty-four. *Woman in the Nineteenth Century* sold out its 1000-copy printing in a week. (Emerson's *Nature* had struggled over several years to break 500, but his essays have endured and flourished in the American consciousness.)

After roughly two years and 250 articles of literary, art, and social criticism, Fuller persuaded Greeley to allow her to travel as foreign correspondent. She began in England and Scotland and ended in Italy, where her life changed dramatically. Still writing copiously, she fell in love with Italian culture and with the much younger Marchese Giovanni Angelo Ossoli. She married him secretly, had a child with him, ran a hospital in Rome while her husband fought with forces defending the city, wrote most of a history of the Roman Revolution, and longed to stay in Italy forever.

With her husband's cause finally quashed and no source of income available to the disinherited marchese, she reluctantly chose to return to the States with her devoted husband and precious toddler son, the manuscript of her history, and the hope of sustaining an income through journalism. Just fifty yards offshore of Fire Island, a storm ravaged their ship and prevented them from learning what sort of social ostracism awaited them. The three Ossolis died in the waves there.

Some controversy now surrounds Margaret Fuller's place in history, but she has found many supporters in the twentieth century. One of them, Laurie James, in her Fuller biography, blames Emerson and Fuller's other Boston colleagues, James Freeman Clarke and William Henry Channing, for creating a watered-down memoir that edited out her stronger writing and less conventional views. They completed it only at the prompting of Horace Greeley. Although even the memoir outsold Emerson's own work, it helped to enshroud Fuller's legacy in a veil of obscurity.

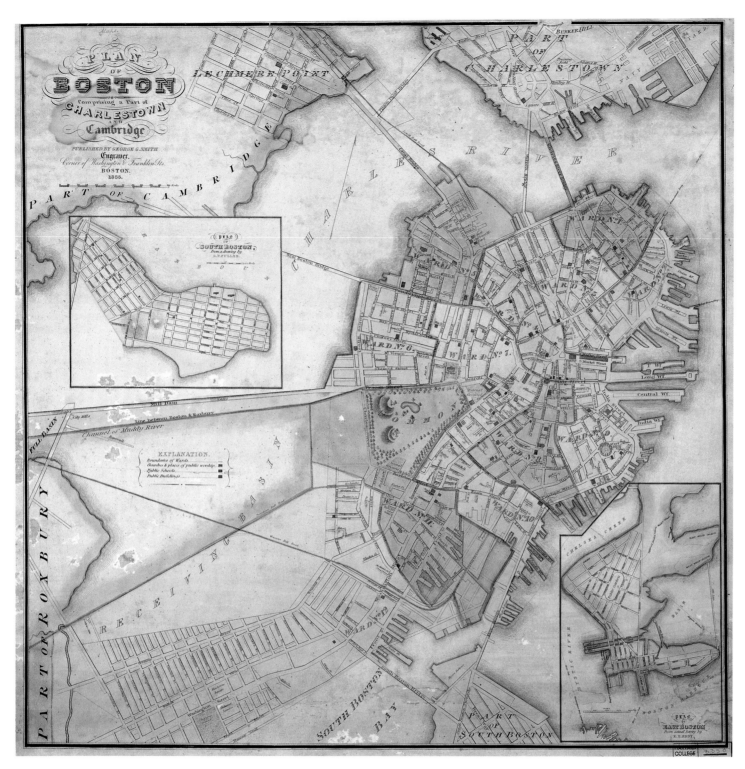

Plate 35

George G. Smith (1795–1878)

Plan of Boston Comprising a Part of Charlestown and Cambridge

(Boston, 1835)

Engraving. 54 × 54 cm.

This map is an updated version of an 1826 map (see plate 33). The revisions on this plan illustrate not only the changes that had occurred since 1826 but also how tracing these changes can be facilitated by using an updated version of the same map.

Since 1826 substantial filling had occurred along the Neck. To spur development south of the Neck, now the South End, Front Street (now Harrison Avenue) had been extended on the west side of the Neck and Tremont Street on the east side and the intervening flats filled in. Other changes concerned the first three railroads in Boston, which opened in 1835, all with depots on made land. The Boston and Lowell crossed the Charles River from East Cambridge to terminals on eight filled acres north of Causeway Street. Both the Boston and Providence and the Boston & Worcester railroads, now Amtrak and the MBTA commuter lines, obtained permission to build their tracks on causeways across the receiving basin (see figure 5 in chapter 7). The Boston and Providence depot was on newly made land approximately where the Park Plaza Hotel is now located. The Boston and Worcester had agreed to construct its depots in South Cove, which was being filled by a group of developers, after it had been obstructed by the opening in 1828 of a free bridge to South Boston on approximately the line of the present Dorchester Avenue Bridge. The filling of South Cove and of South Boston opposite it also began to define Fort Point Channel, the outlet of South Bay. On the central waterfront two new streets—Commercial and Fulton—had been extended from the new Quincy Markets to the North End, much as Broad and India Streets had been filled south of the market area earlier in the century.

The 1835 map included two inset maps of new sections of Boston—South Boston, which had been annexed in 1804 and had begun to develop rapidly after the free bridge opened, and East Boston, an island in the harbor whose owner formed a company in 1833 to develop it as a new residential and industrial section of the city.

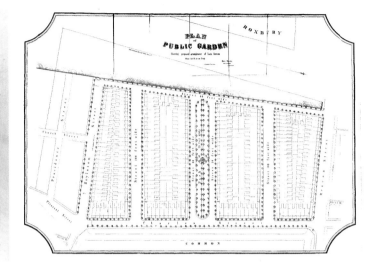

Boston's elegant Public Garden was first a great mud flat at the western base of the gently sloping Common. In 1794, it came to host Boston's ropewalks, a facility that had been destroyed by fire in its earlier location on Fort Hill, nearer the wharves. In exchange for situating there, on town-owned flats, the ropewalk owners were to build a seawall to keep out the tides, and fill in behind it to create new land. In 1799, the remaining gap between the ropewalks and the end of Beacon Street became a trash dump (see plate 32).

Within about thirty years, a solid phalanx of elegant homes had formed along Beacon Street all the way to the water's edge, the ropewalks had suffered two more fires, and the garbage smelled. These incompatible land uses had to be separated. Mayor Josiah Quincy bought back, at considerable expense, the scrap of town land given earlier to the ropewalk owners, with the idea of creating an additional public open space for Boston. By 1837, the city had filled in the dump, remedying a public nuisance, and adding land beyond the dump and the old ropewalks site; this would eventually meet the fill heaped into the Back Bay and would some day become a major public amenity. A group of private citizens led by Horace Gray soon obtained permission to build a botanic garden there, open to the public.

The land, however, became a canvas for the visions of both real estate speculators and civic improvers. Entrepreneurs wanted to divide the land into house lots that would have made it an annex to the future Back Bay development. But eventually the vision of a stately public garden prevailed, with the understanding that such an ornament for the civic realm would, by no small coincidence, elevate real estate values for all current and future abutters.

In 1859, the fate of the land was finally decided. The Commonwealth, busy filling in the Back Bay, offered the city a small wedge of land that brought the tract for the garden even with the future Arlington Street, if the city would agree to keep the land open. A public referendum, heavily supported by the residents of abutting neighborhoods, sanctioned the agreement.

The City Council then appointed a committee to oversee the competition for the design of the public garden. That committee selected George T. Meacham's plan, combining picturesque and formal design approaches, and construction was largely completed in 1861, with minor modifications to the plan made by the city engineer. As shown in an 1869 photograph (at left), the new garden looked unrecognizably barren. It took about thirty years for the carefully chosen specimen trees to mature into the forms Bostonians recognize in today's Public Garden.

(top left) With this 1859 referendum poster, political organizers galvanized the Beacon Hill vote for an act to preserve the lands of the future Public Garden. The measure passed by a vote of 6187 to 99 and the design of the Public Garden soon followed.

(top right) The vision of a Public Garden that began with Mayor Quincy in 1824, and was finally realized in the 1860s, did not prevent hopeful speculators from creating street plans such as this one from 1850 for the expanded site of the old ropewalks.

(bottom) An 1869 photograph of the newly constructed Public Garden.

Plate 36
Nathaniel Dearborn (1786–1852)
A new and complete Map of the City of Boston and Precincts including part of Charlestown, Cambridge, & Roxbury, From the best Authorities
Frontispiece of the *Boston Directory* (Boston: N. Dearborn, 1848–1849)
Engraving. 38 x 43 cm.

George W. Boynton, the city's leading engraver at the time, had engraved similar maps in 1835 and 1839, but created a new plate for this 1848 map. By using a smaller scale than the maps published by Smith (see plates 33 and 35), Boynton was able to include most of the city without inset maps.

Like many *Directory* maps, Boynton's map is not very accurate. The huge Boston Wharf Company wharf shown was based on a plan drawn in 1836 although only a part had been built by 1848. The amount actually constructed can be seen on the 1847 chart of Boston Harbor (see plate 22).

In spite of its inaccuracies, the 1848 map does show some of the land made since 1835. Filling of South Cove had been completed and an additional section, the area where the *Boston Herald* building is now located, had been filled, further defining Fort Point Channel. On the central waterfront, the head of the dock between Central and Long Wharves had been filled in and the Custom House built there. And the area that would later become the Public Garden had been filled.

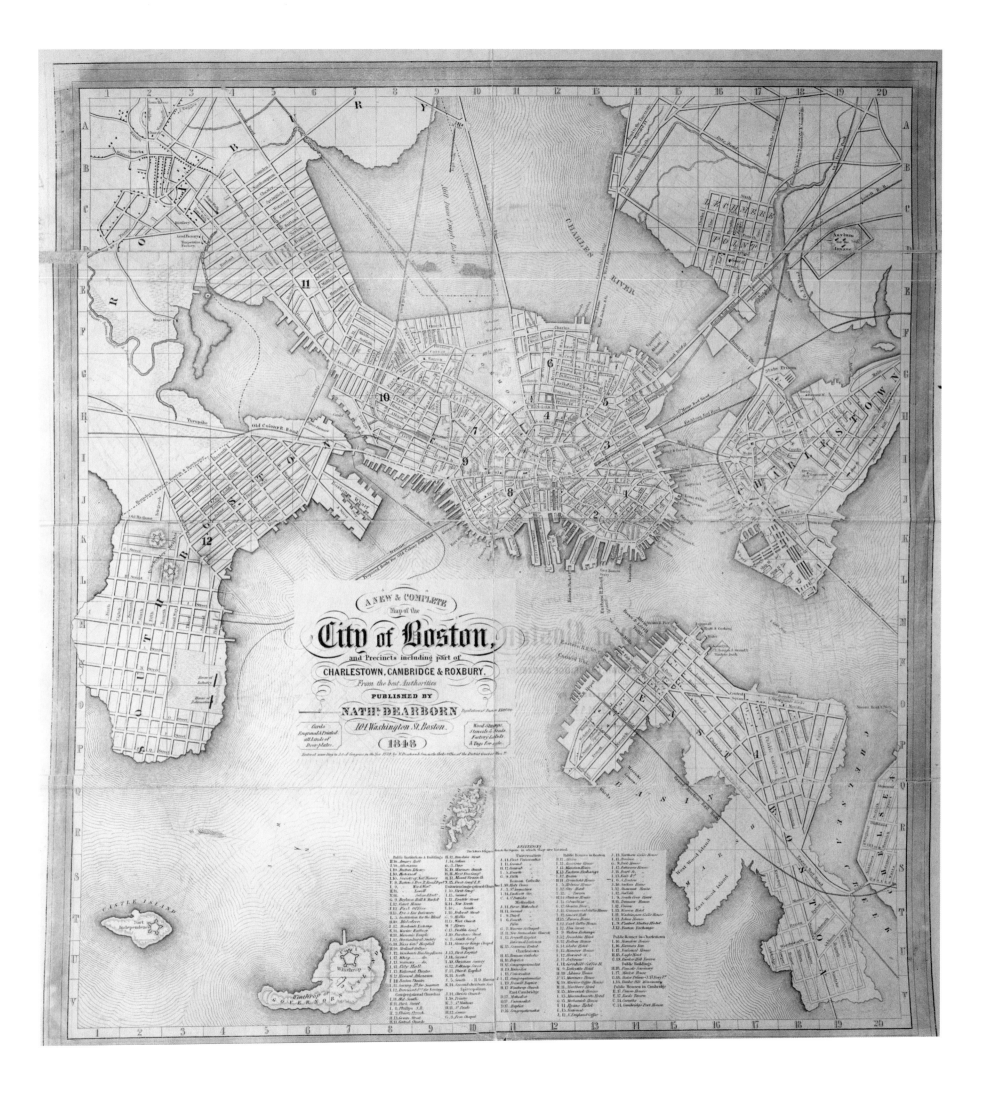

(*above*) The 1854 lithograph portrait of Donald McKay was copied from a daguerreotype by Southworth and Hawes.

(*right*) The *Chariot of Fame,* seen here in an 1854 oil painting by D. McFarlane, came from Donald McKay's East Boston shipyard.

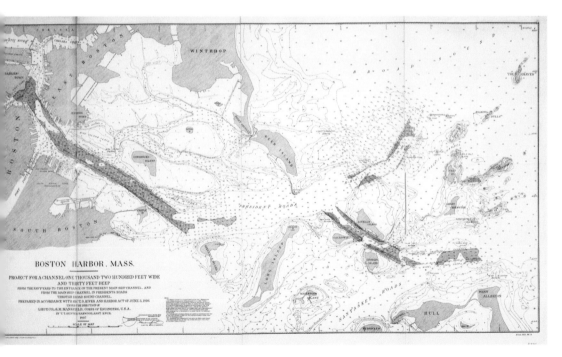

Corps of Engineers, *Boston Harbor, Mass. Project for a channel one thousand two hundred feet wide and thirty feet deep . . .* , 1897. The concern about maintaining proper shipping channels into Boston Harbor continued long after the clipper ships and the establishment of limits to wharf extension. Indeed, larger modern ships needed clearer and better-maintained channels. Nearly half a century after Chesbrough's map (at right) helped define the geometry of the harbor, the Corps of Engineers sought to improve the central shipping channel by dredging it.

THE CLIPPER SHIPS

In a fleeting moment before the maritime prosperity of Massachusetts had expired, and before the refinement of steam ships, the discovery of gold in California kindled a rebirth of the great shipbuilding industry of Massachusetts. With new builders contriving new ship designs, several Boston shipyards and others along the Massachusetts and New England coasts began to produce the most remarkable class of sailing ship ever built—the clipper ship.

The slender, beautiful ships not only clipped through the seas but clipped days off the sailing records of every leg of every journey they undertook. Their records still stand. The *James Baines,* for example—built by Donald McKay for an Australian shipping firm—made the trans-Atlantic journey from Boston to Liverpool in twelve days and six hours. Columbus's first voyage, made in excellent time for his day, had taken thirty-five days from Seville to the Caribbean. English ships bringing the Puritans fared much worse. Many small sailing vessels still take three or four weeks to cross the Atlantic, while the Queen Elizabeth II, with her diesel-electric engine, now travels from England to New York in only six days.

Between 1850 and 1854, the wharves of Boston, particularly those of East Boston, bustled as clipper ships were readied for launching and sail. Donald McKay, a Nova Scotia native who had apprenticed in New York, built the finest of all the clipper ships. The McIntyre map (see frontispiece to chapter 10) illustrates McKay's East Boston shipyard well. With romantic names like the *Flying Cloud, Stag-Hound, Westward Ho!,* and *Romance of the Seas*, they captured more records than any other yard could claim. Boston firms bought them, as did New York firms. (There were also successful clipper shipyards in New York.) British and Australian firms bought the swift, elegant ships—making a historic milestone for Britain: the first purchase of a foreign-made ship.

For Boston firms, the clipper was a packet ship carrying passengers and their baggage or cargoes around Cape Horn to San Francisco. From there, she might make the return voyage with gold and other California cargoes, or proceed to Asian ports. In the packet business, as opposed to the China trade, passenger and cargo each paid its own way and cargoes did not generally belong to the ship owner. Many of the Boston owners who operated clippers did so from New York, a concession to her greater size and superior distribution network.

The excitement over the clippers and their amazing performances under sail died down as they proved burdensome to man, requiring large crews to handle the sails (up to 130 sailors and officers). Their sleek lines sacrificed cargo space, and they were expensive to maintain, requiring frequent repairs that caused costly disruptions of the routes they sailed so gracefully. Even before the end of the age of sail, which was imminent, the shipyards ceased turning out the standard clipper after only four years. Soon, as the age of steam hit with full force, the shipyard owners and workers of Massachusetts were to find their assets and tools idle.

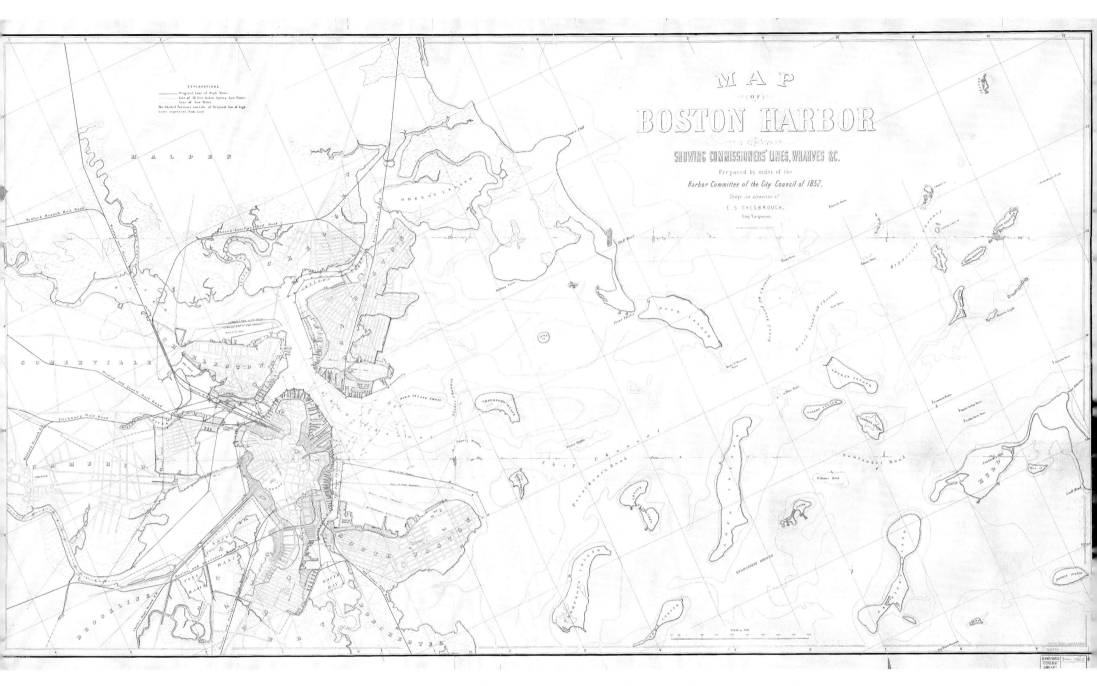

Plate 37

Ellis Sylvester Chesbrough (1813-1886)

*Map of Boston Harbor, showing commissioner's lines,
wharves, &c.*

(Boston, 1852)

Engraving. 60 x 109 cm.

In the middle of the nineteenth century Bostonians were
concerned that filling the flats and building wharves in the
harbor were causing the shipping channels to deteriorate.
In 1852 a city committee asked the city engineer to prepare a map showing both the harbor lines, which limited
how far wharves and fill could extend, and the amount of
the original harbor that had been reduced by filling.

The task fell to Ellis S. Chesbrough, the first, and
very able, city engineer. Chesbrough determined the
amount of fill by reconstructing the original (1630) high
water line—the original shoreline. He based this reconstruction on many maps, among them the 1847 U.S. Coast
Survey of the harbor (see plate 22), Page's 1775 map (see
plate 28), maps of East Boston by R. H. Eddy (an example
appears as an inset map in plate 35), and the work of many
nineteenth-century surveyors. Chesbrough acknowledged
particular difficulty in reconstructing the original shoreline at the foot of the Common because the land there was
so level.

The results of his research are shown on this 1852
map. The original landforms are shown in white and the

filled areas in gray, and one can easily see the amount of
land that had been added by 1852 not only to the Boston
peninsula but also to South Boston, East Boston,
Charlestown, and Cambridge. Chesbrough's reconstruction
of the original shoreline was quickly accepted and reproduced on many subsequent maps. It appeared, for example,
on the 1870 city surveyor's and the 1880 Boston Map
Company maps (see plates 41 and 43) and is still the reconstruction of the original shoreline that is most often used.

Copy photograph of a *carte de visite* portrait of Lewis Hayden, taken by an unknown photographer, ca. 1860.

LEWIS HAYDEN AND THE LAST WALTZ OF THE NORTH AND SOUTH

In the 1850s the U.S. Congress attempted the last legislative compromises between Southerners and Northerners on the divisive issue of slavery. The Fugitive Slave Law of 1850 allowed slave owners' agents to enter Northern states such as Massachusetts, where slavery was illegal, to reclaim their ex-slaves with the help of federal marshals and federal courts. The Kansas-Nebraska Act of 1854 allowed new territories to decide for themselves the question of slavery. The Fugitive Slave Law infuriated many Northerners. The Kansas-Nebraska Act appeased neither proslavery nor antislavery forces. By this time, passions for and against slavery ran too high for compromise.

The Fugitive Slave Law chilled blacks in Northern states—many of whom were fugitives—and stirred abolitionist passions. Boston's well-organized black community of about 2,500—including many fugitive slaves—mobilized against the crisis, devising ways to aid fugitives. Upset but determined, they sought and received the assistance of the anti-slavery portion of Boston's white community in forming a Vigilance Committee to learn of the issuance of warrants for a slave's recapture, and to provide shelter, sustenance, transportation, and financial and legal aid to defeat any ex-slaves' pursuers.

And while politicians and preachers argued the law, and Boston abolitionists such as William Lloyd Garrison and Wendell Phillips hotly denounced it, and the courts began to issue warrants to U.S. marshals, one Bostonian acted with greater conviction than any other. Lewis Hayden, leader of Boston's black community and of the predominantly white Committee for Vigilance and Safety, continually took fugitive slaves into his home—as many as thirteen at a time—despite the penalties for doing so. His home was a station on the underground railway and he was known, in many cases, to smuggle runaway slaves by wagon to the next safe stop on what was usually a route to Canada.

Hayden, a successful clothier, made large and small contributions to ease the difficulties of the fugitives: a carriage fare here, a child's funeral there, or the posting of bail. His Vigilance Committee was able to offer financial and legal assistance to many in need thanks to the financial contributions of black and white citizens, some prominent, such as Ralph Waldo Emerson.

When the first warrant was issued in Boston, for William and Ellen Craft, who had escaped from Georgia, Hayden was instrumental in guarding them and conducting them out of the city to Nova Scotia, whence they sailed to London.

When, several months after the Fugitive Slave Law passed, U.S. marshals finally succeeded in bringing a stunned ex-slave, Shadrach Minkins, to the courthouse in Boston, Hayden led a mob of blacks who abducted him and spirited him away first to Hayden's neighbor, then to Concord and north to the safety of Montreal.

Southern outrage greeted every failed attempt to recover fugitive slaves in Boston. And a racist backlash followed the image of a black mob taking the law—and Shadrach Minkins—into its own hands. President Fillmore scolded the city and called local officials to account. The letter of the law gained wider enforcement, although many Northerners continued to regard the law with contempt.

Hayden was again involved in riots surrounding the trial of fugitive slave Anthony Burns in 1854. But armed soldiers were set against the mob. The verdict returned Burns to inhuman treatment in Virginia but he was eventually purchased by antislavery sympathizers in Massachusetts. He returned to Boston a free man.

After the Civil War ended slavery, Hayden remained an active leader in the black community. Having helped to vanquish slavery, he turned his attention to the racism and prejudice that underpinned it. He fought successfully for the integration of Boston public schools. He endowed scholarships for black students at Harvard Medical School. He helped with the successful petition to the state legislature to erect a statue of ex-slave Crispus Attucks, the first American to fall in the Boston Massacre by British troops (see plate 27 vignette). In 1873, Hayden himself was elected to the Massachusetts legislature.

Hayden's motivations in trying to improve the lot of African Americans, and the intensity of his convictions in repeatedly risking his life, are no mystery. Hayden was born a slave in Kentucky, where his family was sold apart and his mother driven insane by cruel treatment. He first arrived in Boston, with other family members, as a fugitive slave. When he died in 1889, he had not achieved a full victory for his cause, but he had achieved the rare triumph of pressing all his life's energies into the service of his conscience and the healing of his own tragic scars.

Plate 38
I. Slatter and B. Callan
Map of the city of Boston, Mass^ts
(New York and Boston, 1852)
Engraving. 79 x 108 cm.

Eighteen fifty-two was a banner year for important
maps of Boston—a very accurate map of the area surrounding Boston was surveyed by J. C. Sidney, a
reconstruction of the original shoreline of the city and
the area filled to that date was prepared by Ellis S.
Chesbrough (see plate 37), and two maps were published showing every building in the city, the first
since the 1814 Hales. One of these was the map surveyed by I. Slatter and B. Callan and published jointly by Matthew Dripps in New York and L. N. Ide in
Boston. The map was actually engraved in New York,
a reflection of the movement of the lithographic
industry from Boston to New York and Philadelphia.
Like other handsome mid-nineteenth-century city
maps, the Slatter and Callan is bordered with views of
important buildings in the city (see also frontispiece
to chapter 10).

    The Slatter and Callan map is generally more
accurate than the other 1852 map that shows all
structures—McIntyre's *Map of the city of Boston and
immediate neighborhoods* (see frontispiece to chapter
10)—and is an invaluable record of Boston at mid-
century. It also shows all the land making that had
occurred in the city in the four years since the publication of the Dearborn map in 1848 (see plate 36): the
South Bay project, then in progress; filling of the inlet
immediately west of Federal Street (now Dorchester
Avenue) in South Cove; creation of land on the west
side of the peninsula just north of the West Boston
Bridge for the new County, now Charles Street, Jail;
filling west of Charles Street and north of the Mill
Dam, now Beacon Street; and new land in Back Bay
west of Tremont Street.

This photograph, showing the Back Bay in the making, dates from the 1860s. The new buildings in the distance define the east edge of Dartmouth Street and either side of Beacon Street (formerly the old Mill Dam). The smaller, older buildings close by mark the south side of Beacon. The sea-wall on which people are sitting can now be found next to Back Street. Note the camera's shadow in the foreground.

Bird's Eye View of Boston, chromolithograph, ca. 1850, stone drawing by C. Matter, printing by R. Furrer.

Aerial photograph looking east over the Back Bay, 1997. Comparing Furrer's famous nineteenth-century view to the contemporary photograph emphasizes the monumental achievement of the Back Bay.

THE BACK BAY

And this is good old Boston,
The home of the bean and the cod,
Where the Lowells talk to the Cabots,
And the Cabots talk only to God.

In 1910, John Collins Bossidy poked fun at Boston's aristocracy with this adaptation of a toast made a few years earlier at a Harvard reunion. Its wit was born of an outsider's irreverence, for Mr. Bossidy was addressing not Harvard alumni but alumni of Holy Cross.

Bossidy's quip may have represented a new political era in Boston, but in 1860, when Bossidy was born, the Lowells and the Cabots were still having the last laugh. The filling of the Back Bay had begun only a few years before Bossidy's birth and by the time of his toast the last great mansions of the Back Bay had only recently been completed. Within that time, profound political changes had occurred in Boston.

According to some, the Back Bay represented the moneyed Protestants' last stand as the numbers of immigrants (mainly Irish) grew to approach half the city's population, and railroads and horse trolleys made possible the exodus of the affluent to the suburbs. Last stand or not, it was a grand undertaking, enlarging Boston's land mass by 450 acres—more than half the size of the original peninsula—and enhancing her image. The Massachusetts General Court appointed a group of commissioners to plan and oversee this important project.

The Back Bay commissioners were the agents of this last stand. They envisioned the transformation of slime and sludge into "a magnificent system of streets and squares" lined with homes that would command high prices; make a good profit for the Commonwealth of Massachusetts, whose interests they represented, and which held a majority of the flats; and place Boston on a footing with Paris and London. In a public advertisement in 1856, the Commissioners spoke of the need for housing in an otherwise cramped city, and even of a resulting "diminution of rents." However, in making a beautiful, expensive neighborhood, they dealt only with the upper and upper-middle classes. Indeed, in selling the lots and receiving testimony, the Commissioners seemed to be dealing with their colleagues and peers.

To attain their goal of creating a desirable neighborhood, the commissioners forged an early version of zoning regulations. They dictated a minimum height of three stories for the houses to be built, and a set-back from the street of 25 to 30 feet. Architectural ornamentation had to be confined to the "correct taste" and the setback lines.

The commissioners prohibited stables (but did not object to ones placed discreetly on the back alleys) and commercial buildings. They prescribed streets of a grand width, with Commonwealth Avenue as the crowning gem. It was to lead straight from the Public Garden to the pastoral beauty of the suburban lands, with a broad central swath of green, lined with four rows of trees.

The commissioners also donated one seventh of the land to Boston or directly to public cultural institutions in an effort to attract them to the Back Bay. By the time the Back Bay was completed, it was a cultural mecca. Not only plutocrats but members of the intelligentsia such as Dr. Oliver Wendell Holmes bought there. Its streets of English- and Parisian-inspired facades, bounded by the Public Garden, the Charles River, and the cultural and commercial district along Boylston Street, were and are among Boston's glories. The area around Copley Square came to host an impressive array of cultural institutions such as the original Museum of Fine Arts and the Public Library, with educational institutions such as MIT on Boylston Street.

Boston's population continued to grow and diversify, even as the city's commercial vigor waned. The wealthy residents who had helped to create the Back Bay slowly lost their interest in adventurous investments and their political hold on the city. But the Back Bay has survived the many economic and political cycles of Boston as an important and elegant part of the city's identity—still housing the well-to-do near the Public Garden, but changing in character as it meets Massachusetts Avenue and approaches Kenmore Square, with their large student populations and ethnically diverse neighborhoods.

Plate 39

George G. Smith (1795–1878)

Plan of Boston Comprising a Part of Charlestown and Cambridge

(Boston, 1855)

Engraving. 66 x 52 cm.

By the 1850s the map published by George G. Smith (see plates 33 and 35 and figure 4 in chapter 7) had unofficially become the official city map, appearing annually in the *Municipal Register,* a publication that contained the city charter and recent ordinances, rules of the City Council, and a list of city officers.

The shoreline shown on the 1855 Smith map is not much different from that on the 1852 Slatter and Callan, and McIntyre and Chesbrough maps (see plates 37 and 38 and frontispiece to chapter 10), for it depicts the city only three years later, but the Smith map does show planning for a major land-making project that was about to begin—the filling of Back Bay. The tide mills had not been successful and, cut off by the Mill Dam and with the flow of water further impeded by the railroad embankments, the Back Bay, into which all the sewers from surrounding areas drained, had become a stinking cesspool.

By the early 1850s it was determined that the only solution was to fill the bay, and in 1854 the state and the Boston Water Power Company, the two major owners of the Back Bay flats, made an agreement for filling them. This agreement included the street plan shown on the 1855 map. This street grid had been laid out without regard for the railroad tracks, and eventually only the streets east of Dartmouth, which is just west of the point where the tracks crossed, were constructed—the reason that today only the streets from Arlington to Dartmouth cross what is now the Turnpike. The streets west of Dartmouth were then aligned perpendicular to the tracks (see plate 40). The area just south of the Mill Dam and east of the future Exeter Street shown on the map with almost no proposed streets was the state's part of Back Bay; the Boston Water Power Company owned all the rest.

THE BOSTON INTELLECTUAL TRADITION: OLIVER WENDELL HOLMES

Oliver Wendell Holmes, Sr., in his Back Bay study in 1894.

Oliver Wendell Holmes, Jr., strolling in Washington, D.C., ca. 1910.

Although they represent only two generations of intellectual achievement, Oliver Wendell Holmes and his son, Oliver Wendell Holmes, Jr., the Supreme Court Justice, are among the covey of accomplished Boston families that caused Van Wyck Brooks to gush, in *The Flowering of New England*, that Boston "drained a watershed of intellect with which no other could be compared, and it would not let itself be drained in turn."

The first Oliver Wendell Holmes (1809–1894) attended Harvard Law School, as would his famous son, but the elder Holmes turned afterward to medicine. The Paris-trained physician wrote books and poems, lectured, and amused Boston society with his renowned wit. He was a Boston phenomenon whom Sir William Osler declared "the most successful combination the world has ever seen, of physician and man of letters." His only well-known poem, "Old Ironsides," was in the sentimental, heroic mold, but he produced many witty verses. Local admirers often invited him to commemorate an occasion in verse. His mirth and skill as a humorist are evident in a poem he wrote proudly spoofing his own reputation as a wit. It describes the author penning a hilarious poem and giving it to the butler to take to the printer. He watches the butler peek inside and fall down in a fit of helpless, roaring laughter. Finally, it concludes, "Ten days and nights, with sleepless eye, / I watched that wretched man, / And since, I never dare to write / As funny as I can."

OLIVER WENDELL HOLMES, JR.

Like his father, the younger Oliver Wendell Holmes (1841–1935) attended Harvard and Harvard Law School. Emulating his father, he authored a book, *The Common Law*. But unlike his Renaissance-minded parent, the son was single-minded in pursuit of one discipline and career—the law. This made him a national rather than a local phenomenon. President Theodore Roosevelt appointed Oliver Wendell Holmes, Jr., to the Supreme Court in 1902, after Holmes had served two decades on the Massachusetts Supreme Court, the last few as Chief Justice. Arriving with his wife in Washington, he found himself in the company of a number of cabinet appointees such as Henry Adams who, like Holmes, were the Harvard-graduated scions of great Boston families.

Holmes brought with him to the job the family eloquence and wit and left behind a body of finely worded opinions, mainly dissenting. A supporter of civil liberties, he established the "clear and present danger" test for free speech in *Schenk v. United States* (1919). Before it could curtail a person's right to speak his mind, Holmes asserted, the government must prove "a clear and present danger that they [the words used] will bring about the substantive evils that Congress has a right to prevent."

Like his father, Holmes was a philosophical observer of human nature and human destiny. "Certainty is generally an illusion," he wrote, "and repose is not the destiny of man." Like his father he had a lighter side and was also blessed with longevity. On seeing an attractive young woman at the age of ninety, he is said to have quipped, "Oh, to be seventy again!"

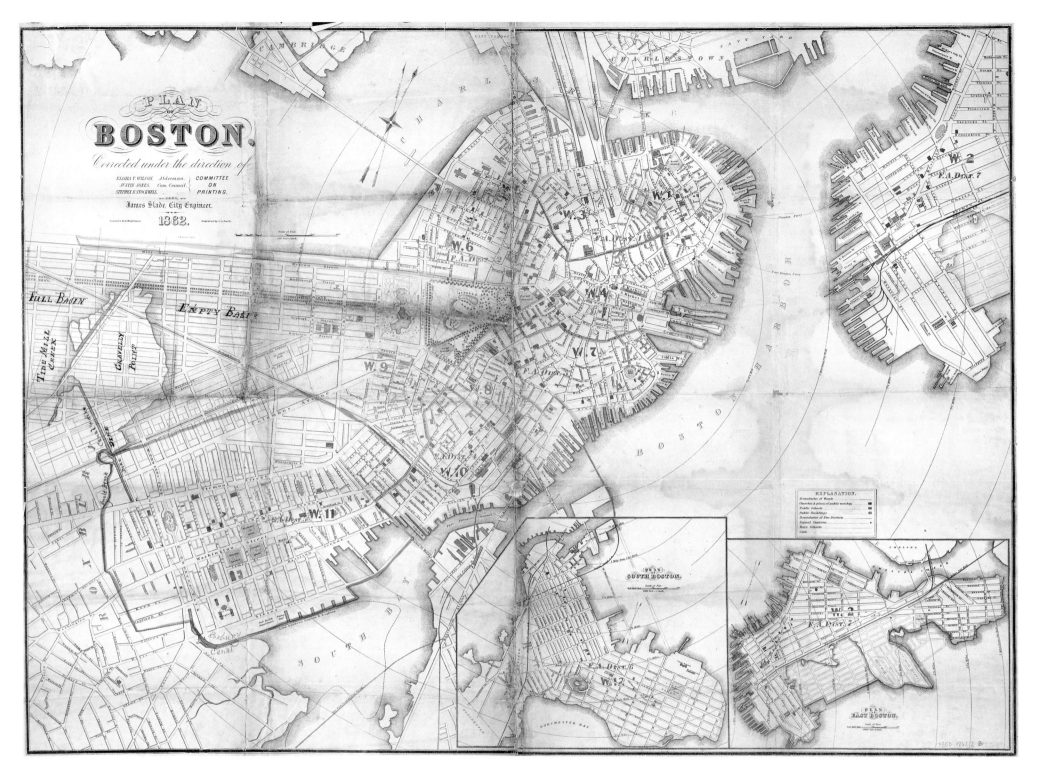

Plate 40
James Slade
***Plan of Boston, Corrected under the direction of
Committee on Printing, of 1861, by James Slade,
City Engineer***
(Boston, 1862)
Engraving. 69 x 98 cm.

In 1860 the Boston City Council decided to have a new map of the city made. It was to be on the scale of 500 feet to the inch, larger than the 1823 Hales map which hitherto served, with updates, as the semiofficial city maps (see plates 33, 35, and 39). The new map, was first published in 1861 and reissued, with updates, every year from 1862 through 1870 with the exception of 1865.

The 1862 edition was drawn by H. M. Wightman, engraved by C. A. Swett, and printed by J. H. Daniels. The map shows many changes since 1855. Filling of Back Bay was underway including Commonwealth Avenue, shown tree-lined and planned as a grand boulevard in order to attract wealthy residents. Huntington and Columbus Avenues, which had been laid out on either side of the Boston and Providence tracks in order to connect the new land with Roxbury and the South End, are also shown. Some areas shown as filled were actually still in progress. This was true of the sections along the Charles River between Beacon Street and the West Boston (now

Longfellow) Bridge and between the latter and the Canal (Lechmere) Bridge, neither of which would be finished until about 1870. The extension of Albany Street between South Cove and the newly filled part of the South End also was being constructed in 1862. The filling in of some docks between the wharves on the central waterfront had taken place and new buildings, such as the still-extant State Street Block (see figure 10 in chapter 7) and the Mercantile Wharf Buildings, had been erected on the made land. On the South Boston Flats, the Boston Wharf Company wharf had been extended to the line of the Boston, Hartford, & Erie Railroad, which had entered Boston in 1855 on tracks that crossed South Bay and South Boston before swinging out over the flats to a depot near present South Station.

Fort Hill on its way to being cut down. This photograph was taken in late 1867 or early 1868 looking down the newly cut Oliver Street just west of its intersection with High Street, approximately where the International Place office buildings are now located. The footbridge had been built in October 1867 to enable students and teachers to get from the south side of Fort Hill, on the right-hand side of the photo, across the Oliver Street cut to the schools on the north side.

In 1871, after five years of cutting down Fort Hill, there was still a sizable hill left. Laborers are digging by hand to fill the horse-drawn tip carts that carried the dirt down to fill the docks cut off by Atlantic Avenue (see also figure 11 in chapter 7).

CUTTING DOWN FORT HILL

It has been said that land was made in Boston by "cutting down the hills to fill the coves," and Fort Hill is a case in point. Fort Hill once rose steeply from the shoreline along what is now Broad Street, covering an area that is part of today's financial district. A seventeenth-century fort at the summit gave the hill its name. After the Revolution, however, Bostonians dismantled the fort and replaced it with a landscaped circle (called, anomalously, a square).

In the early nineteenth century Fort Hill was a fashionable residential area where wealthy merchants built houses. By the 1820s, however, the merchants began to move to newly fashionable areas like Beacon Hill. Institutions such as the Boston Athenaeum and a precursor of the Perkins School for the Blind acquired many of these mansions. The institutions did not remain long either, however, and the mansions were then bought by absentee landlords who, realizing that Fort Hill was near the business district and that land values would probably increase, let the houses deteriorate.

Into this declining neighborhood swarmed Irish immigrants who, fleeing the potato famine in Ireland, poured into Boston in the 1840s. The Irish settled on Fort Hill because it was close to the docks and the railroad yards where many of them worked, an important consideration in the days before horse-drawn streetcars provided inexpensive public transportation. The old mansions on Fort Hill were subdivided, ramshackle housing was built on every available inch of space, and habitations were tunneled into the hill. An 1849 city report graphically described the miserable living conditions on Fort Hill—privies on upper levels drained onto lower areas, cisterns were polluted, and underground dwellings lacked any ventilation. Under such circumstances, it is not surprising that Fort Hill was a center of the 1849 cholera epidemic in Boston.

In 1854 a group of Boston businessmen formed a corporation to cut down Fort Hill. Their ostensible motive was to permit an expansion of the business district and thus increase the city's tax base, but their hidden agenda was to initiate Boston's first slum clearance project. The corporation never acted, but in 1865 the city announced plans to cut just one street—Oliver Street—through the hill. Although the businessmen warned that such a plan was unrealistic, the city embarked on the project in 1866. Cutting through Fort Hill was a formidable task: at Washington Square the cut had to be over 40 feet deep (see illustration). Nonetheless, by 1868 the city had managed to hack Oliver Street through the hill. It quickly became apparent that the businessmen were right—buildings had to be located so far back from the sides of the cut, which were caving in, that the residents were fleeing and the whole hill would have to be taken down after all. But the project could not proceed because there was no place to put the dirt.

At this juncture the city came up with a new land-making project—construction of Atlantic Avenue across the wharves and docks on the central waterfront. Atlantic Avenue was already under discussion as the site for a railroad track, but the need for a place to dispose of dirt from Fort Hill was the final impetus for the project. Both the Atlantic Avenue and Fort Hill projects got under way in 1869; by 1872 Fort Hill had transmigrated into the former docks on the landward side of the new Atlantic Avenue, creating the land where buildings such as the Flour and Grain Exchange are now located (see figures 12 and 13 in chapter 7).

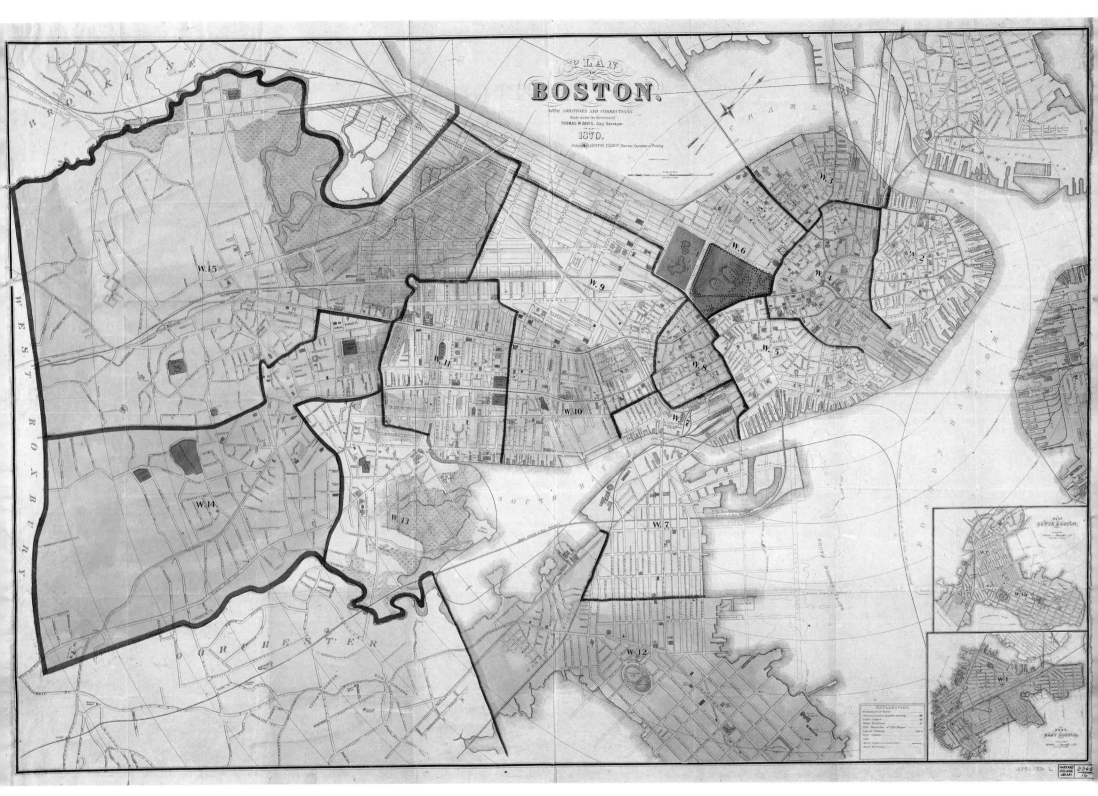

Plate 41

Thomas Wood Davis

***Plan of Boston with additions and corrections, Made
under the direction of Thomas W. Davis, City Surveyor***
(Boston, 1870)

Engraving. 86 × 121 cm.

In 1869 responsibility for the official city map was shifted
to the office of the city surveyor, a position created in the
mid 1860s to handle street widenings. The map had been
enlarged in 1868 to include the town of Roxbury, which
was annexed to the city that year, and was enlarged again
in 1870 when Dorchester was annexed.

A comparison of the 1862 (see plate 40) and 1870
city maps shows several changes. In Back Bay the filled
area extended west of Fairfield Street. On the central waterfront, Atlantic Avenue was being constructed right across

and through the buildings on the old wharves. When it
was completed the docks on its landward side would be
filled in. On the South Boston Flats, the state's attempts to
begin filling these flats is suggested by the proposed street
grid north of South Boston; all that had actually been filled
by 1870, however, was in the vicinity of the Boston Wharf
and the railroad tracks. In South Bay, Albany Street had
been completed and the intervening flats filled, and, on the
South Boston side, new land had been created so that the
Old Colony Railroad tracks could be moved further west.

Weary firemen and volunteers pose for this photograph alongside a steam fire wagon in the aftermath of the still-smoldering fire of 1872.

The devastating effects of the fire can be seen in this panoramic photograph of what was Boston's business district.

THE GREAT FIRE OF 1872

Boston had burned many times—in five great fires and many smaller ones—before the Saturday evening of November 9th, when the Great Fire of 1872 erupted in a dry goods store and hoop-skirt factory on Summer Street, which was deserted for the weekend. The fire raced down Summer Street and every street that intersected it, and in twenty-four hours' time had consumed the entire business district of the bustling Victorian city that was Boston in 1872, at a loss of about $75 million in property.

"There is nothing more remarkable in the dreadful calamity that has befallen our city," read the assessment in the *Boston Daily Globe* on Monday morning, "than the awful rapidity that marked the progress of the flames. . . . Whole blocks were literally mowed down by the flames. . . . Granite was of no more avail against them than so much cardboard. No sooner did the heat touch it than it began to crumble away piecemeal."

Short on horses, water, and manpower, the fire department tried a series of futile measures as they watched the fire advance throughout Sunday. One desperate measure was to explode buildings in the fire's path so they could not burn. By the evening of November 10th, when the fire abated, the business district and

seven wharves along with ships docked beside them were lost in the blaze—leaving sixty-five acres of rubble where 776 buildings had once stood. The blaze devoured most of the area that now lies between Washington Street and the waterfront, including the present-day area of Post Office Square (see figure 3 in chapter 5). Heroic fire-fighting efforts managed to save the Old South Meeting House at the corner of Washington and Milk Streets, but little else.

The magnitude of the disaster was national news, reported in newspapers as far away as San Francisco and throughout New England. The fire was seen as a repetition of that in Chicago the year before.

In Boston, the militia was called on to supplement the police force in dealing with "bands of ruffians" occasionally seen looting in the burned district. The city's most prominent citizens met with the mayor to decide a course of action. A General Relief Committee was formed. Temporary postal facilities opened at Faneuil Hall to substitute for the burned Post Office.

"Let not one discouraging word be spoken," advised the *Globe's* editorial of November 12th, in an exemplar of the best that the high moral spirit of a Victorian culture could offer, "but throw all fault-finding to the wind, no doubt every one did the best, as it seemed to them, in the startling emergency, and let all with open handed liberality strive to help one another to bear the grievous burden which has been visited upon us."

New buildings rose swiftly from the ashes, larger and more handsome than before. In less than a decade, a new business and mercantile district expressed the commercial vigor of Boston. The prevalence of buildings dating from the 1870s in the business district is now the only sign of the fire.

Bostonians had traditionally tightened their fire codes after every fire, beginning in 1649, when they had first outlawed wooden structures—without, however, eradicating them. The fire of 1872 was no exception. Not only wooden structures but even wooden frames inside brick or stone buildings, or used as a roofing material or support, were outlawed, since the flames had licked hardest at the wooden frames of the mansard roofs on many a handsome Victorian building.

"Homeless Tonight or Boston in Ashes," the cover to sheet music for a song commemorating the Great Fire of 1872, reveals the common sentiment of a postfire Boston.

Plate 42

Griffith M. Hopkins & Co.
*Map of the City of Boston, and its
Environs*
(Philadelphia, 1874)
Engraving. 125 x 146 cm.

In 1874 Griffith M. Hopkins of
Philadelphia issued the first real
estate atlas of Boston (see p. 59 and
figure 2 in chapter 5) and also published several maps of the city. This
one includes more of the city than
the 1870 city map (see plate 41), for
it shows most of the recently
annexed Dorchester (1870), West
Roxbury (1874), Brighton (1874),
and all of Charlestown (1874). The
map shows the filling that had
occurred at Commercial Point and
along Freeport Street in Dorchester.
Since 1870, Atlantic Avenue had
been completed across the central
waterfront, and the Boston Wharf
Company had filled more of its
wharf on the South Boston Flats.

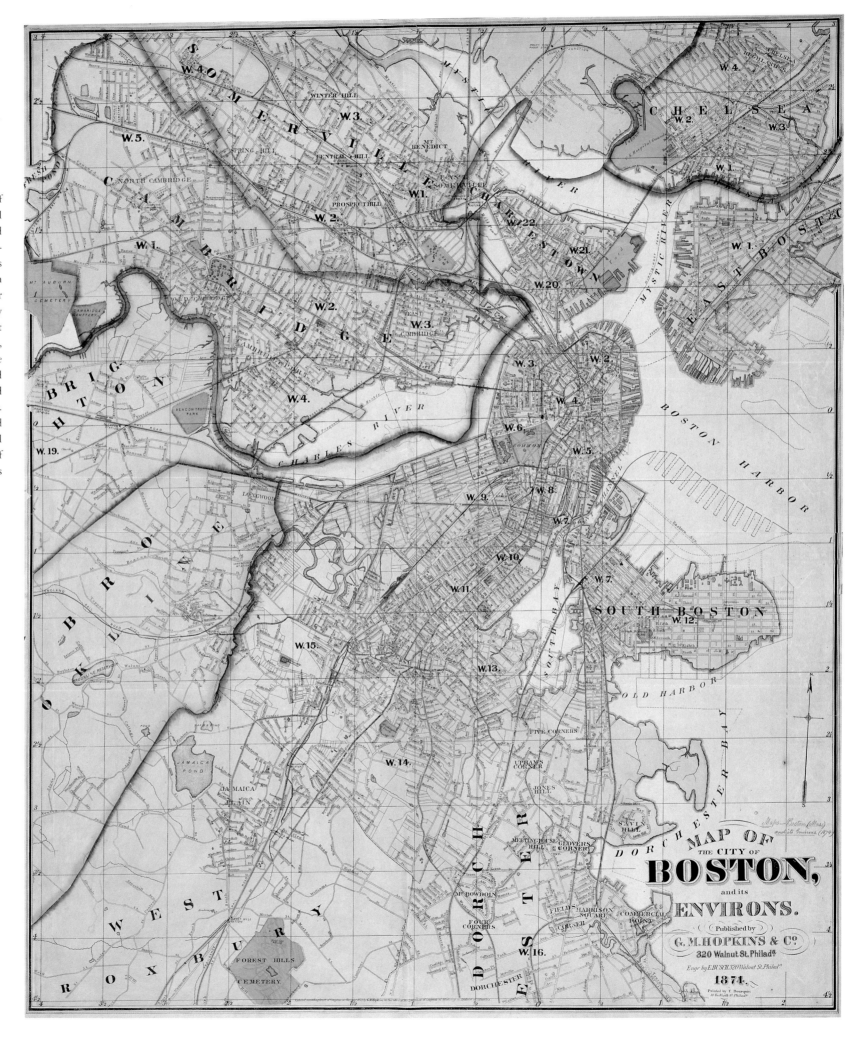

Frederick Law Olmsted in 1890, near the end of his
long and remarkable life.

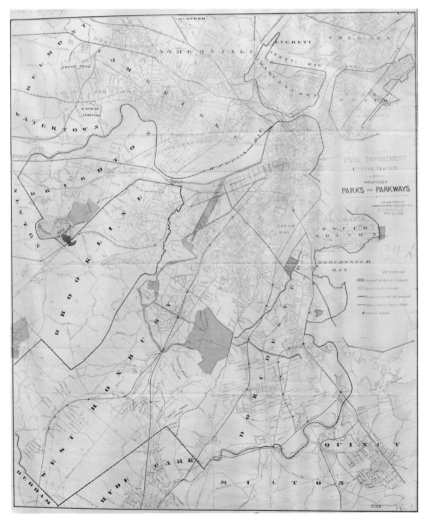

City of Boston Park Department, *Proposed Parks and Parkways,* 1876. This plan was published by the city's first park commissioners. It is the culmination of a period of rumina-
tion, planning, and land acquisition that included consultations with Frederick Law
Olmsted, to whom they were soon to award the job of actually designing and implement-
ing the park system. Compare the general alignment of the commissioners' plan with
Olmsted's eventual plan (see figure 6 in chapter 1 and figure 16 in chapter 8).

OLMSTED AND URBAN NATURE

In the second half of the nineteenth century, the rapid urbanization and industrialization of the United States called for an antidote. This need was reflected in the
themes of nature that characterized Thomas Cole's paintings, Walt Whitman's poetry, and the philosophy of Ralph Waldo Emerson and his fellow transcendentalists.
"Nature," wrote Emerson, "is sanative, refining, elevating," expressing the hope
nature's influence on settlers and town-builders would contribute to a superior
civilization in America.

Meanwhile, Frederick Law Olmsted, landscape architect of Central Park
and other great urban park systems of the same period, arrived to marry benefi-
cent nature to the intractable problems of the city in a most practical way. He has
come to symbolize the park-building era of the late nineteenth century, when
most major American cities were creating great public spaces.

Olmsted understood the purpose of his parks to be manifold. They were to
satisfy physiological, social, and psychological needs, giving relief from city air,
noise, and crowding. They were to provide a fresh-air setting for healthful exercise
and a place for people to satisfy their human urge to mingle, where children could
play, mothers talk, and young men find occupations other than hanging out on
street corners or retiring to bars. In them, the young and old, rich and poor, were
to be uplifted by the beauty of nature, and the brief relaxing of class barriers.

Olmsted was prescient in arguing the benefits of city parks. "It is practically certain that the Boston of today is the mere nucleus of the Boston that is to
be," Olmsted wrote in 1870. "It is practically certain that it is to extend over
many miles of country now thoroughly rural in character. . . . If Boston continues to grow at its present rate even for but a few generations longer, and then simply holds its own until it shall be as old as the Boston in Lincolnshire now is,
more men, women, and children are to be seriously affected in health and morals
than are now living on this continent."

When he arrived in Boston, Olmsted found the park commissioners already
engaged in a program of land acquisition, and he joined them in creating the first
public parks conceived and built as a system. Olmsted's first role was to judge
entries in an 1875 competition for a park system design. He found all of them
lacking, partly because they failed to address the engineering problem of tidal
flow and water run-off at the mouth of the Muddy River. The park commissioners hired Olmsted to supervise the entire endeavor, and he began work in 1878.

Olmsted proposed controls for the flow of the Muddy River and designed a
system of "pleasureways" to connect the pastoral parks he designed. Now called
the "emerald necklace," Olmsted's park system begins at the Back Bay Fens, which
takes up roughly where the greensward of Commonwealth Avenue ends. The
Fenway, Riverway, and Jamaicaway lead from there, along the Muddy River, to a
series of ponds—Olmsted, Ward, and Jamaica. From Jamaica Pond, the Arborway
leads quickly to the Arnold Arboretum, which shares the style of the other parks,
although Olmsted did not design it. A little further along is Franklin Park,
Olmsted's showcase of English pastoral scenery. Construction continued throughout the 1880s and 1890s. Olmsted planned an extension of the park system to the
South Boston shoreline but speculative development compromised the plan.

The growing city has intruded on portions of the emerald necklace: There
is now an interchange over the mouth of the Muddy River and pleasureways have
become heavily traveled commuter routes. But Olmsted's parks continue to serve
Boston as he envisioned, attracting diverse populations and bringing them
together in the enjoyment of nature.

Plate 43
Boston Map Company
Plan Showing the principal portion of Boston From the latest authorities
(Boston, 1880)
Lithograph. 123 × 132 cm.

No edition of the city surveyor's map (see plate 41) was published in 1871, and in November 1872 the lithographic stones for the map were destroyed in Boston's Great Fire. As a result, the city published no maps of the entire city during the 1870s. In 1880, however, two young men working in the city surveyor's office, George F. Loring and Irwin C. Cromack, compiled a new 500-scale map of the city, formed the Boston Map Company, and published it. Even larger than the 1870 edition, the map was printed in two sheets by a New York firm.

The map shows changes that had occurred during the previous decade. In Back Bay, filling was almost complete east of what is now Massachusetts Avenue and had begun west of it where the Back Bay Park (now the Fens), the first of the Boston parks designed by Frederick Law Olmsted, was being created. On the South Boston Flats, the lobster-claw-shaped area of made land with what is now Fan Pier at its tip was the result of the state's South Boston Flats project, which had finally gotten underway in 1873. South of South Boston, the protuberance at the tip of the Calf Pasture, now Columbia Point, was a long pier built over a sewer that ran from the pumping station of the city's new main drainage sewage system to a shaft that descended to a tunnel under the harbor. Sewage flowed through the tunnel to Moon Island, where it was discharged into the ocean.

(top) A 1903 photograph shows subway construction at State Street near the old State House (seen in the background). The utility lines have been labeled, suggesting that this photograph was used as a construction recording document.

(bottom) Boston City Planning Board, *Map of Boston Proper Showing Proposed Railroad Tunnels and Business Streets* (1914). Seventeen years after the opening of the Park Street Tunnel, Boston's planners prepared this plan to address the rising demand for rail service. Two new underground rail lines are proposed, including one (rendered here as a wide blue line) which features six stations between Washington Street and Tremont Street, from North Station to the B&A rail line in the South End. The wide green line indicates a proposed tunnel between North and South Stations with a new "business boulevard" above. This was the forerunner of the Central Artery and, nearly a century later, Bostonians are still discussing adding a rail line as part of the reconstruction of the Central Artery.

BEGINNINGS OF THE BOSTON SUBWAY

In 1897, after only a year and a half of construction, the first subway in the United States opened in Boston. Boston joined London, Budapest, and Glasgow—the only other cities in the world to have underground transit systems at the time. (In 1900, the famous Paris Metro joined the list.)

Boston's progress in rapid transit represented the culmination of decades of experimentation in horse, steam, and electric locomotion for streetcars. By the end of the nineteenth century, over 8,000 horses had been retired from Boston's popular local transportation routes to make way for electric trolleys and electric subway trains. Steam engines—never really well suited to smaller vehicles—had been relegated to conventional railroad lines. But the traffic problems were not solved.

Boston's public transportation system's ridership increased rapidly. In 1895, when construction on Boston's subway began, 406 trolleys were passing along part of Tremont Street at peak hours, making the street nearly impassable. The state legislature had received numerous proposals to build elevated transit lines in and around Boston, but its own commission recommended both an elevated line and a tunnel, and the tunnel was begun.

The new 1.8–mile tunnel connected several stops along what is now the Green Line running from Haymarket through Government Center (then Scollay Square), Park Street (known as "Park Street Under"), and on to Boylston Street. Much of the original tunnel remains in use a hundred years later.

When the first segment of the tunnel, from Park Street to the far edge of the Public Garden, opened on September 1, 1897, there was little fanfare, but the *Boston Daily Globe* welcomed the future with a large front page spread. "CARS NOW RUNNING IN THE SUBWAY," it declared. "Before 9 some thousands of people will undoubtedly have entered the underground system in the public garden, be whirled along at a rate of speed which they have never experienced in the same locality before, and projected out of the earth at the Park st [sic] exit of the subway."

Within two decades tunnels for Boston's Orange Line (under Washington Street), Blue Line (under Boston Harbor), and Red Line (under Beacon Hill) had been completed. With these four interconnecting lines, the central nexus of the modern subway system was mapped out.

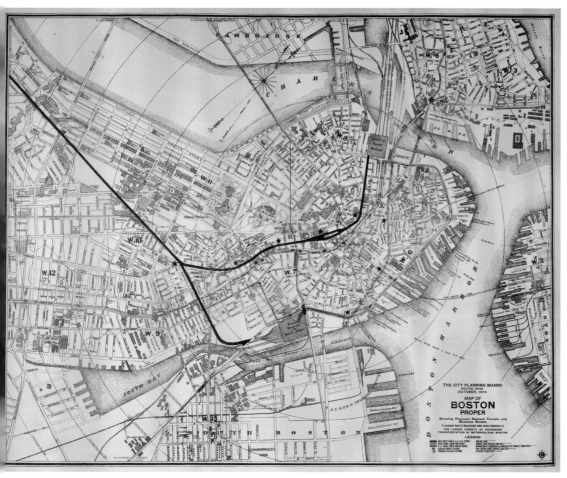

Plate 44
U.S. Coast and Geodetic Survey
Boston Harbor, Massachusetts, **Chart no.**
246, northwest quadrant
(Washington, D.C., 1896)
Lithograph. 89 × 110 cm.

At the turn of the twentieth century the most
accurate maps of Boston's shoreline were actually charts that had been prepared primarily to
aid navigation. This attention to navigational
details is the reason the U.S. Government
charts, which were updated frequently, are such
a good record of changes to the shoreline. The
chart shown here was the first in a new series
put out by the U.S. Coast and Geodetic Survey.
Most of its charts of Boston in the second half of
the nineteenth century were at a scale of
1:40,000 (see figures 8 and 9 in chapter 5). In
1896, however, the Coast and Geodetic Survey
inaugurated a new series of Boston Harbor at a
scale of 1:20,000. This chart, no. 246, was
updated frequently and continued the survey's
tradition of attention to inland as well as maritime detail; it is thus an excellent record of
Boston from 1896 on.

The 1896 chart shows the land making
that had taken place in Boston since 1880.
Perhaps most dramatic was the large amount of
new land on the South Boston Flats, the result
of the state having pressed ahead rapidly with
this project. On the north side of Charlestown,
the huge Mystic Wharf had also been created.
In addition, filling had been done to create new
parks for Boston: Marine Park at the tip of
South Boston, Charlesbank on the river
between the West Boston (now Longfellow) and
Craigie's (now the first Charles River Dam)
Bridges, and Wood Island Park in East Boston.

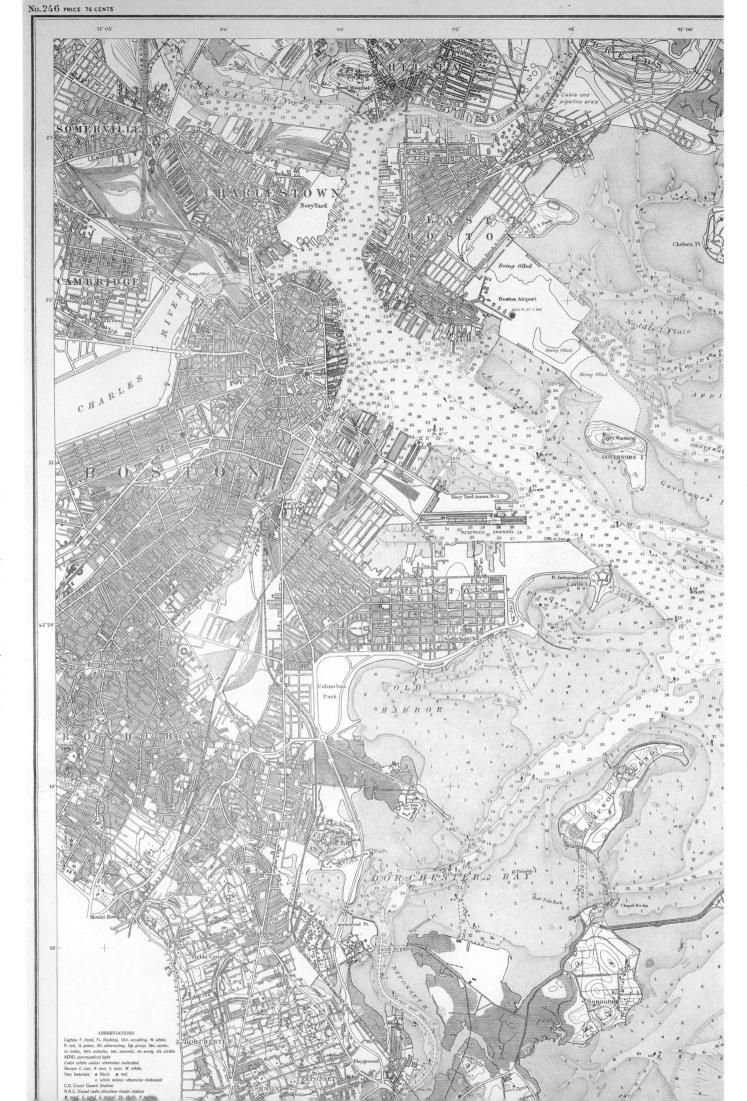

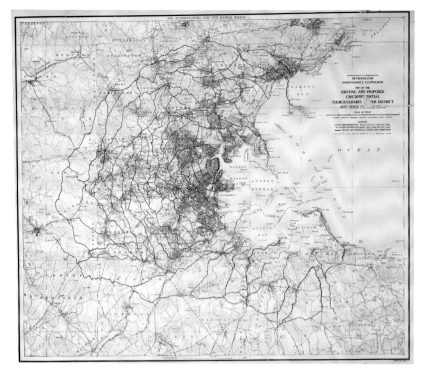

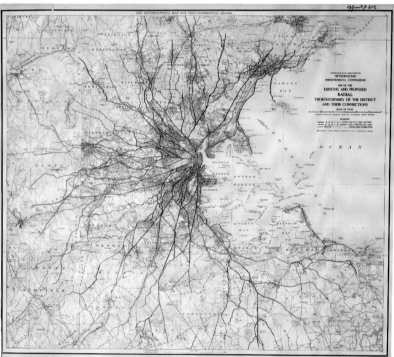

Arthur A. Shurtleff, *Map of the Existing and Proposed Circumferential Thoroughfares of the District and their Connections,* 1909 (top), and *Map of the Existing and Proposed Radial Thoroughfares of the District and their Connections,* 1909 (bottom). Shurtleff's great vision for comprehensive traffic improvements for the growing city scheme was simple, logical, and much ahead of its time. He proposed widening the radial roads emanating from the core and intersecting them with a series of concentric ring roads, formed by connecting fragments of existing roads. A half-century before Routes 128 and 495 would be undertaken, their necessity had been anticipated.

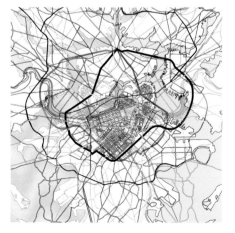

An "Urban Ring," envisioned as a circumferential public transportation corridor that would intersect the radiating subway lines and connect the city's outlying neighborhoods and early suburbs.

RINGS FOR THE SPOKES OF THE HUB

As nineteenth-century Bostonians filled and built, the city expanded out of its long confinement on the island-like Shawmut Peninsula. Radial roadways and rail lines emerging from "The Hub" carried traffic and settlement in every direction except due east into the Atlantic. Great plans had been realized, such as the construction of the Public Garden and the filling of the Back Bay and the South Boston Flats, and visions of civic improvement abounded.

Some of the most breathtaking plans for improvement came from visionary landscape architects who dreamed of rings around Boston, connecting the radial arteries and threading open spaces into the dense city. First, in the mid-1870s, the Boston park commissioners selected Frederick Law Olmsted to create what became Boston's emerald necklace—a sweeping arc of parks and parkways intended to encircle the city from the Public Garden to the mouth of the Muddy River at the other end of the Back Bay, then through Jamaica Plain and Dorchester to the ocean.

In the 1880s, as the emerald necklace was taking shape, Olmsted's ablest disciple, Charles Eliot, proposed a larger series of "public reservations" encompassing the entire metropolitan area. By the turn of the century, the 15,000–acre park system included 30 miles of river frontage, 10 miles of ocean shoreline, and 22 miles of right-of-way for parkways.

The next vision of rings around Boston came to Arthur A. Shurtleff, a landscape architect who devoted much of his youth to considering Boston. He submitted proposals for Copley Square and other public projects, including a treatment of the Common's edge, and for the development of Georges Island in the harbor, and he served on at least one major gubernatorial commission.

Shurtleff made his first proposal for the Boston region in 1907 with a plan produced under the auspices of a forerunner of the Boston Society of Architects. It showed an inner and an outer boulevard. The inner boulevard looped through South Boston, Roxbury, Cambridge, and Somerville. The outer boulevard connected Dorchester, Brookline, Allston, and Harvard Square in Cambridge. Perhaps it was the union of these socially disparate communities, or perhaps it was the focus on transportation and growth that appealed only to planners, but Shurtleff's rings did not fire the public imagination the way the park systems had earlier.

Shurtleff presented his ideas again in 1909 for the Joint Board on Metropolitan Improvements as a lovely web of radial and circumferential routes (at left). These also failed to galvanize civic action.

In 1927, Shurtleff served on a gubernatorial commission with the successors of the Eliot/Baxter coalition. Together, they forged a new proposal: an outlying ring-road that linked the public reservations and parks already assembled. This garnered more interest, but still faltered.

With many intriguing plans unrealized, Shurtleff followed his visionary leanings into writing. In his later life, Shurtleff published, under the name Shurcliff, three small volumes of his own poetic musings about the New England countryside, revealing a deeply philosophical side to his observations of nature and cities.

More rings around Boston were finally built—and one more may come. Following the construction of two beltways at mid-century (routes 128 and 495), political leaders and planners have turned their attention to the idea of a public transit ring, dubbed the "Urban Ring," that would link the radiating subway lines of the hub and connect disconnected neighborhoods.

Plate 45

George Hiram Walker (1848–1927)
Map of the city of Boston and vicinity
(Boston: Walker Lithograph & Publishing
Co., 1908)
Lithograph. 194 x 151 cm.

This large map shows the entire area
encompassed by the city in 1908—
Brighton and West Roxbury had been
annexed in 1874 along with Charlestown,
and the Orient Heights section of East
Boston, which was being developed at the
time, appears in an inset. Although Hyde
Park is shown it would not be added to the
city until 1912. The map also shows the
Esplanade along the Charles, which was
under construction at the time, as well as
projected streets across water in South Bay
and in East Boston.

In 1880, George H. Walker formed
a partnership with his brother, Oscar W.
and established offices at 81 Milk Street,
where they published maps and atlases.
They also had a flourishing business in the-
atrical work and views of residences, hotels,
and factories.

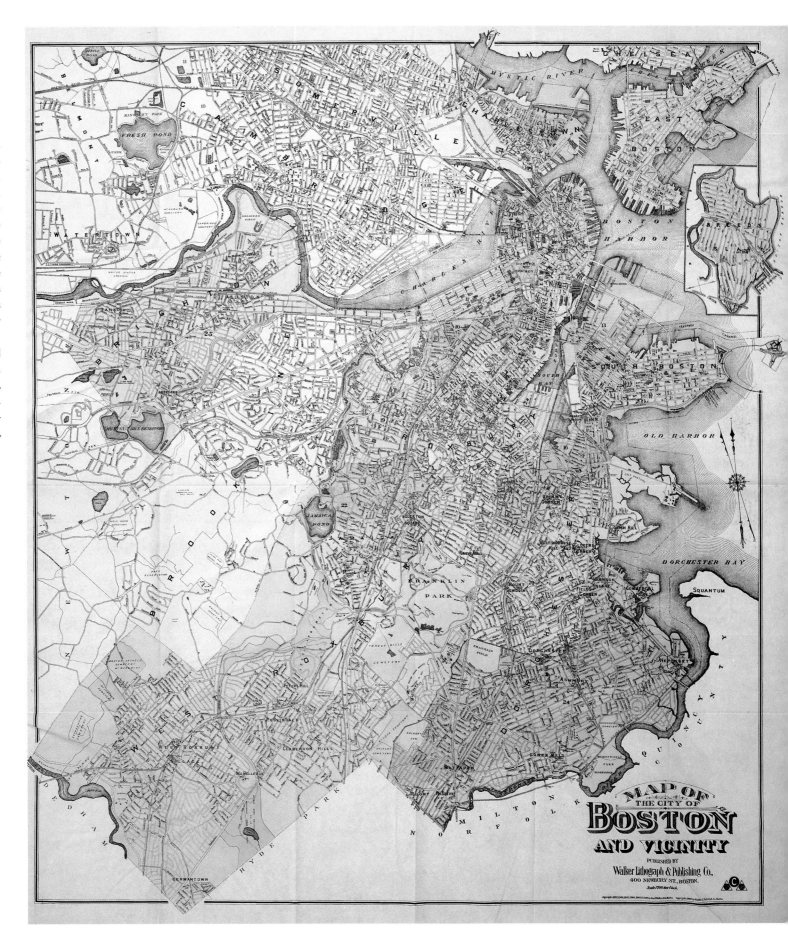

Mayor Curley speaks at Labor Day exercises on Boston Common, September 8, 1931.

MAYOR CURLEY

James Michael Curley (1874–1958) influenced Boston politics for most of the first half of the twentieth century. Between 1914 and 1950, he served four terms as mayor, ran for the office eight times, and served one term as governor and two as a Congressman.

Known for his rich baritone voice and his flamboyant wit, Curley's robust audacity led him to taunt his political enemies, revel in his own cleverness, and reward his friends. He drew on the loyalty of ethnic voters in Boston's outlying residential neighborhoods, whom he thanked with clinics, branch libraries, parks and recreational facilities, roadways, parkways, and bridges—projects that created jobs as well as public amenities. He lived in a middle-class neighborhood in Jamaica Plain, where he built a large, expensive brick house on the Jamaicaway with, rumor had it, city labor.

He despised the Brahmin financiers, who despised him in turn. The old aristocracy lived and worked downtown near genteel institutions and the district of once-posh shops near the Common. Though they could not best Curley, they could stymie his efforts to borrow money for the city, and withdraw their cooperation, initiative, and leadership from city undertakings. He returned their contempt by raising downtown business and commercial property taxes in order to fund projects in the neighborhoods, and he extorted favors from any who requested mercy.

Curley's championing of the "little people" of Boston was probably long overdue. His constituency comprised the diverse groups of minorities that we would now hail as a "Rainbow Coalition." His belief in creating jobs for the unemployed through public works rather than giving them outright welfare might find supporters today.

Still, Curley's politics held disastrous consequences for Boston's downtown and civic spirit. His particularly arrogant Robin Hood pose created a deep divisiveness, alienated the business community from government, and left the downtown, where Curley refused to spend a dime, a deteriorating shambles.

Mayor Curley governed a seedier Boston beset by prohibition, the depression, and corruption. From his poor beginnings in South Boston, he had fought his way into Boston politics with a carefully calculated favor bank, smear tactics, and blackmail. Once elected mayor, Curley flagrantly ran a corrupt, cronyist regime. During the prohibition era, Mayor Curley's liquor supplier, father of a large South Boston family, would regularly arrive by car, using one of his sons as the getaway driver should haste be necessary, and walk into City Hall in an oversized coat lined with liquor flasks.

One of the many charges of corruption leveled against Curley was finally pursued in court. He was convicted of mail fraud during his final term as mayor and sentenced to prison. When he resumed his duties, eager to swagger unhumbled before the press, he slighted the performance of the earnest, mild-mannered city clerk, John Hynes, who had acted as mayor in his absence. The irate Hynes, who previously held no political ambitions, responded by beating Curley in the next three mayoral elections. By the time of his last campaign in 1955, Curley was eighty. Hynes had repaired important relationships with the business community and had begun the rebuilding of Boston that would continue over the next three decades, and Curley had been forced to recognize that Boston was no longer a town in his pocket. The loss of the political power that had compensated him for so much in his life—his hard-bitten childhood and youth, the early deaths of his laborer father, his first wife, and seven of his nine children—left him deeply bitter. He died three years after his last campaign. His proud house on the Jamaicaway still stands, well tended by the city, which now holds the deed, with little shamrocks carved as a defiant motif in every shutter.

Plate 46
George Hiram Walker (1848–1927)
Boston and Surroundings
(Boston: Walker Lithograph and
Publishing Co., 1927)
Lithograph. 74 x 131 cm.

This street plan of Boston represents
one of the later maps produced by the
Walker Company, the last important
lithography firm established in Boston
in the nineteenth century (see plate 45).
This map was intended to be a street, or
traveler's, guide for it was folded and
sold in a paper cover. The map depicts
some of the same land-making projects
shown on the 1934 Coast and Geodetic
Survey chart (see plate 47)—completion of the South Boston Flats project,
Columbus Park in South Boston, and
the projected Old Colony Parkway
(now Morrissey Boulevard) between
Savin Hill and Commercial Point.

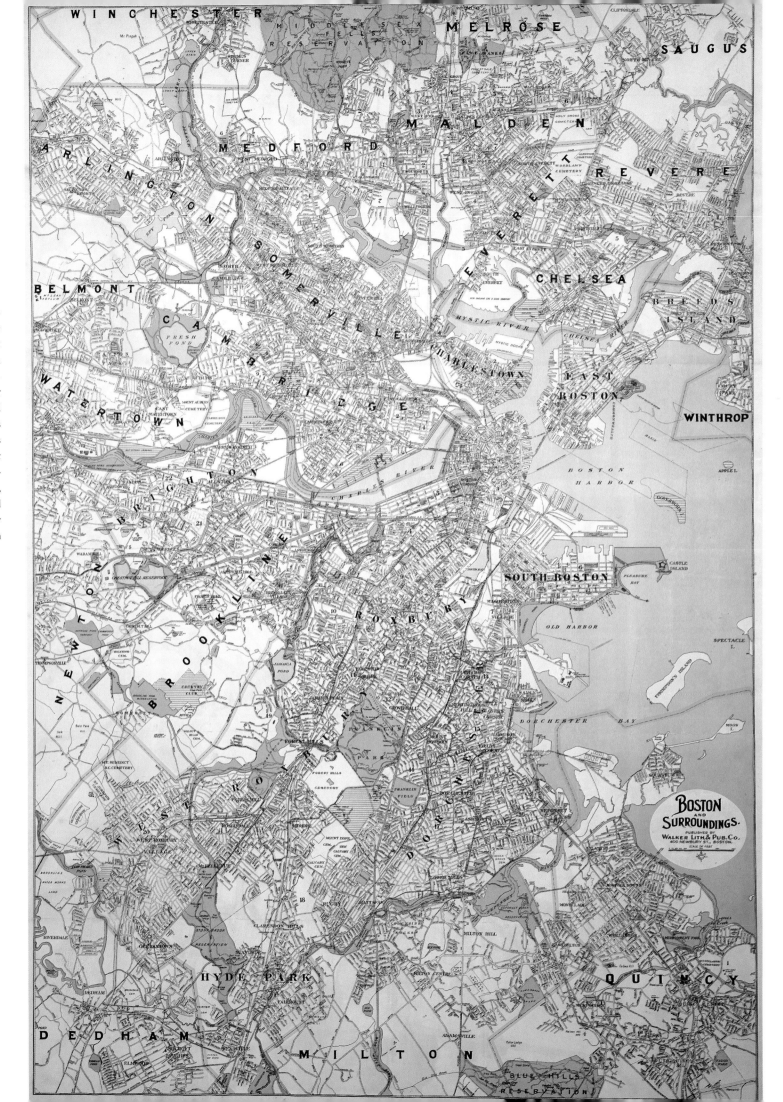

People stand and wait in this depression-era breadline at 42 Hanover Street in the North End, ca. 1931.

BOSTON ON THE EVE OF THE GREAT DEPRESSION: A SOCIAL PORTRAIT

Boston on the eve of the Great Depression was a city divided. As Charles Trout relates in his definitive study, a century of steady immigration had left Boston 20 percent Irish, with perhaps half its citizens claiming some degree of Irish ancestry. From the 1880s through the 1920s a large wave of Italian immigrants pushed the Irish from the North End to South Boston. Smaller groups of Russian Jews and African Americans filled out the mix in the city. Boston's tiny (2.6 percent) black population had come to occupy the South End but had begun moving into Roxbury.

On Beacon Hill and in the Back Bay lived thirty-eight thousand white Anglo-Saxon Protestants of old Boston stock. The political power base of the wealthy conservatives of English descent lay in assorted venues. They held control of prestigious institutions such as Harvard and a small but growing number of highly ranked hospitals, along with myriad cultural institutions such as the Boston Symphony. Many wealthy conservatives had moved out of Boston where they elected men to the state legislature who worked to curb Boston's political power. Other Brahmins—bankers and businessmen who remained or worked in the city—belonged to the five-thousand-member Boston Chamber of Commerce which, with a substantial budget, usually got its way with city government.

The Immigration Act of 1924 closed Boston's doors to further immigration. The act roughly coincided with the end of a twenty-five year period of social progressiveness that attempted to integrate and appreciate minority ethnic groups. Although social leaders with a sense of noblesse oblige continued to work for the "worthy poor," and an annual "racial pageant" on the Common continued to invite different ethnic groups to present the dance, music, or literature of their home countries, the conservatism of the ruling class was deepening at this time.

The increase in social conservatism coincided with a period of economic decline in Massachusetts that eroded prosperity throughout the twenties, setting the stage for the brutal thirties. Although some industries remained vital, textile factories and boot and shoe factories were shutting down or relocating. Transportation-related businesses also declined, losing out to New York as they had for a century in the failure to develop sufficient westbound railroads or an early advantage in steamship construction or use.

In contrast to its weakening industrial capacity, Boston had strong wholesale and retail sales and a strong banking sector, attributable to the large Brahmin fortunes entrusted to Boston's financial institutions. These family legacies were invested conservatively and not in new industrial or commercial ventures. While industrial and commercial initiative waned, this money fueled a world of splendid isolation. In the spring of 1929, in the boatyards of the North Shore, where so many impressive estates were sited, at least 325 large yachts were under construction at a total cost of more than $8 million.

Powerful though the rich were, Boston did not belong to them. The Anglo-Saxon inhabitants of Beacon Hill and the Back Bay were small in numbers compared to the sixty thousand members of the Boston Central Labor Union. And those sixty thousand constituted only a part of the work force. Boston's skilled laborers fought aggressively for higher wages and had attained some of the highest blue-collar wages in the country by 1929.

Unfortunately, it was these workers from Boston's ethnic neighborhoods, and their poorer counterparts, who lost so much ground in the depression. While the overall rate of unemployment in Boston hovered near 30 percent—a figure comparable to that of other major cities—it broke down along ethnic lines. Figures for 1934 show an unemployment rate of 12 percent in the Back Bay and 30 to 40 percent for the ethnic neighborhoods. From these groups come the wrenching depression stories of men who deliberately wounded themselves to get a decent meal and bed at a hospital, or who lined the fishing docks to vie for unappetizing cod parts that their wives could cook into some semblance of a meal.

The displacement of old Bostonians probably accounted to some degree for their disaffection and dwindling sense of social responsibility toward Boston. But a national phenomenon of increasing individualism was also at work and made its own contribution to the great crash of 1929. In the economic sphere, that individualism demonstrated itself as, in the words of John Kenneth Galbraith, "an inordinate desire to get rich quickly with a minimum of physical effort," which many people exhibited through speculative investment that would burst on them like a bubble.

When the depression struck, Boston received less federal aid than other major cities. Although Mayor Curley, elected for a third term at the depression's onset, had been an early Roosevelt supporter, Roosevelt was still considering whether and how to reward his disreputable booster when an investigation of Curley's financial practices began. Nor were the more conservative Democratic leaders of Massachusetts attractive to Roosevelt. To them, his New Deal was socialist anathema.

Boston did not bounce back quickly after the depression. Her population loss was drastic, her industrial base and tax base seriously eroded. Boston would not recover from these losses completely until the renewal campaigns of the 1960s began in earnest.

Plate 47
U.S. Coast and Geodetic Survey
Boston Harbor, Chart no. 246, northwest
quadrant
(Washington, D.C., 1934)
Lithograph. 89 × 108 cm.

The 1934 edition of the Coast and Geodetic
Survey chart no. 246 is an update of the chart
whose 1896 and 1916 editions appear as plate 44
and figure 18 in chapter 7.

A comparison of the 1934 and 1916 charts
(see figure 18 in chapter 7) shows the amount of
land that had been or was being added to the city
in 1934. On the west side of the Boston peninsula additions to Charlesbank park and the
Esplanade were being filled. In East Boston filling of the airport was extending out toward
Governor's Island. Most of the South Bay had
been filled except for a channel on the west side
behind Albany Street and a turning basin at the
south end serving the one remaining wharf. In
South Boston, filling had connected Castle Island
with the mainland, defining the south side of the
Reserved Channel. At the head of Old Harbor,
Columbus Park had been filled, enabling the
Strandway, now Day Boulevard, to be rerouted
along the shore. And south of what is now
Columbia Point, land had been made to enable
Old Colony Parkway, now Morrissey Boulevard,
to cross Patten's Cove north of Savin Hill and the
mouth of Savin Hill Bay south of it.

In the summer of 1958, Defense Secretary Neil H. McElroy (at left in the photograph) examined the Sparrow III rocket, a navy fighter plane, with Charles F. Adams, head of Raytheon, at the Bedford Airport, Bedford, Massachusetts.

A view of route 128, lined with the headquarters of high-technology companies.

BOSTON'S PHOENIX: THE HIGH-TECHNOLOGY INDUSTRY

Viewed from the modern era, the Boston of 1948, portrayed by the Boston City Planning Board map (at right), was a town worn by decades of decline. After her early economic advantage as a founding colony of the nation, Boston's citizens had watched richer soils in new territories supplant their commonwealth's agriculture. After 1850, Boston had progressively fallen behind New York in shipping. By the mid-1920s her industrial advantage of ample immigrant labor had dried up as tighter immigration laws were passed, and her strong stores of old money were no longer a unique advantage as capital became nationally accessible. Her climate was also a drawback, as the national postwar migration to the sun belt showed.

The powerful Brahmins of the nineteenth century stand accused by some contemporary historians of ushering in Boston's decline by failing to pursue new commercial or industrial activity, and by investing their fortunes conservatively rather than taking chances on new enterprises. Instead, they cultivated Boston's cultural and educational institutions with generous endowments. But, as Russell Adams suggests in *The Boston Money Tree,* brahmin-endowed educational institutions such as Harvard (endowed with the Lawrence Scientific School in the mid-

nineteenth century) and MIT (chartered by the state in 1861) would mature and draw talent to Boston like a lightning rod in the twentieth century.

On closer inspection, the dreary Boston landscape of 1948 stirred with potential. That very year, Edwin Land's new Polaroid camera, designed in his Cambridge laboratories, hit the market. By then, Land had been working almost twenty years in Cambridge on problems of light and physics with industrial applications, having started a few years after arriving from his hometown of Bridgeport to attend Harvard. Land's research on the polarization of light so absorbed him that, instead of graduating, he took a permanent leave of absence from Harvard to open a laboratory with one of his Harvard instructors.

Land was one of many fine scientific minds drawn to the Boston-Cambridge area in the first half of the twentieth century. By the time he arrived on the scene, the Raytheon Company, which in the early 1960s would become the state's largest industrial employer (led to greatness by Charles Francis Adams, the fourth descendant of John Quincy Adams to bear that name [see plate 31 vignette], who became CEO in 1938) was already producing tubes for battery-free radios that could run on household current.

By World War II MIT boasted a bountiful enough supply of scientific genius to make it the federal government's single largest defense contractor. Most notably, its scientists pioneered the development of radar and its military applications, such as navigation and bombing. MIT scientists continue to spin off dozens of companies, as they did in those heady early days.

The end of the war produced a period of readjustment for the Massachusetts economy. The old textile industry, temporarily revived by defense contracts for uniforms, lost 100,000 workers within seven years and continued to dwindle. After 1950, the old fishing industry, always a linchpin of the Boston economy, began to suffer competition from frozen imports. But the vibrant electronics and high-technology industries, the Cold War arms race, the space race, advancing consumer technologies, and Boston's growing medical industry eventually provided work for many hundreds of companies. Nearly 150 firms have reportedly splintered off from Raytheon alone. Then, in the 1950s, An Wang and others added computers to Boston's growing list of technologically innovative wares.

Boston's venerable financial institutions remained an important feature of her economy—and saw some innovation as well. A small number of new companies with the plan of funding bold new high-tech enterprises emerged. A young Boston stockbroker invented the money market fund for the small investor. Fidelity Investments, founded in Boston in 1946, eventually became the nation's largest mutual fund company and the world's largest manager of money. Life insurance and law also became important components of the new service-based economy that emerged in postwar Boston as the old industrial base dwindled.

Like all previous industries, the new high-technology industry created a new landscape marked by its infrastructure. Low-rise industrial parks began blossoming around Route 128 shortly after it was completed in 1952, prompting its nickname, America's Technology Highway. The prosperity of these firms changed Boston's skyline, too, as skyscrapers to house corporate headquarters, corporate lawyers, marketing firms, and financial managers went up.

While the map at right indicates only the boundaries of Boston itself, the new Boston soon to emerge in the postwar period would show these boundaries to be meaningless as a large metropolitan area of interdependent communities emerged. These communities experienced growth fueled by technology, financial services, health care, and higher education, all depending on and attracting national and international markets—a further merging of boundaries.

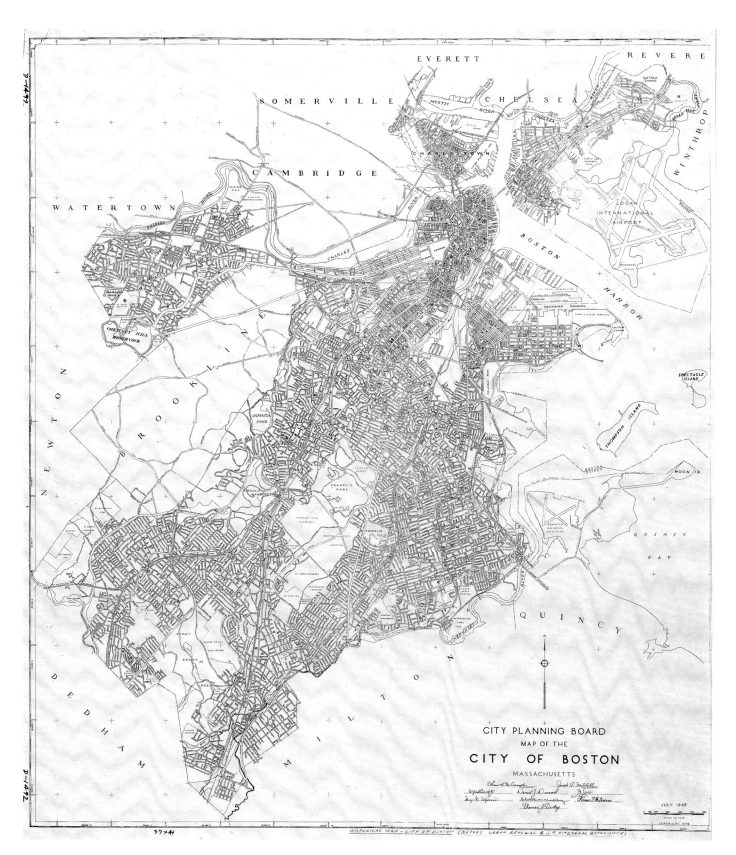

CITY PLANNING BOARD
MAP OF THE
CITY OF BOSTON
MASSACHUSETTS

JULY 1948

HISTORICAL MAP - CITY OF BOSTON (BEFORE URBAN RENEWAL & J.F. FITZGERALD EXPRESSWAY)

Plate 48

Boston City Planning Board
Map of the City of Boston, Massachusetts
(Boston, 1948)

By the middle of the twentieth century maps had become much more utilitarian. The Boston City Planning Board had been established in 1913 as part of a movement to reform city government, an outgrowth of the City Beautiful and City Scientific movements that sought, in part, to create a more rational and professional discipline of city planning. The City Planning Board ceased to exist after it merged with the Boston Redevelopment Authority (BRA) when the latter was established in 1957.

The map shows changes since 1934, most noticeably the tremendous amount of land created at the airport between 1943 and 1947. Some filling had also taken place on the South Boston Flats where the U.S. Navy had created new land, some piers, and a dry dock during World War II. The 1948 map also shows the new land that had been created on the Charles River Esplanade during the 1930s and some, but not all, that had been added to the Calf Pasture (now Columbia Point), which, after many years of having been used as a trash dump, had been greatly increased in size.

Because this is an official city document, only Boston streets are shown, leaving the area of the adjoining towns largely blank. Indeed, it is rare to find plans drawn by municipalities that extend across their boundaries; a bureaucratic limitation for planning efforts that involve more than one municipality.

Edward Logue presents the plans for Government Center at the June 13, 1964, Boston Redevelopment Authority hearing.

Scollay Square in 1930 and 1969, the latter showing the Government Center/City Hall Plaza nearing completion. Few parts of Scollay Square survived the reconstruction. At the lower left portion of both photographs one happily finds Faneuil Hall (see figures 27a and 27b in chapter 8).

BOSTON'S RENEWAL

> *The concept of the public welfare is broad and inclusive. . . . It is within the power of the legislature to determine that the community should be beautiful as well as healthy, spacious as well as clean, well-balanced as well as carefully patrolled.*

With this high-minded opinion, Supreme Court Justice William O. Douglas in 1954 gave the District of Columbia the right of slum clearance and officially welcomed the era of urban renewal in America. In Boston, the first stirrings of renewal began in 1950, when Mayor John B. Hynes was ushered into office. Like many American cities, Boston had grown shabby during the depression and war years, and for four decades political leadership had neglected the downtown.

Hynes determined to reverse this trend. During Hynes's administration, Bostonians greeted the new Freedom Trail, the parking garage under the Common, the new Central Artery, and negotiations for the development of an old railroad yard that eventually became the Prudential Center—Boston's first major construction project in decades. Hynes also demolished a stable lower-income neighborhood in the West End to prepare the way for modern rebuilding (see figures 24 and 26 in chapter 8). This was the first of several neighborhood rebuilding schemes that eventually gave urban renewal a bad name in Boston's working-class neighborhoods, even as it revived the downtown.

Hynes also founded the Boston Redevelopment Authority (BRA) and set a fine example for a worthy successor—John Collins. Mayor Collins made the rebuilding of Boston his administration's raison d'être. His most notable act was the hiring of a forceful urban planner from New Haven, Ed Logue. The Collins-

Logue team laid ambitious plans for Boston that have influenced the city's development to the present day—long after their collaboration ended in 1967.

Under Logue, the BRA became the nation's most powerful redevelopment authority, with the right to condemn large areas of property, make plans, and coordinate and facilitate their completion among the business, development, and financial interests involved. With his impressive record from New Haven, Logue was able to draw extensive federal funding to undertake the renewal of nearly one quarter of Boston's total acreage.

Logue's plan commenced at the geographic heart of the city, where he proposed a new government center, complete with a new city hall and public plaza flanked by other government office buildings. A warren of twenty-two streets in the area of Scollay Square was razed to accomplish this—including many once-proud Victorian buildings that had come to house burlesque theaters and pawn shops, and "Radio Row" from which the Radio Shack stores come. In their place materialized the six superblocks of the new Government Center. Slowly, developers and investors began to return to downtown Boston.

Logue intended to connect Boston's new center to its waterfront—the site and source of so much of Boston's history—and to develop and renovate that waterfront for residential and commercial use. That development has continued auspiciously up to the present day, with such showpieces as the New England Aquarium and Rowes Wharf (see figure 7 in chapter 8), and with the BRA insisting on providing public access to the water's edge through all newly developed parcels.

Between the waterfront and city hall lay historic Faneuil Hall and the Quincy Markets, which Logue identified as a key connecting parcel. Historians and preservationists persuaded him to renovate rather than raze the buildings. In 1970, the BRA began accepting bids for the reuse of the markets, and in 1976 the renovated marketplaces opened to huge crowds that have never abated (see figure 8 in chapter 1).

In the neighborhoods, Logue's success was more mixed, as was that of the whole urban renewal movement. Thousands of families were dislocated in slum-clearance projects. Relatively few were ever able to return to the limited amount of affordable housing constructed in place of the older housing stock. The residents of poorer housing migrated to outlying areas of the city.

Future generations will have to assess more fully the successes and failures of urban renewal. Certainly, under Logue and Collins, Boston was transformed by the stamp of the twentieth century and entered decades of growth and relative prosperity.

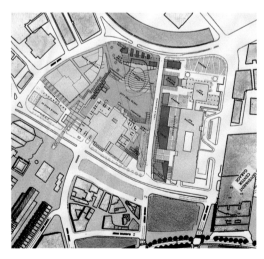

A plan advanced in 1997 by the Trust for City Hall Plaza to reconfigure and reprogram the City Hall Plaza.

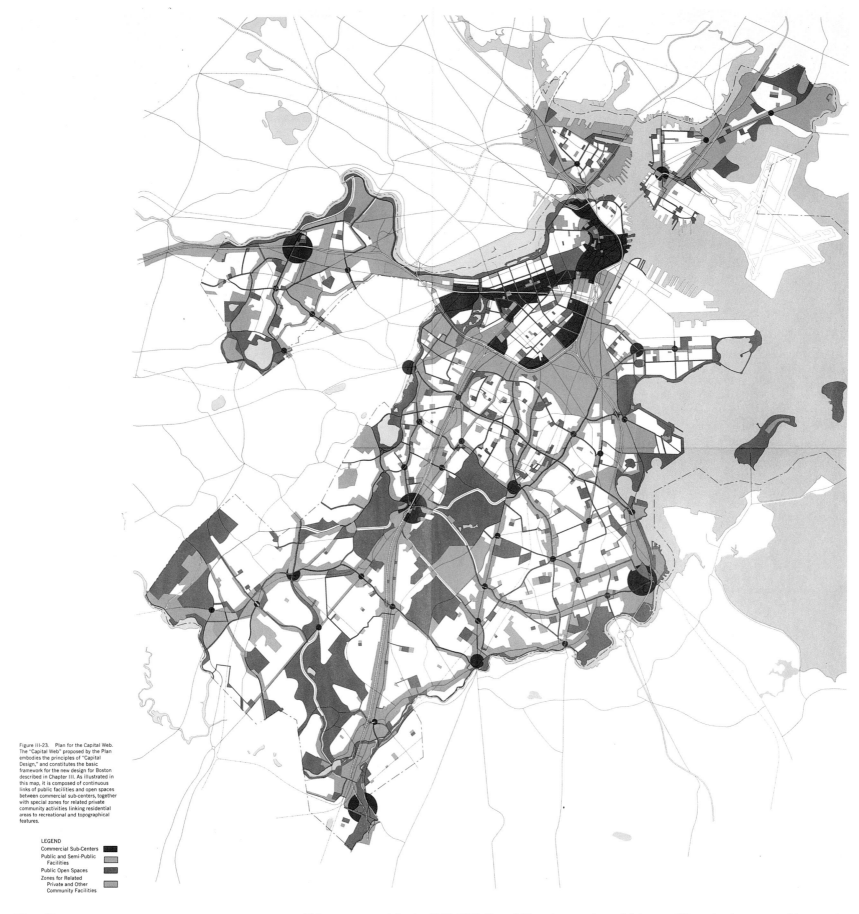

Figure III-23. Plan for the Capital Web. The "Capital Web" proposed by the Plan embodies the principles of "Capital Design," and constitutes the basic framework for the new design for Boston described in Chapter III. As illustrated in this map, it is composed of continuous links of public facilities and open spaces between commercial sub-centers, together with special zones for related private community activities linking residential areas to recreational and topographical features.

LEGEND
Commercial Sub-Centers
Public and Semi-Public Facilities
Public Open Spaces
Zones for Related Private and Other Community Facilities

Plate 49
Boston Redevelopment Authority
Plan for the Capital Web
(Boston, 1965)

This map appeared in the *1965–1975 General Plan,* the most comprehensive city-wide planning document published by the Boston Redevelopment Authority during the urban renewal era. The planning objective illustrated was the establishment of linear development corridors: continuous "seams" of public and commercial uses, along with open spaces that would better connect the neighborhoods of the city.

(top left) This 1954 *Boston Herald* photograph shows sparse traffic on the just-about completed artery as it passes North Station heading south.

(top right) Five years later in 1959, the *Herald* showed the "Evening commuter exodus." While the newspaper blamed this on a temporary bottleneck, the "bottleneck" was never solved. Indeed, photographs taken a few years later—and to the time of the writing of this book—would show equal congestion in both directions during an ever-lengthening "rush hour," which many observe seems to last all day.

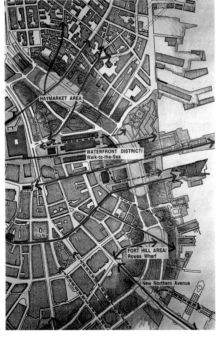

(bottom left) *Boston-2000 Plan,* published by the BRA in 1990, envisions the reuse of the surface of the artery corridor as a linear park once the highway is rebuilt as a tunnel.

(bottom right) A variant to the *Boston-2000 Plan* shows alternating public squares and modestly scaled building parcels. The idea is to restore Boston's fabric of streets and blocks (once severed by the artery) while increasing open space in the downtown.

THE CENTRAL ARTERY

By the 1920s and 1930s, the insurance maps of Boston and neighboring cities began to show gaps in their tidy blocks of building footprints. The parking lot and parking garage, the gas station, and the auto repair shop began to leave their mark on the downtown. The automobile had arrived.

It was around this time that automobile congestion in Boston began to demand the attention of city officials and planners. Indeed, the visionary Arthur Shurtleff had been proffering traffic solutions for two decades by the time the Boston Planning Board issued its *Report of a Thoroughfare Plan for Boston* in 1930.

Chiefly, that report recommended the construction of a tunnel to East Boston and a system of radial highways. It also presented a central artery connecting North and South Stations, originally proposed in 1911 as a "business thoroughfare." Except for the construction of the Sumner Tunnel in 1934, the forward-looking 1930 concept languished in the face of the Great Depression and subsequent world war until Governor Bradford incorporated many of its recommendations in his 1948 *Master Highway Plan.* That plan included the outlines of two beltways around Boston—routes 128 and 495—and the extension of I-95 northward into the city to be intercepted by an inner belt highway. The I-95 extension and the inner belt would eventually be stopped by citizen opposition but not before large portions of the proposed rights-of-way had been cleared. The first segment of the inner belt—the Central Artery—was completed, however.

Construction contracts for the Central Artery were signed in 1951 and after seemingly endless delays—caused by a steel strike, rats, disputes over property rights, and objections from residents of the soon-to-be-ravaged neighborhoods of Chinatown and the historic North End—the artery opened in 1959, by which time it was already well on its way to obsolescence. Dramatic increases in car ownership and usage as well as new commuter patterns loaded the artery almost from the beginning with bumper-to-bumper traffic.

Lewis Mumford was commuting to Boston to teach in 1959 and preparing his manuscript of *The City in History,* with its indictment of modern, automobile-dependant transportation planning. The great scar that the artery left in historic Boston must have been one of the sights that inspired him to blame planners and local authorities for "piling up in . . . cities a population the private motor car cannot handle unless the city itself is wrecked to permit movement and storage of automobiles."

Grumbling about traffic conditions on the Central Artery and its unsightly elevated swath through the city prevailed for more than two decades before action to dismantle it was seriously contemplated. In the 1980s, Massachusetts sought federal funds to widen the Central Artery and bury it, and build a third tunnel under Boston Harbor to Logan Airport. Finally, a Democratic Congress saluted retiring Speaker of the House Thomas P. (Tip) O'Neill by awarding the funds.

By the late 1980s, the Boston Redevelopment Authority was examining schemes for the twenty-seven acres of city land that would become available when the artery was buried beneath the surface—and a debate began about how best to reknit neighborhoods sundered by the artery. That debate continues as the "Big Dig" progresses, the nation's largest public works project. As this book goes to press, reconstruction of the Central Artery is in full swing, with completion projected for 2005. And the imprint of the Central Artery—transformed into either a greensward or a series of neighborhood parks flanked by new buildings—will remain on Boston maps for a long time to come.

Plate 50 ▶

(caption on page 228)

A field of construction cranes stretched across the South Boston landscape as work on the Central Artery/Third Harbor Tunnel Project reaches full swing in 1999.

◄ **Plate 50**

Aerial Photos International, Inc.

{Boston}

(Norwood, Mass., 1999)

At the end of the twentieth century the most accurate depictions of the Boston shoreline are not maps but aerial photographs. This one, taken in 1999, shows much of the city and, when compared with the 1948 map (see plate 48), shows the changes in the intervening half-century. Among the transformations were the new highways: The Central Artery snakes across the Boston peninsula and then, in Charlestown, branches into Route 1 leading to the Tobin Bridge and into I-93 heading northwest. One can also see the extensive work already completed on the Central Artery/Third Harbor Tunnel Project (see photo above). The most dramatic addition of land since 1948 had been at the airport, where fill had been extended in all directions, obliterating Wood Island Park and filling the Bird Island Flats facing South Boston. In South Boston, the piers built by the U.S. Navy in World War II had been filled in to make a pier for imported Subaru cars, and Pleasure Bay at the eastern tip had been completely enclosed. Among the prominent recently completed buildings are the Federal Courthouse and its park at Fan Pier and the hotel and office towers at the head of the Fish Pier, heralding the expansion of central Boston and the Commonwealth flats, recently renamed the South Boston Seaport District. The edges of Columbia Point had been squared off and filled in for the Columbia Point housing project (now called Harbor Point), the JFK Library, and the UMass/Boston campus (see frontispiece to chapter 7). The photograph also shows that South Bay had finally been completely filled in, leaving the Fort Point Channel open only above the West Fourth Street Bridge; the new Charles River Dam on the site of the old Warren Bridge; and the land added to Charlesbank park, including several small islands along the river to compensate for land taken for Storrow Drive construction.

IV

Epilogue

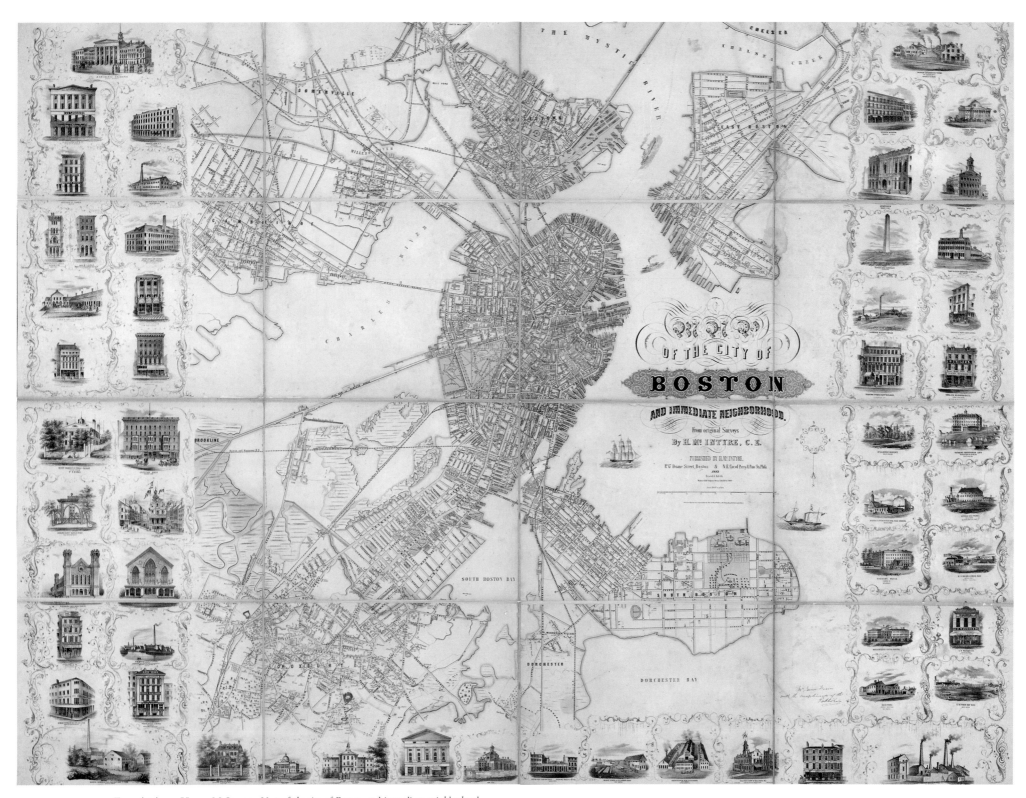

Frontispiece Henry McIntyre, *Map of the city of Boston and immediate neighborhood* (Boston and Philadelphia, 1852).

Map of Good Hope: Boston in the American Imagination

James Carroll

Born in Chicago, raised in Washington, D.C., I came to Boston late, secure in the knowledge of what I would find. That was thirty years ago, and I knew nothing.

The Boston of the American imagination exists only on the poster-sized map of the mind, with its border of oval-framed faces of patriots, politicians, preachers, and poets. The map is entitled, variously, Athens of America, Brimstone Corner, City on a Hill, All Politics Is Local, Ireland West, Berkeley East, Race War North, Birthplace of Bio-Tech, and Banned-in-Boston. The features of the map include painted brick footpaths through early America; prickly borders of tribal neighborhoods; the squared-off glass steeples of faith in financial services; a yawning harbor through which ever fewer fish and a constant current of immigrants funnel; stars marking the desks and workbenches of Nobel laureates; tidal charts of a seasonally shifting student population; the white needles of old churches; the compass rose of politics; and notations for the bus stops of the tourist trolleys.

That Boston retains a mythic vibrancy in the American imagination is never more clear than when one of those blue or red tourist buses chugs by. Its bell clangs, as if in homage to the San Francisco cable car to which it pays kitsch tribute. I have seen visitors to Boston craning from under the rolled-up vinyl windows of those quaint conveyances with expressions of awe on their faces. And what did they behold? The wonder of what, to us, was an ordinary city street. Who'd have thought that ordinary city streets would themselves become exotic in America? Waiting at a corner in my car, I have been blinded by the simultaneous flashes of two dozen Instamatics, as trolley riders pushed their blue-dot buttons on the driver's cue—photographing what? A bow-fronted town house on Beacon Street; an equestrian statue at the foot of Commonwealth Avenue; a narrow lane laid with cobblestones; the gray bent tablets of a colonial graveyard; the home of Parker House rolls. I have caught snatches of the driver-guide's routine: a Beacon Hill Garden Club president, at work in a flower bed on Mount Vernon Street, pointed out as a typical Irish serving girl; a storefront on Charles Street honored as the original 7-Eleven; General Hooker on his horse in the shadow of the State House credited with the invention of prostitution.

Even a transplanted native like me has to ask, What do people see when they come to Boston? Jean-Paul Sartre wrote that a European arrives at an American city feeling wary of being taken in, that a European leaves an American city feeling slightly depressed. But I wonder. It is surely true that the clang of cash registers—or should I say the beep?—competes with the trolley bell in Boston, and that Boston, with nary a nod to Hooker, can tart herself up for tourists: Think of the traffic jam of doodad carts at once-authentic Quincy Market. But the visitors we see, Europeans included, seemed disarmed and interested, uplifted even. By what exactly? There are, of course, the charms of the well-kept downtown residential districts, the relics of history, the minuet of land and sea, the jitterbug of skyscrapers and three-deckers. But charm and history and the scales of juxtaposition do not, of themselves, account for the fascination and respect one senses in the faces of all those visitors, for charm, history, and scale could define the made city of a theme park. If mere quaintness were the draw, then visitors would better seek out the re-created "heritage villages" of bygone days, those oases in time that are staffed by costumed actors—bonnetted schoolmarms, Pilgrim-hatted millers—who say they've never seen a camera, but smile for you anyway.

The map of mythic Boston is clearly drawn and familiar enough. Tourists arrive with it firmly in mind. The Kennedys cross its face like a presidential range, never mind that old Joe made his mark—and fortune—elsewhere, or that none of his progeny was raised here. Boston is the cradle of liberty, never mind that the wealthy merchants who challenged London over taxes had made their fortunes in the slave trade. Contemporary Boston is famous for the Red Sox feud with the New York Yankees, yet even that touches the subliminal nerve of antiestablishment newcomer resentment that took root here, where the name "Yankee" first referred to pinstripes on gray flannel.

Here is the joke: At the dawn of the twenty-first century, Boston lives most vividly in the American imagination not because of the Nobelists in literature who reside here—Derek Walcott, Saul Bellow, Seamus Heaney for part of each year; not because of Henry James, J. P. Marquand, or Edwin O'Connor; not because of Sylvia Plath or Anne Sexton; not because of the great universities that draw the most brilliant minds from the world over; not because, in national election after national election, its politics produce serious contenders for the country's highest offices. Far more humbly, yet more powerfully, perhaps, than ever before, Boston grips the American imagination from the Hollywood set of a long-running television program about a bar. The show's appeal, even in the eternal return of reruns, rests on the image of a place where, as its theme song says, everybody knows your name. That idea points to the most treasured part of Boston's mythic identity, as a place that, despite its character as a true city with all the outsized problems that go with urbanization, has preserved an intangible but real quality of intimacy.

The friendly accessibility of old Boston, especially, is one of its most striking qualities—the way the narrow streets embrace a person strolling, the way low buildings keep the sky a canopy. A regular surprise of lanes and cul-de-sacs that lead only into living rooms, and then windows to look in, make even strangers want to sit. The very geography of the brick city, nearly encircled by a river, harbor and swath of green at a muddy creek, makes it feel like a sprawling outdoor room. There is a wood city too, of course—the clapboard structures of adjacent three-decker neighborhoods like Dorchester, Roxbury, and Mission Hill, and the tidy capes and colonials of West Roxbury, Roslindale, and Hyde Park. Tourists see little of these surrounding enclaves, which draw contours as much from diversity as similarity, but from their varied hilltops a like view of the Prudential Center and the Hancock Tower, which always seem close enough to touch, ties them together. Not for nothing is the literal heart of Boston called the Common.

In other words, the dreamworld of television builds on something the nation already senses about Boston, and the nation has no need to ask, Is this real? But those of us who live here must ask that question, as trolley riders gaze out at us, as if we were figures on the backlot of a Disney studio. The myth of paradise suggests that human beings are always looking back toward a lost golden age that never actually existed. Yet it seems literally true, nonetheless, that a bond of intimacy once marked our national life in ways it no longer does, not only in the town before the age of the strip mall, but in the urban village called the neighborhood before the era of police locks. Hollywood's choice of Boston for this famous sitcom would not have clicked but for that idea America already had of the place. That one could walk in off the anonymous street of an otherwise typical city and be hailed by name may indeed have once been true—no fantasy—even of the Beacon Hill pub that inspired the television series. My wife and I had our wedding party there more than two decades ago, before Peoria had ever heard of the place. That pub was where we went in the early years of our marriage, now and then to be at home away from home. Today, of course, the bar is swamped with dismounted trolley riders from Peoria, Seattle, and Baton Rouge. They want a T-shirt more than a beer, but what they really want is a photo by the sign outside. The difference between myth and reality could be nowhere sharper than at that spot: Ask the homeless men and women who stuff newspapers into their clothing and curl up on benches in the park across the street. Such cheerlessness is as much a part of the human condition here as anywhere, even if television invites us to think otherwise. And, finally, no Bostonian would think of going to the famous bar because in such a place, naturally, no one knows anyone's name, except the movie star's.

And yet. There is no need here to condescend to those who, coming from away, show us what matters in Boston by the photographs they take. To talk of the purely imagined elements of the mental map Americans carry of this city is the farthest thing from debunking these fondly held ideas as "mere myth," as if there were anything "mere" about mythology. What we dream of, whether a lost past or a longed-for future, does, in fact, tell us something quite real about ourselves. Thus, the sentimental fog that wraps even Boston's hard-edged actualities can lift to reveal something deeply authentic. Having wondered for a long time about those trolley riders and what they see, and having been moved by what we see— namely, that fascination and respect illuminating their faces—I eventually recovered the memory of the time when I was one of them. It was a time before trolleys, but I too, like so many citizens who claim the place, was an awed newcomer whose very ignorance of Boston opened me to the core of its truth.

For my first few years here, I was a solitary man who habitually spent days-off alone, and what I did with almost every day of leisure, at least once a week, was walk the streets of this city, inhaling it. The aromas of bread rising from the commercial bakery by North Station, and of fish off the piers along Atlantic Avenue; the unsteady feel underfoot of Tremont Street sidewalks cantilevered by the roots of long-gone trees; splinters of twilight flashing off the sterling white triangles of sailboats on the river; the rattle of the elevated Orange Line on Washington Street, its screech of iron where the track curved sharply at Holy Cross Cathedral; the sad sight of old ladies sitting on porches in the self-made nursing homes on Rockview Street in Jamaica Plain; kids playing stickball against the plywood-boarded door of an abandoned apartment in the D Street projects, how they stopped to glare at me until I kept walking. I remember two trees on Castle Island that, when seen as one shape from back across Pleasure Bay, formed the perfect silhouette of a horse. I remember seeking out and finding the dilapidated clapboard house on a weather-beaten street in Southie, the number telling me it was where Cardinal Cushing was born. I tracked down the site of the original Perkins Institute on Pill Hill, also in Southie, because I so loved the idea of a half-blind Irish girl named Annie Sullivan giving Helen Keller to the world.

In my first few years, I was an itinerant dweller. I lived in the Fenway, around the corner from Symphony Road, which was an open-air arson factory in the late sixties, as well-insured landlords pursued a slum clearance of their own. The smell of charred wood hardly ever left the air. Across the street was a second story window to which neighbors pointed, almost proudly, with a rough tale of the Boston Strangler. It was an edgy neighborhood, but always there were potbellied men and waiflike women carrying fiddle cases to nearby Symphony Hall or the New England Conservatory. It amazed me that some of the best musicians in the world wore shoes as poorly heeled as mine.

On the back side of Mission Hill, I lived on the second floor of a tenement across the hall from a man who told me he was the king of the Gypsies, which I did not believe. Then I saw, on certain days, a train of young women arriving, each with her plucked chicken. Gypsies! I wondered anew about my neighbor, but also about ignorance and stereotype—mine, not his. I lived at various times in Beacon Hill, and in J. P., and in South Boston. My one foray out of town was to a leased apartment on the shore of Nahant—but only because I could look across the harbor at the city I had come to love.

But I could feel hate for Boston, too. My flat in Southie was on Fourth Street, just up from M. Its gracious bay window looked out on the Tuckerman School to which the flashing blue lights of police cars came every morning, an escort for half a dozen African-American second and third graders for whom the simple act of going to school was heroic. I learned an awful truth about my kind when, while serving as a court-appointed bus monitor during the Boston integration struggle of the mid-1970s, a black child said to me, "You're with the FBI, right?"

"Why do you think that?" I asked.

"Because they're the only white folks on our side." The only white folks, the child meant, in Boston. I could see why a child thought so in that terrible season—riding to school sprawled on the floor of a bus for fear of stones or worse—but it wasn't true. The federal judge was on their side, and he was not only white, but Irish. Boston itself had been on their side, having, for example, sent James J. Reeb to die in Selma, Alabama. A Massachusetts governor's mother, Mrs. Peabody, had famously traveled from Boston to join an early civil rights demonstration in Florida, where she was arrested. Boston had trained Martin Luther King, Jr., in theology, and had remained a source of his strongest support. And why not? A court sitting in Boston had made slavery illegal in Massachusetts nearly three decades before Lincoln. But it is also true that the same court first put forward the impossible idea of two school systems for the races, "separate but equal," a notion with a fuse attached to it. Why shouldn't Boston have been the site of the explosion?

The busing crisis, of course, overlays the contemporary story of Boston like a meridian grid overlays a globe, enabling every Bostonian to locate himself or herself in the geography of a city's self-hatred. Busing destroyed the schools, we're told, and laid bare not only the divide of race,

but of class. Busing ruined the educational experience of a generation, and drove middle class whites to the suburbs. The truth of that assessment has become part of the city's conventional wisdom, but it is far from the whole story. Court-ordered integration through busing, by forcing the hand of a recalcitrant, Irish-dominated (as it happened) School Committee, undid the scandal of government-sponsored segregation. In fact, it was the School Committee that had initiated busing—busing black children to predominantly black schools. The court only extended busing to whites. The sacrosanct "neighborhood school" was an ideal for whites, not blacks, who were overwhelmingly assigned to the citywide high schools, while whites were overwhelmingly assigned to "district" high schools. The School Committee rejected every "moderate" remedy, leaving no alternative to busing. By ordering it, the court restored the possibility of civic honor to a community that was in danger of losing its soul.

Busing remains the code-word for the modern tragedy of Boston, tragedy defined as the clash of mortally opposed antagonists neither of whom will surrender—"Never!" was scrawled on the blank walls of Boston for most of a decade—and each of whom is in some way right. It was true what my neighbors in Southie believed—that they were being unfairly forced to bear the burden of a whole society's failure. But at stake in that crisis was nothing less than the answer to the question, Can Boston, which opened its heart to newcomers in the past, do so in the future? Busing was a tragedy—but it was also an answer, and the answer is yes.

Not that the hearts of cities open easily. Except for those native Americans who'd named the place Shawmut before the English came, Boston's successive dominators have, in truth, been slow to open up to others. Thus you could write the history of the place as a chronicle of its antagonisms: Brahmin versus Irish, Irish versus Jews, Italians versus Hispanics, whites perennially versus blacks. There was even the wounding conflict of children versus parents during the generational battle that shocked America in the 1960s, and that took such jagged shape here. That conflict was joined, especially, at Boston area universities by the Pentagon-sponsored scientists whose work underwrote the war in Vietnam, and their very own students who repudiated the war with a fervor that caught the nation's attention. At the Arlington Street Church, an organizing center of the Abolition movement in the nineteenth century, young men turned in their draft cards at a ceremony presided over by William Sloane Coffin and Dr. Benjamin Spock, and after that the Selective Service System was a battleground. For a time, the famous sign at Charles River Park, referred to earlier in this volume, was altered by protester-vandals to read, "If you lived in Hanoi, you'd be dead now." On the Southeast Expressway, the Boston Gas Company commissioned the late artist Corita Kent, a former nun and permanent peace activist, to splash its looming gas storage tank with her trademark rainbow. When she finished—her work remains a landmark on the map of Boston today—drivers whipping by in their cars could spy what some swore was a profile of the North Vietnamese leader Ho Chi Minh. And why not? Hadn't Ho Chi Minh worked in Boston years before as a waiter? I witnessed Boston police officers roughly carting off student protesters with a rebuttal chant of their own; "Ho! Ho! Ho! Chi! Minh!—my ass!" There is a stout young oak tree growing on the hillside in the Boston Common. It was planted discreetly by a group of long-time peace activists, marking the end of the war. The tree is on no map that I know of, but it should be. A stone tablet at its base reads, "For Hai and Sacha, Age 9. For all Vietnamese children who died in the war. And for ourselves. 1975."

The passions of Boston are quite plain to see. The word passion has two senses and both apply. Passion means the intensely felt emotions that give shape to public discourse, and prompt, say, the simple, useless gesture of a tree planting. And passion means the suffering of a people who have chosen, in the phrase of an old Irish saying, contention over loneliness. Such passion is at the heart of fabled Boston politics, which is nothing but the city in dialogue with itself—sometimes conversation, sometimes argument. The reason Boston politicians climb onto the national stage with such regularity is that, as has been true since its first settlers faced west and moved on, Boston cannot conceive of its fate apart from the nation's. Tip O'Neill's dictum, All Politics Is Local, only means that there is no nation apart from its neighborhoods. The nation is the neighborhood writ large—for better and for worse. And the converse is true: The neighborhood is the nation small. In Washington, that is easy to forget, but in Boston impossible.

It was in Boston that citizens first began to think of themselves as having a loyalty larger than to those whose names they knew. Citizenship in Boston, perhaps around the time of Sam Adams or Phillis Wheatley, began to mean more than one thing. Loyalty to the king became a prior loyalty to the people; loyalty to the slave master became a prior loyalty to the human truth of freedom. New England was famous as the home of what would come to be called rugged individualism, but somehow here, a readiness to stand alone—a wish to be left alone—was tempered by a spacious interest in the broader world. Citizenship in Boston, in other words, came to mean a simultaneous sense of membership in—and responsibility for—the United States of America.

The nation, in fact, is an abstraction, and we came to a full understanding of its reach, both far and near, only gradually—indeed, only through the accidents and tragedies, detours and bonuses of history. And gradually we made our commitment, from the near to the far. All of this is quite apparent in those famous tourist walks through Boston. Those ambulatory stories tell it all—from Anne Hutchinson to Wendell Phillips to the African-American soldiers of the Massachusetts 54th to the great Robert Lowell poem about their memorial. Yes, there was busing, but

first there was abolition. Yes, there were Sacco and Vanzetti, but later there was Michael Dukakis, whose principled opposition to the death penalty was the undoing of his presidential campaign. Yes, there was the Brink's Robbery, but there is also Rosie's Place, a shelter for women run by modest idealists who embrace voluntary poverty out of spiritual wealth. What else is America but all of this?

The idea of the nation, like the idea of the universal, remains elusive. It comes alive for us only in a vivid instance of particularity. Boston, exactly because it is not a Hollywood fantasy or a heritage theme park, is precisely such an instance of particularity. That there is a well-known tragic side to life in Boston—that lost generation of school children, a clinging air of racial mistrust, a slant toward tribalism—can by the odd transformation of truth be a consolation to those who face it. Because Boston is tragic as well as charming, human as well as divine, we know it is ours. We flawed citizens claim Boston as home not despite its flaws, but because of them. Thus Boston's local eccentricities, for better and worse—in its characters, but also in the odd turns its story takes—are so widely able to be recognized as intimations of the fate of the very nation, for better and worse. Even the massive, late twentieth century rearrangement of physical space—the depression of the Central Artery is the largest public works project of the era—carries such a weight of intimation, as new buildings go up, and an obsolete highway goes down, and a long-lost waterfront is reclaimed, and disparate ethnic and socioeconomic concentrations are knit together by new means of transport, rapid exchange of information, and, perhaps, unprecedented modes of municipal governance—a Greater Boston?—that these new structures will make possible. When visitors see the signals of this city's reinvention—one by land, twice by the sea—they glimpse what this nation is becoming next.

What do visitors see when they see Boston? They see not the dream of America, but the human reality of it, which is better. One nation under God? In Boston, there are Christians and Jews, but also Muslims, Jains, Buddhists, Hindus, and people for whom the creed is unimportant. Religion is not a ticket here. Through the lens of this city's past, one sees that, generation in and generation out—from those first dissenting Puritans, through the descendants of those who crossed the Atlantic on Boston-owned slave ships, through the Irish, Italians, and Jews who fled a bleeding Europe, to the lately arrived refugees from Latin American and Asian wars, to a new geneation of Jews who've stepped out of Russia, and the new Irish who've come for work—newcomers have always had to possess only one thing for rough acceptance here. They have had to possess a future.

This is Boston's secret—that its famously layered history points beyond itself to all that has not happened yet. Why else have so many of us come here in the flower of youth and refused to leave? Because we are drawn to an open-air museum? Because the statuary moves us? Because the legends teach us moral lessons? We love the provenance, but that does not account for our commitment. Boston is the grande dame and the young rebel both—provenance and prospect. The imaginative spaciousness that accommodates such human range is what people live here for. And visitors glimpse the thing. Jean-Paul Sartre finally acknowledged a grudging admiration for American cities precisely because of this quality. "The cities are open," he wrote, "open to the world, and to the future. This is what gives them their adventurous look and, even in their ugliness and disorder, a touching beauty."

Boston proves that what makes an American—and this is unique to our nation—is a shared future, not a common past. But the future is nothing if not open, and the past is nothing if it does not teach us that. The lesson is dramatically enshrined in the very bones of the city, which is why we love those cobblestones, and Old Ironsides, and the hint of molasses in the air above certain streets in the North End. To go from Paul Revere's house at North Square to Sarah Orne Jewett's apartment on Charles Street to the Bay State Road hotel room—now a Boston University dormitory room—in which Eugene O'Neill died; from Fenway Park to Castle Island to Jordan Hall; from Haymarket stalls to Hancock Tower office suites to one of ten thousand classrooms; from Vilna Shul to Trinity Church to the African Meeting House to the Paulist Fathers' Chapel on Park Street; from a Jain temple to an Orthodox cathedral to a Muslim mosque; from Maison Robert in Old City Hall to Amrhein's on Broadway to the Paramount Deli on the flat of Beacon Hill; from the *Boston Globe* to the *Bay State Banner* to *Bay Windows*; from the people's triumph of Tent City to the imported glitz of Copley Place: from here to there, North End to Southie, West End to Coolidge Corner, Dudley to downtown, the world's great question has its answer.

How do people of diverse racial and ethnic and religious strains live together—not without strain, not just in peace, but in the hope of harmony? Think of the poignant urgency with which that question is being asked now from Belfast to Kosovo, from Kigali to Islamabad. That question is being asked in Jerusalem, which was the first city on a hill, but not the last. And it is true: the eyes of Jerusalem can look this way. Boston is not rid of conflict, and African-Americans in particular may have reason to step warily, but this city's differences are openly faced, and increasingly honored. The eyes of the world, represented by a steady stream of international visitors who lift those vinyl window flaps, ask this question: How to draw *unum* out of *pluribus?* We do it, Boston says, like this.

Thus Boston not only lives in the American imagination; Boston embodies it. The imagination, Coleridge said, is the faculty whose purpose is the reconciliation of opposites. Whether by a fluke of history, or by the deliberate choice of its exemplary citizens, or by lessons painfully learned from dreadful mistakes, the reconciliation of opposites has been

Boston's purpose too, and so it remains. Ask the new immigrants. Ask the children, parents, and teachers of a rededicated Boston Public School system. Ask the city planners whose lessons came the hard way. The ethnic and racial and class boundaries across which so many slings and arrows have been hurled are also sutures that close a social wound. Boston can face the western expanse of a great continent without turning its back on the old world from which so many of its parents came. Boston can prize a parochial quality of life, bitterly cutting down to size every display of worldliness, while also spawning a lettered sophistication that draws the still unbridled young. Opposites? In Boston the has-been and the not-yet are wrestling with each other, and always have. The outcome of the match remains predictably uncertain. And why shouldn't Americans love coming here to watch?

As this volume so elegantly shows, Boston forms the literal center of some of the New World's earliest maps. But Boston itself functions as a map for those who see it now, a metaphoric sketching of the territory of a nation's inner life. A peninsula, a stretch of pasture, cow paths, a set of fingerlike wharves clawing the sea, a constricting grid of streets, the telltale sign of limits and human demands on the earth, demands that seem impossible. The landfill history alone makes Boston a city that walks on water, a city that moves mountains—biblical images of the miraculous. For ourselves, we citizens of Boston make more modest claims. We are proud to feel the gaze of Americans, and grateful to sense their fascination and respect. But what Americans find to love in Boston already belongs to them, as the skilled drawing of a place already belongs to the portion of the earth it represents. Whether the nation sees Boston from the window of a chugging trolley, or on the unscrolled parchment of a spiritual cartography, we are humbled—a word coming from Latin for "of the earth," which also gives us "human"—to be a particular mark of such universal longing. Human longing is for nothing less than the reconciliation of time and place, of past and future, of the many and the one, of the living and the dead. Boston is precious because it lives in the national imagination, and increasingly the world's, just so—as a tattered but still brilliant map of America's good hope.

V

Appendix

Timeline of Boston's Land Making

The massive amount of land created in Boston can be described in various ways. It can, for example, be traced verbally, as in chapter 7, or shown graphically, as in the map overlays in chapter 2 and composite map in the frontispiece to chapter 7. Another way of tracing all the land making that has occurred in Boston is by means of a timeline such as the one on the following pages.

This timeline is divided horizontally into different sections of the city, listed in the left-hand column, and vertically into different time periods, enumerated across the top. By reading across one can trace the specific additions of land to a given section of the city. By reading down each column one can see what parts of the city were being filled at the same time.

Regarding the timeline as a whole, it is evident that "wharfing out"—constructing wharves outward from the shore and eventually filling the slips between them—created land in many parts of the city. Wharfing out began in the seventeenth century along the shorelines of the central waterfront, North End, South Cove, and Charlestown, and by the 1850s the first three areas had been filled almost to their present limits. Wharfing out began later in outlying sections of the city—South Boston, Dorchester, and East Boston—and continued in those areas, as well as in Charlestown, into the twentieth century.

In addition to wharfing out, land was made by many projects organized specifically to create new land. A number of such projects were initiated in the first decade of the nineteenth century in response to Boston's need for more space. In the 1830s the introduction of railroads and burgeoning population prompted another flurry of land making. By the 1850s land-making projects, such as the South Bay Lands and Back Bay, had become larger and were often conducted by the city or state. In the decades following the inauguration of the Boston park system in the 1870s, waterfront areas in many sections of the city were filled to create public parks. Similarly, as a spin-off of the building of the first Charles River Dam in the first decade of the twentieth century, a narrow esplanade was filled along the river and then widened in the 1930s and again in the 1950s during the construction of Storrow Drive. In the 1920s railroads filled in most of South Bay and behind North Station, but most land making during the twentieth century took place in outlying sections of the city, particularly at Columbia Point and in East Boston for the airport. Some filling occurred surprisingly late: The Roxbury Canal behind Albany Street and City Hospital was not filled until the mid-1960s and the last land making on the Boston mainland—the creation of Subaru Pier in South Boston—was only completed in the early 1980s.

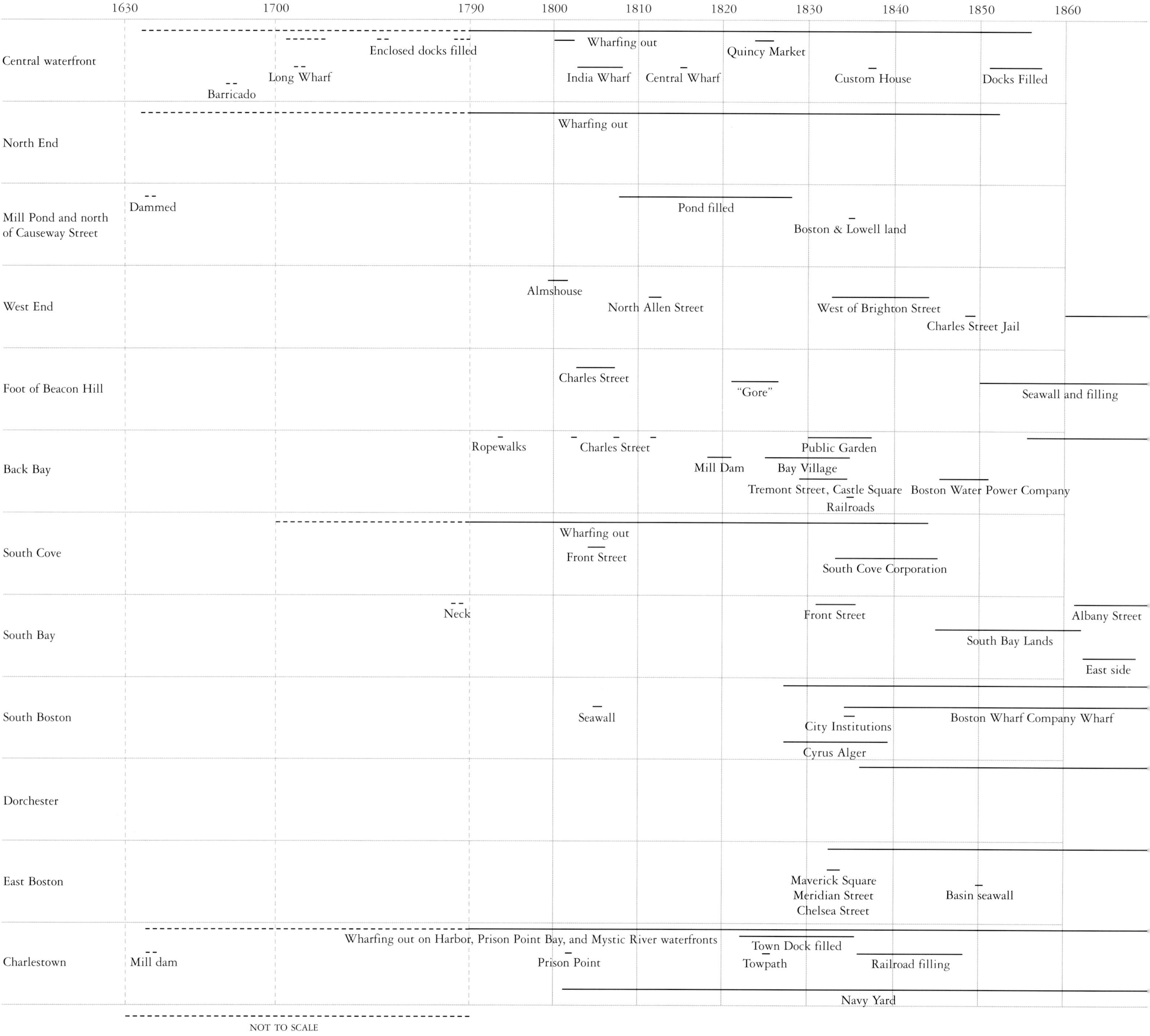

	1630	1700	1790	1800	1810	1820	1830	1840	1850	1860

Central waterfront
Enclosed docks filled · Wharfing out · Quincy Market
Barricado · Long Wharf · India Wharf · Central Wharf · Custom House · Docks Filled

North End
Wharfing out

Mill Pond and north of Causeway Street
Dammed · Pond filled · Boston & Lowell land

West End
Almshouse · North Allen Street · West of Brighton Street · Charles Street Jail

Foot of Beacon Hill
Charles Street · "Gore" · Seawall and filling

Back Bay
Ropewalks · Charles Street · Public Garden · Mill Dam · Bay Village · Tremont Street, Castle Square · Boston Water Power Company · Railroads

South Cove
Wharfing out · Front Street · South Cove Corporation

South Bay
Neck · Front Street · Albany Street · South Bay Lands · East side

South Boston
Seawall · City Institutions · Cyrus Alger · Boston Wharf Company Wharf

Dorchester

East Boston
Maverick Square · Meridian Street · Chelsea Street · Basin seawall

Charlestown
Wharfing out on Harbor, Prison Point Bay, and Mystic River waterfronts
Mill dam · Prison Point · Town Dock filled · Towpath · Railroad filling · Navy Yard

NOT TO SCALE

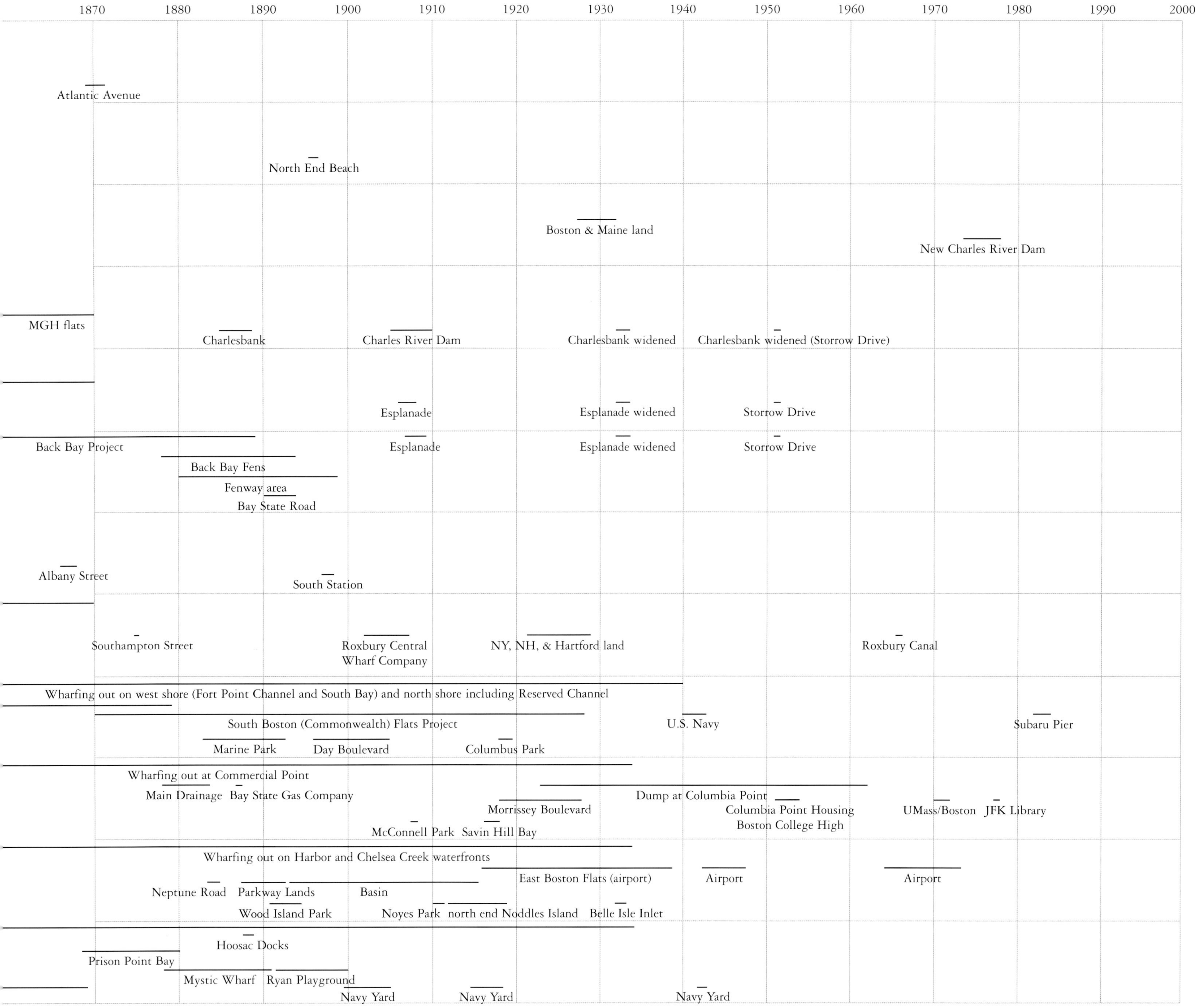

Timeline with years across the top: 1870, 1880, 1890, 1900, 1910, 1920, 1930, 1940, 1950, 1960, 1970, 1980, 1990, 2000

Atlantic Avenue

North End Beach

Boston & Maine land

New Charles River Dam

MGH flats

Charlesbank

Charles River Dam

Charlesbank widened

Charlesbank widened (Storrow Drive)

Esplanade

Esplanade widened

Storrow Drive

Back Bay Project

Esplanade

Esplanade widened

Storrow Drive

Back Bay Fens

Fenway area

Bay State Road

Albany Street

South Station

Southampton Street

Roxbury Central
Wharf Company

NY, NH, & Hartford land

Roxbury Canal

Wharfing out on west shore (Fort Point Channel and South Bay) and north shore including Reserved Channel

South Boston (Commonwealth) Flats Project

U.S. Navy

Subaru Pier

Marine Park

Day Boulevard

Columbus Park

Wharfing out at Commercial Point

Main Drainage Bay State Gas Company

Morrissey Boulevard

Dump at Columbia Point

Columbia Point Housing
Boston College High

UMass/Boston JFK Library

McConnell Park Savin Hill Bay

Wharfing out on Harbor and Chelsea Creek waterfronts

East Boston Flats (airport)

Airport

Airport

Neptune Road Parkway Lands

Basin

Wood Island Park

Noyes Park north end Noddles Island Belle Isle Inlet

Hoosac Docks

Prison Point Bay

Mystic Wharf Ryan Playground

Navy Yard

Navy Yard

Navy Yard

A Boston Chronology

Incorporating the Boston plates illustrated in this book

1614   John Smith explores the New England coast, naming it in *A Description of New England* written a year later during his captivity aboard a French privateer.

1625   Anglican clergyman Reverend William Blaxton settles on the western slope of Beacon Hill on the Shawmut Peninsula (the original part of Boston).

1630   A group of English Puritans of the Massachusetts Bay Company, led by John Winthrop, settle first in Charlestown. At the invitation of Reverend Blaxton, Winthrop and his group move to the Shawmut Peninsula.

1634   The Boston Common is purchased by the town from Reverend Blaxton.

1643   *Book of Possessions,* the earliest thorough survey of land holdings and record of property ownership and transfer, is compiled by order of the General Court (Massachusetts legislature).

ca. 1644   Mill Pond (now the Bulfinch Triangle) is created by damming the marshy North Cove.

1646   North Battery is built at Merry's Point (now Battery Wharf) in the North End.

1666   South Battery (aka Boston Sconce) is built on the present-day site of Rowes Wharf.

1679   Fire destroys eighty homes, giving rise to the mandate that "no dwelling house in Boston shall be erected except of stone or brick"; it is, however, ignored.

1701   Boston's selectmen are empowered to assign and fix names to streets.

1711–1715   Long Wharf is built.

1713   Old State House is completed.

1720   Boston's population reaches 11,000.

1722   **The first state of the famous John Bonner map *The Town of Boston in New England* is published (plate 24).**

1723   The Old North Church is completed.

1728   **William Burgis's *This Plan of Boston in New England* is published (plate 25).**

1740–1742   Faneuil Hall is built and given to the town by merchant Peter Faneuil.

1743   **The seventh state of John Bonner's map is published as *A New Plan of ye Great Town of Boston* by William Price (plate 26).**

1770   Five are killed in the Boston Massacre at the Old State House.

1773   The Boston Tea Party takes place on Griffin's Wharf.

1775   The town's population of 16,000 drops to 6,570 following the outbreak of the Revolutionary War; by 1776 it drops again to 2,720.

1776   The British army evacuates Boston.

George F. J. Frentzel's *Carte von dem Hafen und der Stad Boston* is published (plate 27).

1777   **Thomas Page's *A Plan of the Town of Boston* is published (plate 28).**

Henry Pelham's *A Plan of Boston in New England* is published (plate 29).

1778   **George Le Rouge's *Plan de Boston* is published (plate 18).**

1781   **J. W. F. Des Barres's and George Callender's *{Boston Harbor}* chart is published (plate 19).**

1794   Thomas Pemberton chronicles Boston's history in his *Topographical and Historical Description of Boston.*

1795   **Osgood Carleton's *A Plan of the Town of Boston* is drawn as part of a state survey (plate 30).**

1796   **Carleton's *A Plan of Boston from actual Survey* is published (plate 31).**

1798   The new State House, designed by Charles Bulfinch, opens atop Beacon Hill.

1801   The selectmen, led by Bulfinch, present a plan for developing the Boston Neck into streets laid out in a regular, rectangular pattern.

1803   The Board of Selectmen begins the enforcement of a "brick only" building rule.

Boston's population reaches 25,000.

1803–1807   Charles Street at the foot of Beacon Hill is filled by cutting down Mount Vernon.

1803–1808   India Wharf (now Harbor Towers), Broad Street, and India Street are filled.

1804   Dorchester Neck is annexed and renamed South Boston.

1804–1806   Front Street (now Harrison Avenue) in South Cove is filled.

1805   Charles Bulfinch enlarges Faneuil Hall.

1807–1828   The Mill Pond is filled, primarily using dirt gained from cutting down Beacon Hill (see ca. 1644).

1810	Boston's population is 33,800.
1814	**John G. Hales's** *Map of Boston in the State of Massachusetts* **is published (plate 32).**
1818–1821	The Mill Dam is built on the line of present-day Beacon Street across Back Bay from Charles Street to Sewell's Point (now Kenmore Square) in Brookline, with a cross dam on the line of present Hemenway Street.
1819	**Alexander Wadworth's** *Chart of Boston Harbor* **is published (plate 21).**
1820	Boston's population is 43,300.
1823	America's first municipal sewer and gas lighting systems are begun.
1824	The city reacquires the area of the future Public Garden and votes to keep it forever open and free of buildings.
1824–1826	Quincy Market and North and South Market buildings are constructed on land made by filling in the Town Dock.
1825–1835	Church Street District (now Bay Village) is filled.
1826	**William B. Annin's and George G. Smith's** *Plan of Boston* **is published (plate 33).**
1829–1836	Tremont Street in the South End is filled.
1830	Boston's population is 61,400.
	John G. Hales's *Plan of the City of Boston* **is drawn (plate 34).**
1835	**George G. Smith's** *Plan of Boston* **is published (plate 35).**
1836	Boston Wharf Company begins filling its huge wharf in South Boston.
1837–1847	The U.S. Customs House is built on land made by filling the head of the dock between Long and Central Wharves.
1843	Bunker Hill monument, atop Breed's Hill in Charlestown, is completed.
1845–1862	South Bay lands (Albany Street area south of Malden Street) are filled.
1847	**U.S. Coast Survey's** *Plan of the Inner Harbor of Boston* **is published (plate 22).**
1848–1849	**Nathaniel Dearborn's** *A new and complete Map of the City of Boston* **is published (plate 36).**
1849	A cholera epidemic centered in the Fort Hill area kills 600.
1850	Boston's population is 137,000, of which 46 percent are foreign-born.
1851	A ninety-six-mile sewer system is completed.
1852	**Ellis Sylvester Chesbrough's** *Map of Boston Harbor* **is published (plate 37).**
	Slatter and Callan's *Map of the city of Boston, Mass^{ts}* **is published (plate 38).**
1855	Boston Water Power Company begins filling its part of Back Bay under agreement with the state.
1855	**George G. Smith's** *Plan of Boston* **is published (plate 39).**
1856	The street plan for Back Bay, proposed by the legislative committee on Back Bay, is adopted. It calls for four new streets—Beacon, Marlborough, Newbury, and Boylston—parallel to Mill Dam and on either side of Commonwealth Avenue. These streets and Commonwealth Avenue are intersected at 548-to 600-foot intervals by cross streets.

1858	The state begins filling its part of Back Bay.
1860	Boston's population is 178,000.
1862	**James Slade's** *Plan of Boston* **is published (plate 40).**
1862–1865	City Hall is built on School Street.
1866–1872	Fort Hill is cut down and dirt is used to fill docks cut off by the new Atlantic Avenue.
1868	Roxbury is annexed.
1870	Boston's population is 251,000.
	Dorchester is annexed.
	Thomas W. Davis's *Plan of Boston* **is published (plate 41).**
1872	The Great Fire levels sixty-five residential and commercial acres in the area between Summer and Pearl Streets from Washington Street to the harbor.
1874	Charlestown, Brighton, and West Roxbury are annexed.
	Griffith M. Hopkins's *Map of the City of Boston* **is published (plate 42).**
1877	Trinity Church, designed by H. H. Richardson, is completed at the edge of what would later become Copley Square.
1878–1894	The Back Bay Fens are created by filling the flats of the Muddy River.
1880–1898	The Fenway area is filled.
1880	**Boston Map Company's** *Plan Showing the principal portion of Boston* **is published (plate 43).**
	Boston's population is 363,000.
1882	An incandescent streetlight system is constructed.
1883	The triangular lot bounded by Huntington Avenue, Dartmouth and Boylston Streets, and Trinity Church is purchased by the city and named Copley Square.
1883–1893	Marine Park is filled.
1884	Construction begins on Franklin Park, the centerpiece of the Boston park system designed by prominent landscape architect Frederick Law Olmsted.
1891	Harvard Bridge opens to the public, connecting West Chester Park in Boston with Massachusetts Avenue in Cambridge.
1892	Electrification of the street railway system is completed.
	Boston's population is 448,000.
1895	McKim, Mead, and White's Boston Public Library is completed on Copley Square.
1896	**U.S. Coast and Geodetic Survey's** *Boston Harbor, Massachusetts* **is published (plate 44).**
1897	The Tremont Street subway, America's first subway, opens.
	Boston's population is 550,000.
1898–1900	**U.S. Geological Survey's** *Massachusetts, Boston* **is published (plate 23).**
1899	South Station is completed.
1900	Symphony Hall, another McKim, Mead, and White design, is completed.

1901	The elevated transit structure between Dudley and Sullivan Squares opens.
1904	The East Boston subway tunnel opens.
	The New England Conservatory of Music moves westward to Huntington Avenue.
1905–1910	The Charles River Dam is constructed, creating the Charles River Basin.
1908	George Hiram Walker's *Map of the city of Boston* is published (plate 45)
1909	The Boston Opera House, designed by Parkman B. Haven, is completed.
	The new Museum of Fine Arts in the Fenway, designed by Guy Lowell, is completed.
	Boston's population is 670,000.
1912	Fenway Park opens.
	Hyde Park is annexed, enlarging the city to its present size of 46.1 square miles.
1913	The Dorchester subway tunnel opens.
	The Boston Planning Board is established.
1913–1915	The Customs House Tower is built atop the original 1847 structure. At 496 feet high, it is the tallest structure downtown to date.
1916	MIT moves from Boston to Cambridge.
1918	A worldwide influenza pandemic kills thousands of Bostonians.
1918–1919	Columbus Park in South Boston is filled.
1919	Boston's population is 750,000.
	313 miles of streets are paved.
1927	George Hiram Walker's *Boston and Surroundings* is published (plate 46).
1928	North Station is constructed.
1929	Boston's population is 780,000.
1934	Sumner Tunnel opens, linking East Boston and Boston.
	U.S. Coast and Geodetic Survey's *Boston Harbor* is published (plate 47).
1947	The Metropolitan Transit Authority is established, supplanting Boston Elevated Railway Company.
1948	*Map of the City of Boston* is published by the Boston City Planning Board (plate 48).
1949	The twenty-six story, 495-foot John Hancock Tower is built.
1950	Boston's population peaks at 801,000.
	The Mystic River Bridge opens, linking Charlestown and Chelsea.
	The Boston Planning Board's "General Plan" is enacted, proposing substantial "slum clearance."
1951–1959	The elevated Central Artery is built, severing downtown from the waterfront and the North End.
1957	The Boston Redevelopment Authority, an offshoot of the Boston Housing Authority, is established.

1958–1965	The West End and Scollay Square are razed in two stages in accordance with urban renewal program—creating a vast *tabula rasa* at the center of the city—and eventually replaced by Government Center and Charles River Park.
1960	Boston's population drops to 697,000.
	Edward Logue becomes director of the Boston Redevelopment Authority, ushering the beginning of the major downtown and neighborhood urban renewal program.
1961	Callahan Tunnel opens, linking Boston and East Boston.
	Prudential Center construction begins; the 52-story, 750-feet-high tower, when completed, is the tallest building in Boston, until the new Hancock Tower eclipses it a decade later.
1963	Construction on Government Center begins.
1964	Downtown waterfront urban renewal plan is released, accelerating redevelopment of the central waterfront.
1965	The Boston Redevelopment Authority publishes its *Plan for the Capital Web* (plate 49).
	The downtown office building boom starts, foreshadowing the 20 million square feet of space to be built by 1983.
1966	The John Fitzgerald Kennedy Federal Building, a corner stone of Government Center, is completed.
1968	Government Center is completed with the opening of the new Boston City Hall as its centerpiece.
1970	Boston's population drops to 641,000.
	Governor Sargent declares a moratorium on highway construction, stopping the Inner Belt project and shifting highway funding to expand the MBTA.
1973	Route 93 to Boston is completed.
	The second John Hancock Tower—Boston's tallest at 60 stories and 790 feet high—is completed.
1974	Boston school desegregation is ordered.
	The Charlestown Navy Yard, home of the U.S.S. *Constitution,* is formally closed by the Nixon administration, becoming, instead, the site of an extensive adaptive reuse project as a residential and tourist area.
	Adult entertainment is permitted on lower Washington Street by a zoning variance that establishes the "Combat Zone."
1976	The Bicentennial is celebrated.
	The renovated Faneuil Hall Marketplace opens.
1978–1985	The MBTA Red line is extended northward to Alewife and southward to Braintree. The Orange line is reconstructed to follow the Southwest Corridor alignment.
1979	The John F. Kennedy Presidential Library opens at Columbia Point.
	The Southwest Corridor development plan is adopted.
1980	Boston's population is 563,000.
1984	Copley Place, a large mixed-use development over the Massachusetts Turnpike, is built, leading to the development of Tent City.
1985–1988	A number of neighborhood housing programs are begun including the South End Neighborhood Housing Initiative and the Dudley Street Neighborhood Institute.

1987	Rowes Wharf is completed.
1989	The Midtown Cultural District Plan is adopted.
1990	Boston's population is 575,000, reversing a four-decade decline from the high of 801,000 in 1950.
	The Harborpark District becomes a part of the Boston Zoning Code.
1991	The Central Artery/Third Harbor Tunnel project is approved by the Federal Highway Administration.
1992	The park at Post Office Square is completed; it is rededicated as Leventhal Park in 1997.
1997	The state legislature authorizes planning and funding for a new Boston Convention Center to be located in the Seaport District.
1998	An interim master plan for the Seaport District is announced, initiating a broad public debate about how the area of the Commonwealth Flats should be redeveloped.
1999	**Aerial Photos International shoots the planimetric photograph of Boston (plate 50).**

A Glossary of Map Terms

Anon. Anonymous.

Armillary sphere An ancient astronomical instrument made up of rings showing the positions of significant circles of the celestial sphere.

Astrolabe A circle graduated in 360° with a rotating sighting device called an *alidade.* It was widely used by navigators and astonomers prior to the invention of the sextant to determine the position of celestial bodies.

Atlas A (generally) bound assemblage of maps.

Backing (backed, back) A substance affixed to the verso of a map, using a variety of adhesives, with the purpose of strengthening or flattening the map. It is noted that some maps, particularly sea charts, were issued on a double paper.

Base map Map on which information may be placed for purposes of comparison or geographic correlation. The term *base map* was at one time applied to topography maps, also termed *mother maps,* that are used in the construction of other types of maps by the addition of particular data.

Bench mark Relatively permanent material object, natural or artificial, bearing a marked point whose elevation above or below an adopted datum is known.

Binder's guard (guard, binder's stub) A strip of paper glued to the map along one side of the centerfold. The map is sewn into the atlas using the guard, obviating the need to make stitchholes in the map itself.

Bird's-eye view A perspective view of a town or countryside as seen from an elevation of about 45° above the ground plane.

Blindstamp An impression made in paper using a die that leaves a raised mark.

Border A (usually) decorative device used to embellish the outer limits of a printed map image.

Boundary Monument Material object placed on or near a boundary line to preserve and identify the location of the boundary line on the ground.

Broadside (broadsheet) A single complete sheet of paper printed on one side only.

Burin Tool used by engravers to incise the lines. A graver.

Cadastral Map showing the boundaries of subdivisions of land, often with the bearings and lengths thereof and the areas of individual tracts, for purposes of describing and recording ownership. It may also show culture, drainage, and other features relating to land use and value.

Cartes à figures Maps with figures in small panels around the outer sides. Characteristic of some seventeenth-century maps.

Cartography Science and art of making maps and charts. The term may be taken broadly as comprising all the steps needed to produce a map: planning, aerial photography, field surveys, photogrammetry, editing, color separation, and multicolor printing. Mapmakers, however, tend to limit the use of the term to map-finishing operations, in which the master manuscript is edited and color separation plates are prepared for lithographic printing.

Cartouche Emblemlike device containing title or other information. May be very elaborate or very simple.

Cerography "Wax printing." A technique whereby the image is engraved in wax and a stereotype plate made by electroplating the incised wax.

Chart Special-purpose map designed for navigation or to present specific data or information. The term "chart" is applied chiefly to maps made primarily for nautical and aeronautical navigation, and to maps of the heavens, although the term is sometimes used to describe other special-purpose maps.

Chronometer An instrument for measuring time, used to compute longitude.

City plan (town plan) A map of a city or town as viewed from directly above (normal to) the streets.

Color, contemporary Color that was applied at or about the time the map was printed. Note that the word contemporary refers to the time the map was made, not to the current time period.

Color, later Color applied to a map after it was printed, but may suggest that the color is not recent or modern.

Color, original Color applied to the map at or about the time it was printed.

Color, recent (modern) Color applied to an uncolored map recently, as in last week or last year.

Coloring Any chromatic hue, other than black, added to the map after printing.

Color separation Process of preparing a separate drawing, engraving, or negative for each color required in the printing production of map or chart.

Compass rose The elements of a compass card shown on a map. Rhumb lines radiate from the compass rose.

Composite atlas An atlas, other than a regular edition, that contains an idiosyncratic collection of bound maps not necessarily by the same cartographer.

Contempo The period at or about the time the map was published; not contemporary in the sense of being current or modern.

Continuous tone Image not broken into dots by photographic screen; contains unbroken gradient tones from black to white, and may be either in negative or positive form. Aerial photographs are examples of continuous-tone prints. Contrasted with halftone (screened) and line copy.

Contour Imaginary line on the ground, all points of which are at the same elevation above or below sea level.

Coordinates Linear or angular quantities that designate the position of a point in relation to a given reference frame.

Copper plate (copperplate) The plate, made of copper, that is incised in making copperplate engravings.

Culture Features constructed by man that are under, on, or above the ground which are delineated on a map. These include roads, trails, buildings, canals, sewer systems, and boundary lines. In a broad sense, the term also applies to all names, other identification, and legends on a map.

Datum (pl. datums) In surveying, a reference system for computing or correlating the results of surveys. There are two principal types of datums: vertical and horizontal. A vertical datum is a level surface to which heights are referred. The horizontal datum is used as a reference for position.

Dissected Cut into parts. Large maps were sometimes dissected into rectangles and backed with linen.

Edition The concept of "edition" is difficult to apply to maps. It can be defined by imprint, if one exists. Maps are sometimes described as ". . . being from the *x* edition of the atlas. . . ."

Elevation Vertical distance of a point above or below a reference surface or datum.

Engineering map Map showing information that is essential for planning an engineering project or development and for estimating its cost. It is usually a large-scale map of a small area or of a route (see *Plan*). It may be entirely the product of an engineering survey, or reliable information may be collected from various sources for the purpose, and assembled on a base map.

Engraving Type of printing process wherein the ink is retained in grooves cut with a tool (burin) into a plate. The paper is pressed onto the plate and picks up the ink. An intaglio process.

Etching An intaglio process, but the grooves in the plate are formed by the action of acid rather than by the engraver's burin.

Facsimile The printed reproduction of missing text or image; a close or exact replica of an original.

Feature separation Process of preparing a separate drawing, engraving, or negative for selected types of data in the preparation of a map or chart.

Folio A book consisting of leaves folded once. In maps, it refers to the size of a map, generally about 20 x 25 inches (51 x 64 cm). It is incorrect, but often done, to use this term to describe size.

Formlines Lines, resembling contour lines, drawn to present a conception of a shape of the terrain without regard to a true vertical datum or regular spacing.

Frontispiece The decorative image facing the title page.

Geodesy Science concerned with the measurement and mathematical description of the size and shape of the earth and its gravitational field.

Gore Diamond-shaped sections of maps that are designed to be wetted and laid down on a spherical surface to make a globe.

Graticule Network of parallels and meridians on a map or chart.

Gravure A reproductive printing technique using plates made photochemically.

Grid Network of uniformly spaced parallel lines intersecting at right angles. When superimposed on a map, it usually carries the name of the projection used for the map—for example, Lambert projection, transverse Mercator projection, universal transverse Mercator projection.

Hachure Any of a series of lines used on a map to indicate the general direction and steepness of slopes. The lines are short, heavy, and close together for steep slopes; longer, lighter, and more widely spaced for gentle slopes.

Halftone A picture in which the gradations of light are obtained by the relative darkness and density of tiny dots produced by photographing the subject through a fine screen; a process of simulating a continuous tone image by breaking up the image into small dots, whose size and/or spacing determines image density.

Hydrography Science that deals with the measurement and description of the physical features of the oceans, seas, lakes, rivers, and their adjoining coastal areas, with particular reference to their use for navigation.

Hypsometry Science or art of determining terrain relief, by any method.

Impression Each individual copy of a map is an impression.

Imprint Printed data regarding the publisher, date of publication, and place.

Intaglio printing Printing from a plate where the part to print is below the surface of the plate, as in engraving or etching.

Landmark Monument or material mark or fixed object used to designate a land boundary on the ground; any prominent object on land that may be used to determine a location or a direction of navigation or surveying.

Land use map Map showing, by means of a coding system, the various purposes for which parcels of land are being used.

Latitude Angular distance, in degrees, minutes, and seconds, measured on a meridian, with zero at the equator and 90° at each pole.

Line copy (line drawing) Map copy suitable for reproduction without the use of a screen; a drawing composed of lines as distinguished from continuous-tone copy.

Linen-backed Backed with linen.

Lithography A form of printing invented in 1799. The surface of a plate is treated chemically to accept the inked image which is transferred to paper directly or via an intermediate substrate, as in the case of offset lithography.

Longitude Angular distance, measured westward from a prime (zero) meridian.

Manuscript Written or drawn by hand.

Map Graphic representation of the physical features (natural, artificial, or both) of a part or the whole of the Earth's surface, by means of signs and symbols or photographic imagery, at an established scale, on a specified projection, and with the means of orientation indicated.

Map projection Orderly system of lines on a plane representing a corresponding system of imaginary lines on an adopted terrestrial or celestial datum surface. Also, the mathematical concept of such a system. For maps of the Earth, a projection consists of (1) a graticule of lines representing parallels of latitude and meridians of longitude, or (2) a grid.

Map series Family of maps conforming generally to the same specifications and designed to cover an area or a country in a systematic pattern.

Margin That portion of the paper outside the neatline. The margin is not the border.

Mercator projection A type of map projection in which the meridians are drawn parallel to each other and the parallels of latitude are straight lines whose distance from each other increases with their distance from the equator.

Meridian Great circle on the surface of the Earth passing through the geographical poles and any given point on the Earth's surface. All points on a given meridian have the same longitude. See *Prime meridian.*

Metes and bounds Method of describing land by measure of length (metes) of the boundary lines (bounds).

Monument (surveying) Permanent physical structure marking the location of a survey point. Common types of monuments are inscribed metal tablets set in concrete posts, solid rocks, or parts of buildings; distinctive stone posts; and metal rods driven in the ground.

Mosaic, aerial Assembly of aerial photographs whose edges usually have been cut selectively and matched to imagery on adjoining photographs to form a continuous representation of a portion of the Earth's surface.

nd (ND/ND.) No date.

Neatline The printed line that defines the outer perimeter of a map and separates the body of a map from the map margin.

Offsetting An image transferred from one surface to another.

Orientation Establishing correct relationship in direction with reference to points of the compass.

Original As used here, implies that the map was printed from the original plate at the time the rest of the edition was printed.

Orthophotograph Photograph having the properties of an orthographic projection. It is derived from a conventional perspective photograph by simple or differential rectification so that image displacements caused by the camera tilt and terrain relief are removed.

Overedge Any portion of a map lying outside the nominal map border (neatline).

Overlay Printing or drawing on a transparent or translucent medium intended to be placed in register on a map or other graphic and which shows details not appearing or requiring special emphasis on the base material.

Overprint New material printed on a map or chart to show data of importance or special use, in addition to those data originally printed.

Panorama A comprehensive view of an area, from a seemingly single vantage point, in every direction (usually 180°, and up to 360°).

Parallel of latitude A circle, or approximation of a circle, on the surface of the Earth, parallel to the Equator, and connecting points of equal latitude.

Parchment Vellum.

Photogrammetry Science or art of obtaining reliable measurements or information from photographs or other sensing systems.

Planetable Instrument consisting essentially of a drawing board on a tripod and some type of sighting device with attached straightedge, used for plotting the lines of survey directly from observation in the field.

Planigraphic Printing from a flat surface, such as lithography.

Plat Diagram drawn to scale showing all essential data pertaining to the boundaries and subdivisions of a tract of land, as determined by survey or protraction.

Plan A large-scale map of a small area.

Planimetric map Map that represents only the horizontal positions for features represented; distinguished from a topographic map by the omission of relief in measurable form. The features usually shown on a planimetric map include rivers, lakes, and seas; mountains, valleys, and plains; forests and prairies; cities, farms, transportation routes, and public utility facilities; and political and private boundary lines. A planimetric map intended for special use may present only those features essential to the purpose to be served.

Plate The plate is the prepared surface from which prints are taken. It may be stone, as in lithography, or copper, as in copperplate engraving. The term plate also refers to the actual printed image.

Platemark (plate mark, plate line) The interface between the paper fibers compressed as the plate was printed and the uncompressed fibers that did not get squeezed against the plate as it was printed.

Pocket map A folding map, generally not linen-backed, usually with self-covers and designed primarily for travelers.

Portolan (portolano) A manuscript sailing chart, generally of the Mediterranean regions, usually from the thirteenth through the sixteenth centuries.

Prime meridian The circle connecting the poles that is defined as the meridian of longitude 0°, it is used as the origin for measurements of longitude. The meridian of Greenwich, England, is the internationally accepted prime meridian on most charts. Today, however, local or national prime meridians are occasionally used.

Projection The means, or transform, by which features on the earth's surface can be represented on a flat surface. Each projection introduces some distortion.

Proof An impression taken from the plate as the work progresses to check the image.

Quadrangle Four-sided area, bounded by parallels of latitude and meridians of longitude used as an area unit in mapping (dimensions are not necessarily the same in both directions). Also, a geometric figure of significance in geodetic surveying.

Quadrant An instrument for measuring altitudes, it consists of a graduated arc, which occupies 1/4 of a circle, with an index and usually having a plumb line or spirit level for fixing the vertical or horizontal direction.

Recto The right page of an opened book; the front surface of a map or leaf; the obverse. In Oriental books, which read in reverse, the recto is the left page.

Register The precise alignment of the paper on the several different plates needed to print in colors.

Relief map A map that tries to convey elevation differences by adding a third dimension.

Relief printing Printing from a raised surface, such as woodblock or letterpress.

Reproduction Summation of all the processes involved in printing copies from an original. A printed copy of an original map or drawing made by the processes of reproduction.

Rhumb lines Lines emanating from the compass rose. Sometimes called *wind lines.*

Roller map A wall map mounted on a roller so that it can be rolled up when not in use.

Scale Relationship existing between a distance on a map, chart, or photograph and the corresponding distance on the Earth.

Separate issue A map that was issued by itself; not as part of a book or atlas.

Sextant An ancient nautical and astronomical instrument used to observe altitudes of celestial bodies in order to ascertain angular distances (such as latitude and longitude). Its frame occupies 1/6 of a circle, giving it its name. The sextant was the successor to the astrolabe.

Slipcase An outer case, either box- or envelopelike, into which a folded map can be inserted for protection.

Spot elevation Point on a map or chart whose height above a specified datum is noted, usually by a dot or a small sawbuck and elevation value. Elevations are shown, on a selective basis, for road forks and intersections, grade crossings, summits of hills, mountains and mountain passes, water surfaces of lakes and ponds, stream forks, bottom elevations in depressions, and large flat areas.

State Each significant alteration to a printing plate creates another state of the image.

Steelplate Engraved on steel rather than copper. Sometimes a copper plate that has been iron-plated is called steelplate.

Stereocompilation Production of a map or chart from aerial photographs and geodetic control data by means of photogrammetric instruments.

Stitch holes Small holes in the centerfold made where the map was sewn into the book or atlas. To avoid stitch holes, many binders attached binder's guards to the map and sewed through these.

Survey Orderly process of determining data relating to any physical or chemical characteristics of the Earth. The associated data obtained in a survey. An organization engaged in making a survey.

Thematic map Map designed to provide information on a single topic, such as geology, rainfall, or population.

Topographic map Map that presents the horizontal and vertical positions of the features represented; distinguished from a planimetric map by the addition of relief in measurable form.

Topography Configuration (relief) of the land surface; the graphic delineation or portrayal of that configuration in map form, as by contour lines.

Vellum A prepared and treated flexible sheet derived from animal dermis. Used for writing and binding.

Verso The left page of an opened book; also the "back" side of a map or leaf, or the side on which the image does not appear; the reverse.

Wall map A large map designed to be displayed on a wall, often for didactic purposes.

Watermark An integral design in paper, usually revealing a symbol unique to the individual papermaker. Best seen with transmitted light.

Woodcut (woodblock) An image printed in relief from a carved wooden block. The block is carved, with knives and gouges, on the side grain and blank areas are cut away, leaving raised lines which hold the ink and provide the image. This is relief printing.

Wood engraving The technique of printing from a wooden block that was carved on the end grain. Typical engraving tools, such as the burin, are used and the detail is finer than can be achieved with woodblock technique. Wood engraving is a relief process.

Zenith The point directly overhead.

Compiled from the following sources:

Manasek, Francis J. *Collecting Old Maps.* Norwich, Vt.: Terra Nova Press, 1998.

U.S. Department of the Interior. *Maps for America.* Third edition. Reston, Va.: Geological Survey National Center, 1987.

For Further Reading

AN INTRODUCTION TO MAPS AND MAPPING

Barber, Peter, and Christopher Board. *Tales from the Map Room: Fact and Fiction about Maps and their Makers.* London: BBC Books, 1993.

Brown, Lloyd A. *The Story of Maps.* New York: Little Brown & Co., 1949.

Buisseret, David, ed. *From Sea Charts to Satellite Images: Interpreting North American History through Maps.* Chicago: University of Chicago Press, 1990.

Hodgkiss, A. G. *Understanding Maps: A Systematic History of their Use and Development.* Folkestone, Kent, England: Dawson, 1981.

Manasek, Francis J. *Collecting Old Maps.* Norwich, Vt.: Terra Nova Press, 1998.

Southworth, Michael, and Susan Southworth. *Maps: A Visual Survey and Design Guide.* Boston: Little Brown & Co., 1982.

Stefoff, Rebecca. *The British Library Companion to Maps and Mapmaking.* London: The British Library, 1995.

Thrower, Norman. *Maps and Civilization: Cartography in Culture and Society.* Chicago: University of Chicago Press, 1996.

Turnbull, David. *Maps Are Territories, Science Is an Atlas.* Chicago: University of Chicago Press, 1989.

THE HISTORY OF CARTOGRAPHY

Berthon, Simon, and Andrew Robinson. *The Shape of the World: The Mapping and Discovery of the Earth.* London: George Philip, 1991.

Burden, Philip D. *The Mapping of North America: A List of Printed Maps 1511–1670.* Rickmansworth, Herts, England: Raleigh Publications, 1996.

Cumming, William P. *British Maps of Colonial America.* Chicago: University of Chicago Press, 1974.

Potter, Jonathan. *Collecting Antique Maps: An Introduction to the History of Cartography.* London: Studio Editions, 1992.

Schwartz, Seymour I., and Ralph E. Ehrenberg. *The Mapping of America.* New York: Harry N. Abrams, 1980.

Shirley, Rodney W. *The Mapping of the World: Early Printed World Maps, 1472–1700.* London: Holland Press, 1983.

Tooley, Ronald Vere. *Tooley's Dictionary of Mapmakers.* Tring, Hertfordshire, England: Map Collector Publications, 1979.

Tooley. *The Mapping of America.* London: The Holland Press, 1985.

Wheat, James Clements, and Christian F. Brun. *Maps and Charts Published in America Before 1800: A Bibliography.* Rev. ed. London: Holland Press, 1978.

Wilford, John Noble. *The Mapmakers.* New York: Alfred A. Knopf, 1981.

THE MAPPING OF BOSTON

Boston's Streets, Squares, Places, Avenues, Courts, and Other Public Locations. Boston: Public Works Department, 1989.

List of Maps of Boston Published between 1600 and 1903. Boston: Municipal Printing Office, 1903.

Phillips, P. Lee. "A Descriptive List of Maps and Views of Boston in the Library of Congress, 1630–1865." 1922. Manuscript typescript.

Reps, John W. "Boston by Bostonians: The Printed Plans and Views of the *Colonial City by its Artists,* Cartographers, Engravers, and Publishers." *Publications of the Colonial Society of Massachusetts* 46 (1973): 3–56.

Wilke, Richard, and Jack Toger. *Historical Atlas of Massachusetts.* Amherst: University of Massachusetts Press, 1991.

BOSTON AND ITS HISTORY

Baltzell, E. Digby. *Puritan Boston and Quaker Philadelphia.* New York: The Free Press, 1979.

Beebe, Lucius. *Boston and the Boston Legend.* New York: D. Appleton Century Co., 1936.

Campbell, Robert and Peter Vanderwarker. *Cityscapes of Boston: An American City Through Time.* Boston: Houghton Mifflin, 1992.

Conzen, Michael P., and George K. Lewis. *Boston: A Geographical Portrait.* Cambridge: Ballinger Publishing Company, 1976.

Dalzell, Robert F., Jr. *Enterprising Elite: The Boston Associates and the World they Made.* Cambridge: Harvard University Press, 1987.

Formisano, Donald P., and Constance K. Burns. *Boston 1700–1980, The Evolution of Urban Politics.* Westport, Conn.: Greenwood Press, 1984.

Handlin, Oscar. *Boston's Immigrants: 1790–1865.* Cambridge: Harvard University Press, 1941.

Kennedy, Lawrence W. *Planning the City upon a Hill: Boston since 1630.* Amherst: University of Massachusetts Press, 1992.

Knights, Peter R. *Yankee Destinies: The Lives of Ordinary Nineteenth Century Bostonians.* Chapel Hill: University of North Carolina Press, 1991.

Nesson, Fern L. *Great Waters: A History of Boston's Water Supply.* Hanover, N.H.: University Press of New England for Brandeis University, 1983.

O'Connell, Shaun. *Imagining Boston, A Literary Landscape.* Boston: Beacon Press, 1990.

O'Connor, Thomas H. *Bibles, Brahmins and Bosses: A Short History of Boston.* Boston: Trustees of the Public Library of the City of Boston, 1991.

O'Connor, Thomas H. *Building a New Boston: Politics and Urban Renewal, 1950–1970.* Boston: Northeastern University Press, 1993.

Sammarco, Anthony Mitchell. *Images of America.* Dover: Arcadia Publishing, 1997.

Shand Tucci, Douglas. *Built in Boston: City and Suburb, 1800–1950.* Boston: New York Graphic Society, 1978.

Warner, Sam Bass, Jr. *Streetcar Suburbs: The Process of Growth in Boston (1870–1900).* Cambridge: Harvard University Press, 1962.

Warner, Sam Bass, Jr. *The Province of Reason.* Cambridge: Belknap Press, 1984.

Whitehill, Walter Muir. *Boston: A Topographical History.* Cambridge: Belknap Press of Harvard University Press, 1959.

Wilson, Susan. *Boston Sites and Insights: A Multicultural Guide to Fifty Historic Landmarks in and around Boston.* Boston: Beacon Press, 1994.

Zaitzevsky, Cynthia. *Frederick Law Olmsted and the Boston Park System.* Cambridge: Belknap Press of Harvard University Press, 1982.

An Index of the Maps Illustrated

About the Contributing Authors

David Bosse, formerly map curator at the William L. Clements Library of the University of Michigan, is librarian of Historic Deerfield, a museum of New England history and art. He is the author of numerous articles on the history of American cartography and of *Civil War Newspaper Maps: A Historical Atlas* (Baltimore: Johns Hopkins University Press, 1993).

James Carroll is a Boston writer. He has published nine novels, including *Mortal Friends* and *The City Below,* both set in Boston. His memoir, *An American Requiem,* won the 1996 National Book Award in nonfiction. His column appears weekly on the op-ed page of the *Boston Globe.*

David A. Cobb is the head of the Harvard Map Collection. He has authored several articles on map library management as well as the *Guide to U.S. Map Resources, New Hampshire Maps to 1900: An Annotated Checklist,* and *Vermont Maps to 1900: An Annotated Cartobibliography.*

Alex Krieger is an architect and planner and an authority on the evolution of the American city. A Fellow of the American Institute of Architects, he is a principal of Chan Krieger & Associates, an architecture and urban design firm based in Cambridge, Massachusetts. He serves as chairman of the Department of Urban Planning and Design at the Harvard Graduate School of Design where he has taught since 1978.

Anne Mackin is a planner and writer with a special interest in American history and culture. She has written a number of guidebooks on planning and design, sponsored by arts institutions or public agencies, and articles interpreting Americans' use of their landscape.

Barbara McCorkle is the former curator of maps at Yale University and an authority on the cartography of New England. In addition to her many published articles, she is currently compiling the first comprehensive cartobibliography of the maps of New England published prior to 1800.

Nancy S. Seasholes is an historical archaeologist who became conversant with Boston's land making and historical maps while working as an historian for archaelogical contract firms engaged in the environmental review process. She is a Research Fellow in the Department of Archaeology at Boston University and an independent consultant. Her chapter in this volume is a preview of her forthcoming book entitled *Gaining Ground: Landmaking in Boston, 1630s–1980s.*

Amy Turner is an architect in Cambridge with a special interest in urban form and the mapping of the American city. She has served as curator and exhibit designer for *Mapping Boston: Delineating the City and Its Region,* an exhibition of maps from the Norman B. Leventhal Collection. She was the coordinator of and a contributor to *Windows of Observation,* a catalog and traveling exhibition of theoretical architectural projects.

Sam Bass Warner, Jr., is an urban historian. He has written several books about Boston's history including *Streetcar Suburbs, The Way We Really Live, To Dwell Is to Garden,* and *The Province of Reason.* A professor of history at the University of Michigan (1969–1972), Boston University (1972–1991), and Brandeis University (1991–1994), he is now a visiting professor in the Department of Urban Studies and Planning at MIT and working on a new book describing regional Boston.

Illustration Credits

Chapter 5

frontispiece	With permission of the Harvard College Library, Map Collection
figure 1	With permission of the Harvard College Library, Map Collection
figure 2	With permission of the Harvard College Library, Map Collection
figure 3	With permission of the Harvard College Library, Map Collection
figure 4	With permission of the Harvard College Library, Map Collection
figure 5	With permission of the Harvard College Library, Map Collection
figure 6	With permission of the Harvard College Library, Map Collection
figure 7	With permission of the Harvard College Library, Map Collection
figure 8	With permission of the Harvard College Library, Map Collection
figure 9a	With permission of the Harvard College Library, Map Collection
figure 9b	With permission of the Harvard College Library, Map Collection
figure 9c	With permission of the Harvard College Library, Map Collection
figure 10	With permission of the Harvard College Library, Map Collection
figure 11	With permission of the Harvard College Library, Map Collection

Chapter 6

plate 1	Norman B. Leventhal Collection
plate 2	With permission of the Harvard College Library, Map Collection
plate 3	Norman B. Leventhal Collection
plate 4	Norman B. Leventhal Collection
plate 5	Norman B. Leventhal Collection
plate 6	Norman B. Leventhal Collection
plate 7	Norman B. Leventhal Collection
plate 8	Norman B. Leventhal Collection
plate 9	Norman B. Leventhal Collection
plate 10	Norman B. Leventhal Collection
plate 11	Norman B. Leventhal Collection
plate 12	Norman B. Leventhal Collection
plate 13	Norman B. Leventhal Collection
plate 14	With permission of the Harvard College Library, Map Collection
plate 15	Norman B. Leventhal Collection

plate 16	With permission of the Harvard College Library, Map Collection
plate 17	With permission of the Harvard College Library, Map Collection
plate 18	Norman B. Leventhal Collection
plate 19	Norman B. Leventhal Collection
plate 20	Norman B. Leventhal Collection
plate 21	With permission of the Harvard College Library, Map Collection
plate 22	Norman B. Leventhal Collection
plate 23	With permission of the Harvard College Library, Map Collection

New England Plate Vignettes

plate 1 vignette *(left)*	With permission of the Harvard College Library, Map Collection
plate 1 vignette *(right)*	With permission of the Harvard College Library, Map Collection
plate 2 vignette *(top)*	Boston Athenaeum
plate 2 vignette *(bottom)*	Norman B. Leventhal Collection
plate 3 vignette *(top left)*	With permission of the Harvard College Library, Map Collection
plate 3 vignette *(top right)*	With permission of the Harvard College Library, Map Collection
plate 3 vignette *(bottom)*	With permission of the Harvard College Library, Map Collection
plate 4 vignette	Boston Athenaeum
plate 5 vignette	Norman B. Leventhal Collection
plate 6 vignette	Courtesy of Osher Map Library, University of Southern Maine
plate 7 vignette *(left)*	Norman B. Leventhal Collection
plate 7 vignette *(right)*	Norman B. Leventhal Collection
plate 8 vignette	Courtesy of Massachusetts Archives
plate 9 vignette *(top)*	Courtesy, American Antiquarian Society
plate 9 vignette *(bottom)*	Courtesy Massachusetts Historical Society, Boston
plate 10 vignette *(left)*	With permission of the Harvard College Library, Map Collection
plate 10 vignette *(right)*	Städelsches Kunstinstitut Frankfurt
plate 11 vignette	Boston Athenaeum
plate 12 vignette *(top)*	Courtesy of the Trustees of the Boston Public Library
plate 12 vignette *(bottom)*	Norman B. Leventhal Collection
plate 13 vignette *(left)*	Norman B. Leventhal Collection
plate 13 vignette *(right)*	Norman B. Leventhal Collection
plate 14 vignette	Boston Athenaeum
plate 15 vignette	Norman B. Leventhal Collection
plate 16 vignette	State Historical Society of Wisconsin/ WHi (X3) 29985

Index

COMMON

WITHDRAWN

Beebs S.

Ranford

Essex Street

Pond Street

West St.

Winter St.

Rawsons L.

Burying Place

Beacon St.

Tremount S.

Marlboro S.

Common St.

School Street

Cornhill

Shorts

Summer Street

Bishops Alley

Pond

ills Wharf

ill Point

South Street

Sea Street

Summer Street

Blind L.

WEEKS PUBLIC LIBRARY
GREENLAND N. H.

WITHDRAWN

Milk Street

Queen Street

Darby W.

Long Lane

Crooked L.

Bulls W.

Crooked L.

Tanner

Pudding Lane

Adams W.

Flounders

Cow Lane

Rope Walks

Cooper's L.

Livers L.

G

E des Ship Yard

Tilleys

Belchers L

Oliver Street

Crab Lane

Marchant L.

King Street

Grays W.

Gibbs L.

Marchant Row

Hollaways Yard

Whitehornes W.

Fort Hill

Palmers W.

L. Warehouse

Oliver Dock

Pools W.

Marshalls W.

Hubbard W.

Battery March

Wing's Yard

Olivers W.

Belcher W.

Gibbs W.